DATE DUE

MAY 1 3 1988		
NOV 2 0 1990	OCT 3 0 2001	
	DEC 0 4 2002	
DEC 1 4 1990	DEC 1 3 2007	
DEC 1 2 1991	DEC 1 7 2007	
MAY 6 - 1993		
MAY 1 2 1994		
FEB 2 8 1995		
APR 2 2 1996		
3-17-97 : IL		
APR 2 1 1997		
NOV 1 8 1999		
DEC 0 9 1999		

DEMCO 38-297

THE
PLESSY
CASE

THE
PLESSY
CASE

A LEGAL-HISTORICAL
INTERPRETATION

Charles A. Lofgren

New York   Oxford
OXFORD UNIVERSITY PRESS
1987

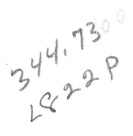

Oxford University Press

Oxford   New York   Toronto
Delhi   Bombay   Calcutta   Madras   Karachi
Petaling Jaya   Singapore   Hong Kong   Tokyo
Nairobi   Dar es Salaam   Cape Town
Melbourne   Auckland

and associated companies in
Beirut   Berlin   Ibadan   Nicosia

Published by Oxford University Press, Inc.,
200 Madison Avenue, New York, New York 10016

Oxford is a registered trademark of Oxford University Press

Library of Congress Cataloging-in-Publication Data
Lofgren, Charles A.
The Plessy case.
Includes index.
1. Segregation in education—Law and legislation—
United States—History.
2. Segregation in transportation—Law and
legislation—United States—History. 3. Segregation in education—
Law and legislation—Louisiana—History. 4. Segregation in transportation—
Law and legislation—Louisiana—History. I. Title.
KF4757.L64   1987   344.73'798   86-16264
347.304798
ISBN 0-19-503852-5 (alk. paper)

2 4 6 8 9 7 5 3 1

Printed in the United States of America
on acid-free paper

For
Jennifer

ACKNOWLEDGMENTS

Speaking as a member of the United States Supreme Court, Justice Robert Jackson once confessed about the institution, "We are not final because we are infallible, but we are infallible only because we are final." (*Brown v. Allen*, 344 U.S. 443, 540 [1953].) His remark comes to mind partly because, viewed historically, his predecessors in 1896 who decided *Plessy v. Ferguson* proved neither infallible nor (one hopes) final. Despite this, or perhaps because of it, *Plessy* provides fascinating material for the historian, offering the opportunity to interpret the interplay of people, law, and ideas, all within the context of an age. My first debt, then, is to the historical actors—some more courageous than others—who gave us the case.

The comment by Jackson, a man given to pithy wisdom, also juxtaposes a reminder: whatever may be the institutionally and constitutionally determined position of U.S. Supreme Court justices, historians are far from infallible. As a result, my efforts are quite unlikely to constitute the final word on *Plessy*. In particular, in plumbing both Southern history and the history of racist thought and race relations in America, I have entered areas in which I was and am clearly a neophyte; and I have felt only somewhat less afield in the intricacies of non-constitutional law into which this book has taken me. All of which is a way of thanking the many scholars on whose studies I have drawn heavily, however much they may conclude—and may show me—that I should have paid closer attention to their work.

Certain of the debts I have incurred require me to make what I choose to call *"sine qua non* awards." One is to the students in a course I taught for several years under the title of "The Supreme Court in American History." As we together read and dissected a fairly standard set of late-nineteenth-century Supreme Court opinions, it dawned on me that *Plessy v. Ferguson* displayed important similarities to a number of cases outside the area of race relations. I followed up that insight (if it can be called such) by outlining a few thoughts to Leonard W. Levy, my good colleague across the street at Claremont Graduate School. In *Plessy*, I argued, the Supreme Court had behaved in a quite consistent and *un*remarkable fashion. In his subdued fashion, Len, who had written on the case and related episodes, disagreed with much that I said but pronounced it worth pursuing. As best as I can reconstruct the history of this book, it was then that I decided definitely to push ahead. For this, as well as for his assistance and subtle prodding on other occasions, he gets the second *sine qua non* award.

Others made important contributions along the way. Librarians and archivists aided my efforts, particularly Marie E. Windell of the Archives and Manuscripts Department, Earl K. Long Library, at the University of New Orleans, which holds the Louisiana Supreme Court's records for the nineteenth century; Lester Sullivan of the Amistad Research Center, New Orleans; Roger F. Jacobs, formerly the Librarian of the United States Supreme Court; Catherine and Mark Phillips, of Pleasant Ridge, Michigan, who checked collections of the Henry Billings Brown papers; Gene Teitelbaum, Professor and Law Librarian at the Law School of the University of Kentucky, which holds part of John Marshall Harlan's papers; R. Russell Maylone, Curator in Special Collections at the Northwestern University Library, which, by virtue of housing the American Economic Association archives, has the distinction of holding the AEA's editorial correspondence with that arch racist of the 1890s, Frederick Hoffman; the staff of the University of Tennessee's Law Library, who tolerated a historian-interloper during two extended stays by me in Knoxville during 1983–84; and the Interlibrary Loan staff at the Honnold Library of the Claremont Colleges. The Chautauqua County Historical Society, Westfield, New York, gave permission to cite and quote from the Albion W. and Emma Tourgée papers, which it holds.

Colleagues in and out of Claremont generously offered leads and assistance, shared ideas, and took the trouble simply to answer letters. The list, far from exhaustive, includes Michael Les Benedict, Arthur Bestor, Alan A. Burns, Patricia Burns, Ward E. Y. Elliott, Edward J. Erler, Don E. Fehrenbacher, Leo J. Flynn, Henry J. Gibbons, Milton M. Klein, Alfred R. Louch, Jonathan Lurie, Alpheus Thomas Mason, James H. Nichols, Jr., John Niven, Otto H. Olsen, Ralph A. Rossum, and Harry N. Scheiber. Well before this book began, James Allen Rogers opened to me some of the complexities of evolutionary thought in the nineteenth century. Pam Martin Greiman provided invaluable research assistance at an early stage. Richard S.

Wheeler carefully read the whole manuscript. Lynn Dumenil, my fellow American historian at Claremont McKenna College, arrived on the scene too late for me to pick her brain, but her own dedication to scholarship set an example that helped prod my final writing. (Next time, she won't escape so easily.) J. Morgan Kousser—who, I strongly suspect, will rip into some of my approaches and conclusions—deserves special mention. Beyond offering suggestions drawn from his own studies of nineteenth-century race discrimination, he subjected earlier versions of Chapters Five and Six to the best critical reading anyone could ask for. It is because I am indebted to all these people that I release each and every one from any responsibility for the final product.

Providing financial support at different stages were Project '87, sponsored by the American Historical Association and the American Political Science Association; the Salvatori Center for the Study of Individual Freedom in the Modern World, at Claremont McKenna College; and Claremont McKenna College's Faculty Research Committee. Two successive Deans of the Faculty at CMC, Colin Wright and Gaines Post, Jr., gave the help that only good deans provide (but still not often enough). Also on the administrative front, I owe a big "thanks" to my colleagues in the Government Department at CMC in their collective capacity. Not only did they make a historian feel at home and even tolerate him as their chairman, but they kept problems from crossing his desk as he was pushing a book to completion.

Jennifer Wood took time from her own writing by volunteering to "word process" early typescript versions of several chapters onto "floppy disks" when I made the transition into the computer age. More important, she wins the third and final *sine qua non* award: she let me know that it was time to finish and gave me the encouragement to do so.

Claremont, California   Charles A. Lofgren
June 1986

CONTENTS

THE
PLESSY
CASE

INTRODUCTION

"The *Plessy* Prison"

I

On Monday, May 18, 1896, the United States Supreme Court handed down its decision in *Plessy v. Ferguson*. At issue was the constitutionality of a Louisiana law, passed in 1890, which mandated "equal but separate accommodations for the white and colored races" on all passenger railways within the state. In an opinion by Justice Henry Billings Brown, a native of Massachusetts, a majority of seven justices upheld the enactment as a reasonable "police" measure. Using a less-than-direct argument, the Court could not say there was no basis for accepting the state legislature's conclusion that the law would promote the comfort of the people and preserve "public peace and good order." But the lone dissenter, Justice John Marshall Harlan of Kentucky, a former slaveholder, saw the inner truth. "The thin disguise of 'equal accomodations,'" he declared, "will not mislead anyone, nor atone for the wrong this day done." The Court's judgment would, "in time, prove to be quite as pernicious as the decision . . . in the *Dred Scott case*."[1]

In castigating the majority's position, Harlan had future company. By mid-twentieth century, a plethora of maledictions—here sampled in the form of a pastiche—centered on "the notorious Supreme Court case of *Plessy v. Ferguson*," which "reduced the Fourteenth Amendment to little more than a pious goodwill resolution" and indeed gave the "ultimate blow to the Civil War Amendments and the equality of Negroes." "It is permissible to doubt

3

whether the . . . Court has ever exposed the fundamentally racialist assumptions behind its reasoning with quite such incontinence, and it is also permissible to hope that it has never [elsewhere] committed itself through such inferior reasoning." In uttering "the climactic Supreme Court pronouncement on segregated institutions" through "one of the most irrational opinions ever announced," Justice Brown in places "slipped into absurdity" and "smuggled Social Darwinism" into the Constitution.[2]

Marking "the Court's acceptance of an overtly racist social policy," Brown's "disastrous excursion into legal philosophy" sentenced blacks for more than fifty years to "the *Plessy* prison." More broadly, it inaugurated a half-century's hiatus in moral leadership in America, announced "the federal birth of the separate but [un]equal doctrine," and itself produced a "catastrophic backlash" against blacks of "almost unbelievable" proportions. It was, in short, "the national decision against equality."[3]

In its specific features, moreover, Brown's majority opinion constituted "a compound of bad logic, bad history, bad sociology, and bad constitutional law." By claiming that "[l]egislation is powerless to eradicate racial instincts," Brown had penned "one of those phrases that live in constitutional history largely because of their inaccuracy."[4] But it was at least clear that the Court had upheld Mr. Plessy's conviction, after dismissing the equal protection arguments that formed the core of his position.[5] Other parts of his case, however, had raised Thirteenth Amendment and due process arguments, the latter involving the claim that the separate car law deprived the light-toned Plessy of property in the form of reputation as a white man. On those fronts, it may have been Plessy's own counsel who had been ill-advised in their approach. Perhaps, too, they were mistaken in allowing the case—an arranged affair—to develop in such a hostile environment.[6]

But at least *Plessy* came down only "over the ringing protest of John Harlan." The Kentuckian delivered "a dissenting opinion of extraordinary force"—"the greatest of his many dissents, and . . . one of the most majestic utterances in American law." Its "most striking aspect . . . [was] the attitudes of racial toleration and the fears of racial antagonism that it expressed . . . ." Because Harlan "recognized the bankruptcy of the Court's reasoning," it was for good reason that a "coming vindication" awaited him—albeit posthumously.[7]

II

It should need no belaboring: Harlan's indignation was the morally correct response in a republic founded on the truth "that all men are created equal." To say that is to affirm that by taking *Plessy* seriously, I hardly intend to resurrect it for the benefit of the late twentieth century, although now and again people are charged with the attempt.[8] Without more, however, simply condemning the decision promotes an understanding neither of it nor of America in the late nineteenth century.

The Plessy case has not been well understood. At the level of "fact," for example, Homer A. Plessy was not appealing a conviction. Nearly as demonstrable, "equal protection" did not constitute the core of the argument made on his behalf. And the connection between his case and the legal ensconcement of "equal-but-separate" (to use the sequence of terms that was more common in the late nineteenth century) turns out to be problematic.

In addition, we confront an initially puzzling phenomenon: the nation's press met the decision mainly with apathy. Why? And why did *Plessy* remain nearly invisible for a long time after 1896? It is true that the early black historian Carter G. Woodson correctly identified it in 1921 as one of the cases that, over a period of fifty years, had substantially qualified the Negro's citizenship. But in 1922, Charles Warren's pioneering history of the Supreme Court neglected it, and his 1926 revision listed it only in a footnote, along with twenty-four other cases "involving rights of Negroes" in the late nineteenth and early twentieth century. Among textbooks, so often the barometer of what recently has passed for scholarly wisdom, Carl Brent Swisher's generally solid survey of constitutional history, published in 1943, failed to mention the case. And as late as 1948, Henry Steele Commager, a historian of assuredly liberal credentials, omitted *Plessy* from his widely consulted *Documents of American History*, first published in 1934.[9]

These omissions suggest several things, not least being the long-term acquiescence of many white Americans in the Compromise of 1877. They also hint that within its historical period, *Plessy* perhaps was *not* especially controversial. But therein lies much of its significance. A decision which is largely commonplace may offer a strategically placed window onto what contemporaries regarded as conventional; or, to change the figure, it may serve nicely as a kind of prism through which to refract and analyze some of the tenets of a period.

Through examining several themes suggested by *Plessy v. Ferguson*, this book has a double thrust. It contributes, I hope, to our understanding of the constitutional-legal context of southern race relations and American racism from the end of the Civil War to the turn of the century; and in doing so it suggests a modest recasting of the controversy over *de facto* versus *de jure* segregation, about which historians have spilled more than a little ink. The book also explores and dissects the case itself within what may be called the legal-racial matrix of the 1890s, with an eye toward explaining why it turned out as it did.

More schematically, the presentation proceeds as follows. To provide background, especially for readers who are not versed in pertinent aspects of what C. Vann Woodward has called "the strange career of Jim Crow," I begin by reviewing transportation segregation in practice and law in the postbellum South (Chapter One). Next, I trace the initial development of a judicial test of Louisiana's separate car law (Chapter Two) and delineate the legal issues emerging at the state level (Chapter Three). Attention then shifts to three "environmental" elements shaping the approaches that courts and counsel took to *Plessy*: the body of law and doctrine that by the early- to mid-1890s had developed around the Thirteenth and Fourteenth Amendments (Chapter Four); current attitudes toward and theorizing about race distinctions (Chapter Five); and non-constitutional case law and related developments concerning transportation segregation (Chapter Six). Finally, I return to *Plessy*, analyzing its presentation before the Supreme Court (Chapter Seven), deciphering the responses of the Court and Justice Harlan (Chapter Eight), and inquiring into the case's broader significance (Chapter Nine).

Two terms (and variations on them) appear frequently in the following pages—"racism" and "the South." Most of us have at least a feel for their meaning, but more specificity may be in order. Covering a multitude of sins, "racism" can refer to prejudice (an attitude), discrimination (an action), theorizing about racial differences that stresses an inferior/superior relationship (a "scientific" doctrine), and a broad system of law and custom embodying each of the preceding elements (a social order).[10] The Plessy case implicated each element and especially the last. Context will establish which emphasis I intend. In using "the South," "southerners," and the like, I generally mean the former slave-holding states and their inhabitants. Additional precision seems unnecessary in a study that does not rest on or aim for sharp quantitative distinctions. Where necessary, I again rely on context to qualify or extend the meaning.

CHAPTER ONE

De Facto to *De Jure*:
Transportation Segregation in the South From the Civil War to the 1890s

I

Historians face at least one special temptation: the pursuit of the ever-receding beginning. The Plessy case increases the urge, for racial separation in the South did not suddenly spring forth fully developed in the late nineteenth century, but rested instead on attitudes and practices running deep into the American past. Even the term "Jim Crow," commonly applied to separate facilities for blacks in the century following the Civil War, dated to the antebellum period. Appearing as early as 1832 in the title of a minstrel show's song-and-dance routine, by 1841 it identified a separate railway car for Negroes in Massachusetts. More importantly, the complex of beliefs that led many white Americans to see blacks as inferior yet threatening beings, perhaps not quite human, predated the founding of the Republic and may even have preceded slavery in England's North American colonies.[1]

But rather than probe the issue of distant beginnings, which continues to attract able scholars, we may take the existence of widespread racial prejudice as a historical "given" at the close of the Civil War, for it assuredly was. A Confederate who returned to New Orleans in 1865, only to find "niggers with arms in hand, doing guard duty," manifested simply an extreme form of the sentiment when he wrote in a personal letter how he hoped "the day will come when we have the upper hand of those black scondrels [*sic*] and we will have no mercy for them[;] we will kill them like

7

dogs. I [was] never down on a nigger as I am now." Not so private, yet more explicit in its denial of black equality, was a resolution by a border state senate. Declaring "[t]hat the immutable laws of God have affixed upon the brow of the white race the ineffaceable stamp of superiority," it held "that all attempt to elevate the negro to a social or political equality of [sic] the white man is futile and subversive of the ends and aims for which the American Government was established . . . ." In the North, to be sure, the bloody war that freed the black race from legalized slavery seems to have lessened racial prejudice, and it stimulated greater recognition of civil rights, but on balance white Americans, North and South, still showed little restraint in disparaging the Negro's intellect, morality, pathologies, and prospects.[2]

Nor it is difficult to identify the form of the "solution" finally devised by southern whites in positions of authority, for by the end of the century the results of anti-black prejudice stood starkly revealed within the South. Negroes were almost fully excluded from the politics of all but some peripheral regions; justice, which had never been especially even-handed across the color line, was even less so; and public facilities, where open to blacks at all, were most often strictly segregated. In particular, transportation facilities were commonly segregated by statute.

We begin instead with the path of southern race relations between the markers provided by the end of the war and the turn of the century. By sighting back, as it were, across three periods of history by conventional labeling (the "Reconstruction," "Redeemer," and "Populist" eras), we can gain an understanding of the institutional trends and arrangements that provided *Plessy*'s context. Even more, we can begin to establish a base line for assessing the importance of the case. Gauging historical significance requires asking "so what?"—what difference did *Plessy* make in the broader scheme of things? And an answer depends, at minimum, on having some appreciation of existing tendencies and of what there was to change.

It is true, of course, that to plumb southern race relations in the late nineteenth century is hardly a novel undertaking, for it lands one in the middle of a historical debate that has now persisted, albeit at a genteel level, for three decades. In 1955, C. Vann Woodward published a short book, *The Strange Career of Jim Crow*, in which he argued that the inauguration of the system of rigid, legally enforced segregation associated with the South in the first half of the twentieth century dated not to the collapse of the Reconstruction experiment in the 1870s, but rather to a period extending roughly from the late 1880s to just after 1900. In later editions of *Strange Career*, Woodward himself has stressed that the South was clearly not an open society on the racial front prior to the 1890s, but critics still maintain that he underestimates the extent of actual, if not legally mandated, segregation during the fifteen or twenty years following Reconstruction. Although a few historians have sought to transcend the controversy, almost everyone uses it as the point of departure. And what critics, defenders, and transcenders alike have taken for granted is that segregation *by law* did come *mainly* in the late 1880s and beyond.[3]

Thus a key dimension of the debate: *de facto* versus *de jure* segregation. What was the importance and extent of segregation *by custom and practice* versus segregation *by statute*? I shall suggest later that, so stated, this dichotomy wrongly characterizes the legal spectrum; yet it indicates the two most obvious elements in the matrix that produced *Plessy*, and it is to them that we turn in this chapter.

II

Responding to an invitation from the editors of the *North American Review*, the English observer James Bryce offered his "Thoughts on the Negro Problem" in December 1891. He had just toured the South, after an absence of seven years, and found that social contact between the races had declined, yet in some areas "the negro [was] allowed to enter the same street-cars or railroad cars" as occupied by whites. In the early 1880s, a northern traveler in the South had seen similar practices. On most railways, he reported, "the negroes were expected and told to take a particular car in each train, and they usually did so; but the rule did not seem to be strictly enforced." "Well-dressed negroes sometimes traveled in the same car with 'first-class' white people, ladies and gentlemen," he added; "and there were usually some white people, poor whites or working folk, in the negro car." Still earlier, in 1867–68, another British traveler, David Macrae, found "'nigger cars' open, of course, to white people and often used as smoking cars, but to which all coloured passengers have to confine themselves."[4]

Reports such as these, including even Macrae's, lend the support of contemporary observers to the conclusion that southern transportation was not rigidly segregated during the quarter-century after the Civil War. Indeed, both Bryce and the northern traveler suggested that railway transportation was perhaps the most open of public facilities within the region, and several modern studies, while recognizing the existence of separation, reach the same conclusion.[5] The easiest conclusion, then, is that what characterized southern transportation as a whole was the lack of a uniform system; but this broad generalization, although undoubtedly accurate, neglects discernible patterns within the region. Contemporaries spotted some of these, and modern scholars have again added detail.

One fairly clear pattern involves types of transportation. Streetcars within cities were probably the least segregated, compared with steamboats and intercity railways. Although streetcar companies had typically excluded blacks from their cars prior to the war, or assigned them to outside platforms, Reconstruction governments were successful in pressuring the companies to change their policies. In many instances, it is true, available evidence is simply too skimpy to indicate for certain if the newly gained access was on an integrated or segregated basis. Another problem is that desegregation of lines in one city reveals nothing necessarily about practice in other cities, particularly at different times, or about other lines in the same city. Yet, as late as 1890, the *Richmond Planet* advised against a rumored plan to segregate a line, contending "we do not know of a city in the south in which discrimination is made on the street cars." In point of fact, this statement was wrong, but still suggests the dominant practice of the period. It is instructive that fewer legal actions for wrongful ejection apparently arose in connection with streetcars than with intercity railways or steamships.[6]

At the opposite pole were steamboats on inland waterways and in the coastal service. Under both Republicans and Redeemers, concludes Howard N. Rabinowitz, they "remained the most segregated form of travel." Particularly significant is evidence from two areas, the Chesapeake Bay region and the lower Mississippi River, where, as we shall discover later in this chapter, railway service remained comparatively open. As early as 1880, the *City of Richmond* maintained "a neat and comfortable dining room for colored passengers in the lower cabin," or so a newspaper claimed. In any event, the facility was racially segregated. By August 1884, four women passengers found the sleeping quarters set aside for blacks on the *Sue*, another boat on the Chesapeake, distinctly unpleasant. Mattresses were defaced, sheets missing or dirty, blankets missing, and washing facilities inadequate. On the lower Mississippi River, separate quarters for blacks, known as "Freedmen's Bureaus," were customary even during Radical rule in the bordering states of Mississippi and Louisiana, although testimony suggests that light-skinned mulattoes occasionally obtained passage in white cabins. In 1887, George Washington Cable, the New Orleans-born liberal critic of the white South, found the name still in use and the pattern probably more rigid.[7]

Most varied were the racial discriminations practiced by regular passenger railways. To understand them, it is useful initially to review the differentiated accommodations that railways typically provided the public, apart from any racial distinctions they enforced.

When traffic justified a minimum of two or three pasenger cars, intercity trains normally offered at least two tiers of service. Immediately behind the engine, or the baggage car if the train included one, was a second-class, low-fare car. (Occasionally, a divided car, called a "combine" by contemporaries, carried both baggage and second-class passengers.) Although sometimes equal in its accommodations to the first-class car or cars further to the rear, often the second-class coach was distinctly inferior, with hard or minimally upholstered seats and less desirable heating, ice-water, and toilet facilities. Whatever its physical comforts, its proximity to the engine meant that when the windows were open, smoke, steam, and perhaps embers permeated its interior. Within the car itself, tobacco smoking was permitted (hence the common label of "smoking car"), and even first-class passengers had to go forward to the car if they wished to smoke. By contemporary accounts, the resulting air was stifling. Profanity and drinking were not unusual among the car's male passengers, and men typically outnumbered women in the car, although it carried both sexes.

Next came one or more first-class cars, which featured more luxurious accommondations, with no smoking allowed. Usually one first-class car would be set aside for "ladies and gentlemen accompanying them." If the train included additional first-class coaches, the latter were open to members of both sexes who paid the higher first-class fare. If not, the conductor or brakeman would sometimes allow unaccompanied males holding first-class tickets to take seats in the ladies' car, if seats were available, but would monitor their behavior. Otherwise, their first-class fares notwithstanding, unaccompanied men had to find seats in the smoking car. (By failing to provide first-class seating to males with first-class tickets, however, the carrier risked legal action.)[8]

How successful were blacks in gaining admission to these different levels of railway service? In The Strange Career of Jim Crow, C. Vann Woodward presented several witnesses whose testimony indicated widespread access. Perhaps the most persuasive of these was T. McCants Stewart, a Boston lawyer who served as a correspondent for the New York Freeman, a Negro newspaper. A black himself and a native of South Carolina, Stewart traveled south along the Atlantic seaboard in the spring of 1885. His interest was the treatment accorded Negroes under the rule of the white Conservatives who had "redeemed" the region from Radical Republican rule. No cover-up of discriminatory practices was likely to come from his pen. "On leaving Washington D.C., I put a chip on my shoulder," he wrote to the Freeman, "and inwardly dared any man to knock it off." But his suspicions proved unfounded, at least with respect to railways. "All along the Atlantic seaboard from Canada to the Gulf of Mexico—through Delaware, Maryland, Virginia, the Carolinas, Georgia, and into Florida, all the old slave States with enormous Negro populations . . . a first-class ticket is good in a first-class coach . . ." As if to obviate the possibility that the first-class coach was a racially segregated first-class coach, Stewart added that Henry W. Grady, the publicist for the "New South" who had recently defended segregated transportation, "would be compelled to ride with a Negro, or walk."[9]

Woodward presented other witnesses with good credentials. One was Thomas Wentworth Higginson, a prewar secret supporter of John Brown and a wartime commander of a Negro regiment. In 1878, Higginson went south on public conveyances to explore conditions in the aftermath of Reconstruction. Carrying with him, as he put it, "the eyes of a tolerably suspicious abolitionist," he should have detected abuse directed toward the

Negro, if there were any. In the states he visited—Virginia, South Carolina, and Florida—he discovered instead that white southerners accepted the presence of Negroes to a degree that compared favorably with the situation in his native New England. He specifically mentioned that he "rode with colored people in first-class cars throughout Virginia and South Carolina . . . ." More testimony came from George Washington Cable, who provided authority for the statement, "In Virginia they [the blacks] may ride exactly as white people do and in the same cars." And Sir George Campbell, a member of the British Parliament, found in his tour of the seaboard South in 1879 that "the humblest black rides with the proudest white on terms of perfect equality and without the smallest symptom of malice or dislike on either side." Even as an English Radical, he was "a little taken aback at first."[10]

The experiences of these four travelers—Stewart, Higginson, Cable, and Campbell—unquestionably establish that some Negroes (and certainly Stewart) rode public conveyances, including first-class coaches, in the company of Caucasians. For despite all the limitations of eye-witness testimony, the four men undoubtedly could identify at least some of the blacks they saw, even if lighter-toned mulattoes escaped their attention. Nevertheless, Woodward has been modest in the claims he makes based on such evidence. In connection with Stewart's account, for example, he uses the phrase "whether typical or not"; and overall, he allows, the evidence is not "conclusive" or "proof of a prevailing pattern. . . . It would be perfectly possible to cite contemporary experiences and testimony of a contrasting character."[11]

In 1890, speaking in Boston before the Women's New England Club, Booker T. Washington offered contrary testimony. To be sure, he claimed that the preceding ten years had seen a lessening of railway discrimination in Virginia, West Virginia, and North Carolina, and "the reformation [was] gradually working its way farther south." But perhaps encouraged by an assurance of privacy "to make statements that were bolder than his customary public utterances," as the editor of Washington's papers has explained, he did not let his probably unwarranted perception of change "farther south" soften his assessment of the current situation. "It is rather hard," he confessed,

> to understand why Southern white people do not object to sitting by the side of a colored person in a street car, and yet if these same persons change from a horse car to a steam car the white person objects to being in the same coach with the negro even though they are thirty feet apart. Notwithstanding the eloquence of the late Mr[.] Grady and newspaper misstatements, the facts are, that in every one of the Gulf states, the Negro is forced to ride in Railroad coaches that are inferior in every way to those given the whites, and they are made to pay the same fare that the whites pay. In many cases the colored people are compelled to ride in the

smoking car, and when this is not the case, one half of the smoking car is portioned off for the colored people, & even in this case the door leading from one room to the other is about as often open as shut.

Washington's own addendum—"it is not the separation that we complain of, but the unequality of accommodations"—underscores his harsh judgment, for it indicates that he was by no means applying a strict integrationist standard to the Gulf states. The addendum also indicates that the improvement he detected in Virginia, West Virginia, and North Carolina did not necessary involve *identity* of accommodations for the Negro.[12]

Washington, who traveled widely, not only thus provided a bleaker assessment, but he also sketched a pattern for the region as a whole. On the one side were the states he associated with improved practices; on the other, the Gulf states plus Georgia, where Washington hinted that black access to first-class cars was the exception.[13] By implication, then, he left South Carolina as the dividing line. The resulting pattern is incomplete, of course, for it omits mention of the border states of the ex-Confederacy, and with respect to one or two states it is probably inaccurate. On balance, though, it proves a serviceable guide.

Prior to the 1890s, Virginia was moving toward less railway segregation, although segregated travel had by no means disappeared. In the first years after the war, common practice was to assign Negroes to second-class or smoking cars, no matter what fare they paid, along with low fare whites. As one result, by the early 1870s some Negroes supported use of separate or Jim Crow cars as a means of obtaining improved accommodations. In January 1871, for example, it was a black legislator who proposed that the House of Delegates establish a committee to seek separate railway cars for Negro passengers. The House rejected the plan, evidently preferring not to disturb the existing smoking car arrangements, but Jim Crow cars began to appear anyway. Other blacks objected, however, and several initiated court actions after being forced to move from first-class accommodations to inferior segregated quarters.[14]

Then, in the late 1870s and the 1880s, properly dressed and behaved blacks evidently came to be accepted into first-class accommodations, just as Stewart, Higginson, Cable, and Washington reported. Charles Wynes, in his study of Virginia race relations, finds that the racial policy of Virginia railways was accurately summarized in this press report, from 1890: "[I]t can be said of railroad travel in Virginia, on some roads at least, that he [the Negro] occupies whatever seats he may be pleased to take in first class car[s]." Of course, the paper's qualifying phrase, "on some roads at least," can hardly be overlooked. The following year, another Virginia newspaper viewed the separate car as sufficiently prominent to remark, "Virginia cannot afford to have the Jim Crow car stand among her other products at the [Chicago] World's Fair"; and the state railroad commissioner publicly acknowledged, albeit indirectly, that some railroads were resorting to the use of second-class cars for all blacks. How extensively this occurred is unknown; and it seems likely, in any event, that most Negro travelers simply did not buy first-class tickets. The result was integrated travel—in smoking cars.[15]

Evidence is less direct, but still persuasive, that practice in Maryland and perhaps North Carolina paralleled Virginia's. Jim Crow legislation was first formally considered in Maryland in 1902 and finally passed in 1904. Even at those late dates, the state's Negroes were sufficiently *unfamiliar* with segregation to cause black leaders, in the course of urging the colored population to oppose the legislation, to take pains to describe the deplorable and humiliating effects produced by such measures further south. North Carolina railways were probably less permissive, but newspapers in the 1870s and 1880s carried reports—some in lurid tones—about blacks riding in first-class cars; and in the 1890s, one argument for legislated segregation in the state was the need to get them off. A white woman explained, for example, that whites should understand how it "feels to get up from a first-class berth in one of the sleepers on the main lines passing Greensboro, to find that a Negro man has occupied the next berth during the night."[16]

In South Carolina, where blacks achieved greatest political success during Reconstruction, racial discrimination on public carriers was an early target of legislation. The resulting equal accommodations law, whatever its limitations, seems clearly to have enabled some Negroes to ride in first-class coaches with whites. Travelers' testimony, as discussed earlier, indicates the practice continued after the collapse of the state's Radical government in April 1877; and as late as 1895 an episode occurred that had a touch of irony. Ben Tillman, one of the race-baiters who gained prominence toward the end of the century, used the occasion of a train ride from Augusta to Columbia to detail his plans for Negro disfranchisement. One of his listeners in the car was a black reporter.[17]

Yet the presence of Negroes on first-class cars in the state may not have been all it seemed to the passing observer, for two reasons. One was the nuances of travel customs. A writer in the *Atlantic Monthly* for June 1877 explained how South Carolina whites would "ride on the same seats in cars with blacks if the latter are traveling in the capacity of servants, nurses, etc. But they would die before doing the same if the latter were traveling as equals." Blacks did ride in the same cars, "although if a negro enters a [first-class] car in which all the other travelers are white[,] the latter, if they do nothing else, plainly evince aversion, and, if practicable, a wide space is left around such intruders." In short, separation within cars provided an alternative to separate cars. The writer also revealed a second feature: "It is not often . . . that any of the blacks besides politicans enter first-class conveyances[,] on account of poverty"; instead, he explained, "second-class tickets are purchased." The practice dated to the Reconstruction period, and by the early 1880s, Iza Duffus Hardy, an Englishwoman who traveled through the state, took it as the norm that blacks would use the cheaper second-class cars. This observation casts a revealing light on an early finding by the Interstate Commerce Commission, which, after hearing testimony about a Negro passenger's journey, concluded: "[I]n South Carolina and some other States, where a large colored population resides, no separation of white and colored passengers is required on railroad trains, but first and second class cars are provided with lower rates of fare for the second class, and . . . both colors may travel in cars of either class, as they prefer."[18]

Georgia's record, at least by the mid-1880s, was less ambiguous. True, T. McCants Stewart cited the state in 1885 as one in which a first-class ticket brought passage on the first-class coach used by whites. Seven years earlier, however, Colonel Higginson had heard that Georgia blacks "were not allowed in first-class cars; but they had always a decent second-class car, opening from the smoking car, with the door usually closed between." Iza Duffus Hardy's description, from her 1883 trip, disclosed other discriminatory practices, along with some legerdemain with labels. Having asked a conductor if blacks were assigned to second-class cars, she was told, "No, no second-class [car] on this train. . . . They'll ride in the forward part of the smoking car . . . . " On another line, evidently also in Georgia, she found a car labeled "For Colored Passengers" and inspected it, reporting, "This car was in every respect exactly like the car reserved for us 'white folk'; the same velvet seats, ice-water tank; every comfort the same—and, of course, the same fare . . . ." The latter arrangement would presumably have satisfied Robert Smalls, a Republican Congressman from South Carolina and a Negro, who claimed in 1884 that blacks "have no objection to riding in a separate car when the car is of the same character as that provided for white people to ride in." But drawing on his own experience, Smalls declared that in Georgia "they have a car called a second-class car; and notwithstanding a colored man may buy a first-class ticket here in Washington, or anywhere else, to go perhaps to New Orleans, yet when he reaches the State of Georgia, he is compelled to go into a 'Jim Crow car,' which is placed next to the locomotive."[19]

On balance, then, we need not accept as completely accurate Henry Grady's boast, made the same year as Stewart's trip, that Georgia's railways provided blacks with equal facilities, but there seems little reason in most cases to doubt the truthfulness of his acknowledgment that they received separate accommodations. Certainly the fledgling Interstate Commerce Commission, which, as we have seen, was not inclined invariably to assert that separation was the rule, agreed with the latter part of Grady's assessment, finding in 1887 that regulations for separate cars "are customary on the railroads of Georgia . . . ."[20]

Elsewhere in the South by the mid-1880s, except in Louisiana and perhaps Arkansas, blacks commonly found themselves segregated into inferior coaches, regardless of the fares they paid. Even during Radical rule, this had been typical, except when the terms of access were still less favorable. One line in Alabama then went so far as to follow the prewar practice of assigning Negroes to the outside platforms of cars. As for Mississippi, it is true that in 1872 one of its United States Senators (a white Republican) bragged, "Colored men can travel . . . and do travel . . . in first class cars, and . . . there is no insult offered them anywhere . . . ." More telling, however, was the experience of a black Republican Congressman who had himself been ordered out of a railroad restaurant in Mississippi. (Interestingly, the same man claimed Mississippi compared favorably with Alabama.) In another well-publicized episode from the Reconstruction period, a conductor ordered Mississippi's black secretary of state out of a "ladies' car." Not surprisingly, such treatment continued after the Radicals fell from power. Exclusion from first-class facilities also became general in Texas and Tennessee. (Regarding the latter state's arrangements, however, Henry Grady sought to turn vice into virtue by noting that Tennessee courts had awarded monetary damages to one black woman who had been denied a first-class seat.) A measure of the region's customs may also be gleaned from the fact that, just as in Virginia early in the preceding decade, some blacks sought a remedy in racially separate first-class facilities. Segregation, as Howard Rabinowitz has remarked, was preferable to the now-forgotten alternative of exclusion.[21]

In detail, what were the accommodations available to blacks in these remaining states? Again, because he hardly carried the taint of extremism, Booker T. Washington is a persuasive witness. In 1885, he offered particulars:

> (a) that in most cases the smoking car and that in which colored people are put are the same; (b) when not put directly into the smoking car they are crammed into one end of a smoking car with a door between that is as much open as closed, making little difference between this and the smoking car; (c) on some of the roads the colored passengers are carried in one end of the baggage car, there being a partition between them and the baggage or express; (d) only a half coach is given to the colored people and this one is almost invariably an old one with low ceiling and it soon becomes crowded almost to suffocation and is misery to one knowing the effects of impure air. The seats in the coach given to colored people are always greatly inferior to those given the whites. The car is usually very filthy. There is no carpet as in the first class coach. White men are permitted in the car for colored people. Whenever a poorly dressed, slovenly white man boards the train he is shown into the colored half coach. When a white man gets drunk or wants to lounge around in an indecent position he finds his way into the colored department.

The fare policies of Alabama's railways constituted Washington's immediate target, but the situation was hardly localized.[22]

Perhaps because of the strength of the New Orleans black community, which had roots in a large free black population before the war, Louisiana provided a contrast to the other Gulf states. During Reconstruction, threats of court action, actual suits, carefully drawn railway charters, and legislative investigations together proved effective in gaining equal accommodations for Negroes, although the practice of assigning them to smoking cars was far from unknown. Openness continued into the 1880s, and George Washington Cable found a marked contrast between the segregation practiced on Louisiana steamboats and the situation on some railways, "where . . . a Negro or mulatto may sit where he will." Two recent historians support Cable's assessment, but note that "many" lines ran Jim Crow cars by the late 1880s. And while another recent study, focusing on New Orleans, finds the practice of Jim Crow cars had become rigid by that date, probably the best evidence that it had not is the difficulty experienced by Louisiana blacks in setting up a test case to challenge the separate car law passed in 1890. As the following chapter describes, at least some of the railways simply did not care to enforce the requirement of separation. Practice in neighboring Arkansas likely fell closer to Louisiana's than, say, to Georgia's or Alabama's. But in both Louisiana and Arkansas, in contrast to Virginia, the trend was unquestionably away from equality of access and accommodation.[23]

Someday, an enterprising historian may undertake the company-by-company or perhaps route-by-route study necessary to determine the exact degree of separation by race, and of discrimination in level of service, on public conveyances in the South during the three decades following the Civil War. Such imprecise qualifiers as "few," "some," "often," "most," and the like, which dot this chapter, will be banished from the resulting account. Until then—and certainly as background for the argument developed in the following chapters—it suffices to say that in the states of the former Confederacy, from the end of the war into the late 1880s and early 1890s, segregation or discrimination existed almost everywhere to an identifiable degree; and in perhaps half the states these practices flourished to the extent that their absence was the exception. If streetcars were less segregated for fifteen or twenty years, that openness was declining by 1890; integrated travel on steamboats had always been the exception; and throughout the period, black travelers on regular railways more often than not encountered either segregation or discrimination in quality of service—or both. Moreover, unlike other public institutions and accommodations, with which Negroes had only temporary contact (as in the case of schools) or could avoid (hotels, restaurants, and places of amusement), reliance on public conveyances was unavoidable for large numbers throughout their lives.[24]

III

Whatever their exact extent, the practices just described largely developed outside the framework of legislative regulations. Southerners nonetheless realized that statutory law offered a tool for shaping relations between the races on public carriers. In particular, an initial wave of separate car laws crested in the late 1880s and early 1890s; and historians, when describing the legal framework of segregation, have commonly focused on this batch of measures, along with comparable legislation in a second wave around the turn of the century. These enactments established the *de jure* segregation that, depending on the historian, either ratified existing *de facto* separation or else carried it further while dashing other options for interracial relations. Yet the story of legislative grapplings with transportation segregation began earlier, in the first year after the Civil War, with brief experiments in railway segregation, and then shifted under Radical governments to a series of equal accommodations laws.

Presidentially established Reconstruction governments in Mississippi and Florida initiated the process of legislative intervention. In November 1865, as part of a broader law regulating the duties of public carriers, Mississippi adopted a provision that penalized railway officials and employees who were found guilty of allowing "any freedman, negro, or mulatto, to ride on any first class passenger cars, set apart, or used by, and for white persons . . . ." The section was not to apply, however, "in the case of negroes or mulattoes, traveling with their mistresses, in the capacity of nurses." Florida's regulation, which was passed two months later as part of the state's comprehensive Black Code, took aim directly at offending blacks, rather than railway officials, and provided punishment for "any negro, mulatto, or other person of color [who] shall intrude himself . . . into any railroad car or other public vehicle set apart for the exclusive accommodation of white people . . . ." The section also banned intrusions into religious and public assemblies, and extended as well to whites entering Negro cars or assemblies. But the penalty—whipping or the pillory—was reminiscent of slave punishments and reveals black, not white, intrusions as the true object of the law.[25]

Significantly, neither Mississippi's nor Florida's law required *any* accommodations for blacks. This, by contrast, was the special focus of a Texas measure in November 1866. Railways in that state had been assigning Negroes to the smoking car, along with low-fare whites; the new law ordered companies "to attach to each passenger train . . . one car for the special accommodation of Freedmen." The only law of the three that came close on its face to the equal-but-separate enactments passed toward the end of the century, it provided no penalties and not surprisingly proved ineffective—railways continued to seat blacks in racially mixed second-class coaches.[26]

After congressionally authorized Radical governments succeeded the Conservative regimes in Florida, Mississippi, and Texas, they replaced these early measures with civil rights legislation that covered all public carriers. Equal accommodations laws were also passed by Tennessee, South Carolina, Georgia, Louisiana, and Arkansas. Adopted between 1868 and 1873, the new statutes varied in details, some forbidding distinctions or discriminations on the basis of color, others outlawing deprivations of full and equal or impartial enjoyment of facilities. The legislation also varied in its intended impact. In Georgia, for example, a brief provision in October 1870 that common carriers "shall furnish like and equal accommodations for all persons, without distinction of race, color, or previous condition," was probably not designed to require integration, although the legislature defeated explicit equal-but-separate amendments. Eight days later, another Georgia law required that railways "furnish equal accommodations to all, without regard to race, color, or previous condition, when a greater sum of fare is exacted than was demanded prior to January 1, 1861, which was at that date half fare for persons of color," which suggests prevention of fare-gouging was the goal. By contrast, the Arkansas law of 1873, one of the most detailed, not only mandated equal accommodations for equal fares, but went further in stressing that passengers were entitled to accommodations for which they themselves were willing and able to pay, a point the second Georgia measure had left silent. Among the different measures, sanctions ranged from authorization of civil suits to fines and imprisonment for derelict employees and forfeiture of corporate charters.[27]

George Washington Cable, despite his attacks on the discriminatory practices of public carriers, later recalled the equal accommodations laws as "freedmen's follies." When judged against the problem these measures addressed, however, several were modestly successful as long as Republican governments remained in office. This was true at least in South Carolina, where, according to historian Joel Williamson, the 1868 law had an immediate effect on common carriers. As noted earlier, steamboats were generally the most segregated conveyances, which gives special significance to the observations of a northern teacher who returned to the state after a short absence:

> We took a small steamer from Charleston for Beaufort. Here we found a decided change since we went North. Then no colored person was allowed on the upper deck, now there were no restrictions,—there could be none, for a law had been passed in favor of the negroes. They were everywhere, choosing the best staterooms and the best seats at the table. Two prominent colored members of the State Legislature were on board with their families. There were also several well-known Southerners, still uncompromising rebels. It was a curious scene and full of significance. An interesting study to watch the exultant faces of the negroes, and the scowling faces of the rebels,—rebels still against manifest destiny . . . .

On South Carolina's railways, close ties between owners and Radical politicians promoted compliance. Yet many blacks continued to receive smoking car assignments, and the colored population pushed for additional legislation.[28]

While South Carolina's equal accommodations laws apparently produced no court actions, Louisiana's legislation did. In New Orleans, Negroes won suits involving a number of areas, not just railways, and the black community had sufficient support within the city's court system to give most white businessmen pause before violating the law. In one noted suit, Mrs. Josephine DeCuir, a black woman who owned a plantation upriver on the Mississippi, won damages from the owners of the steamship *Governor Allen*. At the same time, however, steamship travel remained largely segregated, and streetcars had been desegregated after direct action by blacks *prior* to passage of equal accommodations legislation. Railway compliance resulted, moreover, from ongoing Negro political action as well as from suits and threatened suits. And in the state generally, just as in South Carolina, the practice of smoking car assignments persisted. Not surprisingly, then, Louisiana blacks also demanded further and stronger enactments.[29]

Evidence regarding the Reconstruction-era effects of equal accommodations laws elsewhere is much less complete. During congressional debates over federal civil rights legislation in the early 1870s, several speakers argued that the success of the state measures illustrated the benefits that new national action would bring in other states. The laws of Florida, Mississippi, and Arkansas were singled out for praise in this regard. Against these judgments, however, should be placed more recent conclusions that the laws of the latter two states, like the Texas Act, were dead letters. For the region as a whole, the net effect of the legislation was probably to help nudge white Southerners away from exclusion of Negroes from public facilities and toward allowing segregated access.[30]

What is certain is that the state measures proved largely ineffective as barriers to segregation after the Reconstruction governments fell from power at various dates from the late 1860s through early 1877. In 1884, admittedly, Robert Smalls, the black Congressman from South Carolina, argued that his state's law, in contrast to Georgia's, continued operative. Accompanying this claim, however, was Smalls's remark, noted earlier, that equal-but-separate facilities would meet Negro demands, which makes his assessment of South Carolina's law difficult to evaluate. Five years later, at any rate, the still unrepealed South Carolina legislation did not prevent the Richmond and Danville Railway from formally experimenting with segregated cars on their excursion trains to the state fair. (Perversely, however, the Georgia statute did not lapse into desuetude, for the state railway commission and the Interstate Commerce Commission both gave it an equal-but-separate interpretation.)[31]

IV

Tennessee had been the first southern state to enact a Reconstruction-era equal accommodations law. In 1881, it became the first to move toward legislatively mandated transportation segregation based ostensibly on the equal-but-separate principle. The catalyst was a measure passed six years earlier that had abrogated the common-law duty of common carriers, hotels, and places of amusement to serve anyone who is willing and able to pay and is otherwise presentable in appearance and demeanor. The 1875 law had given operators of public facilities the same right as any private party to discriminate among persons to be carried, admitted, or entertained. Adopted to subvert the federal Civil Rights Act of 1875, which could be interpreted as banning discrimination in facilities that had common-law duties to serve the public, Tennessee's 1875 law in effect legalized the practice of charging blacks first-class railway fares but assigning them to inferior coaches. Then, after a Democratic split within the state led to the election of a Republican governor and a Republican-organized state house of representatives, the four black members of the house, who were all Republicans, sought repeal of the state's 1875 legislation. When they twice failed on close votes, white Republicans in the house compromised on a bill which had already passed the Democratic-controlled senate. Signed by the Republican governor, this became the state's separate car law of 1881.[32]

Because the Tennessee measure has been labeled "the first 'Jim Crow' law," it requires examination. After a preamble that recited the existing practice of indiscriminately assigning Negroes to smoking cars, the law provided that

> all railroad companies located and operated in this State shall furnish separate cars, or portions of cars cut off by partition walls, in which all colored passengers who pay first class passenger rates of fare, may have the privilege to enter and occupy, and such apartments shall be kept in good repair, and with the same conveniences, and subject to the same rules governing other first class cars, preventing smoking and obscene language.

The exact wording is important. The section did not order railways to restrict blacks to separate accommodations, but only to make separate first-class facilities available. Accordingly, the Act was a "Jim Crow" law, but not the kind of Jim Crow law that other southern states began passing in the late 1880s. Indeed, Tennessee authorities either perceived the difference, or lost sight of the 1881 Act, for in 1891 they enacted a new law. In an important respect, however, response to the 1881 measure anticipated the future, for railways simply ignored the law's equality requirement. Significantly, the black members of the legislature seem to have anticipated such a result.[33]

Six years later, southern states began passing mandatory Jim Crow transportation laws in earnest. The legislation came in two waves, one centering on 1890, the other peaking about a decade later. The main focus was railway travel, although some of the later laws added streetcars or steamboats. Of major interst here are the laws enacted prior to the *Plessy* decision in 1896, which included measures in Florida (1887), Mississippi (1888), Texas (1889 and 1891), Louisiana (1890 and 1894), Alabama (1891), Arkansas (1891 and 1893), Tennessee (1891), Georgia (1891), and Kentucky (1892). In the second surge, between 1898 and 1901, laws were passed in South Carolina, North Carolina, and Virginia (each of which also passed subsequent acts). Finally, in 1904 and 1907, Maryland and Oklahoma joined the movement.[34]

Among the nine states adopting measures between 1887 and 1892, the legislation was not entirely uniform. The initial measure, from Florida, departed from subsequent laws prior to *Plessy* in that it regulated only first-class service; railways were required to sell first-class tickets to "respectable persons of color" and to provide them with separate first-class accommodations equal to those offered first-class white passengers. Texas's first measure was also distinctive, for it did not require separate coaches but only authorized them. In this respect, it made no change in the common-law authority of railways, which Chapter Six discusses, but by providing for fines or imprisonment as sanctions against non-complying passengers it significantly altered the penalties for violation. In 1891, three years later, Texas passed a mandatory separate car law. The other states all required railways to provide equal-but-separate service on passenger trains, either with separate cars or by secure partitions to divide cars. All the states established fines and jail terms for railway employees who failed to make the required assignments by race, and all but Georgia included penalties for non-complying railways (or for their corporate officers). All but Florida provided that the lines should deny service to non-complying passengers (usually with accompanying immunity from liability for non-carriage). Of the initial nine states, five additionally imposed criminal penalties (fines or imprisonment) on passengers.[35]

Several exemptions appeared in the legislation.[36] Six states mentioned nurses or personal attendants. Only Florida went so far as to limit the nurse exemption to "female colored nurses"; the other nurse exemptions were sex- and color-blind, but almost certainly this was a distinction without a difference.[37] Arkansas in 1891 pioneered the peace officer exemption, allowing "officers accompanying prisoners [to] be assigned to the coach or room to which said prisoners belong by reason of race," but modified this in 1893 to provide that officers with prisoners would be assigned "to coaches where they least interfere with the comfort of other passengers." (With the modification, railways probably assigned all prisoners, white and black, to the colored coach.[38]) Two other states also exempted peace officers with prisoners. Exemption of railway employees by three states undoubtedly represented an effort to err on the side of caution, for even in states without the provision black employees surely entered white cars. The only significant exemption regarding type of service pertained to streetcars, which five of the nine states specifically excluded from coverage (and which only Georgia explicitly included). The exemption of sleeping cars and luxury "chair" cars by four states only served to relieve the railways of having to provide such facilities for blacks.

The passage of Jim Crow acts by nine states within a five-year period, between 1887 and 1892, suggests that the causes were more than strictly local. Although confident generalization would require close and comparable studies of the circumstances surrounding each of the measures—studies that presently do not exist in sufficient number—several explanations offer insights into the source of the legislation.

The psychological recesses of southern whites contributed two ingredients. Explorations of individual and especially group subconsciousness are almost always hazardous, but W. J. Cash suggested one factor in his classic account, *The Mind of the South*. Discussing the years after the Civil War, Cash asked his readers to "recall the central status that Southern woman had long ago taken up in Southern emotion—her identification with the very notion of the South itself." Once the restraints that slavery had placed on blacks were loosened, whites easily found an excuse for interracial violence in what Cash labeled a "rape complex," or the fear that the promiscuity of black males imperiled the purity of southern white womanhood, and thus of the white race, particularly if blacks moved upward in society. Although Cash's main focus was the resulting physical violence, his insight applies as well to other white attempts to restrict Negro social equality. Indeed, reference by whites to "social equality" became something of a code to evoke fears of black intrusion into private life, or worse.[39]

A second deeply rooted difficulty for the Negro was the race's historical damnation in the white mind. As Joel Williamson has observed, "Freedom for Negroes came simultaneously with the defeat of the South and the beginning of what, in its political phase, was called Reconstruction. In the study of American History we have come to accept the confluence of these two great events as natural . . . . Yet for the future harmony of races the conjunction was hardly less than disastrous." In historical myth, white southerners conjoined black freedom with white defeat, and added a version of Reconstruction that emphasized black misdeeds and buffoonery. The resulting view, in which blacks served nicely as "enemies surrogate for the hated North," quickly became a reflexive part of the mental landscape.[40]

These two elements—white fears about Negro sexual attacks and the link between the black race, bloody defeat, and purported Radical misrule during Reconstruction—probably encouraged and certainly did not restrain anti-Negro actions by the white population. Yet they fail to account for the timing and content of the Jim Crow legislation of the late 1880s and beyond.

At first glance, the reform crusades of the small white farmers, during the late 1880s and the 1890s, offer a better clue of a psychological sort. In *The Strange Career of Jim Crow*, Professor Woodward noted that the white agrarians, who coalesced in many areas into the People's Party and who on occasion even sought to mold a biracial political alliance with black farmers and tenants, eventually turned against the Negro. Drawing on psychological theories about the relation between frustration and aggression, Woodward suggested the small white farmers found the Negro a convenient scapegoat for their own political frustrations.[41] Whether or not the explanation is useful otherwise in accounting for the South's turn to highly overt racism in the 1890s, it fails to fit the chronology of the first wave of Jim Crow legislation: if the Populists had not scored many successes by mid-1892, neither had real frustration yet set in.

In a more direct fashion, however, the agrarian movement in several states probably contributed support to separate car measures. For one thing, legislators with small farmer constituencies likely saw the legislation as a means of obtaining segregated cars for poorer whites, who normally rode the second-class cars that railroad company policy often left unsegregated. Wealthier whites, who were able to afford first-class transportation, already had access to largely segregated cars. In Arkansas, suggestively, the state senate deleted a provision from the law that would have exempted nurses accompanying members of the other race; and the circumstances of the amendment indicate that one motive was resentment against the upper-class whites who could afford nurses.[42]

In addition, the interest of the southern white agrarians in railroad reform may have eased the way for Jim Crow restrictions, which were, after all, a form of railway regulation. Florida's governor had recommended new railway regulations to the same legislative session that enacted that state's Jim Crow law. The next year, in 1888, one of Mississippi's initial Jim Crow provisions was embedded in a comprehensive restatement of the duties that carriers owed passengers and customers. The New Orleans *Daily Picayune* editorialized that the Louisiana measure of 1890 constituted a desirable "railroad reform" and attacked railway opposition to the bill. "In view of the extreme liberality with which the State has treated them," argued the paper, "there should have been at least some concessions from the powerful corporations to the people." And in 1891, the Arkansas separate car law included a couple of non-racial railway regulations; the Texas law came from the same legislature that enacted major railway reform legislation; and Tennessee's emerged from a session that witnessed attacks on railways and trusts (although little actual reform legislation).[43]

In another way, too, political agrarianism may have contributed to the separate car legislation, for the threat of third party action by the small farmers, along with protest channeled through the Republican Party, led the dominant Democrats to push franchise restriction, with black voters as an obvious target if not always the only intended victims. It is suggestive, in any event, that the Jim Crow laws of 1887–92 were enacted during the same period that white Democrats began in earnest to exclude blacks from the political process. Aside from perhaps Georgia and Kentucky, in every state passing a separate car law during this period there was concurrent—and, in fact, generally more vigorous—debate over black disfranchisement, or, as in the case of Louisiana, close attention to debates in neighboring states. In its various stages, moreover, the disfranchisement campaign raised the shrillness of white rhetoric about black incompetence. If this did anything, it must have heightened white convictions about the undesirability of associating with Negroes on conditions of equality.[44]

But the most direct trigger for the initial wave of Jim Crow legislation was increasing black unwillingness to defer to whites. A new generation, raised outside the confines of slavery and the web of antebellum restrictions on free blacks, was coming of age. Negro newspapers perceived growing black assertiveness in the face of indignities inflicted by whites; and among the white population, stories of "uppity" Negroes increased during the 1880s. The immediate context for Alabama's separate car law, significantly, was the threat of a series of black suits directed against the state's railways as a means of improving service. White attitudes made the problem worse, as Texas Governor James S. Hogg candidly admitted when he asked for a stronger Jim Crow law in 1891, stating, "Insolence on the one side, and intolerance on the other, unnecessarily exhibited by the disturbing elements of both races, have borne this fruit." Even incidents of white violence *against* Negroes could be put to use, as in Georgia where one state representative argued that a separate car law would aid in "preventing little riots" on railways. For evidence, he cited an incident involving five black preachers who had boarded a first-class railway coach. When asked to leave, the churchmen refused and a crowd of whites boarded the train and beat them.[45]

By itself, of course, the "fact" of changed black behavior no more "caused" the Jim Crow legislation than did the other ingredients already surveyed; but it evoked interpretations from the politically dominant race that produced the result. Reporting his recent observations in the South, for example, English visitor James Bryce borrowed from Methodist Episcopal Bishop Atticus G. Haygood the assessment that blacks had acquired just enough education to gain new wants but not the "ability to satisfy them." Bryce then added his own gloss:

> This class of half-educated colored people, who can read, but have not yet learned to think, and are beginning to be averse to manual labor, increases daily, while the generation which had the deference, and often the affection, of the slave to his master, will soon have passed away. *It is, therefore, possible that the problem may within the next twenty or thirty years enter into a phase more threatening than the present.*[46]

Could it be that the Englishman had heard such predictions from his white southern contacts? Evidence was accumulating, it seemed, that black uppityness translated into increasing Negro crime rates. Another and not entirely independent element was the racist strand in much of the scientific and social-scientific thought of the period, including predictions of black regression into savagery. We will return to intellectual racism in a later chapter; here it simply needs noting as not only a convenient and conscious rationale for legislated separation but also an element that meshed with the "rape complex" in unquestionably affecting the felt perceptions of contemporary whites who were trying, as people usually do, to understand the world around them. Part of that world was a new black assertiveness, and the resulting interpretations gave urgency to mandatory racial separation.[47]

Further compounding the problem from the perspective of whites, urbanization produced a more permissive environment. Compared with rural areas, opportunity for direct personal control of blacks—that is, for informal, non-governmental maintenance of established interracial relationships—decreased in the cities. In the antebellum South, urban fluidity and mobility had proved to have a corrosive effect on slavery within cities and on black deference toward whites. Local governments then stepped in with ordinances to exclude blacks from hotels and places of amusement and to separate the races in other areas, including public conveyances. In like manner, toward the end of the century, growing southern urbanization, although still low by northern standards, gave one more incentive to racial separation as a means of controlling intrusions by the new black.[48] And certainly one need not have been a city-dweller to have been infected by fears about promiscuously intrusive contacts within urban environments.

The least uncertain element is the immediate source of the verbal formulas used in the separate car acts, for they required no inventiveness on the part of state legislators. In content, they had been repeatedly anticipated in the series of court decisions on non-statutory transportation segregation that Chapter Six explores. At a more popular level, Henry Grady had suggested the way. In 1885, for instance, while arguing for "the segregation of the races" in *all* classes of railway service, he stated: "On railways, as elsewhere, the solution of the race problem is, equal advantages for the same money,—equal in comfort, safety, and exclusiveness,—but separate." And the preceding year, "equal but separate," the exact wording used by five of the nine states passing transportation segregation laws between 1887 and 1892, had appeared in the congressional debate over whether to include race discrimination within the prohibitions of the proposed Interstate Commerce Act.[49]

The need for such a formula was clear. As early as 1870, a federal judge in Baltimore had vaguely linked the Fourteenth Amendment to the requirement for equality in accommodations if separation was to be legal. In 1883, more tellingly, the United States Supreme Court came close to stating that, by its own force, the Amendment forbade states from depriving persons of equality of accommodations on public conveyances. Although the precise point had not been decided by the Supreme Court, the force of the argument was illustrated during the legislative history of Alabama's 1888 law. When one representative proposed striking the word "equal," another responded that without it, the legislation faced judicial reversal.[50]

The statutory mandate of "equal but separate" promised improvement over customary arrangements on many conveyances and may indeed have seemed a victory of sorts to some Negroes. Anyway, it was far from the worst of official policies, as John W. Cell has reminded us, noting the fate of the American Indian.[51] But a group in Louisiana decided nonetheless to challenge that state's Jim Crow legislation.

CHAPTER TWO

Plessy in Louisiana:
The Test Cases

I

Plessy v. Ferguson had its beginnings in black opposition to the Louisiana Separate Car Act, which became law in mid-1890. But a legal challenge to the measure required both organized support and development of an appropriate legal strategy. Chance also played a role. It was the end of 1892 before the state Supreme Court received and ruled on the case, thus completing the Louisiana phase of *Plessy* and giving the issues and arguments in it much of their final cast.

The story begins with the introduction of the separate car bill into the Louisiana legislature at the start of its 1890 session in May. Resistance coalesced immediately.[1] Seventeen blacks, all members of the recently formed American Citizens' Equal Rights Association, denounced the proposed "class legislation" in a memorial filed on May 24. It would violate the basic American tenet "that all men are created equal," they charged, and then asked, "Will it seriously be contended that such a problematical proposition as the ethnical origins of color is a sufficient cause for a deliberate interference with settled rights?" Having challenged one rationale for the legislation, they further anticipated the thrust of later legal arguments when they held that "Citizenship is national and has no color." But appeals to principle failed, and political maneuver proved no more successful in the end. The house passed the bill, and just as soon as supporters of an effort to recharter the state lottery company side-stepped Governor Francis T.

28

Nicholls's veto of the measure and no longer needed the votes of the legislature's eighteen Negro members, the senate added its approval to the segregation measure, which the governor signed.[2]

The new law required "equal, but separate" accommodations for blacks and whites on all passenger railways, other than street railroads. Without attempting a definition of "race" (and without grammatical rigor), it mandated that "[n]o person or persons, shall be permitted to occupy seats in coaches, other than the ones, assigned, to them on account of the race they belong to." The measure went on to describe the duties of "officers of such passenger trains"—that is, of employees like conductors and brakemen—and also of passengers and railroad company officers and directors. Train officers were required to assign passengers to the proper cars or compartments and, upon conviction for making incorrect assignments, faced a maximum twenty-five dollar fine or twenty days in jail. A passenger "insisting on going into a coach or compartment to which by race he d[id] not belong" risked the same penalties. In addition, a train officer could refuse to carry a non-complying passenger "and for such refusal neither he nor the railroad company which he represent[ed]" would be liable for damages in Louisiana's courts. For company officers and directors of non-complying railroads, fines ranged from $100 to $500; and for conductors and other employees on non-complying trains, from twenty-five to fifty dollars. (The sanction against an employee on a non-complying train thus differed from the penalty imposed on an employee who personally made an incorrect assignment.) Exempted from the law's coverage were "nurses attending children of the other race."[3]

Two of the signers of the May 24 memorial had been Louis A. Martinet, an energetic attorney and physician who in 1889 founded the New Orleans *Crusader*, and Rodolphe L. Desdunes, a Customs Office clerk who, like Martinet, was a prominent "person of color" in the city's Creole community. Both men now used the columns of the *Crusader* to attack the separate car law, and Martinet in particular urged a court fight, calling "for the American Citizens' Equal Rights Association to gather funds to test the constitutionality of this law." "We'll make a case, a test case," he continued, "and bring it before the Federal Courts on the grounds of the invasion of the right [of] a person to travel through the States unmolested." Over a year passed, however, before a legal challenge began to shape up, and then it took unexpected turns.

On September 1, 1891, New Orleans blacks organized a "Citizens' Committee to Test the Constitutionality of the Separate Car Law." Formed at the immediate instigation of Aristide Mary, another leading "Creole of color," the group itself was drawn largely from the same community. Although he held no formal office, Louis Martinet seems to have provided much of the Committee's ongoing momentum. (Toward the end of October, he reported that "[i]n addition to my usual labors, I have nearly all the work

[of] our Committee to do & it keeps me busy"; and by early December he reiterated the complaint: "Matters would progress more rapidly if other members of our Committee would take some of this work on them; but they leave it all to me . . . .") The Committee's first requirements were legal counsel and a fund to support a court case.

To secure legal talent, Martinet contacted Albion W. Tourgée, a former carpetbagger in North Carolina, successful novelist, and perhaps the nation's leading white publicist for Negro rights. A skilled lawyer then living in Mayville, New York, Tourgée had already publicized the Louisiana law and black resistance to it in his regular column in the Chicago *Inter Ocean*, after a black from Kansas, visiting in New Orleans, had contacted him in the summer of 1890 about developments there. He now took the case without fee, and on October 10, the Citizens' Committee formally elected him "leading counsel in the case, from beginning to end." He would have "power to choose associates"—Martinet had earlier suggested several nationally known Republican lawyers—and to review and if necessary revise the pleadings of local counsel. Fund-raising also proceeded well. Indeed, the Committee cast a national net, and eventually the group raised nearly $3000.[4]

Obtaining a local attorney proved more difficult. The Citizens' Committee had first hoped to get a prominent New Orleans lawyer, a Republican, whom Martinet described as "the only one, with a good standing at the bar, who we have reason to believe is friendly." To cover the expected several stages of litigation the man asked a total of $3000, and while Martinet did "not think the terms too high, considering that the rights of a people are involved," he told Tourgée that "we do not wish to obligate ourselves beyond our ability to [cover?] obligations." By late October, another local attorney indicated some willingness to take the case. This was Thomas J. Semmes, the leader of the New Orleans bar and a former president of the American Bar Association, who asked a fee of $2500. Eventually, though, Semmes backed out, fearing to draw criticism by supporting the Committee's position. Martinet himself was "glad of this," for he doubted Semmes's loyalties and suspected his heart would not really have been in the case.

The Citizens' Committee then fell back on James C. Walker, who had earlier been passed over because, as Martinet explained to Tourgée, "he is not known much except as a criminal lawyer" and the Committee lacked "faith in his ability for this sort of case." From the beginning, however, Martinet himself thought Walker was impressive, initially describing him as "a friend & a conscientious & painstaking lawyer" and later as "a good, upright, and conscientious man . . . [who] will give us solid work." Helping shape Martinet's assessment was Walker's background in local Republican politics and subsequent disgust at dealings he had seen, as well as the Creole's own professional association with the white attorney in several cases. Also a factor was the absence of black lawyers of sufficient attainment. Excluding himself, Martinet described black members of the bar as "practic[ing] almost exclusively in the police courts. . . . I don't know any of them who could be of assistance. They would rather obstruct." As for his own involvement, Martinet felt too pressed by other business. Besides, even though the Committee had voted that he should be in the case, he had been closely involved in raising the defense fund and wished no one to attribute ulterior motives to him. So Walker was the choice, for a fee of $1000, and on December 29, 1891, Martinet finally cemented the relationship.[5]

Much earlier, in September and early October, Tourgée and Martinet had already begun to explore ways to set in motion a challenge to the law that would take account of both railway practices and existing legal doctrines. One option was to have a mulatto woman who was nearly white attempt to board a white car. By avoiding the problem of seating a male in a car which by railway policy might be reserved for ladies and their escorts, Tourgée presumably sought to narrow the issue to color; and by setting up the case around a light-complexioned Negro, the arbitrariness of the classification would be accentuated, which, as we will discover later, was a point of importance under developing Fourteenth Amendment jurisprudence. But Martinet observed that a nearly white Negro might not be refused entrance to a white car, at least in the New Orleans area, for "people of tolerably fair complexion, even if unmistakably colored, enjoy here a large degree of immunity from the accursed prejudice."

Alternatively, a black could book a seat from out of state and be forced into a Jim Crow car on entry into Louisiana. This would create an interstate commerce issue. But by late 1891, all the surrounding states had similar legislation, which meant the person would probably be assigned a separate car from the beginning of his journey. He or she might, however, move unobserved to the white car after beginning the trip; and either way the law would be suitably violated.

A third approach was "to have a black attempt to buy a sleeper ticket & be refused after a white person ha[d] received one . . . ." Such a refusal on the part of the railway would presumably have been illegal under Louisiana's law (although not under the separate car laws of some other states), which meant this arrangement would not test the constitutionality of the legislation, a consideration Tourgée surely recognized. Yet the approach offered a means of increasing the burden of the law on the state's railways. Martinet cautioned, however, that "at all the railroad offices, so far as I know, berths or sleepers are sold to all who hold first class tickets." In short, a colored person would probably not be refused sleeper service.

Another area receiving attention was the form of the initial legal action. Because the law allowed railway employees simply to refuse to carry passengers who failed to go to their assigned cars, a purposeful violation might not result in criminal charges being filed against the black violator.

Somewhat inconsistent with his view of actual railway practices in the New Orleans area, Martinet feared, too, that if the person making the test were not challenged prior to the time the train started, "they [presumably the employees and perhaps the white passengers] will simply beat & throw him out & there will be no arrest." Each of these possible railway responses— simple non-carriage or forcible ejection—was legally unattractive because it would require a suit for civil damages as the only way of testing the law. Because the law immunized railways and their employees against suits, beginning an action would be difficult, and Martinet expected that even if one were successfully filed, it would prove lengthy.

As a result, an arrest pursuant to the criminal provision of the law became important to secure. "[T]o make this case, Martinet summarized, "the person will have to be refused admission into the 'white' car here before the train starts & attempt to force or gain an entrance . . . ." This "would require some tact," but it could be done in the New Orleans area "without personal danger." The legal focus would then shift to a *habeas corpus* proceeding in federal court, formally to obtain the release of the arrestee, but actually to have the separate car law declared unconstitutional.[6]

By December, after talking with railway officials, Martinet could report hesitant progress in arranging a *habeas corpus* case. "The roads are not in favor of the separate car law," he had found, "owing to the expense entailed, but they fear to array themselves against it." Officers of the first line he contacted admitted that they did not enforce the law. Rather, "[t]hey simply had a coach for colored persons, & the signs required by the law posted up, & the conductors were instructed to show the car to them, and if they refused to go to it[,] they were not to be molested in any way"—a state of affairs Martinet described as "a victory already." Finally, the Louisville and Nashville Railroad agreed to a test. By then, the Citizens' Committee had firmed up a plan: a colored passenger with an interstate ticket would board a train and, by arrangement, the conductor would "direct him or her, for we may have a lady, to the Jim Crow car." When the passenger refused, the conductor would swear out a complaint under the law's criminal provision. But lawyers for the L & N insisted that the Committee itself would have to arrange for a white passenger to swear out the complaint; the conductor would merely be instructed to make the car assignment and "not to use force or violen[ce]."[7] Here matters stood when James Walker entered the case as local counsel.

II

On January 2, 1892, Walker opened correspondence with Tourgée. Although it appears that Martinet had not fully briefed the new counsel on the proposed test case, Walker immediately began assessing the strategy involving a *habeas corpus* action after the arrest of a passenger at the beginning of an interstate trip. But despite everyone's eagerness to move with dispatch, progress was slow. As early as January 21, Walker allowed that "the Committee now & then intimate their impatience at my delay in taking the initiative." The delay partly came from an illness that prevented Tourgée from initially responding to his new associate before mid-January. Partly, too, consultation at a distance was unavoidably time-consuming, and Tourgée did not go to New Orleans to participate personally in any stage of the Louisiana proceedings. Mail between New Orleans and Mayville, New York, typically took three or four days, which meant that a week or more would pass before Walker could obtain answers to the questions he put to Tourgée—and he cleared each step with the senior counsel. Not least, legal planning had to be well advanced before an arrest could be safely arranged.

Finally, in late February, the lawyers obtained their client. He was Daniel F. Desdunes. An octoroon and the twenty-one-year-old son of Rodolphe Desdunes, he had been arrested on the twenty-fourth for taking a seat in a white car on the L & N, having purchased a first-class ticket for the trip from New Orleans to Mobile, Alabama. The timing of the case, not to mention aspects of the two attorneys' legal strategy, now depended crucially on decisions by the District Attorney for the Parish of Orleans. Only after the prosecutor's office filed an information against Desdunes, on March 14, could Walker decide on the final details of the "plea to the jurisdiction" that he and Tourgée hoped would produce the case they wanted. In its final form, this plea—a challenge to the authority of the trial court to hear the case—reflected the assessments that the two lawyers made of three interrelated problems.[8]

Most important, the attorneys had to define the legal-constitutional issues on which they would base their case—a choice that was by no means simple. In particular, a recent ruling of the United States Supreme Court cast doubt on the interstate commerce argument that Martinet had originally banked upon and Walker had endorsed.

The complication came from a decision involving the Louisville, New Orleans and Texas Railway, which ran trains from Tennessee through Mississippi to New Orleans and had been indicted and convicted in Mississippi for failure to provide separate cars, as required by that state's separate car law. First appealing to the Mississippi Supreme Court, the company claimed that the law burdened interstate commerce, but the state court construed the measure as applying only to commerce within the state and concluded that although requiring the railway to add a coach at the state line might increase its operating expenses, "how it [the law] is a burden upon or obstruction to commerce is difficult to perceive." Unlike the Louisiana equal accommodations law invalidated by the federal Supreme Court in *Hall v. DeCuir* (1878), said the court, Mississippi's Act did not purport to regulate interstate carriers "acting under license from the United States and plying the navigable waterways of the same"; and unlike the

Illinois rate regulation struck down in the *Wabash* case (1886), the Mississippi law did not seek to control out-of-state transportation. The company then carried the case to the federal Supreme Court, which, in an opinion by Justice David Brewer, accepted the state Supreme Court's construction of the statute as authoritative, and also agreed with the lower court that the separate car provision "may cause an extra expense to the railroad company[,] but not more so than state statutes requiring certain accommodations at depots, compelling trains to stop at crossings of other railroads, and a multitude of other matters confessedly within the power of the state."[9]

Walker immediately noted the ruling on the Mississippi law, and, before hearing directly from Tourgée, wondered "whether the best openings are presented by the Interstate Commerce Law [*sic*], or by the amendments to the Constitution." Still, his proposal for a test case, undoubtedly influenced by initial conversations with Martinet, stressed that the person who was arrested should hold a ticket for an out-of-state destination.

Tourgée apparently agreed. Having previously explored the interstate approach with Martinet, he approved it in his initial reply to Walker, on January 14. At one point, it is true, he questioned if the federal Supreme Court would read its own decisions as permitting an argument on commerce grounds, but his letter was diffuse, which he himself confessed after pleading he had been ill for a month and was blocked from his office and law books by six feet of snow. He concluded by admitting, "I may have spoken too lightly of the Inter-State Commerce matter," and asked, "[I]s it [the Louisiana law] not an obstruction to Interstate travel, by compelling changes of cars, &c?" He accepted Walker's suggestion that the complaint sworn out against their client should recite that he held a ticket for out-of-state.

Tourgée continued to hold this view. His draft of the plea Walker eventually filed in trial court raised the commerce issue in three of its averments: that the Louisville and Nashville Railway ran passenger trains from New Orleans to Mobile; that the defendant held a ticket for the full trip; and that Louisiana had "no power to distinguish by law between the rights and privileges of citizens of the United States on trains run by common carriers . . . between different states of the Union." Also, when the information filed against Daniel Desdunes omitted to mention the young man's destination, the two lawyers anxiously discussed how to get that fact into the trial court record by other means. Finally, the plea to the jurisdiction that was actually filed, which Tourgée reviewed, stressed both the interstate character of Desdunes's trip and the interstate character of the Louisville and Nashville Railroad as grounds for asserting "the right and privilege" of passenger travel "free from any governmental regulation or control thereof, save by the Congress of the United States, under Art. I Section 8 of the Constitution of the United States."[10]

In light of the U.S. Supreme Court's validation of the Mississippi law, why should both attorneys have seen promise in the commerce argument? The answer probably lies in the narrow holding in the *Louisville, New Orleans and Texas* case. There the Court ruled only on whether requiring railways to furnish separate cars constituted a burden on commerce; it explicitly left open the issue of whether a requirement mandating passenger assignment by race would constitute a like burden. Tourgée and Walker had surely spotted this opening when they agreed that the commerce approach was at least worth pursuing. Still, on balance, neither man saw it as their strongest argument. As Walker observed in late February, just after Desdunes's arrest, "the Statute is craftily worded, seemingly limiting its provisions to such Railway trains as are operated within the limits of this State."[11]

Tourgée took the lead in identifying the other constitutional infirmities of the separate car law. After sketching them in mid-January, he elaborated them at the beginning of March in his draft of the plea challenging the jurisdiction of the trial court, which, in turn, provided the model that Walker followed almost verbatim in the final plea (except for the addition of details developing the commerce argument). Consisting of thirteen averments, Tourgée's handiwork was typical of nineteenth-century pleadings in its reiteration, with only minor variation, of matters of fact and points of law, but its central constitutional argument may be summarized as follows:

> The defendant was a citizen of the United States. As such, because he held all the rights and privileges of citizenship, Louisiana had no authority to condition his rights on grounds of race. In addition, and more specifically, section two of the separate car law, which was an essential part of the Act, impermissibly clothed train officers with the authority and duty to assign passengers on the basis of race and with the further authority to refuse service. The section also made a passenger's "peaceable refusal" to comply a criminal offense. But determination of race was "a scientific and legal question of great difficulty," and as such it was a judicial question that could not be delegated to a train officer. In particular, the penalty of denial of passage could not rest on a train officer's summary decision as to a passenger's race, nor could criminal penalties attach to a failure to submit to his summary decision, for these provisions constituted "the imposition of punishment without process [*sic*] of law and the denial to Citizens of the United States of the equal protection of the laws." Moreover, the rights and privileges of citizenship which were at issue pertained to passage on a public railway within Louisiana and on a common carrier of passengers between states.

This argument only sketched and implied the constitutional "pegs" on which Desdunes's case would hang, for, as Tourgée had explained, the plea to the jurisdiction need lay out just enough of an argument "to prepare a basis" for their full objections to the law, which would come later, on appeal. In the plea that Walker actually submitted, the Amendments that formed the constitutional base for Desdunes's case were nevertheless specified in a final (and fittingly) fourteenth averment added either by Tourgée or by Walker with Tourgée's explicit approval. It read:

> . . . the Statute in question . . . establishes an invidious distinction between citizens of the United States based on race which is obnoxious to the fundamental principles of national citizenship, abridges the privileges and immunities of Citizens of the United States, and the rights secured by the XIIIth and XIVth amendments to the Federal Constitution.[12]

We will return in Chapter Three to the non-commerce issues raised in these averments. Here it suffices to notice that through them Tourgée had ensured that disallowance of the commerce argument would not itself defeat the Citizens' Committee's test case.

There was still another approach to invalidating the separate car law, and that was on state grounds. The Louisiana constitution prohibited multifarious legislation—that is, laws dealing with more than one subject— and Walker proposed early that the 1890 Act violated this restriction. His correspondence does not reveal what he saw as multiple objects, and Tourgée did not find them in the law, but the New Orleans lawyer may have had in mind, for example, its requiring railways to provide separate coaches *and* its relieving them of liability in connection with passenger assignments. In any event, Tourgée would have none of it, cautioning, "If that [question] should be held with us, and this case go off upon it[,] our clients would suffer a virtual defeat. What they want is not a verdict of not guilty, nor a defect in the law[,] but a decision whether such a law can be legally enacted, and enforced in any state[,] and we should get everything off the track and out of the way for such a decision." This proved the only substantial disagreement between the men regarding appropriate arguments.[13]

The two lawyers' second task was to plot an appellate course. From the beginning, both agreed that proceedings would begin in state court, but they realized that a federal ruling was important, and probably necessary, if the Citizens' Committee was to gain the victory it sought. What remained less certain was how to get the case from state court into federal court.

Walker at first questioned whether the route that Martinet and Tourgée had already discussed—a *habeas corpus* action—would suffice, noting the 1886 case of *Ex parte Royall*. This decision strongly suggested that federal judges would hesitate to use their discretion to intervene in state proceedings, before a defendant had exhausted his remedies within the state, when he was charged with a violation of a state law which he claimed deprived him of rights under the federal Constitution. Immediate exercise of the federal judicial power might sometimes be in order, such as "[w]hen the petitioner is in custody by state authority for an act done or omitted to be done in pursuance of a law of the United States," Justice John Marshall Harlan had written, or when the defendant was required in federal court as a witness.

But where special circumstances did not exist, federal judges could properly assume that because state judges were also sworn to uphold the supremacy of the federal Constitution, they would rule on the constitutional claims in the normal course of state proceedings. Citing *Royall*, Walker argued the best course was to take the case arranged by the Citizens' Committee through the local Criminal District Court and then seek relief from the state Supreme Court, from which an appeal would lie to the federal Supreme Court. Another consideration for Walker was his conclusion that the local United States Circuit Court, to which a *habeas corpus* petiton would go, did not offer an especially friendly forum, and he worried about further delays if an appeal from the federal Circuit Court ran to the newly established Circuit Court of Appeals rather than directly to Washington. He recognized, of course, that the "State Courts d[id] not present a more promising alternative," but at least they provided an avenue to the federal high court.[14]

Tourgée nevertheless persisted in a *habeas corpus* strategy. His interest, too, was a quick disposition of the case, but he interpreted *Royall* differently. The question was whether a federal judge would interpret the state trial court's ruling as a *final* ruling, an uncertainty which arose out of Louisiana's appellate rules. Although a conviction for violation of the separate car law was technically not appealable to the state Supreme Court under Louisiana law (because the offense was minor), Walker had observed that the latter court might grant a petition for writs of prohibition and certiorari to "arrest" or stop sentencing in the lower court. (The writ of certiorari in this instance was an ancillary writ to bring the case to the higher court; the writ of prohibition was the primary writ.) By this route, the trial court's judgment was in effect appealable and hence not final. But these writs, Tourgée responded, constituted discretionary and *extraordinary* remedies; and in dicussing the discretion of federal judges with respect to issuance of the writ of *habeas corpus, Royall* referred only to the exhaustion of *ordinary* state appellate processes. By way of analogy, Tourgée pointed out that one need not seek and be refused a state writ of *habeas corpus* (also a discretionary writ) before asking a federal court for the writ. "I think it enough," he concluded, "when our man is in jail and the [state] law denies an appeal."

In early March, Walker finally accepted the strategy. "It was only from an excess of caution that I proposed otherwise," he explained, citing "the indisposition of the Federal Courts to disturb the harmony of their relations with the State tribunals."[15]

The third problem was to perfect a record adequate to support an appeal. Because the separate car law did not explicitly extend to interstate travel, Tourgée and Walker needed the record to show that the measure had been applied to an interstate passenger on an interstate carrier. Because Tourgée in particular had an eye cocked toward a Fourteenth Amendment argument based on United States citizenship, their client's citizenship needed to be established. Tourgée also considered it important to establish that the defendant had held a first-class ticket for carriage, had been well-dressed and well-behaved, and had not been intoxicated or afflicted with any noxious diseases. Although seemingly mundane points, these were essential in order to ensure that a higher court did not conclude that their client had been expelled and arrested on grounds other than race. As Tourgée commented to Walker, "the first effort of the Supreme Court is always to hunt a hole to crawl out of deciding anything they [sic] can possibly evade." The ex-carpetbagger was adamant, too, that the whole separate car law be introduced into the record. Queried by Walker, he recalled he had once had his "fingers pinched . . . for failure to plead the statute in terms." He probably calculated, too, that introduction of the whole Act would facilitate his planned argument that its second section, which improperly imposed judicial functions on train officers, was an essential part of the measure.[16]

As a final touch, after the information filed against Daniel Desdunes turned out to allege that he was "a passenger of the colored race," Tourgée suggested averring that their client had "not more than one eighth of colored blood (which I suppose to be the fact)." Recognizing this fact was probably immaterial under Louisiana law, Tourgée nevertheless saw it as highly relevant to the constitutional arguments about arbitrariness and delegation of judicial authority. He was a little playful, too, adding, "it is a question we may as well take up, if for nothing else, to let the court sharpen its wits on."[17] But even as his suggestion on this last point was in the mail, Walker was filing the plea.

As for *how* to get these facts into the record, Tourgée proposed the solution of having the trial proceed on an agreed set of facts, which as a bonus offered an expeditious way to obtain the final verdict that would facilitate federal *habeas corpus* review under the guidelines of the *Royall* case. But Walker better realized the difficulty they faced, familiar as he was with both Louisiana law and local practice, into which, he remarked, "a certain looseness has crept." Because for the offense in question Louisiana law provided for no direct or ordinary appeal of a conviction within the state court system, the trial court would not keep a transcript. For the same reason, the trial judge need not make specific findings of fact as distinguished from rulings of law. A partial remedy, however, might be the wording of the information filed against Desdunes. After conferring with the prosecuting attorney in early March, Walker briefly expected that the information's wording would follow the language of the affidavit which the arresting officer had sworn out against Desdunes, specifying that the defendant had violated the separate car law while holding an interstate ticket. Tourgée feared, however, that even this appraoch would not sufficiently establish the necessary facts, and Walker himself quickly revised his estimate about the prosecutor's cooperativeness.

As filed, the information omitted mention of interstate travel. For this contingency, Walker and Tourgée's detailed draft plea provided a fallback position. In the course of arguing that the separate car Act was unconstitutional the two attorneys alleged the matters of fact that they considered vital. Their hope was that the prosecutor, rather than question the facts alleged in the plea, would simply demur to it—that is, admit the facts for the sake of argument but question the plea's sufficiency in law.[18]

III

Further planning was cut short when James Walker received notice on Friday, March 18, that Daniel Desdunes would be arraigned on the following Monday in Section A of the Criminal District Court for the Parish of Orleans. After the defendant formally swore out the plea to the jurisdiction, Walker filed it at the arraignment on the twenty-first and supported it with a written brief of points and authorities that was balanced enough to be hardly overwhelming. (He had promised Tourgée, after all, "not to make too strong an argument, except to assist the court with the opportunity to overrule us.") An assistant district attorney then helpfully demurred, as if by script. In this circumstance, Walker had predicted, the judge would "require some days, perhaps a couple of weeks[,] to make up his mind" to disallow the jurisdictional plea, after which a swift trial on a general plea of "not guilty" would lead to Desdunes's conviction. But a quick denial of the plea to the jurisdiction failed to appear. The presiding judge, Robert H. Marr, may have been awaiting the outcome of *Abbott v. Hicks*, an unrelated case on the separate car law pending before the state Supreme Court. Then, on April 19, Judge Marr himself mysteriously vanished, producing further delay until a successor could be appointed.[19]

The ruling still had not come down when, on May 25, the Louisiana Supreme Court decided the *Abbott* case, which originated when a conductor on the Texas and Pacific Railway was prosecuted for admitting a black passenger into a white car. As a defense, the conductor contended that the Negro held a ticket for a destination in Texas and that either the separate car law was not intended to apply to interstate passengers, or if it did apply, it was unconstitutional as a violation of the federal interstate commerce clause. The state Supreme Court agreed, relying heavily on *Louisville, New Orleans and Texas Railway Company v. Mississippi*. There, as we have seen, the federal Supreme Court had upheld Mississippi's separate car law, but on a narrow set of facts, and had intimated that mandatory assignment of interstate passengers by race might be an impermissible burden on commerce.

In *Abbott*, not surprisingly, if not quite accurately, the Louisiana court found "no room for question that the jurisprudence of the United States supreme court holds such [regulatory] statutes . . . to be only valid in so far as they apply to domestic transportation of passengers or goods, and that, as applicable to interstate passengers or carriage, they are regulations of interstate commerce, prohibited to the states by the constitution of the United States." Actually, the federal Supreme Court had *not* held that separate car laws, if they applied only to intrastate carriage, were categorically valid, but simply that they were not invalid on interstate commerce grounds. If the state court muddied this point, it also left unresolved whether the Louisiana law did not apply to interstate passengers because the state legislature had not so intended it, or because the Act was unconstitutional to the extent that it was thus applied. But the court left no doubt that the law could not be enforced against interstate passengers.[20]

Abbott seriously undercut the test case arranged by the Citizens' Committee, for it meant that in all probability Walker's plea to the jurisdiction of the Criminal District Court would eventually be sustained; and indeed it was, on July 9, without a written opinion from the new judge of Section A, John H. Ferguson. Yet the decision could not have been entirely unwelcomed by Desdunes's lawyers. It unquestionably vindicated the conclusions of both Walker and Tourgée that the *Louisville, New Orleans and Texas* case had not foreclosed a commerce-clause attack on the mandatory-assignment provision of the Louisiana law. They may not have fully shared the enthusiasm of Martinet's *Crusader*, that "Reactionists may foam at the mouth, and Bourbon [that is, Redeemer Democrat] organs may squirm, but Jim Crow is as dead as a door nail," but Tourgée himself apparently thought the Pullman Car decision would at least help dismantle segregation on *intra*state lines. In any event, even if litigation progressed no further, the Louisiana court had set an outer limit to separate car legislation; and if a further legal challenge was mounted, the court had clarified the issues still needing resolution.[21]

The efforts of the Citizens' Committee and its attorneys in the winter and spring of 1891–92 had broader significance, too. For one thing, Tourgée and Walker's association had brought them into a confident relationship. Tourgée must have become convinced not only that Martinet's early trust in Walker had been well placed, but also that his own early decision "to defer to [Walker] in all matters of procedure" had been wise.[22] Second, the plea that the two men had developed was available for further use, if stripped of its commerce sections. Finally, and with rather opposite implications for the outcome that the New Orleans blacks desired, the broad-fronted brief against the separate car law was now a matter of public record. State authorities were placed on notice, that is, that their own position (and hence the law) would likely be complicated if they allowed the "fact" of a defendant's racial category to appear in the pre-trial record.[23] In sum, a second test case would require less on-going collaboration between Tourgée and Walker, and would thus allow the New Orleans attorney more room to pursue his own instincts regarding the best appellate procedure; but developing the record necessary to support a successful appeal might prove more difficult.

IV

Even before final dismissal of the charge against Daniel Desdunes, a new effort began. Martinet had promptly telegraphed the outcome of the *Abbott* decision to Tourgée, and on June 1 added, "Walker wants new case wholly within state limits[.]" Tourgée wired back, "approv[ing] anything he [Walker] may advise, only suggesting that time of session of Circuit Court must be considered *if* deemed best to take originally approved course." Then, in sharp contrast to the long delay over commencement of the first test case, the Committee speedily initiated another. Homer A. Plessy, a thirty-four-year-old friend of Daniel Desdunes's father, purchased a ticket on June 7 for the trip from New Orleans to Covington, Louisiana, on the East Louisiana Railway, which operated wholly within the state; and, after insisting on boarding a coach reserved for whites, he was arrested for violation of the separate car law. Like the Desdunes arrest, Plessy's was surely arranged, because despite the allegation in the arresting officer's affidavit that Plessy was "a passenger of the colored race," he, too, was only one-eighth black and, as his counsel later asserted, "the mixture of colored blood [was] not discernible."[24]

In the following weeks, the overt pace slowed markedly. Not until July 20, eleven days after *State v. Desdunes* had formally been dismissed, did Assistant District Attorney Lionel Adams file an information against Plessy (which omitted his race); and the arraignment was then put off until October 13. It may be that Walker had secured Adams's agreement "to shape matters so as to fall in the next session of the U.S. Circuit Court," or so Martinet surmised.

When Plessy finally was arraigned before Judge Ferguson in Criminal District Court, Walker promptly filed another fourteen-point plea to the jurisdiction. In its individual averments, this largely followed the earlier plea, with two main exceptions. One was the omission of the portions referring to the railway's interstate business, the defendant's planned interstate journey, and the resulting interstate commerce issue. The second was the substitution, in the twelfth averment (one of those from which language had been deleted), of the allegation that "[t]he act deprives the citizen of remedy for wrong, and is unconstitutional for that reason[.]" The plea, like the information, did not state if Plessy was black or white. On October 28, in an oral argument which the press reported as taking several hours, Walker further and forcefully developed the case. Again the prosecution demurred. Adams cited the separate car law's requirement for equal accommodations and noted several federal court decisions allowing racial separation in common carriers; apparently, too, he asserted that interracial repugnancies, along with white inconvenience from the foul odors of blacks in close quarters, helped establish the reasonableness of the law.

Three weeks later, on November 18, Judge Ferguson issued a written opinion allowing the demurrer and overruling Walker's plea.[25]

Had he adhered to the original strategy, Walker would now have let the case go to trial on Plessy's "not guilty" plea, followed by a *habeas corpus* action in federal court. Instead, he immediately petitioned the state Supreme Court. But why the shift from the course Martinet had expected as late as mid-July? Unfortunately for the historian, the extant record thins out after the middle of 1892, and speculation must substitute for firm evidence. One clue comes from the likelihood that by autumn Walker had a greater influence on decisions. As we have seen, he had initially regarded the state route to the United States Supreme Court as more expeditious, and had only hesitantly agreed with Tourgée about resorting to a lower federal court. In addition, Tourgée had as much as condoned a departure from the original plan when he telegraphed Martinet in June concerning instigation of a new case. It seems likely, too, that Walker had obtained assurances from Ferguson and Adams that they would not oppose taking the case to the state Supreme Court for review. At least Ferguson's subsequent answer to the court's provisional writ of prohibiton did not question the propriety of the procedure, and Adams's brief supporting Ferguson explicitly endorsed it. (It is suggestive, certainly, that about a year later, in a letter to Tourgée, Walker referred to "my friend Judge Ferguson" in describing the latter's private effort to persuade the Louisiana attorney general to expedite the case before the federal Supreme Court.) Or Walker—probably in consultation with Martinet, for the two surely conferred regularly about the case—may have decided that problems of timing were too great to recommend an action in the local federal Circuit Court.[26]

Not least as a source for the changed approach, the *Abbott* case provided a model for quick review—and more indeed expeditious review than Walker himself had suggested in connection with *Desdunes*. In order to circumvent Louisiana's lack of a provision for direct appeal of such a minor conviction, Walker had originally proposed moving for an arrest of judgment in the Criminal District Court *after* trial but before sentencing. When this motion was overruled, the defendant would then petiton the state Supreme Court for review on writs of prohibition and certiorari. But in *Abbott*, the Louisiana Supreme Court took the case *before* trial, the defendant having petitioned for review, using the same writs, immediately after the trial court judge rejected a plea to the jurisdiction entered during arraignment.[27]

That, it turned out, was the course Walker took in *Ex parte Plessy*, as the case became entitled before the Louisiana Supreme Court. And the new action moved quickly. If anything, the rapidity of the filings before the state high court further suggests planning and preparation prior to Ferguson's ruling. The judge's decision came down on a Friday; Walker filed his petition to halt the trial proceedings (sworn out before Louis Martinet as notary) on the following Tuesday, November 22. Nine days later, he submitted a twenty-two-page printed brief to the state Supreme Court, and Assistant District Attorney Adams filed a thirty-page printed brief on behalf of Ferguson, who was the formal respondent in Walker's action.[28]

The immediate effect of Walker's petition was to stop Plessy's trial. On November 22, Chief Justice Francis T. Nicholls (who as governor in 1890 had signed the separate car bill into law) issued a provisional writ of prohibition, along with an order to Judge Ferguson to show cause why the writ should not be made permanent. In another month, the full court handed down its decision, in an opinion by Associate Justice Charles E. Fenner.

The outcome was predictable. Citing the *Abbott* case, the court agreed that in an otherwise unappealable case where the trial judge had disallowed a plea alleging the unconstitutionality of the law at issue, the court's extraordinary supervisory jurisdiction could properly be invoked. It also found that Plessy's application for writs of prohibition and certiorari "conform[ed] to all the requirements of this rule." But it denied that the separate car law, as construed by Judge Ferguson in his ruling and as explicated by Adams in his brief, conflicted with either the Thirteenth or the Fourteenth Amendment. Walker next petitioned for a rehearing, focusing on several issues that Justice Fenner had not addressed; but on Monday, January 2, 1893, a year to the day after he had first written Tourgée, the court denied the request. The provisional writ now stood dissolved and there existed no further *state* barrier to Plessy's trial.[29]

Homer Plessy could finally invoke the jurisdiction of the United States Supreme Court. The vehicle was a writ of error, which brought up for review the record of the case at the state level. On January 5, Walker took out an application for the writ from the clerk for the federal Circuit Court in New Orleans, and on the same day Chief Justice Nicholls completed the formality of "allowing" it. Paul Bonseigneur, another New Orleans "Creole of color," then executed a bond to guarantee Plessy's eventual court appearance. These steps served to reinstitute the provisional writ of prohibition, thereby further staying the trial proceedings.[30]

With the judicial forum shifting to Washington, we may turn to an analysis of Plessy's constitutional case as it emerged from Louisiana.

CHAPTER THREE

Plessy in Louisiana:
The Constitutional Clash

I

Using the forms and language of the law, Homer Plessy in January 1893 told "the hon[orable] the Supreme Court of the United States" that the record and proceedings of his case in Louisiana contained "manifest error" and "pray[ed]" that the state Supreme Court's provisional writ of prohibition "be made peremptory."[1] While a full understanding of the arguments underlying and supporting this request requires attention to the broader concerns addressed in subsequent chapters, a preliminary analysis of Plessy's legal case is necessary in order simply to identify the broader concerns. Hence we turn in this chapter to surveying and explicating the arguments that Tourgée, Walker, and their opponents had advanced in Louisiana as *Plessy* progressed through two layers of state courts.

The "assignment of errors" that Plessy's attorneys submitted to the Supreme Court in Washington provides a convenient guide. Its usefulness in this respect comes from nineteenth-century rules of pleading which required that an assignment of errors contain considerable detail—indeed, almost redundant detail—for the purpose of covering all the mistakes in law made at the lower court level. (If an individual specification covered more than one topic, the appellate court could disregard the claim.)[2] But just as a guidebook is not the whole trip, we need to flesh out the resulting outline through close attention to the interplay of legal arguments that lay behind the various specifications of error.

44

An overview of the assignment of errors discloses five headings. The most important of these was the first, which contained the attorneys' major specifications or averments under the Thirteenth and Fourteenth Amendments. Headings two through five together dealt with a second distinct subject—the errors allegedly made by the state Supreme Court in reading the separate car law and construing its requirements. Although largely irrelevant to the subsequent deliberations in *Plessy*, owing to the federal Supreme Court's own appellate practices, these latter four headings help illuminate the substance and direction of the debate in Louisiana and cannot be entirely ignored.

Heading one began with the broad allegation that the separate car law violated the Thirteenth and Fourteenth Amendments and then included twelve numbered paragraphs as support. With two or perhaps three exceptions,[3] the paragraphs did not explicitly link the enumerated complaints about the law to the specific protections of the two Amendments, but the constitutional claims are nonetheless discernible in light of the earlier proceedings. Similarly, connections are discernible between several of the individual paragraphs, with the broadest constitutional attack appearing in paragraphs one, four, and five, which together challenged the validity of the doctrine of separate-but-equal itself. We begin with these three paragraphs and the legal dueling that produced them.

II

Paragraph one contained Walker and Tourgée's Thirteenth Amendment argument. The law, they claimed, imposed a badge of servitude by perpetuating "the distinction of race and caste among citizens of the United States of both races." It also promoted "observances of a servile character [which had been] coincident with the incident of slavery [as] heretofore exacted by the white race and compulsorily submitted to by the colored race." In the plea to the jurisdiction that Walker had filed before the Criminal District Court, this argument had been explicated only to the extent of alleging that the act "perpetuate[d] involuntary servitude, as regards citizens of the colored race."

The main elaboration came in the brief that Tourgée and Walker submitted to the state Supreme Court.* This stressed how the separate car law solidified classifications that arose out of the experience of slavery:

*For convenience, the brief is subsequently identified in this chapter as the "Tourgée-Walker brief." Although filed by Walker, it carried the names of both men in the indicated order, and the contents and style of the document suggest Tourgée's strong influence. (Correspondence proving collaboration is missing, but the three months between the filing of the information against Plessy and flurry of activity in October and November 1892 would have provided ample time.)

> What else but a badge of servitude is imposed and perpetuated . . . when a person, seven-eighths white and one-eighth of colored blood, or a person fifteen-sixteenth parts white and one-sixteenth part of colored blood, is subjected to fine or imprisonment by authority of State law, for insisting [contrary to a conductor's judgment] that he or she, as the case may be, should be classed as a white person . . . ?

As authority, the attorneys argued that Justice Joseph Bradley, writing for the federal Supreme Court in the *Civil Rights Cases* (1883), had agreed that the Amendment was intended to eliminate servitudes comparable to legally imposed "burdens and disabilities of a servile character, incident to feudal vassalage in France, and to inequalities and observances exacted by one man from another, badges of slavery, which [that] great nation, in its effort to establish universal liberty, made haste to wipe out and destroy . . . ." The separate car law also sustained the slave regime's practice of separating husbands and wives in mixed marriages, as well as the white parent and his or her mulatto children. "The trouble with this law," they summarized, "is that it perpetuates race prejudice among citizens of the United States, and that the spirit of cast[e] and race is exemplified in the spirit of legislation."

These claims, however, were not sharply focused on the Thirteenth Amendment. The Tourgée-Walker brief explicitly linked the "badge of servitude" argument to *both* the Thirteenth *and* the Fourteenth Amendments. In addition, paragraph one included the charge that the law "abridges the rights, privileges, and immunities of citizens on account of race and color," an assertion which more directly implicates the national citizenship and privileges-or-immunities clauses of the Fourteenth Amendment.[4]

Assistant District Attorney Lionel Adams offered the Supreme Court an alternative reading of the *Civil Rights Cases*. His brief portrayed Justice Bradley as asserting that denial of public accommodations "does not subject [a] person to any form of servitude, or tend to fasten upon him any badge of slavery, even though the denial be founded on the race or color of that person. It is not therefore obnoxious to the provisions of the Thirteenth Amendment." Justice Charles Fenner, writing for the Louisiana Supreme Court in *Ex parte Plessy*, tersely agreed that "the supreme court of the United States has clearly decided it [the Amendment] does not refer to rights of the character here involved."[5]

Paragraph four contained the most conventionally recognizable Fourteenth Amendment argument on Plessy's behalf. It contended that by authorizing train officers to refuse to carry non-complying passengers and by making refusal a criminal offense, the law constituted both a denial of equal protection and a punishment without due process. The equal protection and due process claims of Tourgée and Walker were thus intertwined, but to the extent that the two attorneys had distinguished them in the Louisiana proceedings, the equal protection argument was less central. It was mainly associated with the exemption from liability for damages resulting from non-carriage that the law granted to railway and train officers. This provision, the two attorneys objected, denied a class of people access to a remedy—that is, damage suits—that was available to other persons. The charge implicated a specific feature of the law, not its general scheme; and accordingly it was argued separately in the Louisiana courts and appeared separately under heading one of the assignment of errors, in paragraph eight, as discussed below.

An explicit and broader equal protection argument apparently appeared in Walker's oral argument in Criminal District Court, when he explained three averments in his plea to the jurisdiction which, varying slightly in wording, each denied that a state could distinguish on the basis of race between the rights and privileges of citizens. In response, in his opinion on the plea, Judge Ferguson addressed the allegation that racial separation by itself constituted a denial of equal protection, finding it did not because both white and black passengers were required to take separate quarters and were subject to the same penalties for failure to do so. The conclusion flowed, he asserted, from three lower federal court cases involving common-law damage suits against common carriers; these seemed to indicate that separate-but-equal accommodations met the legal duty of common carriers to provide equal accommodations to passengers who paid the same fare.

In any event, a broad equal protection argument failed to receive significant attention in the proceedings before the state Supreme Court. Despite Ferguson's fairly clear reference to (and rejection of) the claim, the Tourgée-Walker brief mentioned it only in passing. The brief did attack Ferguson's interpretation of the three federal cases that he had examined, but the challenge appeared in the context of a renewed discussion of the separate car law's liability-exemption clause—that is, in connection with the narrow and more technical equal protection claim that the separate car law denied a right of action. Nor did Justice Fenner's opinion suggest that a broad equal-protection claim was at issue. In fact, Fenner avoided all refined analysis of whether the law infringed specific parts of the Fourteenth Amendment. He simply asked, without additional focus, whether it "violates the fourteenth amendment, which provides that 'no state shall make or enforce any law which abridges the privileges or immunities of citizens of the United states; nor shall any state deprive any person of life, liberty, or property without due process of law, nor deny any person within its jurisdiction the equal protection of the laws.'"[6]

More apparent in the exchanges that lay behind paragraph four was a due process argument. Non-carriage of a passenger who refused to take an assigned seat amounted to "a summary punishment," Walker had explained to the Criminal District Court, because punishment imposed by a conductor was devoid of any judicial process and hardly constituted due process. Non-carriage also deprived a passenger of the expected benefits of the ticket he had purchased, a contention Judge Ferguson restated in this manner: "It is urged [by counsel] that the defendant was deprived of his property because he purchased a first-class ticket and never used it by reason of the act of the conductor." But Plessy "was not in a proper sense deprived of his liberty," responded Ferguson, for "[h]e was simply deprived of the liberty of doing what he pleased and of violating a criminal statute with impunity." Nor had the defendant been denied due process; his inability to use his ticket was the result not of the conductor's action but of his own failure to take a seat in the coach where by race he belonged. In his brief before the state Supreme Court, Lionel Adams reiterated this analysis.

In the state Supreme Court arguments, the Tourgée-Walker brief broadened the due process attack to include the penal provision of the law. Following his arrest, Plessy had been jailed before bond was posted. This imprisonment, asserted the attorneys, occurred because their client had insisted on exercising a constitutional right. Observing that Justice Bradley, in the *Civil Rights Cases*, had conceded that "[p]ositive rights and privileges are undoubtedly secured by the fourteenth amendment[,] but . . . by way of prohibition against State laws and State proceedings affecting those rights and privileges," they contended that freedom from arbitrary assignment by race, and especially an assignment without judicial hearing, was such a positive right. A citizen could legitimately resist such an assignment and this action could not be made into a crime, for "[w]ith equal reason might the legislature declare it to be a crime, and punishable, if a man defend his person, his family, or his property, against unprovoked attack and unlawful intrusion." However fleeting, "[t]he imprisonment of a citizen by authority of a State statute which is repugnant to and in conflict with the constitution, is a deprivation of liberty without due process of law."

Ultimately, none of the equal protection or due process claims succeeded. The insuperable barrier was the alleged status of the separate car law as a police measure, well within the state legislature's acknowledged constitutional authority to protect the health, welfare, and morals of the state's citizens.[7]

Paragraph five of the assignment of errors attacked the state's police power arguments. "The statute," it maintained, "is not in the interest of public order, peace, and comfort, but is manifestly directed against citizens of the colored race." Walker's plea to the jurisdiction had not levied the charge so directly, but had laid a basis for it, arguing that the separate car law was void because its "purpose and object . . . as appears on its face, is to assort and classify all passengers . . . according to race, and to make the rights and privileges of all citizens of the United States dependent on said classification . . . ." Linked closely to this assertion was Walker's final and summary averment before Judge Ferguson:

> [the separate car law] establishes an invidious distinction and discrimi-
> nates between citizens of the United States based on race[,] which is

obnoxious to the principles of national citizenship, perpetuates involuntary servitude as regards citizens of the colored race under the merest pretense of promoting the comfort of passengers on railway trains, and in further respects abridges the privileges and immunities of the citizens of the United States and rights secured by the XIIIth and XIVth amendments of the Federal Constitution.

Here emerged the central argument on behalf of Plessy, borrowed almost verbatim from the *Desdunes* plea. Stripped to its essentials, it consisted of the claim that by mandating racial separation the separate car law was categorically unconstitutional. True, the Act was void on due process and equal protection grounds, but it was void on these grounds because it was not a valid police measure; and it was not a valid police measure because it established a classification that, *as a matter of law*, violated (1) the Thirteenth Amendment's ban on badges of servitude, (2) the Fourteenth Amendment's establishment of national citizenship, and (3) the latter Amendment's guarantee against state abridgment of privileges or immunities. These provisions purely and simply outlawed all race distinctions.[8]

The argument was sufficiently elusive, however, to allow both Ferguson in his ruling and Adams on brief to skirt it. Walker's plea, Ferguson recognized, had contended that the law's purpose was not what its title proclaimed ("An act to promote the comfort of passengers on railroad trains") but was instead an attempt "to legalize a discrimination between classes of citizens based on race and color." The judge then shifted focus by defining the sphere of legitimate state legislation through an analogy to the rights and duties of railways as stated in existing case law and as elaborated in the federal decisions he cited and quoted. He explained:

> Clearly railway companies have the right to adopt reasonable rules and regulations for their protection and for the proper conduct of their business and to designate who shall execute said regulations. *It is in the nature of a police regulation.*
>
> If, therefore, said companies have such right, it follows that the legislature, the law maker[,] has the undoubted right to so declare in an expression of legislative will.

A law classifying passengers by race, that is, did not constitute a deprivation of due process because it was a valid police measure. Nor, he continued, did it deny equal protection, for it mandated equal facilities and provided equal punishments for white and black violators.

Overall, Ferguson found that there was no reason to conclude either that the Act's purpose was other than to promote the comfort of passengers or that the law discriminated improperly by race. He never addressed the separate issue of what categorical protections flowed from the Thirteenth

Amendment and from the Fourteenth Amendment's national citizenship and privileges-or-immunities clauses.[9]

Adams went further in his brief before the state Supreme Court, flatly denying that refusal of admission to public accommodations or conveyances, *even on account of race*, constituted a badge of servitude in violation of the Thirteenth Amendment. His source—which Tourgée and Walker had also cited in maintaining the opposite proposition—was the *Civil Rights Cases*. In other respects, Adams only provided additional authorities for holding that separation by race constituted a valid exercise of the police power, so long as equal facilities were provided.[10]

Before the state Supreme Court, Tourgée and Walker elaborated their argument that the separate car law did *not* constitute a valid police measure. "The object expressed in the title of the statute," their brief contended, "certainly was not the incentive that lead [*sic*] to its enactment . . . ." For one thing, if the real purpose of the law had been to prevent interracial collisions, it would not have been "expressly confined to railroads other than street railroads," for who did "not know that contact between white and colored persons on street railways is more immediate, and many thousand times more frequent, than on any other line or system . . . [?]" In addition, the law did not prevent interracial contact when a black occupied the inferior position of nurse. In this respect, there was an example "calculated to dispel every doubt" about the law's true object: if a white man boarded a train with his black wife, their children, and a colored nurse, the nurse could take a seat in the white coach with the husband, whereas the wife and children would have to go to the Negro car. "Thus the bottom rail is on the top; the nurse is admitted to a privilege which the wife herself does not enjoy."

Similarly revealing was the exemption of train officers and railways for liability for damage suits arising from their refusal to carry non-complying passengers. The exemption provision demonstrated that the act was actually designed not for the comfort of passengers but to relieve railways of the risk of liability they incurred if they discriminated among passengers by race. The three cases cited by Judge Ferguson illustrated the risk, argued the Tourgée-Walker brief, for each decision had awarded damages against a carrier.[11]

Perhaps out of awareness that such defects in the statute could be rectified by better drafting, Tourgée and Walker further elaborated the claim that some purported police regulations were unconstitutional simply as a matter of law. To be valid, police measures could "not involve the sacrifice of natural and inalienable rights, nor [could] they make a crime out of a natural right." In immediate context, their brief linked protection of such rights to the Thirteenth Amendment. Later it referred to "the authoritative protection of those *immunities* of petitioner [Plessy] which we believe have have been assailed" and then added, "The establishment of national citizenship by the fourteenth amendment . . . prevents any State from making race or color an element of a crime."[12]

In accepting the separate car law as a valid police measure, the state Supreme Court almost entirely ignored the assessment that Tourgée and Walker had advanced. The *Civil Rights Cases*, as we have already observed, provided Justice Fenner with his (dubious) authority to deny summarily that the Thirteenth Amendment outlawed racial separation. Fenner gave fuller attention to the Fourteenth Amendment, but explicitly and implicitly he also denied its force. Somewhat rearranged in order to give it clarity, his argument took the following form:

The Fourteenth Amendment's national citizenship clause disappeared through sleight of hand. After ruling the Thirteenth Amendment was irrelevant to the police power issue, he observed that "[w]e may, therefore, confine ourselves to the question whether or not the statute violates the fourteenth amendment," but then he quoted *only* the privileges-or-immunities, due process, and equal protection clauses of the latter amendment.

To dispose of these remaining clauses, Fenner first used the federal Supreme Court's decision in the *Louisville, New Orleans and Texas* case to narrow the issue. This case, he claimed, had "definitely decided" that, consistent with the *Fourteenth Amendment*, separate car laws could be made binding on railways. Here he was flatly wrong, but the error made no difference because he correctly noted that the federal high court had explicitly avoided the question of "[w]hether such accommodation is to be a matter of choice or compulsion" *for passengers*. The validity of requiring passengers to use "the separate and equal accommodations provided for the race to which they belong," he allowed, "has not, as yet, been directly presented to, or decided by, the supreme court of the United States."[13]

Fenner next claimed that sixteen state and lower federal decisions had held "that statutes or regulations enforcing the separation of races in public conveyances or in public schools, so long, at least, as the facilities or accommodations provided are substantially equal, do not abridge any privilege or immunity of citizens or otherwise contravene the fourteenth amendment." Yet as Fenner presented his argument, these transportation and school cases, while important for a reason which will become apparent, were superfluous to the issue of whether the compulsory separation of passengers infringed either the privileges-or-immunities or the equal protection clauses.

Instead, he disposed of privileges-or-immunities objections by relying on a line of decisions by the United States Supreme Court beginning with the *Slaughter-House Cases* (1873). These rulings affirmed, as he put it, that the Fourteenth Amendment "created no new rights whatsoever, but only extended the operation of existing rights and furnished additional protection for such rights." His evident meaning, which reflected a conventional reading of the Fourteenth Amendment by 1892, was that the rights protected by the privileges-or-immunities clause were insignificant and few in number. A citizen's other rights flowed from state citizenship and fell under the protection of the state alone, subject to the Fourteenth Amendment's prohibitions on state deprivation of life, liberty, or property without due process of law and state denial of equal protection of the laws.

As for the equal protection clause, no claim could arise under it. As Fenner explained, "The statute applies to the two races with such perfect fairness and equality that the record brought up for our inspection does not disclose whether the person prosecuted is a white or a colored man." Also, if a violation of the Act were proved, the penalty would be the same regardless of Plessy's race.

There remained the question of whether mandatory racial separation conflicted with the Fourteenth Amendment's due process requirement, and it was in this regard that the decisions on transportation and school segregation were especially germane, however much *corroborative* support they incidentally gave to Fenner's conclusions on the other issues.

The sixteen cases, as Fenner described them, had involved statutes, or regulations in the absence of statutes, mandating equal-but-separate facilities on common carriers and in public schools, and had "all accord[ed] in the general principle that, in such matters, equality, and not identity or community, of accommodations, is the extreme test of conformity to the requirements of the fourteenth amendment." No matter that Fenner erred in the latter claim (about half the cases had *not* involved Fourteenth Amendment issues), for what was central to his argument was the reasoning of the cases, which he illustrated with quotations from *Roberts v. City of Boston* (Massachusetts, 1849), a school segregation case, and *West Chester and Philadelphia Railroad Company v. Miles* (Pennsylvania, 1867), a railway separate-car case.

In *Roberts*, Chief Justice Lemuel Shaw of the Massachusetts Supreme Judicial Court ("its great chief justice," Fenner accurately labeled him) rejected the argument that legally mandated segregation would promote race prejudice. "This prejudice, if it exists," Shaw wrote (and Fenner quoted), "is not created by law, and [probably] cannot be changed by law," but Shaw modified his assertion in the very next sentence (which Fenner also quoted): "Whether this distinction and prejudice, existing in the opinion and feelings of the community, would not be as effectually fostered by compelling colored and white children to associate together in the same schools, may well be doubted . . . ." Beneath the expressed doubt lurked the suggestion, which Fenner explicitly noted, that racial mixing might increase race prejudice and, perforce, a prohibition on mixing might lessen it. *West Chester v. Miles* offered similar views. In it, Justice Daniel Agnew upheld a railway company's own regulation mandating racial separation. Race differences, including some of Divine origin, were sufficiently pronounced between blacks and whites, Agnew declared (and Fenner quoted), as to make "their separation as passengers in a public conveyance the subject of a sound regulation to secure order, promote comfort, preserve the peace, and maintain the rights both of carriers and passengers."[14]

Although admitting that the Massachusetts and Pennsylvania decisions had come down prior to the adoption of the Fourteenth Amendment, Fenner claimed they came from states which had comparable guarantees in their own laws. More important, they revealed the "germinal principles" embodied in the other decisions, principles founded on reasoning so cogent "that, notwithstanding the general prevalence of such [equal-but-separate] statutes and regulations, and the frequency of decisions maintaining them, no one has yet undertaken to submit the question to the final arbitrament of the supreme court of the United States." So the very lack of an authoritative decision from the federal tribunal became evidence—but evidence for what?

For Fenner, the silence of the United States Supreme Court, combined with the sixteen cases, testified to a connection between racial separation and the maintenance of "public order, peace, and comfort," in the interest of which the Louisiana legislature had enacted the separate car law. The Act was an exercise of the police power based, like the other acts and regulations involved in the cases he cited, "upon difference of race; and if such difference cannot furnish a basis for such legislation in one of these cases, it cannot in any." Fenner's implication—that race separation arguably promoted the public's welfare in all these instances—led to his conclusion: the separate car law infringed no liberties protected by the Fourteenth Amendment from abridgement without due process. [15]

In summary, Fenner ignored the national citizenship argument, employed federal Supreme Court decisions as authority to dismiss the privileges-or-immunities claim, and found the separate car law mandated equal treatment. By this route, he was able to return to friendly territory— an analysis of the relation between due process and the police power of the states. Here he found enlightenment in some lower court decisions, but, strictly speaking, he did not employ them as precedent for the decision in *Ex parte Plessy*. Instead, they provided a source of evidence bearing on the central question in his analysis of due process and the police power. This was in principle an empirical question: did racial separation promote public health, welfare and morals?

III

The remainder of heading one in the assignment of errors presented by Tourgée and Walker is best understood as an argument in the alternative— even if the principle of enforced separation by race into equal-but-separate coaches was constitutionally permissible as a police regulation, various features of the Louisiana law failed to meet constitutional requirements. These paragraphs—nine in all—resembled the three paragraphs just examined in that they largely avoided explicit invocation of specific constitutional constitutional provisions, but again the related claims and counterclaims during the Louisiana proceedings provide us with clarification.

Paragraph two alleged that the separate car law did not enforce substantial equality in the accommodations furnished to passengers of each race. Without more, this might seem a complaint that separation *by itself* infringed the equal protection requirement of the Fourteenth Amendment. Instead, the paragraph's full wording averred that the law authorized the officers of railroad trains to make passenger assignments without reference to the *quality* of the *separate* quarters. Although the plea to the jurisdiction had not raised the objection, except in broadly contending that the law violated the federal Constitution, Judge Ferguson had hinted at it. In affirming the validity of the Act, he had closely followed the measure's wording, which, by mandating equal-but-separate coaches, *implied* that the law required equal quality in actual seat assignments.

Therein lay the problem, argued the Tourgée-Walker brief before the Louisiana Supreme Court: "too much is left to be supplied by implication, to help out the conclusions of the legislature . . . ." The law left to inference the conclusion that a passenger was obligated to abide by a conductor's assignment *only* if the conductor had assigned him to an equal accommodation; and regarding the conductor's assignments, no appeal existed.[16] In view of the legal rule to construe criminal statutes strictly and leave nothing to implication, the law thereby did not require equality in assignments. Providing further confirmation, the information against Plessy "follow[ed] the statute in keeping silent as to whether the coach to which the conductor assigned [him], was or was not equal in point of accommodations compared with the coach from which he was expelled.[17]

Adams read the law differently. "The clear and specific requirement of the statute," he recited, "is that railway companies 'shall provide *equal* but separate accommodations for the white and colored races.'" (His italics.) For the Court, Justice Fenner agreed that the law provided for "the separation of the races in public conveyances with proper sanctions enforcing the substantial equality of the accommodations supplied to each." The conductor's authority to deny carriage to a passenger who refused to take his assigned seat "obviously" referred to "an assignment according to the requirements of the Act, *i.e.* to the coach to which the passenger, by race, belongs."[18]

Paragraph three reached an issue that Tourgée had in mind from the beginning: the impropriety of classifying octoroons—persons one-eighth black and seven-eighths white—as black, "although color be not discernible in their complexion." But here he and Walker faced a difficulty: the information against Plessy, unlike the earlier information against Daniel Desdunes, did not aver Plessy was a "person of color." Although Walker's oral argument in trial court may have raised the issue, his plea to the jurisdiction had left Plessy's race unmentioned and did not deny that octoroons should be classified as persons of color; and Ferguson's ruling merely noted the information's silence regarding color, then dropped the matter. The first certain mention of the claim appears in Plessy's petition for writs of prohibition and certiorari, which alleged that he was seven-eighths white, "that the mixture of colored blood is not discernible," and that he was "entitled to every recognition, right, privilege, and immunity secured to citizens of the United States of the white race by the Constitution and laws of the United States . . . ." The petiton went on to describe Plessy's eviction from a white car on the East Louisiana Railway, supporting the account with a copy of the complaint that Detective Cain had sworn out against Plessy, which identified Plessy as "a passenger of the colored race."[19]

In the formal "Answer" he filed with the Supreme Court in response to Plessy's petition, Judge Ferguson denied that Cain's affidavit had come before him as evidence or that it formed any part of the proceedings that had so far taken place.[20] Nor had anything else in the proceedings in Criminal District Court revealed or alleged Plessy's color. Not until Plessy's trial, Ferguson maintained, would he know "whether . . . Plessy was a white man or a colored man going into and remaining in a compartment of a coach to which, by reason of his race or color, he did not belong." On brief, Adams bolstered this assertion by explaining that the action for a writ of prohibition was a proceeding between two courts, in which "[t]he only questions . . . legitimately submitted for consideration are those presented by the pleadings and proceedings of the subordinate tribunal." Accordingly, new evidence could not be presented.

In response, the Tourgée-Walker brief denied that Ferguson had no knowledge of Cain's affidavit, for by Louisiana's Constitution and practice, a judge could allow an information to be filed only on a showing of probable cause, and the only evidence that could have supported the information was the affidavit. Yet even if the affidavit were a part of the record, it identified Plessy simply as a colored person and so did not go to the issue of his racial mixture. It is not surprising, then, that Tourgée and Walker finally asserted that his racial composition was constitutionally irrelevant.[21]

Their brief nevertheless probed the implications of classifying a person of mixed ancestry as black. "Reputation is a species of property," it asserted, "and is valuable in proportion as it entails rights and privileges, whether social or political." Politically, blacks and whites enjoyed equal rights before the law, but no one could ignore that whites enjoyed esteem and respect denied blacks. A law that stripped away such a reputation would accordingly be void. The brief did not offer an explicit reason, but implicitly, and quite clearly, its contention was that the invalidity resulted from a deprivation without due process of law.

What Tourgée and Walker saw as constitutional weakness, Fenner's opinion turned into constitutional merit. Whether the conductor's assignment of Plessy deprived him of any rights would depend on whether Plessy had been assigned to a car to which, by race, he did not belong, which would be determined only at his trial. If it turned out that he had been incorrectly assigned by race, then the conductor—not the law—was at fault, for, properly interpreted, the law allowed a remedy.[22]

Paragraph six charged that the separate car law's nurse exemption constituted class legislation and hence violated the Fourteenth Amendment's equal protection requirement. Except as it was covered implicitly in the broad Fourteenth Amendment argument in the plea to the jurisdiction, this claim evidently had not appeared in the Louisiana proceedings prior to the Tourgée-Walker brief. By allowing Negro nurses attending white children to ride in white coaches, ran the argument, "and white nurses, if any such there be, attending colored children," to travel in black coaches, the law did "not apply to all white persons and all colored persons indiscriminately." Neither Adams in his brief nor Fenner in his opinion deigned to mention the issue.[23]

Paragraph seven objected that the law worked "an invasion and deprivation of the natural and absolute rights of citizens of the United States to the society and protection of their wives and children travelling in railroad trains," when the citizens in question were "married to persons of the other race." This accusation, too, first appeared in the Tourgée-Walker brief before the state Supreme Court, where the lawyers explained that Louisiana condoned racially mixed marriages, yet the separate car law required the spouses in mixed marriages to travel in separate coaches, whereas partners in other marriages were not separated. The abridgement of rights in the form of impermissible classification was especially evident when comparing a mixed couple traveling *inter*state with one traveling *intra*state. By the Louisiana Supreme Court's ruling in the *Abbott* case, the law necessarily had no application to interstate travelers; this meant that the first couple could enjoy each other's company, but the second could not. The state high court ignored this argument, too, prompting Tourgée and Walker to renew it in their rehearing brief with the charge that the separate car law was "class legislation."[24]

Paragraph eight protested that by "depriv[ing] the citizen of remedy for wrong," the statute was unconstitutional. The target was the provision that freed railways and train officers from liability for damages for refusing to carry passengers who refused to occupy their assigned seats. The same claim had appeared in the plea to the jurisdiction, where it was identified as an equal protection issue. Clarifying the argument, the Tourgée-Walker brief held that the absolute and unambiguous grant of immunity for damages deprived one class of citizens of the legal remedies available to other citizens. Unfortunately, Lionel Adams had conceded the unconstitutionality of the immunity provision in the hearing before Judge Ferguson, as the latter noted in his opinion on the plea to the jurisdiction. Following an accepted rule of interpretation, Ferguson had then held that one invalid provision did not invalidate the entire law. Justice Fenner in his opinion took a different approach, but with the same effect. He construed the exemption clause to mean that railways were immunized against damages only in instances where passengers had been correctly assigned by race. "It is too clear for discussion," he declared, "that a refusal to carry a passenger because he had refused to obey an assignment to a coach to which his race did not belong would not be exempted from redress in an action for damages."[25]

Paragraphs nine through twelve all focused on the implication of the requirement that train officers assign passengers by race: assignment by race necessitated determination of race. Together, these paragraphs advanced four propositions: (1) Neither the separate car law itself nor existing statute or case law had defined "colored race" and "persons of color," and hence the separate car law necessarily delegated the task of definition to train officers, whose decisions in this regard had the force of law. (2) As common carriers, railways could not "be authorized to distinguish between citizens according to race," because (3) "[r]ace is a question of law and fact which an officer of a railroad corporation cannot be authorized to determine." And (4) Louisiana had "no power to authorize officers of railway trains to determine the question of race without testimony, to make the rights and privileges of citizens to depend on such decision, or to compel the citizen to accept and submit to such decision."

The plea to the jurisdiction had included each of these contentions, which Judge Ferguson interpreted as maintaining that by delegating the determination of race to railway officers, the separate car law deprived persons of liberty and property without due process of law. In reviewing this claim, he concluded it was true that a train officer "determine[d] for the time being the question of color." But the officer made his determination at his own peril, owing to the invalidity of the law's exemption clause; and the officer's decision was "subject to subsequent judicial investigation and determination." Moreover, just as railways possessed undoubted legal authority "to adopt reasonable rules and regulations for their protection and the proper conduct of their business and to designate who shall execute said regulations," so too might a legislature issue analogous rules. Both sorts of rules constituted legitimate police regulations, and neither version deprived a person of lawful liberty. Especially germane here was the *Logwood* case (1885) in federal Circuit Court in Tennessee—a common-law suit against a railroad—which had held that a conductor was the proper person for determining a passenger's seat assignment on the basis of color. Finally, to organize a judicial tribunal on a train to determine race in each instance "would be impracticable—in fact, almost impossible."[26]

Ferguson never reached the question of what would guide the conductor in determining a passenger's race, "a scientific and legal question of great difficulty," as the plea to the jurisdiction had characterized it; and the Tourgée-Walker brief before the state Supreme Court dwelt on the omission. "The statute leaves uncertain and indefinite who are among those classed as persons of the colored race," it charged, noting that Louisiana law and judicial precedent were similarly silent. To underscore the deficiency, the brief quoted legal treatises and court cases from other jurisdictions which not only offered a variety of definitions of what constituted a "Negro," a "mulatto," and a "person of color," but disagreed on how the determination was to be made. The brief also cited authorities for denying that legislatures could delegate their law-making power to private corporations.[27]

Adams found the issue less complicated. He reiterated Ferguson's view that case law established the analogous right of common carriers to separate by race and argued that the determination of race posed no difficulties, as evidenced by two dictionaries. One described "color" as "belonging wholly or partly to the African race," and the other defined "persons of color" as embracing not only "all persons descended wholly from African ancestors, but also those who have descended in part only from such ancestors, and have a distinct admixture of African blood." In the application of these rules for classification, the conductor exercised no judicial function, acting instead in a ministerial capacity, for his duties were "of a peremptory and mandatory nature . . . and in no sense involve[d] the exercise of any degree of judgment." Justice Fenner elaborated that the discretion vested in train officers, which required them "to decide primarily [that is, in the first instance] the coach to which each passenger, by race, belongs," constituted only the discretion that necessarily "attends every imposition of a duty, to determine whether the occasion exists which calls for its exercise." Anyway, the conductor's action could result in no deprivation of liberty or property without due process, because a passenger could resort to a subsequent suit for damages in order to protect his right against misassignment.[28]

Tourgée and Walker had good reason to retort, in arguing for a rehearing, that "as a physical fact, there must be a limit, when color runs out, and in the nature of things, the greater and more extensive population of one race shall absorb the other . . . ." In this circumstance, deciding a person's race *was* "often a question of great difficulty"; and law and fact did become intertwined. In no sense was it the conductor's role merely to determine the occasion for exercising an assigned duty. Nor, given the clear meaning of the plain words of the statute, could a passenger recover through a damage suit.[29]

IV

The final four headings in the assignment of errors contested the state Supreme Court's interpretation of the separate car law. Of these, headings two through four addressed issues of statutory construction. The court had erred, argued Tourgée and Walker, by construing the act as (1) requiring train officers to assign passengers to equal quarters, (2) requiring train officers to assign passengers to the coaches to which by race they belonged, and (3) not exempting train officers from liability for damages in the event of improper assignment by race. To support their position, the two lawyers reiterated that criminal statutes were to be strictly construed.

These disputes took Plessy's attorneys onto soft ground. The rule on strict construction itself was not rigid, as the Louisiana Supreme Court had stressed within the preceding year and a half, when it embraced earlier language of the United States Supreme Court: "The proper course in all cases is to adopt that sense of the words which best harmonizes with the context and promotes, in the fullest manner, the policy and objects of the legislature."[30] Also, far from increasing the burden of the statute on defendants like Plessy, the Louisiana Supreme Court's construction of the Act ostensibly worked to their benefit by imposing stricter standards on train officers and by broadening the remedies available in instances of misassignment. Then, too, federal Supreme Court decisions stressed that federal courts would follow the constructions that the highest court of a state had placed on state laws.[31] Yet, however slim the chances that the federal Supreme Court would review the disputed constructions, Tourgée and Walker pressed the issue, no doubt recognizing that the Louisiana court's reading of the statute seriously weakened their equal protection and due process arguments.

The fifth heading raised a broader issue of interpretation, less the meaning of the statutory language than its implication. Here, quoting and summarizing sections of the law, the two attorneys argued that the state Supreme Court was mistaken in finding that the statute granted no judicial authority to train officers to determine the race of passengers and to impose sanctions. This added nothing to the charge in heading one that the measure delegated judicial functions and thus infringed rights of due process.

Missing from the assignment of errors was any mention of Plessy's health or deportment at the time of his arrest. When planning the Desdunes case, it will be recalled, Tourgée had worried that unless the record clearly showed their client met the usual requirements for passage on a first-class car (proper dress, no noxious diseases, etc.), the appellate courts might avoid the constitutional issues by arguing the record did not show Desdunes was otherwise entitled to a seat. Consistent with this concern, Walker's plea to the jurisdiction in Plessy's case (as in Desdunes's) included averments that Plessy held a valid ticket and met the standards regarding personal appearance, conduct, and condition. After Judge Ferguson directly examined the constitutional validity of the separate car law, neither Adams in his brief nor Fenner in his opinion suggested that non-racial issues mooted Plessy's constitutional claims.

The outcome in Louisiana was hardly unexpected by Plessy, his attorneys, or the Citizens' Committee to Test the Constitutionality of the Separate Car Law. From the beginning the goal had been a ruling from the United States Supreme Court, even though after the decision in *Desdunes*, both Martinet and Tourgée apparently thought desegregation of interstate travel would upset the whole system of railway segregation. Indeed, a victory on federal constitutional grounds in Louisiana would conceivably have disappointed the opponents of the law. Under the existing jurisdictional statute, a case in which a state law was challenged as contrary to the United States Constitution could be carried from the highest state court empowered to decide the issue to the United States Supreme Court only if the state court ruled *against* a claimed federal right.[32] Hence Louisiana (or, formally, Judge Ferguson, who was the opposing party of record in *Ex parte Plessy*) could not have appealed a state court decision in favor of Plessy's claimed rights and against the validity of the law—nor, of course, could Plessy have done so. But Plessy lost in Louisiana, and Tourgée and Walker sought federal review.

The Louisiana proceedings had disclosed three elements which were central to the resolution of Plessy's case. First, and to no one's surprise, the outcome depended on judicial interpretation of the Thirteenth and Fourteenth Amendments. Second, application of the two Amendments involved "tests" that took judges into the realm of "fact"—and, in *Plessy*, almost immediately to "fact" in the form of scientific and popular views of race. Third, current judicial conclusions about the empirical "truths" of race and their implications for transportation rested in part on a series of prior race-related transportation cases involving mainly non-constitutional issues. So, to prepare for an examination of *Plessy* before the United States Supreme Court, as well as for a broader assessment of the case's significance, we turn in the following three chapters to the "environmental" elements of constitutional doctrine, racial "fact" and theory, and non-constitutional case law concerning common carriers.

CHAPTER FOUR

The Constitutional Environment:
Lost Origins and
Judicial Deference

I

Under the Thirteenth and Fourteenth Amendments, what limitations did judges by the mid-1890s typically place on state police legislation? According to myth, state economic and social regulations increasingly came under court attack in the late nineteenth century, while restrictions on blacks went unchecked. To determine the actuality takes us initially to the days of relief, hope, and expectation as the Civil War ended. After that, we turn to judicial interpretations of the new constitutional order.

On January 31, 1865, Congress approved what would become the Thirteenth Amendment to the Constitution: "Neither slavery nor involuntary servitude, except as a punishment for crime whereof the party shall have been duly convicted, shall exist within the United States, or any place subject to their jurisdiction." In contrast to earlier amendments, the text also included a provision affirming Congress's "power to enforce this article by appropriate legislation." Ratified by the end of the year, the Amendment was intended to serve more than simply the interests of blacks. It would eliminate forever the divisive issues of slavery and race—or so its advocates supposed. Still more fundamentally, by eliminating legally defined caste and class, the Amendment would remove "the last moral stain from our national escutcheon—the only disgrace from our flag," as the Chicago *Tribune* put it. It would thus fulfill the promise embodied in the Declaration of Independence and enhance the quality of freedom for all Americans, because slavery had produced closed societies that restricted everyone's liberty. Most tangibly, the Amendment constituted a capstone to recent changes in the Negro's status. While wartime emancipation had already doomed the *existing* institution of slavery, a constitutional amendment would ensure the permanence of freedom. But refined analysis of the freedom it guaranteed was largely absent at first. The Amendment's text, concluded the Boston *Journal* when Congress approved it, "tells the whole story for itself. Every man understands what the new article means."[1]

By late 1865, however, southern whites seemed intent on ignoring the verdict of the war. Revealing their intransigence by electing prominent ex-Confederates to Congress, they had also begun to enact Black Codes reminiscent of earlier slave-control legislation and were subjecting blacks to other, less gentle, forms of local harassment. Through their response to these provocations, congressional Republicans provided later generations with clues to the original meanings not only of the Thirteenth Amendment, but also of the Fourteenth, which Congress soon required the rebel states to ratify in order to gain readmission to the Union.

One measure, proposed in early January 1866, extended the life of the Freedmen's Bureau, originally established a year earlier to assist blacks temporarily in making the transition to freedom. The new Act, finally passed in mid-July over President Andrew Johnson's veto, increased the jurisdiction of Bureau courts in actions involving the freedmen. It further affirmed the rights to make contracts, to participate fully in court proceedings, to acquire, hold, and dispose of property, and "to have full and equal benefit of all laws and proceedings concerning personal property, personal security, and the acquisition, enjoyment, and disposition of estate, real and personal," which were to "be secured to and enjoyed by all citizens . . . without respect to race, or color, or previous condition of slavery." While these provisions produced some questioning of the extent of Congress's authority under the Thirteenth Amendment, they applied only in regions "where the ordinary course of judicial proceedings ha[d] been interrupted by the rebellion." As a result, the law could be defended under the theory that federal authority to suppress the rebellion extended to the restoration of normal civil relations within former rebel territory.

To broaden coverage and to turn the federal court system generally into a vehicle for protection of federally guaranteed rights, the Republicans advanced a second measure, which became the Civil Rights Act of 1866. As first introduced, this forbade any "discrimination in civil rights or immunities among the inhabitants of any State or Territory . . . on account of race, color, or previous condition of slavery," and then included the same enumeration of rights as the Freedmen's Bureau bill. Before final passage on April 9 (over Johnson's veto), the broad language banning all discrimination was deleted, but the enumeration remained. The final version defined as United States citizens "all persons born in the United States and not subject to any foreign power, excluding Indians not taxed." In contrast to the Freedmen's Bureau extension, the bill triggered serious questions about the extent of rights conveyed by the Thirteenth Amendment.[2]

Even before these measures were introduced, Representatives Thaddeus Stevens of Pennsylvania and John Bingham of Ohio had offered constitutional amendments on the topic of federally guaranteed rights. In mid-February, the newly created Joint Committee on Reconstruction reported a variant of Bingham's proposal: "Congress shall have power to make all laws which shall be necessary and proper to secure to the citizens of each State the privileges and immunities of citizens in the several states . . . ; and to all persons in the several States equal protection in the rights of life, liberty and property." Then, when neither house accepted this language, and after the Freedmen's Bureau and Civil Rights bills had been debated and the latter passed, the Joint Committee in April took up a version of Stevens's amendment that declared, "No discrimination shall be made by any State, nor by the United States, as to the civil rights of persons because of race, color, or previous condition of servitude."

Eventually the Committee adopted Stevens's declaratory format for Section One of its draft proposal, but incorporated new language offered by Bingham: "No State shall make or enforce any law which shall abridge the privileges and immunities of citizens of the United States nor shall any State deprive any person of life, liberty, or property without due process of law, nor deny to any person within its jurisdiction the equal protection of the laws." The Committee draft also included sections that reduced representation in the House of Representatives in proportion to a state's denial of suffrage to adult males (Section Two), disqualified from public office ex-Confederates who had violated previous oaths as federal or state officers (Section Three), reaffirmed the validity of the public debt of the United States while voiding the Confederate debt and claims arising from emancipation (Section Four), and retained the congressional enforcement power which Stevens had proposed (Section Five). With the addition (by the Senate) of a citizenship clause at the beginning of Section One, the proposed Amendment received final approval on June 13 and was sent to the states.[3]

This chronology, necessarily simplified as presented here, only begins to suggest the complexities involved in determining what rights the framers of the two Amendments intended them to convey. At minimum, the Thirteenth included the right not to be owned by another, but did abolition of slavery, by its own force, embrace the rights included in the Freedmen's Bureau extension and the Civil Rights Act of 1866? Did it carry still other rights? At minimum, Section One of the Fourteenth Amendment "constitutionalized" the Civil Rights Act, but did it convey other rights? Was it a recognition of the need to remedy deficiencies in the preceding amendment, or was it a detailed (but not necessarily exhaustive) restatement of the Thirteenth? Difficult enough when asked about the framers of the two

Amendments in Congress, such questions become even tougher when we recognize that it was the action of state legislators that gave the Amendments their legal effect. What did they think they were ratifying?

One approach begins with the Thirteenth Amendment. No matter that the debate surrounding its passage was largely silent as to its nuanced meaning, or that the rights specified in the Civil Rights Act began to be associated explicitly with the Amendment only after troubling reports started arriving from the South. A case can be made that in the minds of its supporters it constituted an open-ended grant to do whatever was necessary to eradicate all the vestiges of chattel slavery. The key consideration, Harold Hyman and William Wiecek have argued, is that those responsible for its passage in 1864–65 did *not* see it as merely the first of three steps—as but one of three Reconstruction amendments. Instead, *they* regarded it as a final and sufficient implement for assuring blacks their rightful place in American society. So considered, it established a basis for attacking *all* action, private or state, that deprived Negroes of their rights. Operating in a period of change, as Hyman and Wiecek explain, when legal doctrines had just recently served instrumentalist functions in furthering the anti-slavery crusade, the Republicans "had written the Thirteenth Amendment in an evolutionary, abolitionist context," convinced that formal definitions should not and could not restrict the growth of freedom. By this argument, the Civil Rights Act of 1866 can hardly be taken as a statement of the outer limit of the Amendment's meaning.[4]

In the same vein, Section One of the Fourteenth Amendment needs interpretation in light of the scope of the Thirteenth. In particular, one may plausibly argue, the framers of the Fourteenth recognized that the language they employed in Section One had the capacity for expansion. In *Corfield v. Coryell* (1823), the federal Circuit Court case so often cited in 1866 to explain the meaning of the privileges and immunities of citizenship, Justice Bushrod Washington had as much as admitted that he was only offering a minimum definition. In like manner, John Bingham, one of the Fourteenth Amendment's principal authors, defended the final draft by assimilating it to "the inborn rights of every person." Others amplified the idea. Put differently, Charles Fairman's charge that Section One's wording "in truth . . . had not been [fully] understood even by its framers" may be accurate, but it cuts in an unintended direction: like the Thirteenth Amendment, the Fourteenth had capacity for growth.[5]

That other scholars take more restricted views of the sequence of events in 1864–66 is not so important as is the fact that this expansive interpretation fails to entail a definite answer to a crucial question suggested thirty years ago by Alfred Kelly. If we accept as accurate the view that the two Amendments, separately or together, constituted a charter of equality, the problem still remains: did the meaning of that equality exclude racial classification?[6]

The evidence points both ways. One later survey of northern Republican press reaction to passage of the 1866 Civil Rights Act—which by all accounts constituted a minimum catalog of the Fourteenth Amendment's guarantees—found "a general impression . . . that negroes would, by the provisions of the bill, be admitted, on the same terms and conditions as white people, to schools, theaters, hotels, churches, railway cars, steamboats, etc." Democratic opponents of the measure in Congress, and of the Amendment, had warned against the same results. And examples occurred of blacks asserting the right to enter white facilities, claiming the protection of the Civil Rights Act. True, these episodes are difficult to interpret owing to uncertainty in the record whether the objective was access in place of exclusion, or integrated access in place of segregation. In some instances, however, the goal was clearly integrated access, as in Mobile, Alabama, where a United States Commissioner held that the law entitled blacks to use the same street railway cars occupied by whites. During the war, Congress itself had outlawed segregated street railways in Washington, D.C., which *may* offer insight into the thinking of congressional Republicans on the incompatibility of transportation segregation with equal civil rights.[7]

Yet in debates during early 1866, contrary evidence also accumulated. Challenged to defend the ban in the Freedmen's Bureau bill against "the deprivation of any civil right secured to white persons," Senator Lyman Trumbull of Illinois, who had introduced the measure, not only defended the provision as authorized by the Thirteenth Amendment, but went on to explain why it did *not* apply to state anti-miscegenation laws:

> One of its [the bill's] objects is to secure the same civil rights and subject to the same punishments persons of all races and colors. How does this interfere with the law of Indiana preventing marriages between whites and blacks? Are not both treated alike by the law of Indiana? Does not the law make it just as much a crime for a white man to marry a black woman as for a black woman to marry a white man, and *vice versa?* I presume there is no discrimination in this respect, and therefore your law forbidding marriages between whites and blacks operates alike on both races. . . . I see no discrimination against either in this respect that does not apply to both.

As if to underscore his concept of discrimination, he concluded: "Make the penalty on all classes of people the same for the same offense, and then no one can complain." Trumbull had also introduced the Civil Rights bill, and soon offered a similar, albeit abbreviated, gloss on its ban on "discrimination in civil rights or immunities . . . on account of color," which had not yet been struck out.

In the House, Representative James Wilson of Iowa, chairman of the Judiciary Committee, staked out a comparable position in presenting the Civil Rights bill. Referring to the still-present "no discrimination" clause, he allowed that it "provides for the equality of citizens of the United States in the enjoyment of 'civil rights and immunities,'" and he put the question: "What do these terms mean? Do they mean that in all things civil, social, political, all citizens, without distinction of race or color, shall be equal?" "By no means can they be so construed," he asserted. They did not include the right of suffrage, nor did "they mean that all citizens shall sit on the juries, or that their children shall attend the same schools. These are not civil rights or immunities." Quoting James Kent's *Commentaries,* he "understood civil rights to be simply the absolute rights of individuals, such as—'the right of personal security, the right of personal liberty, and the right to acquire and enjoy property.'" "Immunities" were merely exemptions from officially imposed duty, so no discrimination in this regard meant that "Whatever exemptions there may be shall apply to all citizens alike."

Senator Jacob M. Howard of Michigan similarly explained the Joint Committee's final version of Section One of the Fourteenth Amendment when he presented it to the Senate. Drawing on *Corfield v. Coryell,* he denied "privileges or immunities" were susceptible to easy definition, but held they included at least the rights of freedom from personal restraint, of locomotion, and of security of person and property. He more narrowly interpreted the due process and equal protection clauses as "abolish[ing] all class legislation and do[ing] away with the injustice of subjecting one caste of persons to a code not applicable to another." His example underscored his meaning: "It [that is, the part of Section One containing the two clauses] prohibits the hanging of a black man for a crime for which the white man is not to be hanged." Equality, that is, meant the absence of unequal burdens, a view Thaddeus Stevens had already advanced during debate over an earlier version of the Amendment.[8]

It may be objected that Trumbull and Wilson were not focusing on the Fourteenth Amendment at all, that Stevens was explicating a different version of it, and that none of the men necessarily had to consider the possibly broader meaning of the *Thirteenth* Amendment. The point is, however, that their comments offer insight into how they understood *equality itself;* and their meaning arguably encompassed the permissibility of racial classification within state "police regulations," so long as differential criminal penalties were avoided. For these men, the real problem was "partial state legislation," as Senator Luke Poland of Vermont put it during the Fourteenth Amendment debate. (This conclusion is underscored by the fact that the phrase "no discrimination . . . on account of race" in the initial Civil Rights bill, which Trumbull and Wilson were discussing, was, if anything, *more* explicit than the wording of either the Thirteenth or Fourteenth Amendment.) Also apropos this understanding of equality, although Congress during the war had banned segregation on the District of Columbia's street railways, it had accepted segregation in its schools. Finally, of the thirty states ratifying the Fourteenth Amendment, at least eighteen had laws mandating separate schools or forbidding miscegenation. It may be asked whether a sufficient number of legislatures would have approved an amendment that they understood to invalidate this legislation. At best, then, the record does not reveal an unambiguous rejection of what by the end of the century would be labeled "equal-but-separate."[9]

So both views have at least some historical support. In their constitutional inceptions, the Thirteenth and Fourteenth Amendments arguably rested on an organic view of law and an expansive conception of liberty. The two Amendments *also* arguably failed to exclude legalized racial classifications under the formula of "equal but separate." And while to us these two interpretations seem contradictory in their implications for later developments, in an important sense they point to a common conclusion: the work of future Congresses and courts would prove crucial.

II

In 1873, in the *Slaughter-House Cases*, the federal Supreme Court examined the Thirteenth and Fourteenth Amendments for the first time. The cases came from Louisiana after the state legislature, in 1869, had restricted the slaughtering of livestock in New Orleans to geographically defined facilities run by the Crescent City Live-Stock Landing and Slaughter-House Company. The problem was not that the state's action lacked precedent, for under decisions in several states, abattoirs easily fell within the scope of the state police power. Who, for example, could dispute the need to prevent discharge of slaughterhouse byproducts into the Mississippi River *above* the intake for New Orleans's water supply? But legislative bribery had greased passage of the law, with its most immediate beneficiaries—the seventeen participants in the corporation it established—adroitly distributing shares of stock and cash. (When one of the promised recipients sued for stock owed him, however, the company successfully responded that another of the promoters had absconded with it.)

Claiming, not inaccurately, that the law's real purpose was to restrict pursuit of a common calling rather than to promote health, the butchers who had been left out of the near-monopoly sued to enjoin its enforcement. In turn, the company counter-sued. After conflicting decisions by lower courts, the state Supreme Court sustained the company's charter; but the litigation became tangled further when the federal Circuit Court in New Orleans in effect held for the butchers on the merits, only to rule the next morning that the federal jurisdictional statute provided no authority to enjoin the state court proceedings. The excluded butchers now appealed to the federal Supreme Court.[10]

On first impression, the plight of the butchers seems far removed from the subject matter of the Thirteenth and Fourteenth Amendments. Yet their counsel, former Justice John A. Campbell, who had resigned from the high bench when his home state of Alabama seceded in 1861, arrestingly employed the American and Western European attack on monarchy and privilege over the preceding century in order to interpret the Amendments as banning the Louisiana legislation. Under the influence of the "mighty revolution" of Civil War, he concluded, "[t]he law of freedom became fundamental, and embraced all within the jurisdiction of the United States." Accordingly, the Constitution was changed to provide "an oversight—a censorship that did not previously exist. . . . Conscience, speech, publication, security, occupation, freedom, and whatever else is essential to the liberty, or is proper as an attribute of citizenship, are not held under the guarantee of the Constitution of the United States."[11]

Campbell's bold argument nearly succeeded, garnering four votes on the Court. But Justice Samuel Miller, writing for the five-member majority, agreed with the company's reply that the Amendments were not intended to produce such a sweeping revision of American federalism. Rather, when their "unity of purpose," as disclosed by even "the most cursory glance," was "taken in connection with the history of the times," they pointed elsewhere. Whatever a "microscopic search" revealed about possible meanings of servitude (and Campbell had explored how the French, during their attack on the *ancien régime,* had struck at servitudes in the form of restrictions on employment and occupation), the Thirteenth Amendment's clear target was the personal servitude encapsulated in the institution of Negro slavery. With a similarly restricted focus, the Fourteenth Amendment served to complete the guarantee of freedom to *blacks*, its necessity having been revealed once events in the South had shown "their lives were [still] at the mercy of bad men."[12]

Beyond that, Miller adopted the company's claim that under Campbell's approach, Congress would be able to "pass laws in advance [of state infringements], limiting and restricting the exercise of legislative power by the states, in their most ordinary and usual functions, as in its judgment it [might] think proper on all such subjects." Had the Fourteenth Amendment's originators intended this revolution, making the Supreme Court into "a perpetual censor upon all the legislation of the states, on the civil rights of their own citizens," its language would surely have been explicit on the point. Then there was the actual language of Section One of the Amendment. Having defined *both* United States *and* state citizenship, the Section went on to guarantee *only* the privileges and immunities of United States citizenship against state infringement. Whatever right a citizen had to pursue an ordinary calling, it was a right traditionally associated with *state* citizenship, and so he must look to the state for its protection.

As for conflict between the slaughterhouse legislation and the Fourteenth Amendment's due process and equal process clauses, Miller did little more than pause. The former provision was modeled after the due process clauses of the Fifth Amendment and many state constitutions; and neither federal nor state courts had accepted the interpretation for which Campbell contended. And in view of the framers' intended target for the equal protection clause, Miller "doubt[ed] very much whether any action of a state not directed by way of discrimination against the negroes as a class, or on account of their race, will ever be held to come within the purview of this provision."[13]

Miller's opinion is easily picked apart in much of its logic and evidence. The Fourteenth Amendment's framers, for example, most probably did *not* intend Section One's citizenship clause to establish two categories of citizenship for purposes of interpreting the privileges-or-immunities clause; it served instead to overturn the *Dred Scott* decision of 1857. At least some of them certainly *did* intend to extend federal protection to the full range of rights associated with citizenship, as partially identified in *Corfield v. Coryell.* Furthermore, by Miller's interpretation, the privileges-or-immunities clause was largely nugatory, for the few privileges he described as attaching to United States citizenship—access to federal offices and courts and to seaports, use of navigable waterways, protection when on the high seas and abroad, assembly and petition, and *habeas corpus*—either already carried federal protection or were beyond the ability of states to infringe. A few courts *had* already interpreted due process as a limitation on the police power. The four dissenters thus had little difficulty scoring Miller for his restrictive gloss on privileges and immunities; and one of them, Justice Bradley, averred that "a law which prohibits a large class of citizens from adopting a lawful employment, or from following a lawful employment previously adopted, does deprive them of liberty as well as property, without due process of law."[14]

Dissents, especially memorably vigorous dissents, have a way of becoming law. Those in *Slaughter-House* by Bradley and Justice Stephen J. Field encouraged later litigants and eventually gained a measure of judicial acceptance. In the main, however, it was the majority opinion that foreshadowed the general trend of development over the next two decades.

For one thing, the Thirteenth Amendment quickly atrophied. Functional endorsement soon appeared for Miller's strong hint that the need for the Fourteenth Amendment testified to the Thirteenth's limited coverage. One source was the vicissitudes of legislative drafting in 1870, when Congress adopted a measure to enforce certain Fourteenth Amendment provisions and especially the Fifteenth Amendment's guarantee against denial of suffrage on the basis of race or previous condition of servitude. Originally enacted to implement the Thirteenth Amendment, the Civil Rights Act of 1866 was now explicitly *reenacted* within the new law—which referred to Fourteenth and Fifteenth Amendments but omitted mention of the Thirteenth. Also contributing to the Thirteenth Amendment's practical disappearance was the compilation of existing laws into the *Revised Statutes of the United States,* issued in 1874. This became the standard reference; and in it, the individual sections of the 1866 Act were scattered under different headings.[15]

As for the Fourteenth Amendment, *Slaughter-House* had the effect of reducing Section One to only the guarantees that explicitly referred to *state* infringements. Miller largely eliminated the citizenship clause as an independent source of right. The decision also gutted the privileges-or-immunities clause, which narrowed subsequent focus still further, to determining the sorts of activities that fell within the ban on state action under the due process and equal protection clauses. Although it is true that Miller described the Amendment's primary goal as protection of blacks in their new liberty, these two relatively intact clauses of Section One implicated mainly procedural rights rather than absolute guarantees.

To see how, with this beginning, the Fourteenth Amendment came to provide the primary constitutional context for the Plessy case, we turn next to a series of cases involving black rights.

III

In 1873 Justice Miller had correctly identified protection of the freedmen as the dominant concern of the Fourteenth Amendment's framers and ratifiers. But between *Slaughter-House* and *Plessy*, of the 150 cases the United States Supreme Court decided under the Amendment, only fifteen involved discrimination against blacks.[16] These fifteen were largely distinguishable from the 1896 case, for they probed the state-action limitation on the Amendment's scope; and no question could arise after 1890 that the *state* of Louisiana had mandated transportation segregation. This handful of cases nevertheless contributed essential ingredients to the body of doctrine that figured into *Plessy*, and one of them produced a thoughtful and important critique of dominant tendencies.

An early issue, which served as a catalyst to flesh out the Fourteenth Amendment's meaning in other regards, was the scope of Congress's remedial authority under Section Five. This, as we have seen, empowered the national legislature to enforce the Amendment's provisions "by appropriate legislation," and on several occasions Congress had acted. Among its many objects, the Enforcement Act of 1870 outlawed banding or conspiring together, or going "in disguise upon a public highway, or upon the premises of another, with intent . . . to injure, oppress, threaten, or intimidate any citizen, with intent to prevent or hinder his free exercise and enjoyment of any right or privilege granted or secured him by the Constitution or laws of the United States." Then, faced with further white southern violence aimed especially at black voting, Congress passed additional enforcement measures. One of these—the Ku Klux Klan Act of April 1871, as it was popularly known—slightly broadened the language quoted from the 1870 Act.[17]

The major effort came finally in 1875, from the lame duck session of the Forty-third Congress. Beginning in 1870, Senator Charles Sumner of Massachusetts had tried unsuccessfully to obtain a comprehensive federal guarantee of equal protection through a "Supplementary Civil Rights Bill." Spurred by a variety of motives—among them, Sumner's death in March 1874, lingering idealism, a desire for revenge after steep losses in the election of 1874, and a sense that somehow a new measure might help recoup their party's fortunes—congressional Republicans enacted Sumner's dream in February 1875. Although stripped of the explicit ban on racially separate schools so dear to Sumner—but also lacking the explicit approval of separate-but-equal schools or other facilities that even some Republicans had supported—the Act declared that

> all persons within the jurisdiction of the United States shall be entitled to the full and equal enjoyment of the accommodations, advantages, facilities, and privileges of inns, public conveyances on land or water, theatres, and other places of public amusement; subject only to the conditions and limitations established by law, and applicable alike to citizens of every race and color, regardless of any previous condition of servitude.[18]

These remedial measures rested on a distinction that proved difficult to maintain: a dedication by Republicans to national protection for the civil rights of blacks, but within a general commitment to state responsibility for police regulations. If the Fourteenth Amendment authorized direct federal protection within the states against racially motivated injuries and crimes, what prevented federal intervention to protect a still wider range of personal rights against abridgement? Pointing up the dilemma posed by "states' rights nationalism," as some later students of Reconstruction have labeled it, a foe of restricted protection for Negro rights suggested in 1879 that Thaddeus Stevens would be horrified to learn about the Supreme Court's narrow interpretation of the Fourteenth Amendment. Certainly Stevens had intended more coverage than *Slaughter-House* allowed. Yet, as Michael Les Benedict remarks, "Stevens would have been just as incredulous to learn that he had given Congress or the Supreme Court the power to nullify Louisiana's regulation of slaughterhouses, and that is the nub of the conundrum the Court faced."[19] The problem was even more acute when the issue was federal censure of private rather than state activity.

In this vexatious context, the Court clarified the direction of development with its decision in *United States v. Cruikshank* (1876), which arose after a band of whites attacked a Negro meeting in Louisiana, killing over a hundred people. When the federal Circuit Court in New Orleans divided evenly on whether the multi-count federal indictments against the perpetrators were valid under Section Six of the Enforcement Act of 1870, the Supreme Court had to determine what the law meant when it prohibited conspiring or banding together to deny a citizen rights protected by the Constitution or laws of the United States.

Ostensibly involving only a problem in statutory interpretation, the case further narrowed the Amendment when the Court, in an opinion by Chief Justice Morrison R. Waite, ruled the indictments did not specify constitutional violations, as required by Section Six. Because the prohibitive clauses of the Fourteenth Amendment extended only to state action, they added nothing to a citizen's protection against private injuries. Waite conceded that the national citizenship clause carried with it certain rights that the federal government could protect against all infringements—he mentioned "meet[ing] peaceably for consultation in respect to public affairs and for a redress of grievances"—but then added the apparent qualification that the clause extended only to acts "done because of the race or color of the persons conspired against."[20]

In overturning the Ku Klux Klan Act of 1871, in *United States v. Harris* (1883), the Court again constricted the meaning of state action. *Harris* grew out of a Tennessee lynching in which a mob seized four Negroes from the custody of a local sheriff and murdered one of them. Because, as outlined in the indictment against its members, the mob's action clearly fell within the statutory prohibition on conspiracies to prevent duly constituted state authorities "from giving or securing to all persons . . . the equal protection of the laws," the issue squarely became whether the law itself fell within the terms of the Fourteenth Amendment. It did not, concluded Justice William B. Woods for the Court, because its provisions were intended to apply "no matter how well the State may have performed its duty." In the case at hand, "there [was] no intimation that the State of Tennessee ha[d] passed any law or done any act forbidden by the 14th Amendment," yet under the 1871 law, the lynching was indictable. For Woods, the purpose of Section One of the Amendment—"to place a restraint upon the action of the States"—was "perfectly clear," and the Ku Klux Act did not fit the purpose.[21]

Overall, it is true, the picture was less stark. Lower court decisions accepted the argument that state *inaction* might be interpreted to constitute state *action* for purposes of the Fourteenth Amendment, and in neither *Cruikshank* nor *Harris* did the Supreme Court categorically reject this view. In each case the Court had explained how a properly framed indictment or law might have covered the crime in question, if not under the Fourteenth Amendment, then under the Thirteenth.[22] Not least, even a prohibition limited to state action denied legitimacy to the most blatant forms of legislated race discrimination. On the less auspicious side, however, the state-private distinction meant that if private parties incidentally interpreted state legislation as conferring an inferior status on one racial group, the legislation itself was arguably insulated from attack under Section One.

A more devastating blow came in the *Civil Rights Cases*, a group of five actions decided together in October 1883, which overturned much of the Civil Rights Act of 1875. This decision gains significance because the terms of the 1875 law *probably* invalidated state-mandated segregation of the separate-but-equal variety. (As we shall see in Chapter Six, however, the law did not *necessarily* threaten the doctrine; and here our concern is the constitutional positions that the Supreme Court endorsed by invalidating the law, not the speculative issue of what a validated law would have accomplished.) Justice Bradley wrote the Court's opinion, a point also of significance, for ten years earlier in his *Slaughter-House* dissent, and again seven years earlier on circuit in New Orleans, Bradley had taken positions which, if not inconsistent with his opinion in 1883, suggested broader conceptions of rights.

At one level, Bradley merely reaffirmed the state action doctrine already laid out in *Cruikshank* and *Harris,* underscoring it with echoes of Justice Miller's *Slaughter-House* strictures about how a more expansive interpretation would overturn American federalism. True, he admitted, the federal government need not wait to pass legislation until states had actually infringed rights covered by the Fourteenth Amendment; it would suffice that the provisions of protective legislation be triggered by "the mischief and wrong which the amendment was intended to provide against." But valid legislation could not "properly cover the whole domain of rights appertaining to life, liberty and property, defining them and providing for their vindication." "That," Bradley concluded, "would be to establish a code of municipal law regulative of all private rights between man and man in society." And what kind of law would run afoul of the Amendment? Bradley later mentioned both an act forbidding proprietors of inns and public conveyances from receiving Negroes and one making an "*unjust* discrimination."[23]

More important as a contribution to the constitutional environment was Bradley's *elaboration* of the state-action interpretation. The wrongful acts of individuals, he claimed, if "unsupported by State authority in the shape of laws, [legal] customs, or judicial or executive proceedings," could not impair "the civil rights . . . guaranteed under the Constitution against State aggression." An individual's act was simply a private wrong, or a crime. It might invade the rights of another person, but so long as the harmful actions were not committed through state law or under state authority, the "rights remain[ed] in full force, and [might] presumably be vindicated by resort to the laws of the State for redress." To illustrate this contention, Bradley explained,

> An individual cannot deprive a man of his right to vote, to hold property, to buy and sell, to sue in the courts, or to be a witness or a juror; . . . [for] unless protected in these wrongful acts by some shield of State law or State authority he cannot destroy or injure the right; he will only render himself amenable to satisfaction or punishment . . . .

In the course of these comments, Bradley defined the scope of the rights that private action could not abridge as including those pertaining to an individual's "person, *his property, or his reputation.*" It was almost as if he foresaw and wished to counter the due process argument that Homer Plessy's counsel later raised.

Bradley also administered the *coup de grace* to the Thirteenth Amendment, which lacked a state-action restriction, Congress could enact direct legislation under it, but only legislation aimed at slavery and involuntary servitude or their badges and incidents. And "mere discriminations on account of race or color" did not qualify as badges or incidents of *slavery*, for *free* Negroes in the antebellum period, who "enjoyed all the essential rights of life, liberty and property the same as white citizens," had been subjected to discriminations. Paralleling his delineation of Fourteenth Amendment rights, he asked,

> Can the act of a mere individual, the owner of the inn, the public conveyance or place of amusement, refusing the accommodation, be justly regarded as imposing any badge of slavery or servitude upon [a Negro], or only as inflicting an ordinary civil injury, properly cognizable by the laws of the State, and presumably subject to redress by those laws until the contrary appears?

Such an action, he concluded, violated no Thirteenth Amendment rights. As for legislated distinctions, Bradley conceded that they were not at issue, but even they would "not necessarily" fall before the Thirteenth Amendment "when not involving the idea of any subjection of one man to another." Capturing the tenor of his whole opinion, Bradley declared:

> When a man has emerged from slavery, and by aid of beneficent legislation has shaken off the inseparable concomitants of that state, there must be some stage in the progress of his elevation when he takes the rank of a mere citizen, and ceases to be the special favorite of the laws, and when his rights as a citizen, or a man, are to be protected in the ordinary modes by which other men's rights are protected.[24]

In a powerful dissent, Justice John Marshall Harlan ripped apart Bradley's effort as resting "upon grounds entirely too narrow and artificial." The most significant statement by a Supreme Court justice against racial discrimination prior to his own *Plessy* dissent thirteen years later, Harlan's opinion anticipated much of the approach that Homer Plessy's counsel took in attacking Louisiana's separate car law. Accordingly, it becomes important to explore Harlan's explanation of how "the substance and spirit of the recent amendments . . . ha[d] been sacrificed by a subtle and ingenious verbal criticism."

By the Court's own admission, he noted, the Thirteenth Amendment did more than eradicate the *institution* of slavery; it struck also at "its badges and incidents." Were it otherwise, the Amendment would have embodied form without substance, for the slaveholding region would have been free to curtail "the enjoyment of those fundamental rights which[,] by universal concession, inhere in a state of freedom." And rights created or guaranteed by the Constitution could be protected by the national government, for that was the teaching of *Prigg v. Pennsylvania* (1842). There the Court had upheld Congress's power to enforce the original Constitution's guarantee that an escaped slave "shall be delivered up on Claim of the Party to whom such Service or Labour may be due," *despite* the failure of the fugitive slave clause to specify who should enforce its mandate—if indeed it was a mandate rather than an admonition. If Congress had previously held the power to implement a vaguely stated guarantee designed to protect the institution of slavery, how could comparable power be denied in the case of a grant in an Amendment which *explicitly* conferred enforcement authority? Besides, the Civil Rights Act of 1866, passed before the Fourteenth Amendment had entered the Constitution, testified to the contemporary understanding that the Thirteenth Amendment empowered the national government to strike directly at discrimination based on race.[25]

The Fourteenth Amendment provided further support. Its citizenship clause was "of a distinctly affirmative character." "It introduced all of that race, whose ancestors had been imported and sold as slaves, at once, into the political community known as the 'People of the United States.'" Under Article IV, Section Two, of the original Constitution, blacks had gained the right of equal treatment in all states other than their states of residence, for this clause provides that "the Citizens of each State shall be entitled to all Privileges and Immunities of Citizens in the several States." No less did the new citizenship clause give them freedom from racial discrimination in their home states—that is, "unless the recent amendments be splendid baubles, thrown out to delude those who deserved fair and generous treatment at the hands of the nation." Harlan reminded his brethren that in *Cruikshank,* after all, they had proclaimed that "the equality of rights of citizens is a principle of republicanism." Here, too, a right created by the Constitution fell within the protective authority of Congress, both by the *Prigg* principle and by the terms of the Fourteenth Amendment itself. The enforcement clause of the Amendment said nothing about empowering Congress to enforce only the prohibitive clauses. Rather it applied to the whole Amendment, *including* the citizenship provision.

Nor would acknowledgment of direct national power under either the Thirteenth or Fourteenth Amendment revolutionize the federal system, for the bogey of a national "municipal code for all the States, covering every matter affecting the life, liberty, and property of the citizens of the several States," was simply not creditable. Only discriminations in civil rights fell within the ambit of the two Amendments, and for the purposes of Harlan's argument, those civil rights need only encompass the "exemption of citizens from discrimination based on race or color."[26]

If one rejected both the Thirteenth Amendment and national citizenship arguments, there remained the prohibitive clauses of the Fourteenth

Amendment, and these by themselves sufficed to support the 1875 law—even if they were interpreted to lay restrictions only on positive actions by states. Harlan reviewed existing case law and standard legal treatises to show convincingly that they recognized state-chartered railways as public highways and the keeping of an "inn," within the common-law meaning of the term, as "the exercise of a quasi public employment." Similarly, "places of public amusement," which the law also covered, referred to publicly licensed establishments. There was also the principle the Court had endorsed when, in *Munn v. Illinois* (1877), it had upheld state regulation of private grain elevators: "Property does become clothed with a public interest when used in manner to make it of public consequence and affect the community at large." A proprietor, by conducting a business, granted the public an interest in its use; he might "withdraw his grant by discontinuing the use, but, so long as he maintains the use, he must submit to the control." In short, the activities covered by the law involved agents of the state. It remained true that the prohibitive clauses did not authorize regulation of social relationships, but it was legal right, not social relationship, that was implicated by a person's presence in a place to which by existing legal doctrine all citizens of proper demeanor must be granted access.

The irony of the situation did not escape Harlan. To deny his position, as the Court had done, meant that "we shall enter upon an era of constitutional law, when the rights of freedom and American citizenship cannot receive from the nation that efficient protection which heretofore was unhesitatingly accorded to slavery and the rights of the master." In any event, it was "scarcely just to say that the colored race has been the special favorite of the laws." The now-invalidated Civil Rights Acts of 1875 had applied to all. If in 1883 the black race was the object of "class tyranny," then "[a]t some future time, it may be that some other race will fall under the ban of race discrimination." The majority's decision had stripped the national government of the authority to protect the central constitutional principle of equality of citizenship.[27]

By the time the Court decided the *Civil Rights Cases,* it had also handed down five jury-selection decisions. Although varying in the precise legal issues they presented, these together established that under Section One of the Fourteenth Amendment and related legislation black defendants were entitled to trials by juries from which blacks had not been excluded by reason of race. To that extent, the cases revealed at least a partial commitment to the Amendment's primary purpose as identified by the Court in *Slaughter-House:* "the freedom of the slave race, the security and firm establishment of that freedom, and the protection of the newly made freemen and citizen from the oppressions of those who had formerly exercised unlimited dominion over him."

There remained the problem of making the guarantee effective, and here the Court was less generous in the five cases. It narrowly interpreted the provision of the Civil Rights Act of 1866 that authorized removal of cases from state to federal Circuit Courts when defendants claimed the state courts would deny them their federally guaranteed civil rights. Because this provision, which had been included as Section 641 of the *Revised Statutes,* authorized removal only before trial, it did not cover potential discriminations that might occur during the trial itself. Thus interpreted, the section provided relief from discriminatory state laws affecting the judicial process, but not from the discriminatory acts of officials, for the latter violations would become known only as they actually occurred. For denial of equal protection during a trial itself, blacks would have to depend on the more cumbersome process of appeal through higher state courts and the federal Supreme Court.[28]

With this approach, the Court left open the possibility of further congressional action to implement the Fourteenth Amendment's first section, even while it narrowly read the existing removal statute. Yet the underlying premise, made especially clear in *Virginia v. Rives* (1880), was limiting: Section One's prohibitory clauses covered only state action infringing civil rights. In that regard, the Court merely elaborated the doctrine already laid out in *Cruikshank.* Questions could still arise about what constituted "state action" and "civil rights", but consensus existed that, as Justice Stephen A. Field put it in his dissent in *Ex parte Virginia* (1880), Section One left "political rights, or such [rights] as arise from the form of government and its administration, as they stood previous to its adoption." Employing a significant comparison, he added: "It has no more reference to them than it has to social rights and duties, which do not rest upon any positive law, though they are more potential in controlling the intercourse of individuals." (Field simply differed with the majority in insisting that jury service was a political right and hence not within the scope of Congress's enforcement power.)

If a glimmer of hope emerged from the Court's narrow statutory and constitutional interpretation in the jury cases, it came from Justice William Strong. His opinion for the Court in *Strauder v. West Virginia* (1880) included this analysis of Section One's language:

> What is this but declaring that the law in the States shall be the same for the black as for the white; that all persons, whether colored or white, shall stand equal before the laws of the States and, in regard to the colored race, for whose protection the Amendment was primarily designed, that no discrimination shall be made against them by law because of their color? The words of the Amendment, it is true, are prohibitory, but they contain a necessary implication of a positive immunity, or right, most valuable to the colored race—the right to exemption from unfriendly legislation against them distinctively as

colored; exemption from legal discriminations, implying inferiority in civil society, rights which others enjoy, and discriminations which are steps towards reducing them to the condition of a subject race.[29]

The glimmer proved illusory. In the period between the *Civil Rights Cases* and *Plessy,* the Court decided another five jury selection cases. Only one turned out favorably for the black defendant, although exclusion of blacks from juries almost surely occurred in the others.[30] More ominous still, *Pace v. Alabama* (1883) revealed that Justice Strong's translation of the negative clauses of Section One into positive rights did not bar state anti-miscegenation laws. In Alabama, adultery or fornication between a man and woman of the same race carried a maximum penalty of two years imprisonment at hard labor; when parties of different races were involved, the penalty was two to seven years at hard labor. Writing for the Court, Justice Field conceded that the equal protection clause undoubtedly was intended "to prevent hostile and discriminating state legislation against any person or class of persons"; but Alabama's code did not discriminate. The sections in question punished *different* offenses, one involving persons of the same race, the other involving persons of different races. The penalties in the former instance were the same whether the parties were both white or both black; those in the latter instance applied "to both offenders, the white and the black." "Whatever discrimination is made in the punishment prescribed in the two sections," Field held, "is directed against the offense designated and not against the person of any particular color or race."[31]

IV

The possibility remains that the Supreme Court lagged notably behind lower courts in recognizing the rights of blacks under the Fourteenth Amendment. Because the Court's jurisdiction, dating back to the Judiciary Act of 1789, did not include review of state decisions *upholding* claims under the federal Constitution or laws, state courts were free to adopt interpretations of the Amendment more favorable to Negro defendants or petitioners than the federal Supreme Court was willing to endorse. Also, opportunities for Supreme Court review of cases from lower federal courts were somewhat limited.[32] Existing studies, while not yet as complete as one might wish, strongly suggest that on balance, however, state courts and lower federal courts took a similarly restrictive view of the Amendment by the mid-1890s. From a review of race-related Fourteenth Amendment cases at the state level between 1870 and 1890, Jonathan Lurie has found that "most frequently the judges ignored the new enactment altogether." Tellingly, when counsel cited the Amendment, they did so more often to support segregation. "It seems fair to conclude," Lurie has written, "that almost a generation after ratification of the fourteenth amendment there was no legal consensus that it had altered the basic relationship between a state citizen and the state or local government in respect to civil liberties." Lurie's focus, it should be noted, is the East, North, and West—regions which, despite continuing racism, manifested less opposition in law to black rights than did the post-Reconstruction South.

Another study reaches a more mixed conclusion. J. Morgan Kousser has identified eighty-two state and lower federal cases on racial discrimination in schools between 1834 and 1903, about three-fourths of which were decided in the period extending from the ratification of the Fourteenth Amendment to the United States Supreme Court's decision in *Plessy*. Blacks prevailed in somewhat more than half of all the cases in which winners could be determined, but typically did so on state grounds; judges who supported black rights observed proper professional restraint by relying on broad federal grounds only when necessary. Nevertheless, approximately 40 percent of the total number of cases turned on federal constitutional issues, and of these, a scant fourth went in favor of blacks. In only one—an obscure Pennsylvania ruling from 1881—did a court squarely hold that the Fourteenth Amendment itself outlawed segregated schooling. (Other favorable rulings on federal grounds supported such outcomes as separate but actually equal schools, integration *if* districts failed to provide equal facilities, and better school funding arrangements.)

Kousser rightly observes that looking only at the cases involving federal constitutional issues seriously misrepresents the total legal environment confronting blacks, as does focusing solely on court action to the neglect of legal gains won directly from school boards and state legislatures. And putting those caveats aside, the proportion of black court victories in cases decided on federal grounds appears higher in the years 1868–96 than during the period from 1834 to 1903 as a whole. But on Kousser's evidence, the restrained judicial style of the pro-black-rights judges *did* keep them from building a major body of anti-segregation case law based explicitly on the Fourteenth Amendment. The *judicially defined* Amendment, as it emerged in the state and lower federal case reports, remained quite hospitable to the principle of separate-but-equal.[33]

Whatever their overall direction, *lower* court decisions on the rights of blacks could not require the federal Supreme Court to accept state-legislated racial segregation under an "equal but separate" formula. Nor did the Supreme Court's own Thirteenth and Fourteenth Amendment decisions on Negro rights mandate acceptance of the doctrine. Yet, by the early 1890s, the Court had turned neither Amendment into a tool to cut broadly at the badges and incidents of slavery; it had effectively derailed the efforts of Congress in that direction; and it had analyzed "servitude," "citizenship," "due process," and "equality" in ways that enshrined form above substance.

Meanwhile, the Court had also decided about 135 Fourteenth Amendment cases unconnected with race. These elaborated a doctrine that could serve to legitimate the racial classifications which its Negro-rights decisions had not effectively prohibited.

V

Initial failure does not foreclose ultimate success. In the *Slaughter-House Cases,* the New Orleans butchers had not established the Fourteenth Amendment as a barrier against a state-authorized monopoly. But seventeen years later, in 1890, a railroad company successfully invoked it against a state rate-setting commission; and in 1894 a railway bondholder used it to enjoin enforcement of a rate order by another state's commission. As early as 1877, the Supreme Court in *Munn v. Illinois* had given a possible clue to the future in the dictum that "[i]f no state of circumstances could exist to justify . . . a [regulatory] statute," then the Court might declare the law void under the Section One of the Fourteenth Amendment.[34]

By sighting along these and a few other markers, one can fashion an account of how business enterprise capitalized on the Fourteenth Amendment to avoid state regulation, at the very time black Americans were meeting only the most limited success—and more often failure—in *their* efforts to use the Amendment. Because it accentuates judicial insensitivity, if not judicial complicity in the spread of rapacious capitalism at the expense of the less fortunate, this line of interpretation makes for good drama; and later Supreme Court justices as well as historians have embraced the account.[35] Since early in the twentieth century, however, other students of the period have recognized that development was less bifurcated. It is revealing that not until 1897 did the Supreme Court clearly overturn a legislatively enacted police measure; and from 1887 through 1900—the period when unbounded laissez faire supposedly gained constitutional sanction—over 90 percent of the Court's Fourteenth Amendment decisions went in favor of the state.[36] In reality, the approach that the Court took to state economic and social regulations paralleled and anticipated its treatment of restrictions on blacks.

Because the Fourteenth Amendment constituted a limitation, the place to start is with the power it purportedly limited—the police power. Offering a definition of the police power in 1873, the *Slaughter-House* majority relied especially on *Commonwealth v. Alger* (1851), by Chief Justice Lemuel Shaw of Massachusetts, and *Thorpe v. Rutland* (1855), from Chief Justice Isaac F. Redfield of Vermont, the two antibellum cases that, by the 1870s, had become the most frequently cited decisions on the subject. In his *Treatise on Constitutional Limitations,* Thomas M. Cooley, the leading legal commentator of the late nineteenth century, began his discussion of the police power with the same two cases. *Alger* and *Thorpe* therefore are particularly germane. Shaw gave this explanation:

> We think it is a settled principle, growing out of the very nature of well-ordered civil society, that every holder of property, however

absolute and unqualified may be his title, holds it under the implied liability that his use of it may be so regulated, that it shall not be injurious to the equal enjoyment of others having an equal right to the enjoyment of their property, nor injurious to the rights of the community. . . . Rights of property, like all other social and conventional rights, are subject to such reasonable limitations in their enjoyment, as shall prevent them from being injurious, and to such reasonable restraints and regulations established by law, as the legislature, under the governing and controlling power vested in them by the [state] constitution, may think necessary and expedient. . . . The power we allude to is . . . the police power, the power vested in the legislature by the constitution, to make . . . all manner of wholesome and reasonable laws . . . not repugnant to the constitution, as they shall judge to be for the good and welfare of the commonwealth, and of the subjects of the same.

Redfield put it succinctly: under the police power, "persons and property are subjected to all kinds of restraints and burdens, in order to secure the general comfort, health, and prosperity of the state, of the perfect right, in the legislature to do which no question ever was, or, upon acknowledged general principles, ever can be made . . . ."[37]

The Latin maxim *sic utere tuo ut alienum non laedas*—use your own so as not to injure another—stated the basis of the power. Rights within society, ran the argument, did not encompass the commission of acts tending to the detriment of others, which meant that a person could not complain about restrictive regulations that promoted the health, welfare, or morals of the community. Put somewhat differently, such regulations did not infringe an individual's rights, for the harmful acts they restricted fell outside the scope of one's rights. As Chancellor Kent had explained, as if to anticipate the case before the Supreme Court in 1873, "Unwholesome trades, slaughter houses, operations offensive to the senses, the deposit of powder, the application of steam power to propel cars, the building with combustible materials, and the burial of the dead, may all be interdicted by law, in the midst of dense masses of population . . . ."

These examples did not exhaust the subjects of the police power; Shaw remarked in *Alger* that it was easier to illustrate the power "than to mark its boundaries, or prescribe limits to its exercise." Moreover, contemporaries were not always rigorous in distinguishing the police power from the power of eminent domain—that is, the power of government to take property for public use in return for compensation—although strictly defined, the latter authority pertained to acquisition of property that itself would be used by the public. Nor did lawyers and judges neatly distinguish regulation of the uses to which property might be put, or of the activities in which a person might engage, from limitations on the rates individuals or enterprises might charge. Also, contrary to some later historical accounts, state and local governments had broadly exercised the police power prior to the Civil War, and they continued to do so in the ensuing years, typically with increased vigor as the century progressed. Consumption of alcohol, drug usage, school attendance, oleomargarine and other food products, occupational and professional qualifications, commodities trading, insurance sales, railway rates, working hours and conditions (especially of women and children), lotteries and gambling, prostitution, Sunday business operations—all were subjects of state legislation.[38]

Even the two principal dissenters in *Slaughter-House,* Justices Field and Bradley, recognized and accepted the sweep of the police power, in language paraphrasing Shaw and Redfield. Their quarrel with the majority lay elsewhere. They claimed, for one thing, that Louisiana's regulation did not actually promote the public health, or, more accurately, that a much less restrictive measure, not involving a monopoly grant, would produce the desired results. As Bradley put it, the monopoly aspect was "onerous, unreasonable, arbitrary and unjust. It ha[d] none of the qualities of a police regulation." He conceded, though, that the "portion of the act which requires all slaughter-houses to be located below the city, and to be subject to inspection, etc., is clearly a police regulation." The second area of disagreement with the majority was over the role of the Court. Field and Bradley concluded that the justices might second-guess the state legislature in assessing whether specific legislative provisions would promote the public interest. Miller, for the majority, implied the judiciary had no concern with the wisdom of the means employed by the legislature to achieve the legitimate police goal of abating the problems associated with abattoirs.[39]

A case decided the following day, April 15, 1873, underscored the extent of a state's police power. Myra Bradwell, the publisher of a legal newspaper in Chicago, had sought admission to the Illinois bar. Finding that the Illinois legislature intended to limit the practice of law to men, the state Supreme Court denied her application, and Bradwell took her case to the federal Supreme Court on writ of error, contending that pursuit of the calling was a privilege or immunity of United States citizenship under the Fourteenth Amendment. Bradwell again lost, on an eight-to-one vote, with the Court's majority doing little more than cite the just-decided butchers' case. Here, though, three of the four *Slaughter-House* dissenters agreed with the majority holding, but on different grounds. Justice Bradley's separate opinion, which was joined by Justices Field and Noah H. Swayne, took as its premise the natural differences between men and women, differences long recognized by the civil law. "The paramount destiny and mission of woman are to fulfill the noble and benign offices of wife and mother. This is the law of the Creator." A second observation about fundamental relations followed: "In the nature of things it is not every citizen of every age, sex, and condition that is qualified for every calling and position." And then came the conclusion: "It is the prerogative of the legislator to prescribe regulations founded on nature, reason, and experience for the due admission of qualified persons to professions and callings demanding special skill and confidence. This fairly belongs to the police power of the state . . . ."[40]

The question, then, was not about the existence of the police power, but rather how to define its boundaries. In 1877, the Court offered an important hint. While upholding state authority to regulate grain elevators, Chief Justice Morrison R. Waite had written in *Munn v. Illinois:*

> For us the question is one of power, not of expediency. If no state of circumstances could exist to justify such a statute, then we may declare this one void, because in excess of the legislative power of the State. But if it could, we must presume it did. Of the propriety of legislative interference within the scope of the legislative power, the Legislature is the exclusive judge.[41]

Waite thereby offered a test of constitutionality that, taken literally, demanded proof of the *complete* non-applicability of a challenged law to the public health, welfare, or morals before the regulation would be invalidated as a police measure. Unless entirely farfetched, the measure was valid. Still, although this made the presumption of constitutionality practically irrebutable, the formulation conceded the possibility of a Fourteenth Amendment barrier.

Meanwhile, the legal profession had concluded that the possibility of a barrier was more than hypothetical. "[T]he docket of this court," observed Justice Miller a few months later, "is crowded with cases in which we are asked to hold that State Courts and State Legislatures have deprived their own citizens of life, liberty or property without due process of law." In another eight years, in an opinion that also revealed the large overlap between the due process and equal protection claims that might be raised under the Fourteenth Amendment, Justice Field discerned still greater emphasis on due process arguments.

What is more significant, both Miller and Field held that this use of the Amendment revealed a "strange misconception" about its scope, to use Miller's language (which Field quoted). In view of Field's position in *Slaughter-House* and his general image as a stalwart defender of laissez faire, his comments in 1885 are particularly noteworthy. At issue was a Missouri law providing double damages against railways for failure to fence their lines. Denying that any consequential lessening of a railroad's property values brought the law "under the objection of depriving a person of property without due process of law," Field found it

> hardly necessary to say [but said so anyway] that the hardship, impolicy, or injustice of state laws is not necessarily an objection to their constitutional validity; and that the remedy for evils of that character is to be sought from State Legislatures. . . . This court is not a harbor where refuge can be found from every act of ill advised and oppressive state legislation.

Beyond that, the provision for double damages constituted a rational means of protecting society from injury, for the actual injury from any single neglect of duty might be too small to justify an aggrieved party's suit against the railway. Regarding the related argument that the law singled out railroad companies with respect to their liability in civil suits, contrary to the equal protection clause, Field found it was "an untenable" as the due process argument. The Missouri statute treated all railway companies equally: they were "subjected to the same duties and liabilities under similar circumstances."[42]

In the late 1880s and early 1890s, two pairs of cases provided important elaborations of how the Fourteenth Amendment might limit the police power. In each pair, the first case seemed to read real force into the prohibitions of Section One, only to have the second case quickly and substantially qualify the conclusion. The initial pair, involving the power of states to prohibit the manufacture and sale of alleged food products, consisted of *Mugler v. Kansas* (1887) and *Powell v. Pennsylvania* (1888). The cases arose after Kansas adopted a general prohibition on alcoholic beverages in 1881 and Pennsylvania outlawed the manufacture and sale of oleomargarine through laws, passed about the same time, "to Prevent Deception in Sales of Butter and Cheese" and "for the Protection of the Public Health and to Prevent Adulteration of Dairy Products and Fraud in the Sale Thereof." Convicted in their respective states for running a brewery and for selling margarine, Peter Mugler and William Powell appealed to the Supreme Court when lower courts upheld the two laws. Justice Harlan wrote both majority opinions.[43]

In *Mugler,* Harlan unquestionably used language that, taken alone, claimed for courts the role of independently judging whether purported police legislation *really* promoted public health, welfare, and morals. Simply because the legislature's task was "to determine, primarily [that is, in the first instance], what measures are appropriate," it did "not at all follow that every statute enacted ostensibly for the promotion of these ends is to be accepted as a legitimate exertion of the police powers of the State." "The courts are not bound by mere forms, nor are they to be misled by mere pretenses," Harlan declared. "They are at liberty—indeed, are under a solemn duty—to look at the substance of things, whenever they enter upon the inquiry whether the Legislature has transcended the limits of its authority." Observing this guideline, Harlan readily established the evil of intoxicating drink. (The "fact" of alcohol's danger was "within the knowledge of all"; and "statistics accessible to everyone" revealed "that the idleness, disorder, pauperism, and crime existing in the country are, in some degree at least, traceable to this evil.")

According to a later author, *Mugler* "definitely established the due process of law clause as a restriction upon state legislation of a substantive character affecting life, liberty, or property and thus closed the period of groping and uncertainty as to the application of the various phrases of the first section of the [Fourteenth] Amendment." Yet Harlan's comments on the judiciary's duty of independent review did not stand alone, for his task was not so easily completed. Beer, Peter Mugler had contended, was not an intoxicating drink, but rather a food beverage that, by the Kansas law, could not be manufactured even for personal use. In response, Harlan did not debate beer's proper classification but instead endorsed the deference to legislative judgment that he earlier had disclaimed. It was "not for the courts, upon their views as to what is best and safest for the community, to disregard the legislative determination of that question." It was sufficient that general prohibition was a useful means to eliminate intoxicating drink; exceptions (other than for scientific, medical, and industrial purposes) could cripple attainment of this legitimate end.[44]

The following year, Harlan held that the principles just laid down in *Mugler* governed *Powell*. He then restated those principles, but in doing so emphasized that "[e]very possible presumption is in favor of the validity of a statute and this continues until the contrary is shown beyond a rational doubt." True, he admitted, Powell had offered testimony to prove that his margarine was entirely healthful and the trial court had refused to hear such evidence. But even if Powell's product was healthful, most margarine *could* still be harmful; and the Court could not say "that such is not the fact." The determination lay with the legislature, as did the decision of whether to guard the public health through regulation of production, or through outright prohibition that would eliminate the need for inspection in a situation perhaps making for easy evasion. Accordingly, Powell suffered no arbitrary deprivation of liberty or property, and hence no deprivation without due process of law. Nor was he denied equal protection, for the law placed the same burdens on all those who manufactured the product.[45]

Compared with *Munn,* the decisions in *Mugler* and *Powell* together placed judges under more of an obligation to render an independent judgment on the relation between a purported police measure and the public health, welfare, and morals—but not much more. Indeed, *Powell*—which Harlan himself characterized as a gloss on *Mugler*—arguably asserted that if a *conceivable* link existed, then the measure infringed no liberty or property interests. Serving, too, to underscore the leeway thus accorded legislative discretion was a strong dissent by Justice Field that stressed the need for more rigorous review.[46]

Soon the Court confronted a different kind of regulation. *Chicago, Milwaukee, and St. Paul Railway v. Minnesota* (1890) overturned an attempt by Minnesota to establish a railroad commission with rate-setting authority that, as the state Supreme Court construed the law, was final and unreviewable in court. Without deciding whether the rates set by the commission were so low as to be confiscatory and hence a deprivation of property, the federal Supreme Court found that the statute creating the commission did not require such essential ingredients of due process as notice to affected parties, a hearing, and the opportunity to examine witnesses. As a result, the absence of an opportunity for court review of the commission's orders meant that its rates *might* be low enough to constitute a deprivation of property, and this would be a deprivation in the absence of due process of law.

The Court had limited the manner in which states could regulate railways, and by implication it had done more. In dissent, Justice Bradley charged that the *Chicago, Milwaukee* decision overturned *Munn.* By his reading, the Constitution required that "the invasion [of individual rights] should be clear and unmistakable" in order to qualify as a deprivation of property without due process, but, he lamented, Justice Samuel Blatchford's majority opinion had rejected this standard and had made courts, not legislatures, the judges of the reasonableness of legislation.[47] Were they approached in the same manner, all regulations to promote community health, welfare, and morals faced the likelihood of invalidation.

Two years later, in *Budd v. New York,* the Court clarified that it had *not* overturned *Munn. Budd,* too, involved a limitation on rates—in this instance for handling grain in floating and shorefront facilities in cities exceeding 130,000 population—but the New York scheme differed from the invalidated Minnesota law in that the state legislature itself had set the permissible rate. Again speaking for the Court, Justice Blatchford identified this as a crucial difference and thereby limited the holding in *Chicago, Milwaukee* to that case itself. "What was said [there] . . . as to the question of the reasonableness of the rate of charge being one for judicial investigation," Blatchford explained, "had no reference to a case where the rates are prescribed directly by the legislature." Not denying that some legislative regulations might be so stringent as to deny Fourteenth Amendment rights, he found that nothing in the record of *Budd* and the two related cases before the Court suggested either a deprivation of due process or a denial of equal protection. His language implied that only the most blatant legislative infringements would trigger invalidation. A shrill dissent by Justice David Brewer, Field's nephew who had joined the Court in 1889, accentuated the conclusion. "The paternal theory of government is to me odious," proclaimed Brewer, adding that the Court's action brought Edward Bellamy's utopian novel *Looking Backward* closer to reality.[48]

The same lax posture emerged in *Reagan v. Farmers Loan and Trust Company* (1894), even though here the justices unanimously invalidated a rate schedule ordered by the Texas Railway Commission. The legislation establishing the commission took account of the rule laid down in *Chicago, Milwaukee* that rate-setting procedures must accord due process; and Justice Brewer, now writing for the Court, found no fault with the overall regulatory scheme entrusted to the commission. Hardship might flow from the requirement that a challenged rate remain in effect until the Commission completed its own review; yet it was "not to be supposed that the legislature of any state, or a commission appointed under the authority of any state, will ever engage in a deliberate attempt to cripple or destroy institutions of such great value . . . , but will always act with the sincere purpose of doing justice to the owners . . . , as well as to other individuals . . . ." Also, the Act provided that a dissatisfied party could seek relief through court review. Despite the fact that the Supreme Court had received *Reagan* after a federal Circuit Court had enjoined the commission's operation and had as much as established a presumption against the validity of the agency, Brewer reversed the lower court decree concerning the commission itself.

The difficulty instead lay with the specific tariffs promulgated by the Texas commission. The Circuit Court had found that these rates forced a well-run railway to operate at a loss. After reviewing a record rich in detail, the Supreme Court agreed that the facts admitted by the state "sustain[ed] a finding that the proposed tariff [was] unjust and unreasonable." This outcome indicated little *overall* hostility to state police regulations, although, as revealed by his dissents in other cases, Justice Brewer himself took a harsher view.[49]

That the *Reagan* decision constituted no abandonment of a permissive attitude by a majority of the Court becomes still more certain from two other cases decided during the same term. In one of these, *Brass v. North Dakota* (1894), a five-to-four majority sustained a legislative grain elevator regulation against due process and equal protection challenges. The majority opinion, by Justice George Shiras, went so far as to observe that while in some earlier cases it may have been true that judges commented on the wisdom of the laws involved, "and that some of the reasons given for sustaining them went rather to their expediency than to their validity," this approach tended to obscure "the real question at issue, namely, the power of the legislature to act at all."[50]

The second case was *Lawton v. Steele* (1984), in which Justice Henry Billings Brown spoke for a six-to-three majority to uphold a New York measure prohibiting use of fishing nets on portions of Lake Ontario. This allowed Brown—who had joined Brewer's dissent in *Budd* but had voted with the majority in *Brass*—to describe the outlines of the police power. Because, as it turned out, Brown would write the Court's opinion in *Plessy* just over two years later, his summary deserves quoting at length. The power, he wrote,

> . . . is universally conceded to include everything essential to the public safety, health, and morals . . . . Under this power it has been held that the state may order . . . the prohibition of wooden buildings in cities; the regulation of railways and other means of public conveyance, and of interments in burial grounds; the restriction of objectionable trades to certain localities; the compulsory vaccination of children; the confinement of the insane or those afflicted with contagious diseases; the

suppression of obscene publications and houses of ill fame; and the prohibition of gambling houses and places where intoxicating liquors are sold. *Beyond this, however, the state may interfere wherever the public interests demand it, and in this particular a large discretion is necessarily vested in the legislature to determine, not only what the interests of the public require, but what measures are necessary for the protection of such interests.* [Emphasis added.]

Two tests needed satisfying to justify exercise of the police power: "the interests of the public generally, as distinguished from those of a particular class, [had to] require such interference"; and the means had to be "reasonably necessary for the accomplishment of the purpose, and not unduly oppressive upon individuals." But a police regulation did not fail merely because it incidentally burdened individuals who proved innocent of any violation: although Brown did not state the point so directly, his use of examples suggested it was enough that innocent parties have judicial recourse to vindicate their rights.[51]

During the period Plessy's case was making its way through the courts, the United States Supreme Court thus proved reluctant to overturn state police legislation on Fourteenth Amendment grounds. Majority dicta and dissenting opinions may have suggested the possibility, but in truth the decided cases established what a recent scholar has called "the principle of conditions," which stressed that the constitutional legitimacy of police measures turned on social and economic facts. In addition, the same cases showed that the Court usually deferred to legislative judgment about the existence of such facts.[52]

VI

By comparison, state courts were somewhat less lenient toward the police power. As explained earlier, existing federal law did not allow Supreme Court review of state court decisions which *upheld* claimed federal rights. A state decision *overturning* a state police measure on Fourteenth Amendment grounds was thereby insulated from federal Supreme Court reversal—even if the Supreme Court itself would likely have accepted the challenged act. As an illustration, New York authorities had no judicial recourse when the state Court of Appeals struck down a state prohibition on the manufacture and sale of oleomargarine that was substantially the same as the Pennsylvania ban soon upheld by the federal Supreme Court in *Powell v. Pennsylvania*. After the latter decision, the New York court rightly observed that its own earlier— and contrary—decision remained good law.[53]

This jurisdictional limitation allowed an independent body of state case law to develop that attacked state interference with personal activity and use of property. As early as 1885, the year Justice Field complained that Fourteenth Amendment cases were clogging the Supreme Court's docket, over thirty state appellate decisions had accumulated to narrow or prohibit use of the police power on due process grounds. Moreover, the line between due process and equal protection was indistinct. As analyzed by the courts, the same impermissible regulation of an activity or group typically *both* infringed liberty *and* constituted an arbitrary classification—that is, one unrelated to any legitimate state interest under the police power.

However, the hostility of the state courts is easily overemphasized. They generally limited their censorship to a fairly narrow range of measures, consisting mainly of employment regulations affecting male workers; and differences existed from state to state and occupation to occupation, so that in this area, too, more laws were upheld than struck down during the 'eighties and 'nineties. Judicial deference to legislative judgment remained the rule. Judges revealed a commitment to "public rights," as Harry N. Scheiber has shown, along with their more publicized attachment to the vested private rights associated with property and contract. As a result, state courts not only failed to elaborate a unified body of law opposed to regulation of perceived societal ills; they largely shared the Supreme Court's lax attitude toward police legislation.[54]

The negative decisions, although not typical, are nevertheless doubly revealing. They offer an inkling of why, despite the generally permissive environment confronting legislative regulation, Plessy's counsel could find at least some encouragement for an attack on the Louisiana separate car law. When examined carefully, they also disclose more fully how "the principle of conditions" nonetheless posed a substantial barrier to attacks on police measures.

An important example is *In the matter of Jacobs* (1885), judged by Morton Keller to be "the most notable" of the state labor decisions. In *Jacobs,* the New York Court of Appeals rejected a state prohibition on manufacturing cigars on any floor of a tenement house occupied as a residence. As characterized by the Court of Appeals, the law made it a crime for the owner or renter "to carry on a perfectly lawful trade in his own home," deprived him of the advantages of working in circumstances that allowed "the supervision of his family and their help," and reduced his competitive edge. As a result, "[i]n the unceasing struggle for success and existence which pervades all societies of men, he may be deprived of that which will enable him to maintain his hold, and to survive." "It is therefore plain," concluded the court, "that this law interferes with the profitable and free use of his property by the owner or lessee of a tenement-house who is a cigarmaker, and trammels him in the application of his industry and the disposition of his labor, and thus in a strictly legitimate sense it arbitrarily deprives him of his property and of some portion of his personal liberty."[55]

As for the contention that the law was nonetheless a legitimate police measure to promote the public health, the Court of Appeals laid down this test: "the courts must be able to see that it has at least in fact *some* relation to the public health, that the public health is the end actually aimed at, and that it is appropriate and adapted to that end." But as the Court of Appeals surveyed the law in question, its purpose was to regulate manufacturing, not to promote health. In contrast to a limitation on occupancy in tenement houses or to a construction code, the law's specific focus on tobacco failed to qualify it as a health measure. "[J]udicial notice of the nature and qualities of tobacco," disclosed for the court the product's "general use among civilized men for more than two centuries," as well as its use "in some form by a majority of the men in this State, by the good and bad, learned and unlearned, the rich and the poor." In its presentation of the case, the state had not claimed the manufacture of cigars harmed either the public health or the health of those engaged in the manufacturing. No evidence before the court indicated that manufacturing in one room harmed those in other rooms, and certainly not when, as in the *Jacobs* case, the odor of tobacco did not permeate to the other rooms.

In addition, as the Court of Appeals read it, the law *on its face* was obviously not directed to the public health. It allowed cigarmakers "to manufacture cigars everywhere except in the forbidden tenement-houses," including crowded private houses and factories, as well as in all tenement-houses outside of New York and Brooklyn, the only two cities meeting the Act's size requirement. (The law applied only in cities exceeding 500,000 population.) Then, too, it excluded from its coverage the first floor of any tenement-house that included a tobacco shop, yet surely if tobacco caused harm to residents, the harm would be even greater from the large quantities kept and processed in a shop adjoining a residence.[56]

The Court of Appeals pushed the attack still further, hinting that, *as a matter of law,* certain regulations exceeded the police powers of the state. This seeming implication flowed from the court's treatment of the constitutional prohibition against deprivation of liberty or property without due process. Specifically regarding the "liberty" portion of the guarantee, the court said:

> Liberty, in its broad sense, . . . means the right not only of freedom from actual servitude, imprisonment or restraint, but the right of one to use his facilities in lawful ways, to live and work where he will, to earn his livelihood in any lawful calling, and to pursue any lawful trade or vocation. All laws therefore which impair or trammel these rights . . . or restrain his otherwise lawful movements . . . are infringements upon his fundamental rights of liberty, which are under constitutional protection.

No matter that the court included the adjective "lawful" at key points, or that it added the qualifying phrase "except as such laws may be passed in the exercise by the legislature of the police power." The tenor of the language insinuated a nearly absolute guarantee.[57]

The idea of an absolute limitation on the police power emerged yet more forcefully in other cases, two of which may be usefully—but more briefly—examined. *Godcharles and Company v. Wigeman* (1886) required the Pennsylvania Supreme Court to review a state law prohibiting use of "store orders" or company script to pay workers in manufacturing industries. In *Ritchie v. People* (1895), the Illinois Supreme Court confronted an eight-hour law for women employed in the apparel manufacturing industry. In each instance, the state high court overturned the challenged legislation.

Each decision ringingly affirmed "liberty of contract" as a constitutionally protected right. In *Godcharles,* the Pennsylvania Supreme Court was terse: the challenged sections of Pennsylvania's law were "utterly unconstitutional and void, inasmuch as by them an attempt has been made by the legislature to do what, in this country, cannot be done; that is, prevent persons who are *sui juris* from making their own contracts." Although the case was not explicitly decided under the Fourteenth Amendment (the court cited no state or federal constitutional provisions), counsel had reminded the court, in arguments reported with the case, that Pennsylvania's restriction on special laws had been interpreted as meaning "[e]qual privileges for all, exclusive privileges for none." The court unquestionably saw a federal issue when it denounced the law as "an insulting attempt to put the laborer under a legislative tutelage, which is not only degrading to his manhood, but subversive to his rights as a citizen of the United States."

Ritchie elaborated the argument, drawing authority from over a dozen earlier state cases, including *Godcharles* and especially *Jacobs*. According to the Illinois Supreme Court, these left the meaning of due process "quite clearly defined." The Illinois eight-hour restriction violated both state and federal constitutions because of its unequal and arbitrary impact. "The legislature," explained the court, "ha[d] no right to deprive one class of persons of privileges allowed to other persons under like conditions." Even if the Act were interpreted to cover all women in all manufacturing areas, and not just the apparel industry, there was "no good reason" why it should not also cover other employments. But still more fundamentally, the law interfered with an inherent freedom of contract, being "a purely arbitrary restriction upon the fundamental right of the citizen to control his or her own time and facilities. It substitute[d] the judgment of the legislature for the judgment of the employer and employee in a matter about which they are competent to agree." Nor did the focus on *female* workers exempt the statute from invalidation, for the guarantees of the Fourteenth Amendment's first section extended to "citizens" and "persons"—categories each covering women.[58]

Language of this sort attracted contemporary attention, which is not surprising in view of the proliferation of police measures in the 'eighties and 'nineties. The line of cases which included *Jacobs, Godcharles,* and *Ritchie* in fact dominated the newspaper coverage given state courts and probably received disproportionate notice in the professional legal literature.[59] Attorneys seeking to attack purported police measures relating to race would doubtlessly have been familiar with the arguments employed in these cases and, with the lawyer's eye for analogy, would have seen in them some hope for persuading courts to recognize the rights of blacks.

The claims made on behalf of liberty of contract were perhaps bold enough to obscure what a close reading reveals: embedded in the explanations of limitations on the police power were acknowledgments of legislative authority. In *Jacobs,* although the New York court's survey of conditions in the cigarmaking business precluded its finding "at least some relation" between the statute and publice health, the judges conceded that if a law "ha[d] some relation" to public health, safety, or comfort, then it was "not subject to review by the courts." In its brevity, *Godcharles* omitted any discussion of circumstances that would legitimate a police measure; but *Ritchie,* besides paraphrasing the "some relation" test employed in *Jacobs,* provided amplification. The Illinois court explained that "the power of the legislature to thus limit the right of contract must rest upon some reasonable basis, and cannot be arbitrarily exercised. . . . [S]uch power is based in every case on some condition, and not on the absolute right to control."[60] In other words, the presence of a connection between a law and the ends of public health, safety, or comfort established that the legislation was "reasonable."[61]

The state cases unquestionably asserted a role for the judiciary in determining reasonableness. Even so, the threshold requirement for strict judicial scrutiny was substantial. A court would closely examine a legislative judgment only in the absence of a commonly acknowledged or easily perceived connection between (a) the law in question, along with whatever classifications it embodied, and (b) the public welfare. Moreover, *Jacobs* in particular revealed the sort of evidence that judges might take into account on the issue of reasonableness, for the New York Court of Appeals reviewed both a form of expert opinion (a report by the Secretary of the Treasury) and common knowledge.

In a word, *Plessy*'s overall constitutional environment was ominous. The judiciary's application of the Thirteenth and Fourteenth Amendments to issues of Negro rights was timid or lacking: the origins of the Amendments had been forgotten. In addition, only a minority of non-racial cases in state courts seriously qualified the police power, while at the federal level the Supreme Court's *occasional* endorsement of what has come to be called "substantive due process" still lay almost entirely in the future. (Indeed, until the 1920s, the Court's Fourteenth Amendment decisions went in favor of challenged state legislation by a nine-to-one margin.)[62] Especially troublesome was the "reasonableness" test that judges applied to police regulations, for it potentially implicated the Negrophobic portions of a large body of contemporary opinion on the supposed facts of race.

CHAPTER FIVE

The Intellectual Environment: Racist Thought in the Late Nineteenth Century

I

"The life of the law has not been logic: it has been experience," wrote Oliver Wendell Holmes, Jr., in what has surely become his most quoted passage. More influential than syllogisms were "[t]he felt necessities of the time, the prevalent moral and political theories, intuitions of public policy, avowed or unconscious, even the prejudices which judges share with their fellow men." Whatever its limitations, Holmes's insight in 1881 suggests that an understanding of the Plessy case requires attention to the views white Americans held of blacks in the late nineteenth century. The conveniences and conventions of the day might be expected to shape and even override syllogisms rooted in the Constitution.

Holmes added that the law's "form and machinery, and the degree to which it is able to work out desired results, depend pretty much upon its past."[1] In the 1890s, the legal order's recent past encompassed a body of doctrine, associated especially with the Fourteenth Amendment, that practically mandated consideration of some of "the felt necessities of the time." As detailed in the preceding chapter, so long as state legislation was not discriminatory on its face, its permissibility turned on its "reasonableness," which depended on answers to two interrelated questions. One was of law: did the legislation seek legitimate police power objectives? The other was of "fact": did the legislation employ means arguably calculated to obtain those objectives? And if the means embodied in the legislation would *conceivably* promote objectives within the state's broadly defined police powers, then the legislation's objectives could be so construed and thus considered legitimate. In probing the latter question, to be sure, judges stopped short of including explicit social science citations, for the dominant judicial "style" of the late nineteenth century limited the extent to which courts displayed their reliance on the world of "fact." The kind of reference that Chief Justice Earl Warren would use sixty years later in *Brown v. Board of Education* was definitely a thing of the future. In the end, however, police power issues were crucially but not restrictively empirical: given conceivably existent facts and factual relationships, would the Court *necessarily* have to deny that legislators could conclude the measure in question promoted public health, welfare, or morals?[2]

Twentieth-century critics of the federal Supreme Court's decision in *Plessy* have attacked Justice Henry Billings Brown for trafficking in poor social science in his majority opinion.[3] The same charge might be levied against the Louisiana judges who denied Plessy's claim at the state level. But did their handiwork rest simply on those "prejudices which judges share with their fellow men," as Holmes had put it over a decade earlier? Or did the Louisiana separate car law rest on "empirical" foundations having scientific respectability in the 1890s, discredited though they are in more recent times?

An answer involves examining those elements in the popular and particularly scientific thought of the late nineteenth century that arguably supported the state's position in *Plessy*. If this approach seems to bias the result in favor of the separate car law, it should be recalled that the reasonableness standard on which Louisiana's argument turned did not require that a consensus exist with respect to relevant factual findings, or even that the preponderance of evidence support them. The standard required only enough of a base to give color to the conclusion that the legislation conceivably had other grounds than mere prejudice.

Historians cannot generalize about the views of late nineteenth-century Americans as confidently as they can about public opinion since the 1930s, when sophisticated polling techniques appeared.[4] Nonetheless, sufficient evidence exists to indicate that the ideas of black intellectual and moral infirmity and racial antipathy had broad acceptance among individuals and groups whose views dominated public forums. Popular writers and politicians, both southern and northern, enunciated such positions, and their sentiments matched more systematic elaborations by students of the emerging (and not well differentiated) social sciences, as well as by natural scientists, especially biologists, who extrapolated the social implications of their opinions. Even Negro spokesmen offered views *seemingly* consistent with dominant white expressions. Depicting this body of thought and opinion runs another furrow through ground well-tilled by intellectual and social historians of race in America,[5] but detail is necessary. Whatever

Homer Plessy's antagonists may have lacked, under the reasonableness standard they did not lack contemporary warrant.

II

The Negro's intellectual inferiority was one of the tenets of the southern paternalism that C. Vann Woodward has identified as a kind of official ideology for the "Redeemers" who dominated southern politics and society in most places and at most times during the years from the 1870s into the 1890s. True, a few paternalists regarded the Negro's inferiority as temporary, quickly remediable by education, but these "modified equalitarians" were overshadowed by southerners whose paternalism rested on the premise of long-run Negro retardation. Thomas Nelson Page, a major contributor to the "moonlight and magnolias" version of antebellum southern history, voiced the more common sentiment. Dismissing a few (unspecified) instances of achievement by blacks, he sweepingly claimed "that such cases of intellectual development are exceptional instances, and that after long, elaborate, and ample trial the negro race has failed to discover the qualities which have inhered in every race of which history gives the record, which has advanced civilization, or has shown capacity to be itself greatly advanced."

The litany continued. White southerners broadly identified the Negro's moral characteristics as including poor work habits, leading the Birmingham (Alabama) *Age-Herald* to editorialize: "The Negro is a good laborer when his labor can be controlled and directed, but he is a very undesirable citizen." Others concurred that blacks provided useful menial labor, but were unreliable, uppity, and unsocialized, as well as menacing because of their criminal tendencies. The popular view further stressed that Negroes displayed low standards of cleanliness, had abnormal sexual proclivities, and were afflicted disproportionately with diseases then commonly associated with filth.[6]

Pervasive as these views were in the South, perhaps the more significant consideration is that the attitudes crossed sectional lines. Henry M. Field of Massachusetts, a Presbyterian clergyman and brother of Associate Justice Stephen J. Field, provides a noteworthy example. His *Bright Skies and Dark Shadows,* a travelogue of Field's 1889 journey through the South, allowed the possibility of modest Negro improvement through education and described the black race as physically more vital than did some southern publicists, but otherwise offered the same stereotypes, with shifts only in emphasis. Underscoring his observations about the South, Field wrote that in his home state of Massachusetts the Negro was free from white hostility, but still "[t]he whole race has remained on one dead level of mediocrity." Typifying journalistic comment, another northerner asserted,

> The fact is, and the sooner the fact is recognized the sooner we shall be rid of dangerous illusions, that the negroes constitute a peasantry wholly

untrained, in, and ignorant of, those ideas of constitutional liberty and
progress which are the birthright of every intelligent voter; they are
gregarious and emotional rather than intelligent, and are easily led in any
direction by white men of energy and determination.

From a comparison of northern and southern opinion, Alton Hornsby has
concluded that the Negro was portrayed in both sections as a "physical and
mental inferior, generally lazy, untidy, prone to immorality and crime,
politically inept, excessively pious, but fun-loving."[7]

Events on the political front helped draw forth further aspersions about
Negro mentality and morality. Beginning with Georgia's poll tax in 1871,
southern states gradually moved beyond fraud and intimidation toward
formal exclusion of black voters, initially by statute and then by constitutional convention. The disfranchisement crusade reached its first peak in the
period 1888–93, with the enactment of procedurally complex and restrictive
registration laws, complicated multiple ballot box and secret ballot arrangements, literacy tests, and understanding clauses. Because the disfranchisers'
motives included the desires of Democrats to suppress a continuing threat
from opposition parties, and because Negroes constituted a major element of
the opposition's strength, anti-black rhetoric served the cause of restriction.
"This ballot system must be so arranged as to effect one object," confessed
the president of Mississippi's convention in 1890, "for we find the two races
now together, the rule of one of which has always meant economic and moral
ruin; we find another race whose rule has always meant prosperity and
happiness to all races." The allusion to black governmental incompetence
played nicely, of course, on a leading tenet of white southern belief, which
increasingly commanded northern support as well. Negro rule during
reconstruction, as Thomas Nelson Page put it, had resulted in "[s]uch a riot
of folly and extravagence, such a travesty of justice, such a mummery of
government, as was never witnessed save in those countries in which he [the
Negro] has himself furnished the illustration."[8]

At the national level, faced with over a decade of informal southern
efforts to exclude or manipulate black voters, the Republican administration
of Benjamin Harrison came into office in 1889 mildly committed to enact
new federal protection for voting. Representative Henry Cabot Lodge of
Massachusetts proceeded to introduce an elections bill that received overwhelming support from Republicans in both houses (and none from the
Democrats). Although the measure eventually failed to come to a vote in the
Senate because of a filibuster and Republican maneuvers to enact silver and
tariff legislation, the prospect of federal intervention occasioned more debate
about the Negro's civic fitness. Democratic Senator John T. Morgan of
Alabama minced no words: "The inferiority of the negro race, as compared
with the white race, is so essentially true, and so obvious, that to assume it
in argument, cannot be justly attributed to prejudice." For the "natural
incongruity" between the races, he held that separation was the only

solution. If northern readers doubted southern testimony on the point, they could turn to E. L. Godkin, the northern liberal editor (though in fact no liberal on racial matters), who prophesied that Negro electoral participation could "not only prevent industrial progress, but put their [*i.e.,* southern] civilization itself in some peril." Several months later, the same premise appeared in the reflections of the distinguished English observer, James Bryce. Lodge's "Force Bill" represented for Bryce "an attempt to overcome nature by force of law." "The Negroes have been unable to protect themselves in the exercise of the suffrage," he confidently explained, "because they are naturally inferior to whites—inferior in intelligence, in tenacity, in courage, in the power of organization."[9]

In some southern locales during the early 1890s, whites in the People's Party attempted to cooperate politically with Negro voters. Although the white Populists often carefully avoided endorsing the Negro's social and intellectual equality, their efforts at biracial politics drew predictable retorts. In Arkansas, for example, a state Democratic campaign song demeaningly limned the intelligence of the Populists' black supporters:

> The Australian [secret] ballot works like a charm,
> It makes them think and scratch,
> And when a negro gets a ballot
> He has certainly got his match.
> . . .
> They go into the booth alone
> Their ticket to prepare.
> And as soon as five minutes are out
> They have to git from there.

Replying to local Populist condemnations of lynching, a Democratic newspaper offered the reassurance that practical Arkansas farmers had not "suddenly become . . . defenders of Negro rapists and criminals."[10]

Publicists and politicians did not stop with the attribution of differing endowments to the two races, nor with the assignment of the black race to an inferior position. Race differences, they claimed, produced relatively immutable instinctive behavior. Debating the position of the Negro in the South with George Washington Cable in 1885, Henry W. Grady had reminded a national audience of the result of the intellectual and moral differences between the races. There was, he held, "an instinct, ineradicable and positive, that will keep the races apart, that would keep the races apart if the problem were transferred to Illinois or Maine, and that will resist every effort of appeal, argument, or force to bring them together." The instinct toward separation guaranteed the integrity of each race, an integrity that was crucial because "the hybrid would not gain what either race lost." Put differently, amalgamation posed a threat that the races resisted. Perhaps, however, white perception of Negro inferiority merely indicated prejudice. On this point, Senator Morgan extended Grady's reasoning: "If it is prejudice, it is rare prejudice, which affects nearly all the white race, and proves the existence of a deep-seated race aversion." The same premise about innate racial instincts had earlier led a Southern Baptist editor to argue against the efficacy of civil rights legislation on grounds that it was "very difficult, if not impossible, to regulate or change social ideas or customs by means of legislation." Henry Field, too, placed man's "natural instincts" on racial matters beyond the power of human contrivance to eradicate.[11]

Ironically, in view of his having led the final serious attempt, in 1890, to hold the white South to a semblance of the standard demanded by the postwar radical Republicans, Henry Cabot Lodge offered one of the fullest summations of race differences for a lay audience. By 1896 Lodge was in the Senate, pushing for immigration restriction, and in March, about a month before oral arguments in *Plessy,* he spoke at length on the bill he had earlier introduced to add a literacy test to existing restrictions. Lodge frankly defended his proposed test on grounds that it favored the English and northern and western Europeans, as against the eastern and southern Europeans and Asiatics who created many of the social and economic problems in congested urban areas; he then examined the core idea of race-based restriction by "look[ing] into the history of our race."

Focusing on the status of the English, French, and similar groupings as distinct races, Lodge explained that the true test of race was not the ethnologist's findings about original divisions, for "to the scientific modern historian, to the student of social phenomena, and to the statesman alike," these were "of little consequence." Instead, "absolutely vital" were "the sharply marked race divisions which have been gradually developed by the conditions and events of the last thousand years." Such events within historical time had established "artificial races" like the English, each of which was identified not "merely or ultimately [by] its physical appearance, its institutions, its laws, its literature, or even its language." Those characteristics were, "in the last analysis, only the expression or the evidence of race"; what distinguished races themselves was "something deeper and more fundamental than anything which concerns the intellect."

Lodge elaborated the crucial "something" in this fashion:

We all know it instinctively, although it is so impalpable that we can scarcely define it, and yet it so deeply marked that even the physiological differences between the Negro, the Mongol, and the Caucasian are not more persistent or more obvious. When we speak of a race, then, we . . . mean the moral and intellectual character[istic]s which in their association make the soul of a race, and which represent the product of all its past, the inheritance of all its ancestors, and the motives of all its conduct. The men of each race possess an indestructible stock of ideas, traditions, sentiments, modes of thought, an unconscious inheritance from their ancestors, upon which argument has no effect. What makes a race are their mental and, above all, their moral characteristics, the slow growth and accumulation of centuries of toil and conflict. These are the qualities which determine their social efficiency as a people . . . .

In addition, once a race had developed through centuries of shared experience, the only way its defining qualities could be weakened was "by breeding them out." If interbreeding occurred in situations where "the people of alien or lower races of less social efficiency and less moral force" approached the higher race in numbers, the higher race would be lowered rather than the lower raised.

With respect specifically to the problem of immigration, the saving feature was that the "great race instinct" of (white) Americans would "assert itself and shut the immigration out." Although Lodge did not address the issue of black-white racial contact, his remark needed little translation to provide a comparable solution for the South. If "race instinct" promoted the correct policy of shutting out certain "artificial" races then the desirability of separating "natural" races was hard to deny. Lodge's strictures hardly endorsed the notion of white solidarity, but their content—and even more, their premise—nevertheless supported black-white division. [12]

Invoking science along with history, Lodge had capsulized the racial views of many northerners and southerners alike. Yet he held that racial groups took on distinguishing characteristics and developed instinctive behavior within historical time, all as a result of the inheritance of characteristics acquired through distinctive shared experiences—a view now rejected. If this premise had a base in expert opinion during the late nineteenth century, then so did many contemporary lay comments on race relations in the South, and so, too, did Louisiana's argument in *Plessy*. Lodge claimed his position rested on good scientific authority. Did it?

III

Of comparatively recent origin, scientific racism first appeared in the United States during the 1830s and 1840s, concurrent with heightened Southern interest in finding new justifications for the institution of black chattel slavery. By the end of the century, despite the idea's arguable guilt by early association, probably a majority of American social and natural scientists concerned with race accepted the concept of racial differences and would have rejected George Washington Cable's claim in 1888 that even if "the black is 'an inferior race,' . . . how, or how permanently inferior, remains unproved." For these "experts" the evidence for nearly permanent Negro inferiority was conclusive. This preponderance of opinion had its roots in the antebellum emergence of what became known as the "American School" of anthropology. [13]

The question of racial hierarchy intrigued the founders of scientific ethnology in America, whose focus encompassed significant aspects of what would become physical anthropology, as well as the cultural anthropology their subject more directly anticipated. Pioneering the field was Dr. Samuel George Morton, a Philadelphia physician who had received his medical training in both the United States and Scotland and made significant contributions to paleontology and geology. Strategically placed and with a growing number of contacts, Morton amassed a substantial collection of skulls, which he measured to determine their capacities and shapes. In *Crania Americana,* published in 1839, he reported that skulls differed by race, descending in cranial capacity, or internal volume, a supposed indication of brain size, from Caucasian through Mongolian, Malay, and American Indian, and finally to Ethiopian. Although not linking capacity directly to intelligence, his description of the different races' "moral" characteristics (a category Morton defined broadly enough to include intellectual qualities) implied a descending mental ranking in the same order. Morton also directed his attention to the sources of the racial differences he observed. Rejecting environmental influences, he came openly to espouse a theory of separate creations—that is, polygenism or non-common ancestry, rather than monogenism or common ancestry.

The arrival at Harvard in 1845 of the biologist and paleontologist Louis Agassiz lent powerful scientific respectability to Morton's views. Solidly trained in Europe, with an established reputation there, and quickly recognized as America's leading biologist, Agassiz defended polygenism throughout the biological kingdom. He also accepted the notion of Negro inferiority, although apparently without any love for slavery.

It was another of Morton's associates and correspondents, Dr. Josiah S. Nott of Mobile, Alabama, who most clearly linked polygenism with Negro inferiority and slavery. Whether Nott pursued anthropology in order to defend slavery, or defended slavery because of his scientific conclusions, is a matter of dispute. What is beyond doubt is that while contributing little empirical data beyond anecdotal evidence from his medical practice and from hearsay accounts, he proved a skillful publicist and not a bad ethnological theorist. By the late 1850s he had even managed to silence some leading southern critics who objected to polygenism on biblical grounds. A continuing outlet for Nott's essays was *De Bow's Review,* the widely read journal published in New Orleans by J. D. B. De Bow, who persistently rested his vision of a progressive South on "the peculiar institution."

Yet, for all his effort, Nott was probably not essential to establishing the proslavery implications of the "American School." In 1844, before the Mobile physician began active participation, Secretary of State John C. Calhoun obtained ethnological data directly from Samuel Morton in order to elaborate a defense of slavery during his dispute with the British Foreign Minister, Lord Aberdeen, over American claims to Texas.[14]

By the eve of the Civil War, Agassiz firmly established polygenism in American biology, and Morton's associates thoroughly swept the field of ethnology, although Morton himself died in 1851. But a challenge came in 1859, from abroad, with the publication of Charles Darwin's *The Origin of Species*. It is true that the book initially met a cool reception from the American scientific community, for several reasons. Telling attacks on prior theories of evolution created doubt; Agassiz held preeminence and defended his conviction that fossil and other evidence pointed to static plant and animal species; biblical accounts of creation continued to have some appeal to American scientists; and the war itself caused distraction. By the late 1860s and early 1870s, however, American scientists had shifted position. The emerging American evolutionists often departed from details of Darwin's view, but polygenism was routed, a defeat made certain by Agassiz's death in 1873.

Antebellum conclusions about race nevertheless showed remarkable postwar vitality. As scholarly disciplines took on firmer definition in the latter part of the nineteenth century, practitioners in several fields developed a more systematic science of man. They also manifested an ongoing, shared, and even more elaborate commitment to the idea of race differences.

One reason was the ease with which ethnology deflected the Darwinian challenge. Existing craniometric evidence supported evolutionary arguments for Negro inferiority, just as it had lent itself to polygenist speculations. Skull measurements of historical races, as well as more anecdotal evidence, now testified to the different levels of advancement attained by different races descending from a common source, but the relative standing of the races in relation to each other remained undisturbed. Nor was it likely soon to change. As Josiah Nott explained in 1866 when he publicly announced his acceptance of evolution (although, on examination, not Darwinian evolution), the new theory left intact the idea of Negro inferiority in the foreseeable future, for even by its tenets change occurred only over "millions of years." In short, as George W. Stocking has described, polygenist *theorizing* about race disappeared, but a kind of *de facto* polygenist *thinking* persisted.[15]

Another reason was the particular variety of evolutionary commitment displayed by American social scientists. Until approximately the turn of the century, practitioners in the emerging disciplines commonly employed biological analogies which incorporated the teleological, progressive evolutionary viewpoint of Herbert Spencer, rather than the unpredictable development increasingly implied by biological Darwinism. Similarly, the mechanism of evolutionary change that many social scientists expressly or implicitly accepted was not selection from random mutations at the individual level within population groups but rather the widespread inheritance of acquired characteristics within broad social or cultural groups. The social scientists, that is, tended toward Neo-Lamarckianism, a position that allowed the heritability of changes produced directly by environmental influences. Their orientation in turn mirrored the dominance of Neo-Lamarckians within American biology during the period. Indeed, the theoretical and experimental work in biology necessary both to solve major problems with Darwin's idea of natural selection and to destroy the basis of Neo-Lamarckianism did not occur until the 1890s and later. Gregor Mendel's genetic discoveries of the 1860s lay hidden, for example, until 1900, and August Weismann's theorizing about the isolation of the environment-confronting protoplasm from the heredity-determining germ plasm within biological organisms came only a few years earlier. Lord Kelvin's temperature-based estimates of the Earth's age, which denied the vast expanse of time necessary for natural selection to work, remained a barrier to full acceptance of Darwinian evolution until they were undercut by discoveries shortly after the turn of the century.[16]

Thus enamored of progressive, Neo-Lamarckian evolution, social scientists sought out stages. They typically conceived of different cultures and societies as occupying lower or higher places along a unilinear scale. Races received comparable positions, because of the association of "race" with distinctive mental, linguistic, and cultural traits, as well as with physical traits. Not that the social scientists always held that physical traits of races "caused" non-physical traits. (It is significant, though, they most often asserted a causal connection between the physical and the non-physical in discussions of Negroes.) But to the extent that racial groups, as defined physically, manifested particular non-physical characteristics, the latter would become hereditary, given the social scientists' Neo-Lamarckian premises. One result was that differing behaviors, temperaments, and personalities became instinctive for particular races in the same way that intelligence level varied by race. Then, although further evolutionary change might occur more rapidly than it would if natural selection were the operative mechanism, patterns of thought and behavior embedded in racial inheritance through thousands of years would not yield within several generations.

Accompanying the commitment to an evolutionary model, "[a]nother trend, equally irresistible, swept through the human sciences" in the late nineteenth century, as Stephen Jay Gould has observed. This was a fascination with numbers, the belief that truth would emerge when sufficient precision in measurement had eliminated human subjectivity. "Evolution and quantification formed an unholy alliance," Gould comments; "in a sense, their union forged the first powerful theory of 'scientific' racism . . . . " In the 1860s in Europe, the Parisian physician and anthropologist Paul Broca founded a school of craniometry dedicated to the proposition that careful measurements of brain size and of various cranial angles could explain the intellectual differences between the human races and sexes. In an effort to explain criminal behavior, others, especially the Italian Cesare Lombroso, expanded anthropometry to include additional bodily measurements.[17] Americans, too, succumbed to the allure of numbers and initiated serious work about the same time Darwin's *The Origin of Species* began receiving attention in the United States.

Activity by the United States Sanitary Commission during the Civil War led to the accumulation of an unprecedented body of anthropometric data, leading to "perhaps the greatest irony" of the war, as John S. Haller has put it. Employing refined instruments and statistical techniques, the Commission conducted over 15,000 examinations, about three-fourths on white servicemen, and the remainder on full-blooded Negroes, mulattoes, and American Indians; these produced data on age, race, measurements of various parts of the body, and ratios between the measurements. Other comparative information came from 405 wartime autopsies on white and black soldiers, and still more from questionnaires sent to physicians examining recruits. As interpreted in studies after the war, the wartime results showed that blacks, in contrast to whites, had physical statures closer to those of anthropoids, along with smaller brain weights and generally weaker physical constitutions. By providing an empirical base that was no longer tainted by the proslavery sentiments of the antebellum American investigators, the Commission had bolstered the scientific respectability of the prewar findings of Negro inferiority. The war that freed the slaves thus contributed to the argument for black inferiority. The wartime experience with anthropometry, moreover, gave impetus to postwar investigations that contemporaries read as supporting the same conclusion.

The firm place that the idea of race differences gained within American social science emerges strikingly from a study by George Stocking. Reviewing twenty-one scholarly journals from the late 1880s to approximately 1915, Stocking identified 552 articles dealing with race, by 228 different authors, whose positions he then analyzed on several issues. These included the existence of racial and cultural hierarchies, the relationship of mental differences to race, the role of race in determining cultural differences, and the inheritance of acquired characteristics (that is, Neo-Lamarckianism broadly construed). Of special interest with respect to the question of what constituted good social science at the time of *Plessy v. Ferguson* are the fifty authors whose journal publications began to appear in 1896 or earlier.[18] Table I on page 104 summarizes their views.

Although problems in defining "social science" and in distinguishing between important and more ephemeral social scientists make it impossible to draw highly refined conclusions from these data, the figures are still highly suggestive. The scientific racism prominently advanced by individual scholars was hardly atypical within the whole group of social scientists who discussed race. Indeed, Stocking's close textual analysis of journal articles *and* of other writings indicates that his quantitative data understate the *intensity* of the social scientists' acceptance of racial differences and instincts and of

TABLE I Attitudes on Race-related Issues among Social Scientists Whose Articles Began Appearing in 1896 or Earlier

Issue	Number with discernible views (total N = 50)*	Of those with discernible views, number (percent) expressing	
		Explicit or implicit agreement	Questioning attitude, but not necessarily disagreement
A racial hierarchy exists.	31	29 (94%)	2 (6%)
A cultural hierarchy exists.	26	26 (100%)	0 (0%)
Differences exist between the mental traits (intelligence, temperament, etc.) of races.**	32	30 (94%)	6 (19%)
Hereditary racial differences cause cultural differences.**	23	19 (83%)	6 (26%)
Acquired characteristics may be inherited.**	27	26 (96%)	4 (15%)

*Not all the authors who discussed race revealed positions on each issue or on any of these issues.

**Several authors revealed *both* explicit or implicit agreement *and* a questioning attitude on these issues.

SOURCE: Data included in George W. Stocking, Jr., "American Social Scientists and Race Theory, 1890–1915" (Ph.D. diss., Univ. of Pennsylvania, 1960), viii–xxxvii, 602–17.

race as a relatively permanent social and cultural determinant.[19] As a result, examples of "expert" opinion in the late nineteenth century convey an even fuller sense of the period.

Daniel G. Brinton's presidential address in August 1895 to the prestigious American Association for the Advancement of Science provides a broad and timely overview of scientific racism on the eve of the federal Supreme Court's deliberations in *Plessy*. Brinton took as his subject "The Aims of Anthropology," a field which "includ[ed] the study of the whole man, his psychical as well as his physical nature, and the products of all his activities, whether in the past or in the present." Although accepting a "psychical unity" throughout the human species, he quickly branded as "erroneous" the contention that external conditions and individual faculties, rather than "ethnic or racial peculiarities," were "the factors of culture-evolution." On the contrary, "each of the great races, each ethnic group, ha[d] its own added special powers and special limitations"; all races were not "equally endowed."

Focusing on the deficiencies of "the black, brown, and red races," Brinton held that no race could "escape the mental correlations [sic] of its physical structure" and that some manifested "a peculiar mental temperament which has become hereditary and general, of a nature to disqualify them for the atmosphere of modern enlightenment." These less able stocks possessed "an inborn morbid tendency, constitutionally recreant to the codes of civilization, and therefore technically criminal." To speak of "a racial mind, or temperament of a people," he averred, was as accurate as to describe distinguishing physical traits. Not least, after disavowing "the indiscriminate enforcement of general prescriptions as has hitherto been the custom of governments," Brinton concluded that the differences between mankind's "component social parts, its races, nations, tribes . . . , supply the only sure foundations for legislation; not *a priori* notions of the rights of man . . . ."[20]

Other writers contributed detail. Sociologist Franklin H. Giddings elaborated a theoretical basis when he described a "consciousness of kind" which "within the class of the animate . . . marks off species and races." This consciousness provided a "determining principle" around which "all other motives organize themselves in the evolution of social choice, social volition, and or social policy." The implications of the principle had already been charted by Harvard paleontologist and ethnologist Nathaniel Shaler, whose "intellectual rationalizations, *a priori* values, and race analyses mirrored the cumulative mind of the century's intellectual concepts of race," according to John Haller. Shaler explained that racial antipathies, to the extent that they existed, would have "a very important bearing on the matter of the future relations of the African and European races on this continent." And they clearly did exist. Even "devoted friends of the negro" had confessed to Shaler "that they abhorred the sight of him; that his black face and other peculiarities of countenance made the most painful impression on their minds." Adding difficulty was the certainty that as a new generation of whites and blacks came of age in the South, the "old harmony" produced by enforced closeness under slavery would disappear.

Nor was progress likely. In 1886, Shaler had seemed hopeful that proper training would "open to the abler members of the [Negro] race higher places in life" and so create individuals who "would be a most valuable bond of union between the races." But by 1890 he feared that even with Negro self-improvement, "the two races are doomed to live separate though they may live parallel lives." Later the same year he remarked, "the negro type of today is almost certainly nearer to the anthropoid or pre-human ancestry of men than the other marked varieties of our species, such as the Aryan, Tartars, or Semitic folk."[21]

Owing to his southern upbringing, Shaler perhaps carried suspect credentials. This could be said less easily of social statistician Frederick

Hoffman, who completed his *Race Traits and Tendencies of the American Negro* during the year prior to the final decision in *Plessy v. Ferguson*. In his preface, Hoffman claimed that "[b]eing of foreign birth, a German, [he] was fortunately free from a personal bias which might have made an impartial treatment of the subject difficult." Yet the body of his 330-page study— which was expanded from a shorter essay at the urging and with the assistance of the American Economic Association's editorial staff—began with the observation that "[t]he natural bond of sympathy [typically] existing between people of the same country, no matter how widely separated by language and nationality, cannot be proved to exist between the white and colored races of the United States." Despite thirty years of Negro freedom, "the two races [were] farther apart than ever in their political and social relations." By Hoffman's concluding chapter the picture was bleaker still: "The central fact deducible from the results of this investigation . . . is plainly and emphatically the powerful influence of *race* in the struggle for life." What appeared between those remarks by one of the most important racist spokesmen of the late nineteenth century was no more flattering, as we shall see; and Hoffman personally confided that his views had a more solid base than "the many foolish utterances" of an optimistic character by spokesman like Albion Tourgée—whom he specifically mentioned to the AEA's editor.[22]

In addition to general aversion and consciousness of kind, students of race traced black-white antipathy to a number of specific factors. One of these was the Negro's "moral deficiencies," which included a variety of alleged social pathologies. From his review of (as he admitted) sketchy statistics on the black as both agricultural and industrial laborer, Frederick Hoffman indentified a key failing: an ingrained pattern of indolence. With some exceptions, the Negro's efficiency was low compared even with that of recent white immigrants, a condition that education had proved little able to remedy. As further manifestation of economic deficiency, the Negro had "prove[d] himself an unscrupulous tax-dodger," which Hoffman saw as "only another proof of his tendency to acquire the vice rather than the virtue of the white man's civilization." In sum, as he read the record, "The great majority leave the earth as poor as they entered it, and as fully satisfied with a degree of comfort too low to prove of economic advantage to the state." Historian Philip A. Bruce completely agreed. Nathaniel Shaler saw promise in the Negro as agriculture laborer, but little on the industrial front.

Poor work habits constituted perhaps the least of the black's instinctive vices. Far more serious was sexual excess. This failing manifested itself partly in illicit relations between Negro men and women. The "immorality and vice" that were "a habit of the vast majority of the colored population" surfaced, for example, in Washington, D. C., where more than a quarter of the Negro births were illegitimate. The rate of venereal disease—three times the rate among the white population in Washington and Baltimore—

testified to the same infirmity. One source of the problem was both sexes' lower mental development and their genital anatomies, which, among males, caused sexual furor resembling the behavior of bulls and elephants. Despite the wantonness of the female of his own race, moreover, the Negro male had an unquenchable lust for white women. The result was a high incidence of rape by black men of white women, which in turn caused whites to resort to lynch law—an understandable response that tended to undermine the morality of the whole white community.[23]

Freed from slavery and possessing no inner moral direction, the black race showed an overall crime rate, both in southern states and in northern cities with large black populations, that ran a least three times the proportion of Negroes in the population. To some extent Hoffman conceded that, at least in Chicago, the social and economic conditions in the section into which the race was crowded were perhaps a contributing element, but it was "not all a result of the 'conditions of life.'" Various immigrant groups encountered similar conditions, but among them the rate was "almost always, excepting the Irish, in proportion to the population." Writing under the auspices of the philanthropic Slater Fund, which supported Negro education in the South, Henry Gannet detected the same imbalance. The Negro criminal possesed two redeeming features, however. He lacked the mental concentration to commit crimes requiring much forethought or attention to detail, and when he committed capital offenses, he was more easily apprehended, "owing to his characteristic negligence."

Another Negro trait, the experts claimed, was greater susceptibility to disease. Drawing on published material as well as on his own investigations, Hoffman demonstrated to his satisfaction that the rates of consumption, scrofula, and venereal disease, and of related deaths, ran at least three times the rate among whites and was increasing, which "became a matter of greatest social and economic importance." As with the race's criminal propensities, this characteristic made it a threat to a white community in close association with it. More serious, "the root of the evil [lay] in the fact of an immense amount of immorality, which is a race trait," and which made the disease rate "inevitable." (By the late 1880s, argues Lawrence J. Friedman, the view that blacks carried contagious diseases "was rapidly gaining adherents, perhaps because of greater familiarity with the germ theory of disease.")[24]

Hoffman and other students of the Negro held a dim view of the race's future. One cause lay in the black's mental limitations, which restricted the possibilities of improvement through education. Despite the support given Negro schooling since the Civil War and the accompanying rise in black enrollment and literacy, concluded Hoffman, "*the race* as a whole ha[d] gone backwards rather than forwards." As Philip Bruce described the problem, the Negro's moral infirmities shaded into mental, and vice-versa; blacks overall bore "the same moral relation to the Caucasian as a child does to an adult." The "principal element of doubt" in contemplating the race's future was thus not whether its fundamental character would change, for that had proved fixed, but rather whether its traits "will be held in check by circumstances, or whether they will override circumstances, however strong the opposition offered."[25]

Themselves menacing and indicative of race weakness, these moral infirmities broadly endangered the white race when racial interbreeding occurred. The mulatto might be mentally superior to the black of unmixed blood, but was still inferior to the unmixed white and had a weaker physical constitution than either. In 1890, a warning issued from Edward D. Cope, an American- and European-trained academician of broad interests who had just moved from a chair in zoology and botany at Haverford College to a position in geology at the University of Pennsylvania:

> The highest race of man cannot afford to lose or even to compromise the advantages it has acquired by hundreds of centuries of toil and hardship, by mingling its blood with the lowest. . . . We cannot cloud or extinguish the fine nervous susceptibility, and the mental force, which cultivation develops in the constitution of the Indo-European, by the fleshy instincts, and dark mind of the African. . . . The greatest danger which flows from the presence of the negro in this country, is the certainty of the contamination of the [white] race.

Frederick Hoffman added copious detail on the effects of hybridization. (He saw little threat from intermarriage, but feared the results of prostitution.)

By the mid-1890s, census data added a new dimension to the argument. Miscounting of blacks in the censuses of 1870 and 1880 had produced figures showing that black population growth exceeded white, a threatening trend that Philip Bruce in 1889 had explained would continue "[f]or a half century, at least," until population pressure on land greatly increased. But the 1890 count revealed a black growth rate below the white race's. "The plain language of the facts" demonstrated for Hoffman in 1896 that a "gradual extinction of the [Negro] race will take place." If the earlier censuses had bolstered arguments for control of the Negro, the new evidence hardly led to more favorable conclusions. It simply proved the race's overall degeneracy and confirmed the accuracy of Bruce's earlier prediction that the race would experience a "reversion" to type—a lower type that lacked the inborn traits of moral character needed to compete successfully in a struggle with the Anglo-Saxons.[26]

Lest contemporaries should overlook the implication of such forebodings, several commentators were explicit: the Negro's well-established infirmities, along with the Caucasian's instinctive reactions, warranted separation of the races. One assessment came from Joseph LeConte, a Georgia-born geologist, botanist, and sociologist who had moved to the University of California in 1869 and there established his reputation as a leading American scientist. Whether or not George Fredrickson is strictly correct in arguing that LeConte offered "probably the decade's most sophisticated application of *Darwinian* theory to the American race problem," he surely proposed one of the most elaborate "scientific" justifications for classification by race.

In a paper delivered to the Brooklyn Ethical Association in 1892, LeConte explored the potential of sociology for guiding race relations. Science, he explained, had passed successively in development from mathematics to mechanics, astronomy, physics, and chemistry, "reducing all to law"; then had moved its focus in the present—nineteenth—century to biology and psychology; "and finally even now, to sociology—the science of social organization and social progress, the highest of all." Each of the earlier areas had displayed a progression of understanding that sociologists would have to heed in order to give practical significance to their own work. Art, "the material embodiment of certain underlying rational principles," preceded the scientific understanding of rational principles; but, when understood scientifically, those principles allowed further improvement in art. "Empirical art," which was "the outcome of the use of intuitive reason . . . [and] works without understanding itself," thereby became "[s]cientific art, [which,] because it understands itself, is of necessity infinitely progressive . . . ." Now passing from the empirical to the rational stage of development, sociology could provide the means of preventing the retrogression in the arts of politics and social organization that would result from a "more or less blind, unreasoning, passionate conflict" between the various elements and forces comprising society.

With respect to the issue of race relations, the need of sociology was to recognize the role that classification had played in all the sciences, because "[t]hings and phenomena can not be dealt with as individuals, for they are too numerous and diversified . . . ." The scientist had to begin with "an arbitrary, artificial, provisional classification of some sort, to enable him to manage his material"; this led to fuller understanding and refined classifications better corresponding to natural classifications, and ultimately to such a complete understanding that "classes shade into each other more and more until division lines disappear." "Any classification [was] better than none" in the pursuit of rational knowledge, but those most closely corresponding to natural groupings were most justifiable. Earlier class and caste lines within society having been unmasked as "unnatural and oppressive," social organization now demanded a more rational basis. And so arose the requirement for modern sociology to understand that "race-classes" not only provided a further basis for scientific advancement, "but are more natural and rational than many others, because founded on a real natural difference—i.e., a difference in the grade of evolution; and moreover, where the difference is as great as it is between the Anglo-Saxon and the Negro, the class distinction seems absolutely necessary, at least for the present."

The natural line between races, LeConte cautioned, "can not be broken down, and . . . ought not, until we understand better than we do now the effects of race mixture." With this warning, he qualified his earlier suggestion that the "marginal varieties of primary races may approach sufficiently near to mix with advantage." Adequate evidence simply had not accumulated to reveal if race mixing would prove beneficial, or if "the law of organic evolution, the law of destruction of the lower races and the survival of only the higher, must prevail and the race-line must never be broken down." His immediate purpose being an explication of principles that would allow "the adjustment . . . of the relation of the two races in the South on a just and rational basis," LeConte did not examine the full range of practical measures the white South might take. Nonetheless, two justifications for observance of the color line flowed from his presentation. Classification by race would protect the white race from contamination, and it would aid in amassing the scientific knowledge necessary to save the colored race from the otherwise inevitable oblivion it faced in the social struggle.[27]

Frederick Hoffman similarly left little to the imagination. Emphasizing the extent to which interracial contacts weakened the colored race, he explained that misplaced white charity and philanthropy only accentuated the Negro's dependence and his lack of the traits of self-reliance and chastity that were so vital to race survival. In existing circumstances, the black faced certain extinction in his struggle with the Anglo-Saxon or Aryan race, which was so superbly equipped "solely on account of its ancient inheritance of virtue and transmitted qualities which are determining factors in the struggle for race supremacy," an inheritance, Hoffman stressed, that was "not . . . the result of easy conditions of life." Not convinced that the Negro could survive in any case, he held that if the race had a chance, it would only come as blacks realized both that "[i]ntercourse with the white race must absolutely cease," and that only an "independent struggle" would produce the "higher morality," the "economic efficiency," and "the predominating trait of the white race, the virtue of thrift."

Another indication of "expert" opinion in the 1890s was the reaction to such open espousals of Negro inferiority and of racial separation. Robert C. Bannister has thoroughly analyzed how a variety of reformers in the late nineteenth century used the label "social Darwinist" to tar proponents of a laissez-faire economic order, whereas actually most "conservatives," whether in the academic or industrial worlds, did *not* employ Darwinian justifications. The picture differed significantly concerning the issue of race. There Bannister found that "few if any critics charged racial theorists . . . with perpetuating a monstrous social Darwinism or the equivalent." In reality, however, when LeConte, Hoffman, and other students of race relations variously classified blacks within an evolutionary scheme, prophesied future race development on the basis of evolutionary science, and argued the need for social control in order to mitigate the unpredictable effects of race conflict, they advanced a more genuine social Darwinism. But in response, as Bannister puts it, "no one was apparently willing to blow the whistle," or at least not before the turn of the century.[28]

IV

To say *no one* objected is not literally true. Among other dissenters, Frederick Douglass levied a withering attack on the idea of Negro inferiority in all its manifestations. Even before the war, at Western Reserve College in 1854, the ex-slave had scored the "scientific" core of polygenism in a talk entitled "The Claims of the Negro Ethnologically Considered," his first scholarly presentation before an academic audience. He continued to subject claims about the black's natural incapacity and interracial aversion to a combination of logic and ridicule, scorn and counter-evidence. "If the white man were really so constituted that color were, in itself, a torment to him," Douglass chided, "this grand old earth of ours would be no place for him. Colored objects confront him here at every point of the compass." Theories of mulatto degeneration, he said, ran head on against common observation. He praised Abraham Lincoln not only for his statesmanship in making the compromises necessary to win the war which destroyed slavery, but also for the Great Emancipator's own freedom from prejudice in his personal dealings with Douglass. Linking the mandate for equality embodied in the 1875 Civil Rights Act to the Declaration of Independence, the Golden Rule, and the Sermon on the Mount, Douglass related how the voice of America at its founding "announced the advent of a nation, based upon human brotherhood and the self-evident truths of liberty and equality."

But Douglass died in 1895, and while he lived his influence was waning, his call for integration and racial assimilation becoming more suspect. For in the dawning "age of Booker T. Washington" some prominent Negroes manifested views that were recognizable reflections of white racial thought, particularly when culled for damaging implications.[29]

Booker T. Washington's later critic, W. E. B. DuBois, identified Washington's Atlanta Exposition Address, on September 18, 1895, as the event that more than any other made him "the one recognized spokesman of his ten million fellows and one of the most notable figures in a nation of seventy millions." A key to his success on the occasion was his double thrust. As one theme, Washington rejected the exclusion of blacks from the life of the South, stressing instead the asset they constituted. If only the white South recognized, supported, helped educate, and justly utilized this native resource, the last vestiges "of sectional differences and racial animosities and suspicions" would disappear. Cooperation, he argued, "coupled with our [resulting] material prosperity, will bring into our beloved South a new heaven and a new earth."

Conveying a quite different message, Washington's second theme constituted, as his biographer states, "a sweeping concession to the white South's desire for segregation"—a concession that could not have displeased contemporary white racial theorists. Its core was this assertion: "In all things that are purely social we can be as separate as the fingers, yet one as the hand in all things essential to mutual progress." A bit later Washington added a distinctly evolutionary touch: "The wisest among my race understand that the agitation of questions of social equality is the extremist folly, and the progress in the enjoyment of all the privileges that will come to us must be the result of severe and constant struggle rather than of artificial forcing." Other passages contributed to the theme, although less obviously. He reminded his audience of such homey Negro traits as patience, dedication, loyalty, and harmless chicken thievery. Admitting the propriety of the Negro's beginning "at the bottom of life . . . and not at the top," he cautioned whites that the black third of the South

> will aid you in pulling the load upward, or they will pull, against you, the load downward. We shall constitute one third and more of the ignorance and crime of the South, or one third its intelligence and progress; we shall contribute one third to the business and industrial prosperity of the South, or we shall prove a veritable body of death, stagnating, depressing, retarding every effort to advance the body politic.

One need only eliminate favorable options within the passage, and the remainder echoes the stark situation that Frederick Hoffman had begun to publicize.[30]

Washington had preached much the same message over a decade earlier, in 1884, when he addressed the National Education Association in Madison, Wisconsin. Implicitly endorsing the myth of unjustifiable Negro "uppity-ness," he conceded to the educators that "[t]he teachings of the Negro in various ways for the last twenty years have been rather too much to array him against his white brother . . . ." Having "had no standard by which to shape his character," the black man naturally had fallen prey to "poverty and ignorance," which had "made him untruthful, intemperate, selfish, caused him to steal, to be cheated, and made the outcast of society, and he ha[d] aspired to positions which he was not mentally and morally capable of filling." But Negro morality was "slowly but surely improving," and as new interracial bonds developed, whites found "that all Negroes are not liars and chicken thieves." An example of good will and sensible action on the part of southern whites came from the Railroad Commission of Alabama, which had responded to a black's complaint of inadequate railway service by ordering "every railroad in the State [to] provide equal but separate accommodations for both races."[31]

Louis R. Harlan rightly identifies Washington's concessions on segregation as part of a subtle argument. Playing to the white South's social prejudices and stereotypes of the Negro was a device to draw forth support for the industrial education Washington thought so essential to the race's future; and Washington did not neglect mentioning the positive duty of whites to uplift the Negro, if only as a matter of white self-interest. These features of his public statements, along with his behind-the-scenes work to combat discriminatory and proscriptive practices, suggest that however mistaken his public acceptance of separation, Washington's limitations were of means rather than of ultimate goal. Unfortunately, it was his seeming endorsement of separation and his caricaturing of the Negro, not his broader vision, that caught the eye of white Americans, north and south, who sought an escape from the strife commonly associated with the race issue.[32]

Washington's emergence coincided with an emphasis by black businessmen and professionals on Negro self-help and racial solidarity. Expressed through organizations that included farmers' conferences, business groups, churches, fraternal orders, and women's clubs, these doctrines accentuated the idea of Negro separatism. Until about 1900 even black intellectuals, many of whom later moved toward the Niagra Movement and the National Association for the Advancement of Colored People, gave Washington's views substantial support. Whether or not such groups accurately mirrored the opinion of less articulate blacks is uncertain, but it is also beside the point, for the opinions of the Negro elites undoubtedly proved more visible to the dominant whites.

Spokesmen for Negro solidarity did not fail to demand recognition of civil and legal equality, but some also endorsed segregation. "We prefer separate schools with colored teachers to mixed schools without them, every time," announced the black editor of a Methodist newspaper, in 1886, as Ohio debated segregated schooling. A black school principal held that separate schools would benefit the race, claiming "[t]he mere fact of separation does not necessarily involve inferiority." In 1888, William Harper Councill, a Negro educator in Alabama, opposed demanding improved railway accommodations for the race, despite having previously sought relief from the Interstate Commerce Commission for being excluded from a first-class coach. A year earlier the Washington *Bee* quoted Negro lawyer John H. Smythe as arguing:

> The Negro is now a distinct, and ever will be a distinct race in this country. Blood—not language and religion—makes social distinctions. We are therefore bound by every drop of blood that flows in our being, and by whatever of self-respect you and I individually or collectively possess, to make our selves—not on the pattern of any other race, but actuated by our peculiar genius in literature, religion, commerce and social intercourse—a great people.

In 1895, another black Methodist editor disapproved "the growing disposition on the part of the Negro to force his way into white institutions where he is not wanted." The races were "peculiarly constituted," making separate institutions an "absolute necessity."[33]

Given his eventual prominent opposition to Washington, W. E. B. DuBois is perhaps the most interesting example. As early as his undergraduate days at Fisk University during 1884–88, DuBois held the southern Negro community responsible for its degraded condition. In 1891, while a graduate fellow at Harvard, he argued that Henry Cabot Lodge's "Force Bill" incorrectly assumed that "law can accomplish anything," and added:

> We must ever keep before us the fact that the South has some excuse for its present attitude. We must remember that a good many of our people . . . are not fit for the responsibility of republican government. When you have the right sort of black voters you will need no election laws. The battle of my people must be a moral one, not a legal or physical one.

During the early 1890s, it is true, DuBois attacked the inequities of southern labor arrangements, stressed the importance of a broad liberal education for blacks, and called for equal treatment in the civil and political spheres. Again, however, the relevant point is that, *taken selectively,* his comments provided confirmation for the position that Negroes constituted a distinctive group, too often with debilitating characteristics and needing segregated institutions.[34]

Decades later, Robert Penn Warren aptly, if not quite completely, summarized the traits which many white Americans for years had attributed to "Sambo." The Negro, he wrote, with the keen sense of the poet-novelist, was viewed as

> the supine, grateful, humble, irresponsible, unmanly, banjo-picking, servile, grinning, slack-jawed, docile, dependent, slow-witted, humorous, child-loving, childlike, watermelon-stealing, spiritual-singing, blamelessly fornicating, happy-go-lucky, hedonistic, faithful black servitor who sometimes might step out of character long enough to utter folk wisdom or bury the family silver to save it from the Yankees.

Transcending sectional lines, the Sambo image developed early and "lived on—in white eyes—as Pullman porter, bootblack, yard boy, sharecropper, waiter, barber, elevator operator, the Three Black Crows, and Step-and-Fetchit"; it was "eternal and immutable."[35] As a description of opinion in the late nineteenth century, Warren's portrait fails in only one respect: it inadequately emphasizes the black race's alleged inborn pathologies. But adjusted to include a larger dose of sexual threat and criminality, the Sambo image clearly had a substantial presence in the thought of white America in the 1890s—a presence that carried legal significance.

Although embodying no unified, internally consistent doctrine, popular and scientific opinion provided broad grounds for concluding that racial separation was "reasonable" in the sense of arguably conducing to maintenance of public health, welfare, and morals. George Fredrickson has outlined six "white supremacist propositions" on which "almost all shades of white opinion" showed "widespread, almost universal, agreement" between the late 1830s and World War I. His listing, certainly accurate for the 1890s, can be cast in the form of an extended—and loose—syllogism that summarizes the racist thought of the period and thus the case for reasonableness: (1) Blacks are significantly different from whites. (2) These differences result in black inferiority, especially in moral and mental characteristics. (3) Change in these respects will occur very slowly, if at all. (4) Given inbred racial differences, race mixing is deleterious to both whites and blacks, and at best produces a hybrid inferior to the former. (5) Race antipathy is inevitable, especially if blacks intrude themselves on the superior group. (6) Therefore, an integrated society is impossible in practical terms. "The subject of race inferiority," agrees John Haller, "was beyond critical reach in the late nineteenth century . . . ."[36]

CHAPTER SIX

The Transportation Law Environment: Access by Leave, Not Right

I

Only in an unrealistically narrow sense can "law" be associated simply with *legislative* enactment. This is particularly true in Anglo-American jurisdictions, where courts have played leading roles in defining the legal relations and obligations between private parties as well as the rights and duties of individuals vis-à-vis the community. When courts shape and employ doctrines that endorse and even mandate particular activities, they create law or extend its domain. The result gives some parties legal rights and remedies and restricts the access that others have to legal redress for injury. "Deciding cases," comments the leading historian of American law, is "part of lawmaking."[1]

So it was with separate-but-equal. As an element in transportation *law* in the United States, the doctrine did not originate in the separate car legislation that southern states began to adopt in the late 1880s, but instead emerged through a series of state and federal judicial cases dating from the 1860s into the early 1890s. Arising when regulation of public or common carriers through statutes and commissions was still in its infancy, most of these cases involved ordinary common-law suits against transportation companies or their agents.[2]

Some of the decisions and opinions that emerged as influential by the end of the period came from state appellate courts, others from federal trial and appellate courts. Typically, a passenger sought to recover monetary damages for an allegedly discriminatory act. Even the majority of federal cases had a common-law basis. They came into federal courts not because they involved distinctly federal issues, but rather because aggrieved parties invoked either the federal judiciary's diversity-of-citizenship jurisdiction (that is, its authority to hear suits between citizens of different states) or its admiralty jurisdiction, which includes private suits associated with transportation on the sea and inland navigable waters. In either instance, the federal courts turned to common-law doctrines for rules of decision. Claims based substantively on federal law entered into a few of the federal cases, but even in these instances the federal courts often employed the common law in crucial ways.[3]

The immediate backdrop for these cases was the common law of common carriers. By the 1860s, American courts had held that these carriers must conduct their affairs in a reasonable manner, in the sense of promoting the welfare of their customers and of the public generally as well as advancing the interests of the proprietors. Through a case-by-case process, largely in the absence of legislation, this requirement derived from the premise that by offering their services to the public in general, carriers became quasi-public businesses, and so were subject to judicial supervision on behalf of the entire community. Applying the requirement, courts held that a public carrier of passengers was obligated to carry and provide equal service to all those who sought passage and who paid or offered to pay the established fare. Reasonable exceptions included persons of known bad character and deportment, persons afflicted with contagious diseases, and those intent on harming the carrier or other passengers. As regards persons given passage, moreover, a carrier had the right and duty to establish rules and regulations that were reasonable in the same sense, and could eject a passenger who refused to abide by the carrier's reasonable rules.

Some rules pertained to safety, such as the prohibition against riding on train engines; others looked more broadly toward passenger comfort and convenience and community welfare. Different classes of accommodations, graduated by fare, were thus reasonable, for they secured basic transportation to the less affluent, while they provided additional comforts to persons able to pay higher fares. Even passengers paying the same fare could be classified and separated on reasonable grounds, so long as they received substantially equal accommodations. What constituted a reasonable ground for separation might be in doubt, but not the principle, which received endorsement in the nearly universal legal acceptance of "ladies' cars"—separate first-class cars for women and their male escorts.

So long as a carrier's rules and regulations were reasonable, were published or otherwise made known, and were regularly rather than capriciously enforced, a passenger had no basis, in either contract or tort law, to sue a carrier in connection with their enforcement. Reasonable rules, that is, when properly publicized and enforced, constituted both a part of the contract for passage between carrier and passenger, and a statement of the duties that carrier and passenger owed to each other and to the public. Accordingly, if a passenger was assigned to particular accommodations pursuant to a carrier's reasonable regulations—or if, for failing to abide by a reasonable regulation, a passenger was ejected from a particular accommodation or put off a train or boat entirely, but with no undue force being used against him—he could not recover damages in court.[4]

Consistent with these legal doctrines, railways offered differentiated service on intercity trains, typically providing at least a ladies' car and a smoking car, as described in Chapter One. River and coastal steamers provided comparable tiers of accommodation. But what of blacks in the postwar era? On its surface, anyway, the common-law framework as it emerged from the antebellum period failed to settle the question of where they legally now could be assigned.

II

The doctrine of reasonableness and the existence of ladies' cars both entered into the Northern case, from Pennsylvania in 1867, that produced the earliest regularly reported judicial endorsement of the separate-but-equal doctrine in transportation law. Within thirty years, both state and federal courts accorded high authority to *West Chester and Philadelphia Railroad Company v. Miles*. In one sense, it is this later attention that gives *Miles* its importance, but an appreciation for the foundations of later developments requires a close look at the case itself.

At issue was a rule or regulation of the West Chester and Philadelphia Railroad Company that required blacks to sit at one end of the company's cars. One day, Vera E. Miles, "a person of color," decided instead to take a seat toward the middle, and when the conductor asked her to move to the end she "positively and persistently refused to comply." Finally, after first warning Mrs. Miles that further noncompliance would lead to her removal from the car, the conductor ejected her. When Mrs. Miles sued, a jury awarded her damages, and the railway appealed to the state Supreme Court. The trial court judge had erred in his charge to the jury, claimed the company; he had declined to instruct that Mrs. Miles could not recover damages if the seat to which she had been assigned by the conductor "was in all respects a comfortable, safe, and convenient seat, not inferior in any respect to the one she was directed to leave." Rejecting this version of a separate-but-equal instruction, the trial judge had instead ruled that separation by race was not lawful, adding "that the defendant could not compel the plaintiff to change her seat simply on account of her color." Finding this instruction to the jury had been faulty, the state Supreme Court reversed the lower court judgment. Justice Daniel Agnew wrote its opinion.

Agnew began with a deceptive concession and then moved to the issue of reasonable distinctions. "[N]o one," he admitted, "can be excluded from carriage by a public carrier on account of color, religious belief, political relations, or prejudice." But the railway company claimed no right to *exclude* Mrs. Miles. It argued instead that assigning her, on the basis of color, to a seat equal to the one she was asked to leave was reasonable, took account only of racial *differences*, and did not imply racial *inferiority*. In assessing this claim, Agnew employed a convenient analogy, observing, "The ladies' car is known upon every well-regulated railroad, implies no loss of equal right on the part of the excluded sex, and its propriety is doubted by none." This practice suggested a "simple question": could a carrier, "in the exercise of his private duty of property, and in due performance of his public duty, separate passengers by any other well-defined characteristic than that of sex?"[5]

The answer required initially a fuller discussion of a carrier's *general* right and duty to regulate the seating of passengers, which Agnew, accurately stating existing doctrine, linked to two sources. The first was the carrier's private interest in his own property. Its protection required the seating of passengers "so as to preserve order and decorum, and to prevent contacts and collisions arising from natural or well-known repugnancies, which are likely to breed disturbances by a promiscuous sitting." Nor could a passenger object to such arrangements, for the passenger's "right . . . is only that of being carried safely, and with a due regard to his personal comfort and convenience, which are [similarly] promoted by a sound and well-regulated separation of passengers."

The second ground for separation was the carrier's duty to promote the public's "interest in the proper regulation of public conveyances for the preservation of the public peace." A conductor had the duty and means of suppressing tumults once they began, but "prevent[ing] difficulties among passengers by regulations for their proper separation" was much easier than quelling them.[6]

Having established what was largely unexceptionable—that carriers could classify and separate passengers "in proper cases"—Agnew then examined the reasonableness of race as a criterion for separation. Was there "such a difference between the white and black races within this state [that is, Pennsylvania], resulting from nature, law, and custom," that separation by race promoted the interests of owners, passengers, and public in the maintenance of order, decorum, convenience, and comfort?

The apparent neutrality of the question was misleading. Even before stating it, Agnew had provided an answer, in the midst of discussing the public's general interest in regulation. There he had written:

> The danger to the peace engendered by the feelings of aversion between individuals of the different races cannot be denied. It is a fact with which the company must deal. If a negro takes his seat beside a white man or his wife or daughter, the law cannot repress the anger or conquer the aversion which some will feel. However unwise it may be to indulge the

feeling, human infirmity is not always proof against it. It is much wiser
to avert the consequences of this repulsion of race by separation than to
punish afterwards the breach of the peace it may have caused.

Elaboration came later, in the form of three not entirely consistent
propositions: God had implanted instincts toward race separation; "[t]he
tendency of intimate social intermixture is to amalgamation, contrary to the
law of races"; and the natural geographic separation of races testified to their
natural differences.[7]

Pennsylvania's own institutions offered further confirmation. In particular, in a "solemn decision" in 1837, Chief Justice John Gibson of the state
Supreme Court had employed "his remarkable intellect" to demonstrate
"that the *status* of the negro never fell within the term 'freeman' in the
[state's] several constitutions; and that the emancipation act of 1780 did not
elevate him to the citizenship of the state." In 1838, moreover, a state
constitutional amendment had maintained the distinction between white
and black. Finally, the state's blacks separated themselves from whites in
private and public life; they "fill[ed] no civil or political stations, not even
sitting to decide their own causes"; the school laws of the state "provide[d]
for separate schools when their [the Negroes'] numbers are adequate"; and
separation was the rule in military service. "Law and custom having
sanctioned a separation of races," Agnew concluded from his review, "it is
not the province of the judiciary to legislate it away. We cannot say there was
no difference in fact, when the law and the voice of the people said there
was." At the time Mrs. Miles was ejected from her seat, there had been a
"natural, legal, and customary difference between the black and white races
. . . which made their separation as passengers in a public conveyance the
subject of a sound regulation to secure order, promote comfort, preserve the
peace, and maintain the rights both of carriers and passengers."[8]

As regards transportation law, Agnew had advanced a novel view in
upholding the acceptability of separation by race so long as the resulting
accommodations were equal. In the context of regularly reported cases,
however, the novelty was *not* the disallowance of Mrs. Miles's claim that *all*
distinctions based on race were illegal. Instead, it was recognition, really
without argument, that common carriers had to provide *equal* accommodations. Although anticipated in 1849 by Chief Justice Lemuel Shaw in the
Massachusetts school case of *Roberts v. the City of Boston*, the requirement
went beyond the holding of the Michigan Supreme Court in *Day v. Owen*
(1858), the leading antebellum case involving racial separation in transportation. *Day*, too, had turned on a reasonableness test, formulated in this
fashion:

> All rules and regulations must be reasonable; and to be so they should
> have for their object the accommodation of the passengers. Under this
> head we include everything calculated to render the transportation most

comfortable and least annoying to passengers generally; not to one or two, or any given number carried at a particular time, but to a large majority of the passengers ordinarily carried.

Reiterating, the Michigan court stressed that "the law would defeat its own object if it required the carrier, for the accommodation of particular individuals, to incommode the community at large." Under this test, a steamship company was justified in assigning its few black passengers to the deck rather than allowing them in the cabin occupied by whites. The *Day* rule, that is, had been separate-and-unequal.[9]

Yet only in a limited sense did Agnew break new ground when he endorsed separate-but-equal. The railway did not claim the right to assign Mrs. Miles to inferior quarters, and Mrs. Miles specifically contested the rule of separation per se, not the permissibility of *either* separate-and-unequal *or* separate-but-equal.[10] As a result, the only attention Agnew gave to the requirement of equality of accommodation was in restating the jury instruction that the railway had requested in the trial court, and in maintaining, categorically, that separation did not imply inferiority. The necessity of equality where accommodations were racially separate thus passed into the law of common carriers almost without comment and clearly without explicit argument. But explication was perhaps unnecessary. Implicitly the doctrine flowed from Agnew's analogy of ladies' cars: they were permissible partly because other first-class passengers had access to equal accommodations, at least in theory. More broadly, the law of common carriers generally required equality of treatment for passengers paying equal fares. The separate-and-unequal rule of *Day v. Owen* had been the aberration. Rather than invent doctrine, Agnew had adapted it.

The more important contribution of *West Chester v. Miles* to transportation law consisted of Agnew's remarks about the *reasonableness* of racial separation. This is ironic, because by November 1867, when the decision came down, the Pennsylvania legislature had outlawed racial discrimination on the state's railways, and Agnew himself noted that he had "pronounce[d] the law only as it stood when the case arose," prior to the legislation.[11] The Fourteenth Amendment to the federal Constitution, ratified the following year, similarly undercut the portion of Agnew's argument that rested on the state-imposed disabilities of Negroes. Far from impairing the authority of *Miles*, these problematic aspects simply disappeared from view.

The case itself did not fade; its fate testifies to the precedential toughness of announced law that corresponds to broader preconceptions.[12] By 1890, state and federal courts had extensively cited, quoted, and paraphrased *Miles* in the course of implanting the separate-but-equal doctrine into the common law of carriers of passengers. What proved especially serviceable were Agnew's comments about inherent race instincts, differences, and repugnancies, which so nicely harmonized with "scientific" theorizing about race.

Separate-but-equal in transportation law received further confirmation three years later, in the case of *Chicago and North Western Railroad Company v. Williams*, and more obviously so because the Illinois Supreme Court detoured into dicta to discuss the doctrine. The real issue in *Williams* was exclusion. Although regularly reserving one of the two first-class cars on its passenger trains "for the exclusive use of ladies, and gentlemen accompanied by ladies," the railway set aside neither a car nor separate seats for black passengers, and evidently had no uniform rule at all concerning the seating of black passengers in the ladies' car. Nevertheless Anna Williams, a black woman holding a first-class ticket, had been forcibly prevented from entering the ladies' car on one of the company's trains even though it had vacant seats. She sued successfully. The record contained no suggestion "that she was not a woman of good character and proper behavior," and evidence revealed that the only objection to her taking a seat in the ladies' car was her race. As in *Miles*, the railway appealed.

The state Supreme Court easily upheld the verdict for Mrs. Williams. In the absence of a rule on the seating of black passengers, the company's agents had acted wantonly and capriciously in preventing Mrs. Williams from boarding, and hence unreasonably and wrongfully. The court went further, however, asking whether a rule excluding black women from the ladies' car would have been reasonable, had such a rule existed and been enforced. *Miles* provided a possible answer; the Illinois court extracted from the Pennsylvania case the holding that it was

> not . . . an unreasonable regulation to seat passengers so as to preserve order and decorum, and prevent contacts and collisions arising from well known repugnancies, and therefore a rule that required a colored woman to occupy a separate seat in a car furnished by the company, equally as comfortable and safe as that furnished for other passengers, was not an unreasonable rule.

Having omitted Justice Agnew's suspect argument drawing on the Negro's *antebellum* civil and political disabilities in Pennsylvania, the court concluded: "Under some circumstances, this might not be an unreasonable rule." Still, the court quickly abandoned the hypothetical problem and returned to the case before it, reaffirming, "At all events, public carriers, until they do furnish separate seats equal in comfort and safety to those furnished for other travelers, must be held to have no right to discriminate between passengers on account of color, race or nativity, alone."[13]

Although Mrs. Williams won her case, separate-but-equal did not lose. True, the Illinois court only said in the end that a railway regulation which fell short of mandating equal accommodations would definitely *not* be reasonable, which did not necessarily mean that a rule for separation incorporating the requirement of equality would be reasonable. But the fine distinction emerges only on close reading; and *Williams* had the effect of stripping Justice Agnew's opinion in *Miles* of its more obviously dated language.

Explicit endorsement of *Miles* came the same year from the federal Circuit Court in Baltimore, Maryland, where the Baltimore City Passenger Railway charged blacks its standard fare but excluded them from the interiors of its cars and relegated them to the cars' outside platforms. When Alexander Thompson, a resident of New York, sued for damages after being ejected from one of the company's cars, counsel for the railway sought support from the Pennsylvania decision, claiming that threats to public order arising from racial mixing and race repugnancies established the reasonableness of the railway's policy. But without hearing arguments to support the proposition, Judge William F. Giles ruled no, holding that in view of the abolition of slavery and the Fourteenth Amendment's grant of citizenship to blacks, exclusion had become unreasonable. After quoting extensively from *Miles*, Giles ruled further that in the absence of "legislation prohibiting the carrier from making any distinction between passengers on account of race or color," separation by race was itself reasonable, so long as blacks received seating equal in comfort and convenience to that assigned whites. But in the case before him, the admitted facts revealed the company had not provided such seating, and Thompson received a directed verdict with damages. The company responded by announcing it would open specified cars to blacks, designated by the sign "COLORED PERSONS ADMITTED INTO THIS CAR."[14]

The victory proved hollow, for whites commonly occupied the cars set aside for blacks and prevented blacks from entering. In this circumstance, John W. Fields, a Negro from Lynchburg, Virginia, boarded a car reserved for whites on February 27, 1871. Testimony differed on what then happened, but Fields claimed he was ejected, the driver throwing his fare money after him. When the resulting case came before the Circuit Court in Baltimore, the company pleaded that it provided separate cars for blacks, equal in comfort and convenience to those for whites. To this Fields's counsel first demurred. The recent amendments, he contended, gave Fields a right to ride in any of the railway's cars, but the court overruled the demurrer. Then, after testimony about the facts of the dispute—the availability and quality of cars open to blacks—counsel for both Fields and the railway requested and received separate-but-equal jury instructions from Judges Giles and Hugh L. Bond, who together presided over the trial. The judges added that "if the jury find from the evidence . . . that the defendant refused . . . to transport him [Fields] because of his color only, then the plaintiff is entitled to recover." Awarding damages to Fields, the jury evidently accepted Fields's account of his ejection, found that it had occurred on account of race, and concluded that the four out of fourteen cars formally set aside for blacks on the day of the incident did not constitute accommodations as convenient or comfortable as those provided whites.[15]

In 1964 a federal Supreme Court justice implied that *Fields* was a strike against separate-but-equal. Concerning the immediate effect of the decision, the assessment is accurate, for the verdict in the case prompted the Baltimore City Passenger Railway to open all of its cars to blacks.[16] But to interpret *Fields* as asserting the legal doctrine that equality requires identity of accommodations is to misread the case badly. The law announced in *Fields*, no less than in *Thompson*, displayed no tentativeness in endorsing separate-but-equal as an appropriate common-law standard: the jury instruction allowing recovery for refusal to transport on account of race was issued along with explicit separate-but-equal instructions and addressed the separate issue of exclusion. Later, in fact, Judge Giles had occasion to offer his own gloss on the two cases, which he saw as turning on the same issue. Falling within the Circuit Court's diversity-of-citizenship jurisdiction, he explained, they rested on the principle that, once admitted to citizenship, blacks could not be denied privileges exercised by other citizens. In short, exclusion constituted denial of the rights of citizenship; separation into equal facilities did not.[17]

But doctrine had not yet hardened. Prior to *Miles*, at least two state trial court decisions—one in New York (1855) and the other in California (1863)—had come down in favor of black plaintiffs who challenged their exclusion from cars on street railways. In each case, the judges had instructed the jury that as a common carrier the company had no right to exclude colored persons. But the factual situations underlying the cases made it problematic to extract from them a clear rule against merely segregated transport, and the rulings attracted little professional attention, perhaps because neither case was apparently reported outside the press.[18]

In 1873, two regularly reported decisions came down denying the legitimacy of separate-but-equal in transportation. One was in a federal case that developed out of a well-publicized incident in February 1868. Catherine Brown, a black woman who had charge of the ladies' restroom of the United States Senate, had purchased a standard ticket, as provided to whites and blacks alike, for the train from Alexandria, Virginia, to Washington, D.C., on the Washington, Georgetown, and Alexandria Railroad. Declining to enter the car set aside for blacks, she instead tried to board the white ladies' car even though, according to later court testimony, the two cars were "alike comfortable." Enforcing the railway's standing regulation, the conductor forcibly kept Mrs. Brown out of the car for whites, and she made the trip in the colored car. When Mrs. Brown subsequently sued for damages, the company asked the trial court in the District of Columbia to charge the jury that Mrs. Brown could not recover if it found both that the denial of access to her had actually been in accordance with the company policy and that "all the cars were equally safe, clean, and comfortable." The trial court refused to give the requested jury instruction, Mrs. Brown won damages, and the company appealed to the United States Supreme Court.

The case now turned on the proper interpretation of the railway's federal charter. Originally incorporated in Virginia, the company had received congressional approval in 1854 to extend its line into the District of Columbia. Then, in 1863, another federal grant authorized a further extension into the District; at the insistence of Senator Charles Sumner, this second modification provided "that no person shall be excluded from the cars on account of color." The Supreme Court had to determine what the provision meant.

Taken literally, the 1863 language could be interpreted as prohibiting only the outright exclusion of Negroes from the company's trains. But if Congress had intended such a limited reading, Justice David Davis argued for the Court, the provision would have been meaningless, because economic self-interest dictated that the company carry paying blacks in some fashion, and evidence indicated the company had always done so. Rather, Congress's concern had been "the discrimination in the use of cars on account of color, where slavery obtained . . . and not the fact that the colored race could not ride in the cars at all." As the Court read the record—accurately, it seems—"Congress . . . told this company, in substance, that it could extend its road within the District as desired, but that this discrimination must cease, and the colored and white races, in the use of the cars, be placed on an equality." The Court accordingly upheld the award to Mrs. Brown.[19]

The other 1873 decision, more sweeping in scope, came from the Iowa Supreme Court in *Coger v. North Western Union Packet Company*. Meeting practically every point raised six years earlier by Justice Agnew in the *Miles* case, Iowa's Chief Justice Joseph M. Beck provided a statement for identity of treatment far more compelling than Agnew's arguments for segregation— yet less influential.

At issue was the denial of first-class steamship facilities to one Mrs. Coger, a schoolteacher who was one-quarter black. On her homeward voyage along the Mississippi River from Keokuk, Iowa, to Quincy, Illinois, Mrs. Coger had first attempted, unsuccessfully, to purchase a ticket for a first-class stateroom and meal privileges on the *S. S. Merrill*, but eventually settled for a ticket giving her only transportation. Once on board, she made another attempt to obtain the desired meal ticket, using her maid as an intermediary. This was also abortive, but she finally found another passenger, presumably white, who was able to purchase the ticket for her; and when the dinner hour arrived, she took a seat at the table for white women. A ship's officer then asked her to leave, telling her that her dinner would soon be served on the guards of the ship or in the pantry.

But Mrs. Coger proved feisty and determined. For the ensuing fracas, the appellate court's description is doubly revealing, suggesting both Mrs. Coger's dedication and the broader environment of racial (and sexual) assumptions within which her legal case developed:

> She refused [to leave the table], and thereupon the captain of the boat was sent for, who repeated the request, and, being denied compliance, he

proceeded by force to remove her from the table and the cabin of the boat. She resisted so that considerable violence was necessary to drag her out of the cabin, and, in the struggle, the covering of the table was torn off and dishes broken, and the officer received a slight injury. The defendant's [that is, the company's] witnesses testify that she used abusive, threatening and coarse language during and after the struggle, but this she denies. Certain it is, however, that by her spirited resistance and her defiant words, as well as by her pertinacity in demanding the recognition of her rights and in vindicating them, she has exhibited evidence of the Anglo-Saxon blood that flows in her veins. While we may consider that the evidence, as to her words and conduct, does not tend to establish that female delicacy and timidity so much praised, yet it does show an energy and firmness in defense of her rights not altogether unworthy of admiration. But neither womanly delicacy nor unwomanly courage has anything to do with her legal rights and the remedies for their deprivation. These are to be settled without regard to such personal traits of character.[20]

When Mrs. Coger sued, the trial judge predictably instructed the jury that common carriers had a right and duty to establish reasonable regulations to promote the accommodation of passengers, the interests of the community, and their own business operations. He added as a matter of law, however, that "all persons, unobjectionable in character and deportment, who observe all reasonable rules and regulations of the common carrier, who pay or offer to pay first-class fare, are entitled, *irrespective of race or color*, to receive upon the boats of the common carrier first-class accommodations." To obviate any remaining confusion, he reiterated that Mrs. Coger "was entitled to the same rights and privileges . . . that other passengers upon the same boat, similarly situated, of purely Anglo-Saxon origin, were entitled to." It followed that the company's rule for colored passengers to "take their meals in the pantry or on the guards of the boat, is not a reasonable but an unreasonable rule, and must be disregarded . . . ." The steamship line appealed after the jury returned a verdict for Mrs. Coger.[21]

Writing for the Iowa Supreme Court, Chief Justice Beck described the sole question as "in a word, are the rights and privileges of persons transported by public carriers affected by race or color?" Answering with a clear "no," he found the company's rule denied the equality mandated by natural law, Christian doctrine, and the court's own recent decision in *Clark v. Board of Directors* (1868), which outlawed segregated schools in Iowa. The same equality inhered in the Iowa's constitution, which declared, "in language most comprehensive, and incapable of misconstruction," that "[a]ll men are, by nature, free and equal." Beyond these sources, Mrs. Coger's rights rested on the guarantees of the Fourteenth Amendment and the federal Civil Rights Act of 1866. "The peculiar privilege of the colored man intended to be guarantied by these constitutional and statutory provisions," concluded Beck, is equality with the white man in all affairs of life, over which there may be legislation, or of which the courts may take cognizance. He is secured in life, liberty and property, and the remedies provided by law to enforce the rights pertaining thereto. As to all these, there cannot be laws imposing disabilities upon him, or depriving him of equal benefits, equal advantages, and equal protection, with other citizens.[22]

Beck admitted that federal protection did not extend to social rights, but Mrs. Coger had not complained that she had been deprived of the company of whites. She was deprived instead of "the advantages of the contract made with other passengers[,] . . . her rights of property were invaded, and her right to demand services to which she was lawfully entitled was denied." The presence of people in a steamer's cabin simply did not establish what is called society, nor did it "create social relations." The variety of persons typically found in such cabins offered ample proof that mixing of passengers neither conveyed nor diminished social status. Quite the contrary, argued Beck: "It cannot be doubted that she was excluded from the table and cabin, not because others would have been degraded and she elevated in society, but because of prejudice entertained against her race, growing out of its former condition of servitude . . . ." The very object of the postwar amendments and the Civil Rights Act was "to relieve citizens of the black race from the effects of this prejudice, to protect them in person and property from its spirit." Considering this body of law, Beck had no difficulty agreeing that the company's regulations for colored passengers were unreasonable as a matter of law. Reviewing the factual evidence, moreover, he discovered no grounds to disagree with the jury's finding that Mrs. Coger had been ejected from the ladies' table solely because of her color.[23]

Neither of these 1873 cases proved very important. *Brown* too obviously applied only to the narrow circumstances of travel on the Washington, Alexandria, and Georgetown Railroad, as controlled by a particular congressional act. In rejecting the doctrine of separate-but-equal in *Brown*, the federal Supreme Court did not address the issue of whether separation by race was reasonable in other circumstances, a consideration the Interstate Commerce Commission stressed fifteen years later when it distinguished the case. Perhaps Justice Davis had meant to signal more when he noted in his statement of the facts of the case that the incident involving Mrs. Brown, in February 1868, had occurred *prior* to the adoption of the Fourteenth Amendment. With the Amendment in force, that is, perhaps all classification by race would be impermissible, whether or not specific legislation forbade it. But if this was Davis's intended implication, it remained undeveloped.[24]

In a sense *Coger* picked up where *Brown* left off. Its use of recent federal constitutional and statutory provisions was clear and convincing. The meanings Chief Justice Beck assigned these enactments were certainly the meanings that some of the framers or authors had intended; and given these meanings, Beck's conclusions were hard to fault. There can be no doubt, moreover, that the Iowa court meant to strike at segregation of both the equal and unequal varieties.

Yet few arguments are invulnerable. Isolated sentences in *Coger* did harmonize with the separate-but-equal doctrine,[25] and nowhere did Beck *explicitly* define equality as by itself inconsistent with separation. Probably the closest he came was in using the *Clark* decision, which disallowed segregated schooling, but *Clark*, it could be argued, rested on the conclusion that, properly interpreted, the state school law positively denied local districts the option of establishing racially segregated schools. Finally, the factual situation in *Coger* allowed the decision to be distinguished away: to uphold the jury's award, the court need not have considered the validity of separate-but-equal, since that standard, too, would have allowed Mrs. Coger to recover. As a commentator remarked, looking back on *Coger* from 1893, "in this case . . . the accommodations set apart for blacks were obviously inferior . . . ."[26]

III

Soon courts did not have to quibble over legal and factual distinctions in order to qualify and limit the reach of *Brown* and *Coger*. In *Hall v. DeCuir* (1878), the United States Supreme Court itself concluded that separate-but-equal was permissible within the common law of common carriers in America. This decision federalized the interpretation of the reasonableness doctrine that the Pennsylvania Supreme Court had advanced in *Miles* a decade earlier and, in a very real sense, constitutionalized it as well.

Under the title *DeCuir v. Benson*, the case began in the state courts of Louisiana, one of several southern states to adopt civil rights legislation during the Reconstruction era. Louisiana's equal accommodations Act, passed in 1869, mandated that the rules and regulations of common carriers could "make no discrimination on account of race or color," and provided for private lawsuits and punitive damages as one remedy for violations. Its basis was Article 13 of the state's constitution of 1868:

> All persons shall enjoy equal rights and privileges upon any conveyance of a public character; and all places of business or public resort, or for which a license is required by either State, parish or municipal authority, shall be deemed of a public character, and shall be open to the accommodation and patronage of all persons without distinction or discrimination on account of race or color.

Notwithstanding these provisions, Mrs. Josephine DeCuir, a black woman, was denied a berth in the ladies' cabin of the steamship *Governor Allen* when she took passage in July 1872 from New Orleans upriver to her plantation in Pointe Coupe Parish, Louisiana. As allowed under the state legislation, Mrs. DeCuir sued John C. Benson, the captain of the *Governor Allen*, and when she won, Benson appealed. Louisiana's legislation, he claimed, unconstitutionally regulated interstate commerce and abridged *his* Fourteenth Amendment rights to liberty and property. He argued, too, that despite the state civil rights law, common carriers legally had a right to issue reasonable rules and regulations, including rules assigning Negro passengers to separate quarters equal to those given whites. (On the last point, evidence from the trial proceedings revealed that such rules were customary on Mississippi riverboats.)[27]

In an opinion by its Chief Justice, John T. Ludeling, the Louisiana Supreme Court dismissed Benson's commerce claim almost summarily, contending that the state's 1869 civil rights Act "was enacted solely to protect the newly enfranchised citizens of the United States, within the limits of Louisiana, from the effects of prejudice against them." With no more detailed explanation, Ludeling concluded that the Act "does not, in any manner, affect the commercial interests of any State or foreign nation or of the citizens thereof." The Fourteenth Amendment argument received fuller attention. In well-established law, Ludeling explained, common carriers were prohibited from abitrarily discriminating between passengers, and owners of common carriers held their property on the condition they would abide by that restriction. Accordingly, Louisiana's Act compromised no liberty or property rights. Instead, to treat Mrs. DeCuir differently from a white passenger abridged the rights and privileges that *she* possessed under the Constitutions and laws of both the United States and Louisiana. To affirm this conclusion, Ludeling quoted and explicitly adopted language from *Coger*. As for Benson's claim that common carriers still might require separation by race, Ludeling commented sharply: "it can not be pretended that a regulation, which is founded on prejudice and which is in violation of law, is reasonable."

Had Mrs. DeCuir's case progressed no further than Louisiana's highest court, Ludeling's 1875 opinion could conceivably have added weight to the attack on separate-but-equal begun by the 1873 decisions in *Brown* and especially *Coger*. This conclusion must remain speculative, however. The state court averred that "in truth" Mrs. DeCuir would have had the same grounds for suing Captain Benson in the absence of the state's 1869 Act, which was to say that the law was not essential to her suit. Yet Ludeling's opinion tied the rejection of separate-but-equal most clearly to the existing law, and it seems likely that this linkage would have severely limited the precedential value of *DeCuir v. Benson* in cases not covered by legislative enactment. And the Chief Justice may have recognized Louisiana's distinctive legal climate, for he implied as much when he wrote, "it is settled, *in this State at least*, that colored persons now have all the civil and political rights which white persons enjoy."[28]

In light of the case's subsequent history, a more serious flaw was an omission in the opinion. By holding, as already explained, that because the state Act involved civil rights it simply did not regulate commerce, Ludeling sidestepped the opportunity to rule that the law pertained only to commerce *within* Louisiana. In turn, he gave no attention to analyzing and disposing of two factors that arguably gave Mrs. DeCuir's trip an *inter*state character, even though it was entirely in Louisiana, below the portion of the Mississippi River which forms the Louisiana-Mississippi state boundary. The *Governor Allen* operated under a federally granted coasting license—the same authorization that had immunized vessels from New York control in the celebrated Marshall Court case of *Gibbons v. Ogden* (1824). Also, when Mrs. DeCuir took passage, the ship's overall voyage was interstate, from New Orleans to Vicksburg, Mississippi.[29]

The captain now appealed to the United States Supreme Court, and when he died his heirs continued the action as *Hall v. DeCuir*.[30] In 1878 the federal court reversed the Louisiana ruling. Its opinion, by Chief Justice Morrison R. Waite, focused formally on the interstate commerce question, but in a way that encompassed a different issue—the content of the common law of common carriers.

Waite's argument was subtle. At a superficial level, he held that the Louisiana Act regulated interstate commerce and to that extent was invalid. But it was not merely the law's interstate reach that invalidated it, for under the "selective exclusiveness" doctrine of *Cooley v. Board of Wardens of the Port of Philadelphia* (1851), some activities technically in interstate commerce were open to state regulation until such time as Congress acted. "The line which separates the powers of the States from this exclusive power of Congress," Waite conceded, "is not always distinctly marked, and oftentimes it is not easy to determine on which side a particular case belongs." He then discussed how the 1869 Act directly burdened and interfered with interstate commerce by encroaching on the area of exclusive congressional control. The manner in which Louisiana obligated a carrier to accommodate passengers on the intrastate portion of an interstate voyage could not but affect passenger arrangements for the overall voyage, especially when different states might establish different rules.[31]

Waite's approach thus closely paralleled Chief Justice John Marshall's in *Gibbons*.[32] He *almost* held the state law invalid as impermissibly trenching on Congress's exclusive sphere. But, like Marshall, and crucial to the overall meaning of *Hall v. DeCuir*, Waite concluded with a significantly different argument. Logically, he could have done little else, for the hypothetical example he used to illustrate the burden Louisiana had imposed on interstate commerce was the confusion that would arise if a carrier first fell under Louisiana's regulation and then, further on, under another state's rule mandating separation. But one could argue that the Louisiana rule against segregation was less burdensome. In any event, *some* rule—public or private—would have to apply, and the commerce clause itself may provide no basis for preferring one over another, so long as none of the competing rules is federally imposed.

On Waite's analysis, the central problem was not that the state law infringed on an area of exclusive congressional authority. Rather, it infringed on a commercial regulation *adopted by Congress*. This was true because Congress's

> power of regulation may be exercised without legislation as well as with it. By refraining from action, Congress, in effect, adopts as its own regulations those which the common law or the civil law, where that prevails, has provided for the government of such business, and those which the States, in the regulation of their domestic concerns, have established affecting commerce, but not regulating it within the meaning of the Constitution. In fact, congressional legislation is only necessary to cure defects in existing laws, as they are discovered, and to adapt such laws to new developments of trade.

To remove any remaining ambiguity, Waite quoted from Justice Field in a case from 1875: congressional "inaction . . . [was] the equivalent to a declaration that inter-state commerce shall remain free and untrammelled." In context, Waite's evident meaning was that observance of the common law of common carriers would accomplish that goal, and hence the common law was federal law.[33]

Nor did Waite's argument stop there, for it entailed the conclusion that, in content, the law thus adopted by Congress embraced the reasonableness of separation by race, so long as accommodations were equal. He explained that "congressional inaction left Benson at liberty to adopt such reasonable rules and regulations for the disposition of passengers upon his boat, while pursuing her voyage within Louisiana or without, as seemed to him most for the interest of all concerned." And the record of the case, as summarized by Waite, left no doubt that Benson's rules and regulations required racial separation.[34] Waite, that is, accepted the interpretation which Justice Agnew had elaborated in *Miles*, but again stripped of Agnew's dated rhetoric.

Hall v. DeCuir had even greater effect because of Justice Nathan Clifford's concurring opinion, which occupied twenty-six pages in the official report, compared with just under four pages for Chief Justice Waite's opinion for the Court. Although labeled only a concurrence "in the judgment" of the Court, Clifford's opinion disagreed with Waite's in no important way, but rather supplied a mass of supporting detail, citation, and quotation. One historian has even confused or at least conflated the concurrence with the opinion of the Court.[35]

Clifford surveyed the Court's commerce decisions, described the privileges conveyed by the federal coasting license that the *Governor Allen* ran under, assessed the permissive effect of congressional silence with respect to carrier-imposed commercial regulations, and elaborated the status of reasonable regulations within the common law of carriers. A substantial and favorable paragraph on the *Miles* case concluded with this summary: "it is not an unreasonable regulation to seat passengers so as to preserve order and decorum, and to prevent contacts and collisions arising from natural or well-known customary repugnancies which are likely to breed disturbances, where white and colored persons are huddled together without their consent." Conceding that "[s]ubstantial equality of right is the law of the State and of the United States," Clifford quickly added: "but equality does not mean identity, as in the nature of things identity in the accommodation afforded to passengers, whether colored or white, is impossible, unless our commercial marine shall undergo an entire change." Congress had passed no legislation forbidding separation of passengers; and "in locating his passengers in apartments and at their meals it is not only the right of the [ship's] master, but his duty, to exercise such reasonable discretion and control as will promote, as far as practicable, the comfort and convenience of his whole company." When kindred questions had arisen about segregated schooling, Clifford claimed that state decisions had upheld its reasonableness.

In particular, Clifford dismissed *Coger* as carrying no authority as precedent. On his view, the Civil Rights Act of 1866 and the Fourteenth Amendment only granted Negroes the guarantee of citizenship, thereby reversing *Dred Scott*. The measures did not destroy the freedom from state regulation that the federal Coasting Act conferred on vessels licensed under it.[36]

In *Hall v. DeCuir*, both opinions contained a curious oversight. By 1878, as Louis Pollak has observed, "inaction" did not accurately describe Congress's stance, for the national legislature had passed a new Civil Rights Act, signed into law by President Ulysses S. Grant on March 1, 1875. As quoted earlier, Section One of the new measure guaranteed equal access to public carriers and accommodations.[37] In view of this provision, it may be argued that Waite's majority opinion (if not Clifford's concurrence) should have taken a cue from *West Chester v. Miles*. There Justice Agnew finally conceded that he had announced the law only as it had stood when the case arose, but that Pennsylvania's new civil rights measure would govern future cases.

The historian interested in the roots and significance of *Plessy* may ask how a comparable addendum by Waite would have affected the development of racial segregation in transportation law. Answering the question takes us again to *Civil Rights Cases* (1883) and their background.

A short answer derives from the actual fate of the Civil Rights Act of 1875, which the Supreme Court invalidated in 1883 as exceeding Congress's enforcement authority under the Thirteenth and Fourteenth Amendments. On this analysis, whatever the reason for Chief Justice Waite's overlooking the 1875 Act in his opinion in *Hall v. DeCuir*, the omission only prophesied the measure's historical insignificance.[38]

Such a response suggests a recasting of the question: *If* the Civil Rights Act had withstood constitutional challenge, *then* would its application have legally negated the outcome of *Hall v. DeCuir*?

Here another short answer suggests itself. Because on its face the Act banned discrimination, its effective enforcement *of course* would have outlawed segregation premised on the common-law reasonableness of separate-but-equal accommodations. This answer comes readily because Justice John Marshall Harlan, the dissenter in the *Civil Rights Cases*, almost certainly would have interpreted the Act in this way, had he been called on in 1883 to fashion an opinion that upheld *and* construed the measure. His known views during the 1890s, when he twice dissented from decisions upholding separate-but-equal, indicate that he defined the doctrine as *in*consistent with equality. His dissent in 1883 pointed in the same direction. Noting the Court's earlier comment in *Hall v. DeCuir*, that "if the public good requires such legislation [as Louisiana had adopted in its 1869 equal accommodations law,] it must come from Congress, and not from the States," Harlan portrayed the 1875 federal law as sharing the goal of the invalidated Louisiana measure. In Harlan's view, that is, by *equality* of accommodations Congress had meant *identity* of accommodations.[39]

It is conceivable, however, that Harlan is not a sure guide to how the Court would have construed the 1875 Act, although he himself contended that his brethren agreed with him about its meaning.[40] Evidence from three areas hints that had the law been constitutionally validated, it might not have struck at separate-but-equal.

One source is the majority opinion in the *Civil Rights Cases*. Justice Bradley did not tarry over the question of the Act's meaning and paraphrased its language only to the extent necessary to illustrate that the law unconstitutionally struck at individual acts of discrimination. "Its effect," he wrote, "is to declare, that in all inns, public conveyances, and places of amusement, colored citizens, whether formerly slaves or not, and citizens of other races, shall have the same accommodations and privileges in all inns, public accommodations, and places of amusement, as are enjoyed by white citizens; and *vice versa*." But his use of the phrase "the same accommodations" fell considerably short of entailing a particular understanding or meaning. By contrast, counsel for the Negro plaintiffs in one of the cases being decided had restated the measure's meaning with this emphasis: "The right is to 'full and equal enjoyment' of the *very same* 'accommodations, advantages, facilities, and privileges' . . . ."[41] Also hinting at a restricted reading were the examples that Bradley used to illustrate what the law prohibited. They involved *exclusion* from accommodations, not assignment to separate-but-equal quarters. Finally, Bradley implied, if he did not quite state, that the common law's embodiment of separate-but-equal met the standard of equality mandated by the act. "Innkeepers and public carriers, by the laws of all the States, so far as we are aware," he asserted, "are bound, to the extent of their facilities, to furnish proper accommodations to all unobjectionable persons who in good faith apply for them."[42] Yet by 1883 it was obvious that common law, which was still largely the pertinent law in most states, at least sometimes allowed carriers (and innkeepers) to separate by race.

Lower court rulings contribute a second source of doubt about the meaning that the Supreme Court would have given a validated Civil Rights Act. By the end of 1877, it is true, new case filings under the 1875 Act had declined markedly, owing to lack of federal interest in enforcement and adverse constitutional rulings by trial courts.[43] Several federal judges nonetheless sought to explain the coverage of the Act.

Within two months of the law's passage, Circuit Judge Robert Dick construed its language while charging a federal grand jury in North Carolina. Its guarantee of equal accommodations, he said, duplicated the state's existing common-law guarantees, which

> require[d] innkeepers, common carriers, etc., to furnish accommodations to colored men, equal to those provided for white men, when the same price is paid. . . . Railroad companies may have first class coaches for colored men, and first class coaches for white men. If white men are protected from the intrusion of colored men, colored men must likewise be protected from the intrusion of white men, as the legal rights of both classes are the same. . . . If a traveller gets inn accommodations and comfortable transportation according to the price paid, he has no just cause for complaint, and the innkeeper and common carrier discharge the obligations imposed upon them by the law.

This led Dick to doubt the constitutionality of applying the federal measure within the state. The *law* of North Carolina, by his analysis, simply did not "discriminate against the negroes as a class, or on account of their race."

But Dick recognized the presumption of constitutionality that attached to federal legislation and drew back. "Although the constitutionality of the civil rights bill may be questioned," he explained, "the act cannot properly be regarded as an oppressive exercise of legislative power. It only reenacts the law already in force in this state, and furnishes new remedies . . . ." To reach this conclusion, he had already elaborated his operative and revealing premise:

> Any law which would impose upon the white race the imperative obligation of mingling with the colored race on terms of social equality would be repulsive to natural feelings and long established prejudices, and would be justly odious. There is no principle of law, human or divine, that requires all men to be thrown into social hotchpot in order that their equality of civil rights may be secured and enforced. The civil rights bill neither imposes nor was intended to impose any such social

obligation. It only proposes to provide for the enforcement of legal rights guaranteed to all citizens by the laws of the land, and leaves social rights and privileges to be regulated, as they have been, by the customs and usages of society.[44]

District Judge Thomas H. Duval illustrated a more direct approach to the same conclusion in instructing a federal trial jury in Texas. There President W. E. Dodge and other officers and employees of the Houston and Texas Central Railway Company stood indicted for denying Milly Anderson admission to a ladies' car "for the sole reason that she was a person of African descent." Having explained the citizen's essential "liberty of locomotion," Duval amplified both the ancillary right "that he or she shall be conveyed on and over the great public lines of transportation" and the correlative obligations of common carriers. "This right of the citizen, and this duty of the common carrier," he declared, "is recognized and exists by the common law of the land, and it is only to protect this right, and enforce this duty, that congress passed the [Civil Rights Act's equal accommodations] provision . . . ." Race or color justified no discrimination in passenger assignment. If, however, the car to which Mrs. Anderson had been assigned was equal in every respect to the other car, "and was as fit and appropriate at that time for white female citizens as for colored female citizens," then the railway had not discriminated. Like Judge Dick, Duval accepted separate-but-equal as conforming to the requirements of the 1875 Act, and this view seems to have been the dominant one among lower federal judges who confronted the issue.[45]

Other federal courts simply resorted to common-law standards, ignoring the Civil Rights Act. One such case developed out of an episode along the coast of Georgia in September 1878, after a black woman, Mrs. Green, had boarded the *City of Bridgeton* at Darien, Georgia, on the steamboat's run from Palatka, Florida, to Savannah. Accompanied by her three-year-old nephew, Mrs. Green took a seat on the upper aft deck, which she regarded as the only section of the boat with adequate conveniences for a woman with a young child. The purser nonetheless ordered her to the lower deck. Not wishing to take quarters she regarded as unfit, but unwilling, too, to be ejected forcibly, she left the boat at its next stop. For its failure to carry her properly and for "the pain, indignity and humiliation" she had suffered, she sued the carrier in federal district court.

Falling under the court's admiralty jurisdiction, the suit required Judge John Erskine to determine the governing federal law. He easily found it in *Hall v. DeCuir*, from which he paraphrased Justice Clifford's paraphrase from *West Chester v. Miles*. Racial separation, Erskine wrote, "was not an unreasonable regulation, for it prevented contacts and collisions arising from natural and well known repugnancies, which are likely to breed disturbances where white and colored persons are huddled together without their consent." Nor did separation imply inequality, for equality of rights did not require identity. Here Erskine drew support from Judge William B. Woods's recent ruling on school segregation in New Orleans: "Any classification which presumes substantially equal school advantages, does not impair any rights, and is not prohibited by the constitution of the United States." Confronted with conflicting evidence on whether the lower deck's facilities equaled the upper deck's, Erskine found they did and ruled against Mrs. Green.[46]

A happier outcome marked an 1882 case that originated when the Cincinnati Southern Railway Company denied a ladies' car seat to one Mrs. Gray, instead assigning the Negro and her sick child to the smoking car on its train from Lexington, Kentucky, to Cincinnati. Judge Philip B. Swing acknowledged his uncertainty whether to turn to the Civil Rights Act or to the common law for governing rules, and simply said he would "briefly state the law as applicable to [the case]." What followed was a short summary of common-law principles. Swing allowed that under their right to issue reasonable regulations, carriers "perhaps" had the right to separate by race, if they provided first-class accommodations to those paying first-class fares, but because here the inequality of the assignment was unquestioned, the point did not require resolution. Finding, evidently, that Mrs. Gray had purchased a first-class ticket, and that seating had been available on the ladies' car, the jury awarded her $1000 in damages. This was double the maximum civil award allowed by the federal statute, which further indicates the common-law rather than statutory basis for the action.[47]

Of these two cases, if *Gray* is more satisfying to the late twentieth-century critic because of its outcome, *Green* is the more instructive. Under either standard—separate-but-equal or equality-means-identity—Mrs. Gray stood to win, the inferiority of Cincinnati Southern's smoking car having been well-established. But the condition of the separate quarters assigned to Mrs. Green on the *City of Bridgeton* was in dispute. For her, the stricter standard of identity was more likely to lead to a favorable decision. Accordingly, if the Civil Rights Act would have supported the argument that equality required identity of accommodations, it is difficult to understand why her counsel did not advance it; and the ample discussion of the case in Judge Erskine's opinion discloses no such argument on behalf of the black woman, although the opinion does summarize her testimony stressing the inferiority of the cabin assigned her.

If arguments involving the requirements of the Civil Rights Act did enter into *Green*, the case is noteworthy for another reason. Mrs. Green lost, but it seems likely that in most cases arising under the statute, the weaker separate-but-equal standard, *if* fairly applied, would have produced convictions or civil damages. Exclusion from equal facilities, not separation, was typically the immediate complaint. In the transportation case included among the five cases that the Supreme Court decided as the *Civil Rights Cases*, for example, the aggrieved Negro couple had unsuccessfully requested a separate-but-equal jury instruction, and, had the Act been held constitutionally valid and had other issues not figured into their case, they should have won with such an instruction.[48] Realistically, though, as John Hope Franklin has noted in reviewing enforcement of the Civil Rights Act, the weaker standard "presented new opportunities for evasion."[49]

The legislative history of the 1875 law adds a final hint as to why, even if the measure had survived its constitutional test in 1883, it perhaps would not have upset the *Miles* standard of separate-but-equal as federalized in *Hall v. DeCuir*. Because this is not the place to offer yet another full account of the long journey of the Civil Rights bill through Congress, suffice it to sketch conflicting evidence on the resulting law's "original" meaning.

In 1870, when Senator Charles Sumner first introduced his bill to supplement the guarantees of the 1866 Civil Rights Act, *he* certainly intended it to outlaw racial separation, and so did some of his Republican allies. During the ensuing five years of legislative debate, Democratic opponents, joined by a handful of Republicans, just as surely castigated the bill as having the same object, which they tagged as enforced "social equality" between races.

In the middle were the bill's other Republican supporters. Both genuinely concerned about widespread southern mistreatment of blacks in public facilities, and eager to tap whatever political capital would accrue to their party from renewed fervor over the civil rights issue, these Republicans sought *some* increased federal protections. But the racial incidents they complained of in floor debate largely involved relegation of blacks to clearly inferior facilities. Some of the same Republicans disclaimed any intention to create new rights beyond the common law's requirement of equality; they protested they were not proposing enforced racial mixing. Indeed, the need was not new rights, they asserted, but new federal *remedies*.

Eventually, Sumner's death in March 1874 triggered Senate passage of the bill. House action came only later when many House Republicans found themselves lame ducks after the autumn election of 1874, and hence unencumbered by worries about constituents who cared little for civil rights. Even so, the final Act was shorn of the prohibition on segregated schools that Sumner had so strongly desired. As adopted, the equal accommodations section may have guaranteed more than simply a right of access to equally good facilities, enforceable in federal court, but this interpretation was ensured neither by its language nor by its legislative history.[50]

In sum, the Tennessee editor who in October 1881 defended separate-but-equal railway service as "conform[ing] in every respect to the principle of the civil rights bill, which is not mixed but equal accommodations," did not lack a plausible case and even some authoritative company.[51] It cannot be said with great confidence that constitutional validation of the Civil Rights Act of 1875 would have set transportation law on a course departing from the common-law doctrine that Chief Justice Waite defined in *Hall v. DeCuir*.[52]

IV

Whatever protections would have followed from further enforcement of the Civil Rights Act, its invalidation removed them, and in 1885 the persistence of earlier doctrine was confirmed in a case involving *The Sue*, a steamboat running between Baltimore and the Virginia shore. After purchasing a first-class ticket for a night passage, in August 1884, a black woman of "unobjectionable character and conduct" found herself refused sleeping quarters in the ladies' cabin to the aft of the boat, but assigned to the same deck's forward cabin, which she knew from experience was filthy and without common conveniences. She chose instead to sit up all night in the boat's saloon cabin. In defense of the assignment, the boat's owners, two women, would later claim that by well-publicized regulations, the aft cabin was for white women, while the forward one was for "female colored passengers." The resulting suit came within the admiralty jurisdiction of Maryland's federal district court.

Counsel for the Negro "libelant," or plaintiff in a maritime tort action, argued that as a matter of law the steamboat's officers had *no* right to separate passengers on the basis of race for any purpose, the Reconstruction amendments having made racial distinctions on carriers unreasonable as contrary to declared national public policy. Judge Thomas J. Morris rejected this position "[i]n view of the authoritative interpretations of those amendments." He did not identify the "authoritative interpretations" but probably meant the *Civil Rights Cases* and *Hall v. DeCuir*. The former decision unquestionably interpreted the coverage of the Thirteenth and Fourteenth Amendments in a restrictive fashion, and Clifford's lengthy concurrence in *DeCuir* denied that the Fourteenth Amendment altered Congress's tacit approval of common-law regulations.[53]

The decision accordingly turned on the common-law reasonableness of separation by race on the Chesapeake-Potomac waterway. Morris allowed that "one or two cases have been cited in which such separations have been held unreasonable," but this he attributed to differing circumstances, for the reasonableness of separation could not be maintained where "facts do not exist which give reasons for the separation." But in some circumstances segregation *was* reasonable under common law; "it is not too much to say," he ventured, "that such is the decided leaning of the supreme court of the United States, as expressed in the opinion pronounced in *Hall v. DeCuir*." Paraphrasing although not citing Justice Agnew's disclaimer in *Miles*, he stated, "It is the duty of all courts to declare the law as they find it to be, not as individual judges may think they would like it to be." As for the instant case, testimony indicated the prevalence of segregation "on all the numerous night lines of steamers on the Chesapeake and adjacent water," a practice which complied "with the demand of the great majority of their passengers." Just as passengers' demands for smoke-free quarters established the reasonableness of carriers' rules against indiscriminate smoking on railway cars, widespread sentiment for racial separation created a strong presumption in support of *its* reasonableness.

Finally, though, Morris avoided ruling outright that segregation specifically on *The Sue* met the test of reasonableness, for besides promoting general comfort, separation "must not deny equal conveniences and opportunities to all who pay the same fare." Discrimination by color was a rule "which it must be conceded goes to the very limit of the right of a carrier to regulate the privileges of his passengers, and it can only be exercised when the carrier has it in his power to provide for the passenger, who is excluded from a place to which another person, paying the same fare, is admitted, accommodations equally safe, convenient, and pleasant." The forward cabin for blacks was equally convenient in location, Morris concluded, but otherwise its inferiority was plain. It was cleaned less often, its bed-coverings were seldom changed, and it lacked a stewardess; "no disinterested person would have gone into the forward cabin in its actual condition in August, 1884, who had the option of the other one, quite irrespective of all questions of color or race." The carrier not having provided quarters equal in "comfort, convenience, or safety," Morris awarded damages to the libelant.[54]

Another instance of common-law standards producing an award to a black woman came in North Carolina. White passengers had unceremoniously ejected Elsi L. Britton from a white second-class accommodation, a smoking car, on the Atlantic and Charlotte Air-Line, with no interference from the train's conductor. After the trial-court jury held for the railway, the state Supreme Court announced that separate-but-equal was good law, but found that the trial record disclosed that the railway's officials themselves had conceded that the conductor had orders to allow blacks into the white second-class cars if they insisted on admission. Its enforcement having been optional and thus capricious, the regulation for separation had no validity; Mrs. Britton's right to a seat in the white smoking car was as good as anyone else's. She had a similar right to protection by the railway's agents, particularly when earlier rowdy behavior by whites had warned the conductor to expect trouble.[55]

So, too, in Texas, where Mrs. Lola Houck, pregnant and by outward appearance white, but "with some degree of negro blood in her veins," traveled to visit her sick infant. The train she took had two cars, with the rear one, which she persistently tried to enter, reserved exclusively for whites. "[T]he other, the front car, was known in Texas as the 'the Jim Crow Car,'" wrote Judge Aleck Boarman, summarizing undisputed testimony, "and was for the use of colored people, though white people often rode in it." The train's bootblack having tipped off the brakeman about Mrs. Houck's race, the official artfully managed to keep her locked out of the rear car while letting more whites slip in. Rather than going to the colored car, Mrs. Houck proceeded to ride on the rear car's outside platform, getting drenched in the "ugly, rainy September day." She subsequently fell ill, suffered a miscarriage, and successfully sued for damages.

Reviewing the legal instructions and evidence from her trial, Judge Boarman denied the Southern Pacific's motion for a retrial. True, the company had introduced sufficient evidence about the character of passengers along its Texas route to establish that racial separation was reasonable. But the jury had heard ample testimony to conclude, as Boarman put it, that the Jim Crow Car "was nothing like as comfortable to ride in" as the white car and "was occupied by boisterous passengers, both white and colored, who were smoking and drinking, as is usually the case in such cars . . . ."[56]

Yet the standard of separate-but-equal by no means invariably guaranteed legal redress to blacks. One person learning this was Ida Wells, who in 1883 insisted on a seat in the white ladies' car of a Tennessee train. By statute in 1875, as we discovered in Chapter One, the state had abrogated common-law rights and remedies against public carriers. Then, in 1881, Tennessee had reenacted the common-law standard and remedies in legislation requiring railways to provide blacks paying first-class fares with first-class accommodations equal to those given whites paying the same fare. The latter measure, however, did not change the practice of the state's railways; and as a matter of routine—and of public notoriety—they continued to charge blacks the higher first-class fare and then assign them to second-class cars.

When Miss Wells, a Negro schoolteacher who went on to a career as a civil rights advocate, received such treatment, she sued—with initial success. Although another passenger disputed her testimony about people smoking in the car to which she was assigned, the train's conductor corroborated it, and two trial court judges, one in a magistrate's court and the other in a state circuit court, evidently accepted her version, for they each awarded her damages. But the state Supreme Court held against her when the company appealed and her own attorneys argued her position on separate-but-equal grounds. In effect calling the smoking testimony a draw, despite the lower court rulings, the high court stated, "The two coaches were alike in every respect as to comfort, convenience, and safety; were furnished and equipped alike, and with like accommodations." As the Missouri Supreme Court explained in a similar case, "If the regulation was good and just, no rights guaranteed her were denied."[57]

Robert A. McGuinn, the pastor of a Negro Baptist Church in Annapolis, was another victim of the common-law standard. Having purchased a first-class ticket for passage from Baltimore to Millenbeck, Virginia, on the steamer *Mason L. Weems*, McGuinn boarded and at suppertime took a seat, as directed by a waiter, at a table already occupied by three white passengers. When the whites complained, the boat's captain asked McGuinn to shift to another table and tried to move his chair, but the clergyman demanded that his first-class ticket be honored. The captain then had another table set for McGuinn's unhappy companions and they moved. Later, after several passengers threatened to pitch him overboard, the clergyman sat up all night rather than take a sleeping berth. The next morning he disembarked at a landing prior to his destination.

But had McGuinn been legally harmed? No, said Judge Morris, who reiterated the law as he had announced it four years earlier in *The Sue*. Although in refusing to eat with McGuinn, "a well-behaved, educated minister of the Christian religion," the other passengers displayed "foolish" sentiments, his table accommodations equaled theirs. Regarding the other indignities directed at the pastor, the evidence was insufficiently conclusive.[58]

V

In the late nineteenth century, summaries of transportation law also came from two less traditional but still influential sources. One was the quasi-judicial Interstate Commerce Commission, established through the Interstate Commerce Act of 1887. The other included commentaries and related reference materials used variously within the legal profession.

Created to police discriminatory and unreasonable rates and practices on interstate railways, the I.C.C. briefly buoyed the opponents of Jim Crow. The Commission's potential worth in this regard had received recognition as early as December 1884, during the lame-duck session of the Forty-eighth Congress, when the House of Representatives debated an early version of the Interstate Commerce bill. Congressman James E. O'Hara, a Negro Republican from North Carolina, initially offered an amendment to outlaw discriminatory treatment of passengers holding the identical class of tickets. This passed on a 134 to 97 vote. Although his alteration did not mention race, O'Hara's stated purpose was to strike at racial separation. After other congressmen argued that the amendment only restated the common law and thus would condone railway regulations classifying passengers by race, Clifton R. Breckinridge, a white Arkansas Democrat, proposed a further amendment to ensure the common-law interpretation. This passed, too, 137 to 131.[59]

With opponents of the bill in any form not above tapping a divisive issue, the House then accepted still another round of contradictory amendments. The resulting provision was a farce:

> . . . any person or persons having purchased a ticket to be conveyed from one State to another, or paid the required fare, shall receive the same treatment and be afforded equal facilities and accommodations as are furnished all other persons holding tickets of the same class without discrimination. But nothing in this act shall be construed to deny to railroads the right to provide separate accommodations for passengers as they may deem best for the public comfort or safety, or to relate to

> transportation relating to points wholly within the limits of one State: *Provided*, that no discrimination is made on account of race or color; and that furnishing separate accommodations, with equal facilities and equal comforts, at the same charges, shall not be considered a discrimination.

Eventually no legislation passed prior to adjournment. The law finally adopted by the next Congress omitted any language directed specifically to race discrimination, although its third section forbade common carriers from giving "any undue or unreasonable preference or advantage to any particular person . . . in any respect whatsoever," and from subjecting "any particular person . . . to any undue or unreasonable prejudice or disadvantage in any respect whatsoever."[60]

In its first three years, the Commission heard three disputes under Section Three involving racial discrimination. One pitted William H. Councill, the principal of Alabama's Colored Normal and Industrial School, at Huntsville, against the Western and Atlantic Railroad Company. In the other two, William H. Heard, the pastor of an African Methodist Episcopal Church in Charleston, South Carolina, challenged the Georgia Railroad Company. Both men had held first-class tickets and had been ordered into compartments designated for blacks.[61]

Councill's experience was the more violent. It occurred on a train from Chattanooga, Tennessee, to Atlanta, Georgia, during a trip that had already taken him from Cincinnati through Kentucky and Tennessee on lines that did not separate passengers by race. Councill had taken a seat in the first-class white ladies' car, in which unaccompanied white males were permitted so long as seating was available. Then, without identifying themselves, a Western and Atlantic conductor and brakeman asked him to move to the portion of the train's forward passenger car set aside for blacks as an allegedly first-class compartment. When he stayed put, a white passenger borrowed the brakeman's lantern and, as the assailant later recalled in a deposition, told Councill that

> there was to be no more foolishness, that I did not want to hurt him, but he had to go. . . . I grabbed him in [sic] the collar and struck him over the head with the lantern. I knocked him out of his seat and pulled him out. He fell to the floor and as he raised up he came toward me, and I let him have it again with the lantern. I hit him several times before I conquered him and rushed him right out of the car into the darkies' car. He was willing to go by the time I got through with him.

Heard, by contrast, had gone peaceably to assigned compartments when denied admission to white cars on two different occasions on the Georgia Railroad's Atlanta-to-Augusta run, the second incident occurring *after* the I.C.C. had ruled favorably on his first complaint.[62]

Not surprisingly, in view of Councill's own conciliatory stance on racial issues, which included a commitment to Negro self-help within a segregationist framework, his attorneys admitted the railway's right to classify by race, arguing that the line had failed to meet the concomitant requirement of equality. Heard's counsel went further, claiming that only *identity* of accommodations would guarantee conformity to the requirements of Section Three. The Commission granted relief to each man in the form of cease-and-desist orders to the respective railways; these required the lines to abandon the practice of "furnishing to colored persons purchasing first-class tickets . . . accommodations which are not equally safe and comfortable with those furnished other first-class passengers." In other words, in the interpreting Section Three of the Interstate Commerce Act, the Commission held that the standard of separate-but-equal was non-discriminatory.[63]

In reaching this conclusion, it turned to and quoted existing case law and elaborated what was by the late 1880s a standard version of the doctrine of separate-but-equal, with arguments targeted both at those who would settle for less and those who demanded more. "The undeniable fact of a difference in color," it maintained, "is one for which government and law are not responsible. It exists by a fiat transcending human knowledge, and has existed through the epochs of history." But just as the law could not give "sole regard to the wishes or conceptions of ideal justice of colored persons," it could not defer entirely "to the prejudices or abstract convictions of white persons." Evidence for the reasonableness of a compromise—segregation on terms of equality—came from public life:

> The people of the United States, by the votes of their representatives in Congress, support the public schools of the country's capital city, and here white and colored children are educated in separate schools. Congress votes public moneys to separate charities; men, black and white, pitch their tents at the base of Washington's Monument to compete in the arts of war in separate organizations. Trades unions, assemblies, and industrial associations maintain and march in separate organizations of white and colored persons.

The Commission found, too, as further proof of reasonableness, that regulations for separate cars, "either as a safeguard against disturbance or for other good reasons," were "customary on the railroads of Georgia, Tennessee, and neighboring states." Finally, a close reading of the Interstate Commerce Act was pertinent. Section Three applied to both persons and property, yet no one would seriously maintain that railways could not sort goods for purposes of shipment. Rather, the Act's "fair meaning," for both property and passengers, was "complied with when transportation and accommodations equal in all respects and at like cost are furnished and the same protection enforced."[64]

But evidence disclosed that the railways immediately involved in the cases had *not* met the required level of equal service for both races. In each instance, they had run two passenger coaches, the rear one for white women and their escorts, and open to unaccompanied white males if seating was available. These ladies' cars were modern, with separate toilets for each sex, adequate heating and lighting, carpets, and upholstered seats. The forward cars, by contrast, were combination affairs, the rear half for smoking by both sexes and races, the front part for Negroes of both sexes, with a divider and door between the halves. In two of the three cars that figured into the complaints, physical facilities were distinctly inferior, and in one of them the whole car shared one toilet—"the one necessity of railroad travel which adds to the convenience without contributing to the cleanliness of the car."

In all three instances, smoke invariably wafted into the colored compartment, either through the usually open door to the smoking section or around the partition. There was "about as much tobacco smoke in one compartment as the other." (To many people, the Commission correctly acknowledged, "the fumes of tobacco are peculiarly sickening," and especially to "those unavoidably subject to nauseous sensations like seasickness.") As if that were not serious enough, the Georgia Railroad reversed the designation of the forward car's two compartments on alternative trips, so that each half became successively fouled "by persons who chew tobacco and smoke and expectorate tobacco juice on the floor, and saturate the seats, wall and ceilings with the ordors [sic] and fumes of tobacco." Cleaning between trips effected little improvement. On both of Heard's journeys, whites from the smoking compartment came into the colored compartment to share a drink of whiskey, using the compartment's watercup.[65]

For good reason, then, the Commission noted the irony of southern railway transportation. Blacks were "put in a badly furnished car, popularly designated as the 'Jim Crow car,' of which only half is at their service, with liability to interruption and annoyances," and were asked "to call that equality of accommodations." But the agency's rulings undeniably accepted the compatibility of separation itself with equality, and its position in this respect soon found its way *back* into court rulings.[66]

Separate-but-equal received further currency through resource materials intended for the legal profession in the face of a rapidly growing body of case law. These included not only legal treatises, which summarized and interpreted decisions in specific areas, but also the case annotations that law book publishers and law journals appended to the reports they printed.

One of the leading treatises, by Isaac Redfield, was in its fourth edition by 1869, when it noted that the *Miles* case in Pennsylvania had maintained the legal right of carriers to issue regulations separating passengers by race. But the same right had been denied in other cases, Redfield observed (without naming the cases), and the Reconstruction Amendments "[h]ad been supposed by some to settle this question." Overall, he saw "no sufficient reason why any such discrimination should be made," adding hopefully that

> when the unfortunate animosities growing out of the former existence of
> slavery in the country shall have effectually subsided, it is to be hoped

that any such question will cease to be raised. Persons of the highest culture and refinement, as a general thing, feel less sensitive on this subject than others, and their example will constantly tend to lead others in the right path.

The same comment appeared in the fifth edition, in 1873; but for the sixth edition, issued in 1888, the reviser added an explanatory footnote—the usual method of incorporating changes—which allowed that Redfield had been a poor prophet. Repeating the common formula "that equality of accommodation does not mean identity of accommodation," the note flatly recognized separate-but-equal as authoritative doctrine.

Thomas M. Cooley displayed a comparable shift in outlook as he reviewed tort law. Admitting in 1880 that case law allowed separation, he nevertheless characterized the doctrine as "not so plainly justified." In 1895 he omitted the qualification. (Meanwhile, in 1887–89, he had sat on the *Councill* and *Heard* cases while serving as first chairman of the Interstate Commerce Commission, and had written the headnotes for the report of the first *Heard* case.)[67]

With few or no qualifications, other treatises and commentators recognized the right of carriers to separate by race. An example was Robert Hutchinson's first edition in 1882, which included an especially long footnote singling out the contrary view in Iowa's 1873 *Coger* case as "one which cannot be maintained in light of recent decisions." Annotating a separate-facilities case from South Carolina, Owen Wister similarly interpreted the case law and a few statutes from the vantage point of 1893. He saw "very clearly the history of a national prejudice, and our progress *from* an inhuman and unenlightened attitude *through* an over-sentimental attempt to correct this [during the early Reconstruction period] . . . , *to* a poised and temperate level of common-sense." As evidence of the progress he detected, he explained that by the late 1870s, if not earlier, "courts most usually declare[d] that in any community where the relations between the two races are of such a character that a compulsory herding of them together is likely to result in breaches of the peace or discomfort, in such circumstances it is wise and proper that they should have equally good but separate accommodations." In these views, Hutchinson and Wister had considerable company.[68]

Viewed narrowly, the cases discussed and cited in this chapter may not seem particularly significant. Over a period of about twenty-five years, from the late 1860s into the early 1890s, fewer than twenty-five state appellate and federal decisions endorsed separate-but-equal in transportation where not compelled by statute. By origin none came from courts in Virginia, Florida, Alabama, Mississippi, or Arkansas, while one of the most important—*West Chester v. Miles*—came from a northern state, as did two others. Most of the cases turned on interpretations of common law rather than on arguably more weighty constitutional principles.

Such a view is misleading, however, for it neglects the trend of the cases and commentaries, toward acceptance of separate-but-equal. As a statement of current state public policy, the Pennsylvania Supreme Court's *Miles* ruling (1867) had been reversed by the state legislature even before the pro-segregation decision was handed down. Though technically deciding a narrow statutory issue in *Brown* (1873), the United States Supreme Court likewise displayed obvious impatience with the argument that separate-but-equal was reasonable. The same year, Iowa's *Coger* decision boldly denied that racial separation had a place in post-Civil War America. But *Coger* marked both the peak and, for practical purposes, the end. In 1875, when Louisiana's highest court found transportation segregation conflicted with that state's civil rights legislation, it only set the stage for the federal Supreme Court's landmark ruling in *Hall v. DeCuir* (1878). Whatever limits *DeCuir* had as strict precedent for cases not involving interstate commerce, it provided convincing authority for concluding that American common law recognized the reasonableness of separate-but-equal.

Questions may be raised whether *Hall v. DeCuir* (and *Miles* before it) correctly stated pre-existing common law. The Iowa Supreme Court in *Coger* had not been alone in denying the common-law status of segregation: similar positions had emerged in trial courts and in congressional debates in the 1860s and 1870s, when Charles Sumner and other lawyers flatly held that separation by race was impermissible under the common law. Also questionable was the failure of courts to acknowledge claims that the Thirteenth and Fourteenth Amendments established, as a matter of law, the *un*reasonableness of separation.

But these questions are irrelevant in an important respect: regularly reported case law, as it continued to develop in the field of transportation, accepted separate-but-equal, so long as carriers met certain conditions. Substantial equality in facilities and treatment was one requirement, and company rules mandating separation had to be publicized and generally enforced. Somewhat less specific was the need to show that separation promoted peace, order, convenience, and comfort; in practice this meant evidence about prevalent opinions and customs. Once these requirements were fulfilled, the legal consequence followed that separation was reasonable and permissible. The grip that this version of reasonableness (and of equality) had on jurists was underscored in the systematizing efforts of treatise writers and commentators, who largely came to accept separate-but-equal as the teaching of American courts.

Outside the South, it is true, state common law proved open to modification through legislation. By 1890, at least sixteen northern and western states had enacted equal rights measures, mostly after the Supreme Court had invalidated the federal Act of 1875. Although courts perhaps tended to narrow the coverage of these laws, blacks won cases. Most important, several state courts specifically rejected separate-but-equal accommodations as meeting the requirements of the state Acts.[69]

By contrast, the common-law reasonableness of separation met no comparable legislative challenge within the South. Not only did southern legislatures fail to pass new equal rights laws; existing Acts proved no bar to segregation. In Alabama, for instance, the state railway commission upheld separate car arrangements as meeting that state's statutory requirement of equality. Georgia's Reconstruction-era equal accommodations law received the same twist. (Not without reason, it would seem, several states saw no need to repeal their equal accommodations legislation when they finally mandated separate railway cars by statute.)[70] In short, the decisions favorable to segregation stood available to be tapped; and because they constituted the kind of sources that courts traditionally cited, they were even more readily available than the racist pronouncements found in the literature of contemporary science and social science.

For another reason, too, the case law is important, as Frederick Douglass and George Washington Cable understood. Immediately after the United States Supreme Court struck down the 1875 Civil Rights Act, Douglass recognized that a southern railroad conductor now had more power than the national government: "He may order the wife of the Chief Justice of the United States into a smoking car, full of hirsute men and compel her to go and listen to the coarse jests of a vulgar crowd." In 1888, with Georgia's separate car *statute* still three years in the future, Cable wrote that Georgia, *by law*, forbade integrated first-class railway travel.[71]

Douglass engaged in hyperbole, and Cable misstated the actual content of the law which still governed Georgia's railways in the area of racial separation, but the two men shared an important insight. *De jure* segregation did *not* depend on legislation, contrary to the apparent operating premise of historians who associate it with statutory mandates and then typically go on to argue about the degree of earlier, supposedly *de facto* segregation. True, a great deal of *un*lawful segregation existed on carriers prior to the separate-car enactments beginning in 1887–92—and Douglass's hypothetical example would likely have fallen into that category. This, however, resulted not from the unlawfulness of separate-but-equal but from the failure of carriers to observe the equality portion of the doctrine. In the absence of effective state legislation forbidding it, segregation that met the requirements of separate-but-equal was legally acceptable and those experiencing it had no legal remedies. Without doubt, southern practice varied considerably; and access to accommodations without distinction by race—to the extent it existed— was significant for the traveler. But within the South such access translated into access by leave, not by right.

CHAPTER SEVEN

Plessy Before the
United States Supreme Court

I

The Louisiana courts had given Homer Plessy the decision he needed. The highest court in the state "in which a decision in the suit could be had," to use the language of the United States Supreme Court's jurisdictional statute, had ruled in favor of the validity of a state statute challenged as contrary to the federal Constitution and against "a right, privilege, or immunity . . . claimed under the Constitution." The filings necessary to invoke the federal Supreme Court's jurisdiction on writ of error were complete by the end of February 1893. Yet a decision in *Plessy v. Ferguson* did not come down until May 1896, a delay that would *seem* to demand explanation. In the meantime, the constitutional, scientific, and common-law doctrines surveyed in the preceding three chapters took firmer shape.

One step in presenting the case was quickly accomplished. Within a month of the final Louisiana decision, Albion Tourgée had arranged for former Solicitor General Samuel F. Phillips to serve as co-counsel. Phillips, an old friend of Tourgée, had argued for the government in the *Civil Rights Cases* in 1883 and was now in private practice in Washington, D.C. Besides eventually submitting a brief of his own in *Plessy* and participating in the oral argument before the Supreme Court, Phillips supervised the printing of the record from Louisiana and the brief prepared by Tourgée and James Walker.

Perhaps most important, as an experienced and active practitioner in the capital, he could advise Tourgée on procedure and keep him posted on the case's status before the Court.[1]

Another early decision was to seek an expedited hearing before the Supreme Court. Existing law gave priority on the Court's docket to criminal cases being heard on writ of error, and the Court's own rules of procedure provided for advancement of hearings in such cases on motion of one of the parties, although at the discretion of the Court. Evidence on the decision to seek advancement is skimpy, but in early 1893 Louis Martinet, Tourgée, and Walker seem to have anticipated a hearing by the end of the year and even discussed plans for both Martinet and Walker to join Tourgée in Washington at the time of oral argument. On May 1, however, Phillips advised Tourgée "that it might prejudice the chances for an advance if we made the motion without the concurrence of the Louisiana authorities. The ground[s] upon which we *alone* can press for the advance are not plain." Accordingly, he postponed application until the beginning of the Court's new term in October, "hoping we can secure that cooperation in the mean time." Nonetheless, he anticipated a hearing before Christmas—if the Court finally did agree to advance the case. As late as October, Walker still sought Louisiana's agreement, using an interesting intermediary. But his report to Tourgée was gloomy: "My friend Judge Ferguson of the Crim[inal] Court has had a private interview with the Aty. Genl. in the hope of prevailing upon him to join in our application . . . but nothing has come of it so far."[2]

Whether Louisiana would agree became moot. In late October, probably before he had seen Walker's letter, Tourgée decided "to leave the case to come up when it will and not attempt to advance it." As he analyzed the Court, "Of the whole number of Justices there is but one who is known to favor the view we must stand upon." Four were inclined against Plessy, although argument or public sentiment could make the difference. That left another four who would "probably stay where they are until Gabriel blows his horn." Time had to serve as an ally. Slowly the justices who had ruled against the black race in various cases would change their minds or leave the bench; slowly, too, public opinion might shift. "The Court has always been the foe of liberty," Tourgée reflected, "until forced to move on by public opinion." It had finally accepted needed policies in the *Granger Cases* (1877), upholding regulation of railway rates and grain elevators, and in *Mugler v. Kansas* (1887), validating state prohibition of alcoholic beverages, "because the general sentiment of the country was so unmistakeably expressed as to have an *enlightening* effect." In any event, it was "of utmost consequence that we should not have a decision *against* us[,] as it is a matter of boast with the Court that it has *never reversed itself* on a *constitutional* question." Although Tourgée's reading of history on the last point was inaccurate, it underscored the seriousness of the problem he foresaw. Meanwhile, he thought, a new national newspaper advocating the cause of equal rights and aimed at blacks and whites alike might "get the ear of the country."

The decision to delay represented a distinct change in approach. Knowing Martinet himself would "be surprised to hear" of it, Tourgée put off telling Walker until the Citizens' Committee had given its approval. The Committee raised no objection, however, for earlier in the year it had again reaffirmed Tourgée's "full control" of the case; and so Phillips in Washington did not file an application for advancement.[3]

A hearing in *Plessy* now awaited the Court's normal progress through its docket. Although passage of the Circuit Court of Appeals Act in 1891 had reduced the number of cases coming to the Supreme Court (many cases from federal trial courts now went to the new Courts of Appeals), in the early 1890s about three years still elapsed between the filing of a case and argument, with a decision coming a month or so later. Because the writ of error had been filed at the beginning of 1893, by the end of the year the attorneys could estimate that the case would likely come to hearing no earlier than the October 1895 term of the Court, running into the spring of 1896. By the summer of 1895—on schedule—a hearing appeared probable during the following term, although in January 1896, Phillips concluded that whether the case would actually be reached was *"just upon a balance."*[4]

By then, however, Martinet, Tourgée, Walker, and Phillips all agreed that yet further postponement, at least until after the autumn presidential election, could only aid their case. Martinet speculated that if Congressman James Reed of Maine were the Republican Party's nominee and were "elected by a large majority[,] men's minds on questions of rights might be changed." (Reed in fact had advocated civil rights for blacks, and throughout the early and mid-1890s was an object of Tourgée's correspondence.) But if the Court did reach the Plessy case during the current term, Louisiana would have to cooperate in order to put off the case until the following term, for the Court's rules provided that a case would be heard if *either* party was ready for argument. And the state's agreement seemed unlikely. "I have not the faintest hope," reported Walker on April 9, 1896, "that the Aty. Genl. of La. will accede to the suggestion . . . to put off the Plessy case until next term. . . . [He] is now in the midst of a hot campaign in the interior of the State." Walker's assessment was correct. The Attorney General, Milton J. Cunningham, had already sent the state's printed brief to the Supreme Court in Washington, advising its Clerk that the Court should take the state's argument "on submission"—that is, on the basis of the brief, without Cunningham's appearance at oral argument.[5]

Near the beginning of April, the only serious failure occurred in the coordination of Plessy's case by mail. It was probably on March 28 that the office of the Court Clerk telephoned Phillips that the Court would reach *Plessy* on Wednesday, April 1, or the day after. When Phillips arrived at

Court on Wednesday, he learned that the case would not come to argument (although it might on Thursday). Because he also discovered that Tourgée was not present, he wrote to the lead counsel explaining that his brief addressed some technical points which Tourgée and Walker had not stressed in theirs. Evidently receiving Phillips's letter on Friday, April 3, Tourgée worried less about different theories for approaching the case than about the likelihood that he had missed the oral argument altogether. Shooting off two indignant letters to the Court Clerk, he protested that his clients, "an association of about 10,000 colored men of Louisiana who raised the money to prosecute these and other cases," had been deprived of the counsel they wished, and "I am put in the attitude of neglecting a case over which I have exerted the most scrupulous care and to which I have given years of labor and study." The Clerk had informed the other attorneys about the schedule but not Tourgée, who complained, "Just how you could do this without notifying me I do not quite understand."[6]

Phillips had slipped in not contacting his colleague, for the Clerk's office promptly informed Tourgée that standard practice was to notify only local counsel, when they appeared on a case, and to depend on them to reach any out-of-town associates who wished to take part in the argument. But no matter. Another letter from the Clerk's office, probably arriving in Mayville on the eighth or ninth, brought news that the Court had called but not actually reached *Plessy* on Thursday, April 2; it would be the first case called on Monday, the thirteenth. On April 10, Tourgée boarded the train for Washington.[7]

The case went to hearing on the thirteenth. The Court already had two briefs on Plessy's behalf—one from Tourgée and Walker, and one from Phillips. Whether Tourgée and Phillips engaged in any last-minute coordination prior to oral argument remains unknown. What is certain is that neither Walker nor Martinet participated; Walker's health would not permit a trip to Washington—and he probably could not have arrived in time anyway, which likely also explains Martinet's absence.

The Court also had Louisiana's brief, which was supplemented at the oral hearing with an argument by Washington attorney Alexander Porter Morse. In the absence of firm evidence, it seems at least plausible that Attorney General Cunningham made final arrangements with Morse rather late, probably when he himself decided not to appear, for Morse filed as a counsel of record only on April 1. (The other attorneys had all filed by the beginning of the term.) A native of Louisiana, the new participant maintained an active Washington practice that had included appearances in 1877 before the commission on the disputed Hayes-Tilden presidential election and on two occasions before international arbitration commissions. In the current term of the Court, he also represented Louisiana in another appeal involving a civil rights issue. Morse's written brief, which apparently had not been printed by April 13, came in two days later.[8]

II

The major statement of Plessy's position appeared in the brief submitted by Tourgée and Walker; this included separate sections by each man after a short introduction stating the case, reprinting the assignment of errors, and listing nineteen "questions arising."* Tourgée's portion was the more important, detailing Plessy's chief constitutional claims. But Walker's section contributed significant material; and for the fullest understanding of the case presented against the separate car law, recourse to Tourgée's notes for his oral argument is essential, even though we cannot be certain he covered all his intended points.

Tourgée established his premises by reciting the Thirteenth Amendment and then Section One of the Fourteenth Amendment, which he divided into "affirmative" and "restrictive" provisions. The former provisions comprised the grants of national and state citizenship; and the latter, the privileges-or-immunities, due process, and equal protection clauses. This division, he noted as a preface to what followed, "more readily . . . show[ed] the construction for which . . . [Plessy] contends." His argument then appeared in twenty-three numbered sections of unequal length, labeled "points of plaintiff's contention." These did *not* neatly follow either the assignment of errors or the "questions arising." Taken as a whole, the "points of contention" contained two broad but partially intertwined arguments. The shorter argument began first and emphasized violations of two of the Fourteenth Amendment's negative provisions. The second argument focused on the Amendment's affirmative provisions, as well as the Thirteenth Amendment and the Declaration of Independence. Compared with the arguments of Tourgée and Walker in Louisiana, the affirmative rights argument more clearly revealed the unorthodox thrust of Plessy's case within the contemporary doctrinal climate.[9]

The following pages unravel, synthesize, and assess the case thus presented. The argument is here cast in the form of an extended outline, which has the effect of sharpening certain distinctions that Tourgée and Walker left implicit or only partly developed.

The Restrictive Rights Argument

A. The separate car law violated Fourteenth Amendment rights to equal protection.

1. Despite the state Supreme Court's construction of it, the statute's

---

*To avoid confusion, it needs emphasizing that this was *not* the "Tourgee-Walker brief" submitted to the Lousiana Supreme Court in 1892 and so labeled in Chapter Three, although Walker's section of the brief discussed in the present chapter included large segments lifted from the earlier Louisiana brief.

language exempted train officers and railways from *all* civil liability for enforcing the Act. By so denying a person put off a train his right of action for wrongs committed against him, such as the deprivation of liberty under the guise of an unconstitutional police regulation, the Act denied equal protection of the laws. Moreover, the denial of a right of action to recover damages made the whole Act "null and void" because it was essential to the overall scheme of the law. Without it, companies would not dare enforce the measure. The accuracy of this conclusion about railway behavior was "for the [federal Supreme] Court to determine upon its knowledge of human nature and the conditions affecting human conduct, in regard to which it would be idle to cite authorities."[10]

2. Similarly, when properly construed, the statute gave arbitrary finality to a conductor's decision regarding a passenger's race. As Walker briefly mentioned, this denied to passenger-defendants in criminal actions the defenses that other defendants would have open to them.[11]

3. While the law required railways to provide equal but separate accommodations, in practice the accommodations offered blacks might not conform to that standard. Notwithstanding the Louisiana Supreme Court's contrary construction, the law imposed criminal liability on a passenger who refused to accept a seat assignment, even if the assignment was to an inferior accommodation. (But this claim emerged only implicitly; the pertinent language came in a discussion of the law's true purpose, as a part of Tourgée's later affirmative-rights argument. When Walker implied such a claim, he did so in a largely due-process context.)[12]

4. The law's nurse exemption made the measure, in the words of the assignment of errors, "amenable to the charge of class legislation." (But here, too, an equal protection claim was only implied in the context of establishing the law's real purpose. Still, Tourgée and Walker had used the nurse exemption argument in an equal protection context before the Louisiana Supreme Court, and the record of its action was before the federal Supreme Court.)[13]

B. The separate car law deprived passengers of due process rights.

1. Determination of race was "wholly impossible to be made, equitably and justly by any tribunal, much less by the conductor of a train without evidence, investigation or responsibility." Race-mixing had blurred racial lines, and in most cases actual pedigrees were impossible to determine. In addition, neither federal nor Louisiana law had "define[d] the limits of race—who are white and who are 'colored'?" Hence, the determination depended on the conductor's arbitrary judgment. Nor, as Walker elaborated, did other jurisdictions offer a consistent guide, with Michigan, for example, defining as "negro" a person with no more than three-fourths white and no less than one-fourth Negro ancestry. In North Carolina, by contrast, possession of one-sixteenth or more colored ancestry marked one as a Negro, and in Georgia the required proportion was one-eighth. In one South

Carolina case, a court had held that in doubtful instances, the matter was mostly for the *jury* to decide, "by reputation, by reception into society, and by the exercise of the privileges of a white man." But under the Louisiana separate car law the determination depended on the conductor's arbitrary judgment. Tourgée probably added orally that the information against Plessy was itself faulty on similar due process grounds. By not specifying the defendant's race, it failed to indicate the charge against which he had to defend himself, and neither existing law nor science filled the void.[14]

Several federal cases explored a comparable due process issue, Walker noted. In *Chicago, Milwaukee, and St. Paul Railway Company v. Minnesota* (1890), the Court had invalidated a non-reviewable rate order of the Minnesota Railroad Commission because it "deprive[d] the company of its right to a judicial investigation, by due process of law . . . ." Then, in *Budd v. New York* (1891), it upheld a New York freight rate, noting that the state legislature itself had set the rate after determining it was reasonable. Under the Louisiana separate car law, Walker explained, the conductor's orders regarding seat assignment were comparable to those of the Minnesota commission—final, conclusive, and unappealable to the courts. In contrast to the New York legislature's definition of a reasonable rate, the Louisiana lawmakers had not provided a statutory definition of "Negro." By the doctrine of these and related cases, the law deprived persons of liberty and property without due process.[15]

2. The conductor's arbitrary assignment without due process worked a deprivation of property in the form of reputation. Anyone assigned to the colored car would "inevitably be regarded as a colored man or at least suspected of being one." Whether reputation is a form of property was "for the court to determine from its knowledge of existing conditions," but Tourgée suggested relevant questions:

> How much would it be *worth* to a young man entering upon the practice of law, to be regarded as a *white* man rather than a colored one? Six-sevenths of the population are white. Nineteen-twentieths of the property of the country is owned by white people. Ninety-nine hundredths of the business opportunities are in the control of white people. . . . Indeed, is it [reputation] not the most valuable sort of property, being the master-key that unlocks the golden door of opportunity?[16]

3. The provision allowing a conductor to refuse to carry a passenger who declined to accept the conductor's seat assignment summarily deprived the passenger of liberty without due process, for it denied the passenger access to a place he had a right to occupy. The same provision deprived a passenger of property, for he was "denied the enjoyment of . . . the ticket purchased by him to the point of destination." Such action served "to seize, convert and destroy his property by pretended force of law."[17]

4. The Act deprived persons of their natural liberty to associate with spouses and children by keeping apart spouses of different races, and white parents and mixed children.[18]

An Evaluation

With one exception, Plessy's direct equal protection and due process claims depended on acceptance of the construction that Tourgée and Walker gave the separate car law. But the state Supreme Court had ruled that the exemption from civil damage suits that the law granted to railways did not apply in cases of wrongful assignment. This construction obviated the first and most explicit equal protection claim—that the law deprived a class of people of a right of action available to others. Similarly, the state court had denied that the law imposed criminal liability on a passenger who refused to abide by either a racially incorrect assignment or an assignment to an unequal seat; this undercut the second and third equal protection claims (if, indeed, the third had been intended as an equal protection claim).

The only equal protection claim not arguably negated by the state court's construction involved the nurse exemption, for the state court had not addressed it. Even if this claim were upheld, however, the main machinery of the law would remain operative, for the exemption was not an invariable feature of the southern separate car laws. It is not surprising, then, that Tourgée apparently did not explicitly advance the nurse issue before the federal Supreme Court as a distinct equal protection argument, mentioning it instead to show the true purpose of the statute in connection with his affirmative rights argument.

Tourgée and Walker each put more emphasis on direct due process arguments, but these, too, were weakened by the state Supreme Court's construction of the law. Once the conductor's decision about a passenger's race became, in effect, judicially reviewable, it was no longer final and arbitrary. The process established by the law now accorded with the criteria laid out in *Chicago, Milwaukee, and St. Paul Railway Company v. Minnesota*; and even if Louisiana had no existing statutory definition of "colored," its courts could evolve one through judicial proceedings, just as courts in other jurisdictions had done. So whatever a person might be deprived of pursuant to the law, the deprivation no longer occurred without due process, and the law did not block access to recourse by way of civil suits. True, Plessy's due process claims turned partly on the premise that a person's right to occupy a seat on a common carrier could not be qualified *in any way* on grounds of race, but that was the very point involved in Tourgée's affirmative rights argument. To the extent, that is, that the contention about an unqualified right was essential to the due process argument, the argument turned on a more fundamental issue.

Probably because the restrictive rights argument depended so much on a rejection of the Louisiana Supreme Court's reading of the law, Walker put considerable stress in his section of the brief on the deficiencies of this construction, reiterating the arguments made earlier in the process of requesting a rehearing at the state level. With the same object, Tourgée probably argued orally—by pulling out of context two quotations from earlier cases—that federal courts need not follow state court construction of state laws. But in view of Supreme Court practice, chances were less than slim that the Court would adopt the statutory readings that were crucial to Tourgée and Walker's claims about equal protection and due process violations. With an eye toward that eventuality, Tourgée went on to assert that mandatory racial classification was "still such an interference with the personal liberty of the individual" as to infringe his Fourteenth Amendment "rights as an equal citizen of the United States and of the State in which he resides."[19] That shifted the focus to the second line of argument.

The Affirmative Rights Argument

A. The national citizenship clause, which contains the affirmative provisions of the Fourteenth Amendment, by itself conferred broad positive rights, despite there "hav[ing] been, both on the part of the Court and of textual writers, an inclination to overlook the force and effect" of the clause. The clause bestowed national citizenship on every person born or naturalized in the United States, and conferred "Statal [sic] Citizenship, as *an essential* incident of national citizenship." Because both categories of citizenship derive from federal authority, "[t]he State [was] thereby ousted of *all control over citizenship*," and the rights attaching to each category of citizenship were federally guaranteed. "The United States having granted *both* stands pledged to protect and defend both." The negative provisions of the Amendment's first section, "which are supplemental of the positive ones [that is, the citizenship grants]," further strengthened this guarantee, for they "were not intended to be construed by themselves, but in connection with and as supplemental to the affirmative provisions—[and] taken together they constitute this section [as] the *magna carta* of the American citizen's rights."[20]

B. But even by themselves the negative provisions of the Amendment ousted the states from exclusive jurisdiction over the rights of state citizenship "and establish[ed] the appellate or supervisory jurisdiction of the United States in all matters touching the personal rights of citizens." This was made clear by the construction that the Supreme Court had put on an analogous clause of the antebellum Constitution, the fugitive slave clause, in *Prigg v. Pennsylvania* (1842). On its face, the latter clause only declared that a state could not discharge a fugitive from service due under the laws of another state, but instead must deliver him up; it did not explicitly confer federal judicial jurisdiction. In *Prigg*, however, the Court determined that by virtue of the clause, as Tourgée summarized, "the Courts of the United States had jurisdiction to consider and pass upon the validity of the acts of a State touching the rendition of fugitives from labour—to undo or invalidate all that mig[h]t be done or attempted by virtue of State authority, in regard to the condition of one claimed as a fugitive from labour . . . ." Homer Plessy, wrote Tourgée, "only ask[ed] that the rule of construction adopted . . . *to perpetuate the interests of Slavery*, be *now* applied *in promotion of liberty* and for the protection of *the rights of the citizen*."[21]

C. The citizenship that was so broadly given positive federal protection by Section One of the Fourteenth Amendment had, as its "prime essential" and "very essence," the "*equality* of personal right and the *free* and secure enjoyment of all public privileges." The Amendment put on the plane of equal right all those earlier-recognized categories of persons—citizens, slaves, and "that strange non descript, the 'free person of color,' who had such rights only as the white people of the state where he resided saw fit to confer upon him, but [who] could neither become a citizen of the United States *nor of any State*."

To explore the "equality of personal right" thereby conferred, Tourgée turned to *Louisville, New Orleans and Texas Railway Company v. Mississippi* (1890), where the Court had decided that a state may compel a railway "to provide separate cars or compartments[,] equal in character and accommodation, to be used by individuals of different races," but had explicitly reserved judgment on the question of whether individuals could be compelled to use the separate coaches. "The gist of our case," declared Tourgée, taking advantage of the opening, "is the unconstitutionality of the assortment; *not* the question of equal accommodation . . . ." For if the principle of assortment were allowed on railways, what would prevent its application to citizens elsewhere?

Seeking to demonstrate the absurdity of the result, Tourgée pushed the point:

> Why may it [the State] not require all red-headed people to ride in a separate car? Why not require all colored people to walk on one side of the street and the whites on the other? Why may it not require every white man's house to be painted white and every colored man's black? Why may it not require every white man's vehicle to be of one color and compel the colored citizen to use one of different color on the highway? Why not require every white business man to use a white sign and every colored man who solicits custom a black one? One side of the street may be just as good as the other and the dark horses, coaches, clothes and signs may be as good or better than the white ones.

"The question," he concluded, "is not as to the *equality* of the privileges enjoyed, but *the right of the State to label one citizen as white and another as colored* in the common enjoyment of a public highway as this court has often decided a railway to be." In this respect, there could be no doubt that the separate car law made race per se the essence of a crime, for a man of one race became guilty of a crime by "taking his seat and refusing to surrender it . . . while another person belonging to another race may occupy the same [seat] without fault."[22]

D. The foregoing interpretation of Section One was "in strict accord with the Declaration of Independence, which is not a fable as some of our modern theorists would have us believe, but [is] the all-embracing formula of personal rights on which our government is based and toward which it is tending with a power that neither legislation nor judicial construction can prevent." Because the Declaration had "become the controlling genius of the American people," it "must always be taken into account in construing any expression of the sovereign will . . . ." Consistent with the Declaration's avowal of an inalienable right to the pursuit of happiness, when courts construed the powers of the federal government, they had to give preference to the advancement of individual right and the eradication of caste distinctions.[23]

E. Seemingly contrary language in leading cases interpreting Section One did not negate the claim of an absolute right against racial classification, nor did such language remove the Supreme Court's jurisdiction over the claim.

1. Prior to the adoption of the Fourteenth Amendment, to be sure, "[the] idea that certain phases of personal right were *wholly excluded* from the jurisdiction of the general government, was entirely correct." In fact, the idea "was so unique as to become a sort of feti[s]h in our legal and constitutional thought." But the Amendment gave the Court "jurisdiction to decide whether a State law is promotive of the citizen's right or intended to secure unjust restriction or limitation thereof." This proved such "a shock to established preconception" that in order "[t]o avoid giving full and complete effect to the words of this amendment, the theory of exclusive state control over 'police regulations' was [re]formulated in what are known as the 'Slaughter House Cases' . . . ." The resulting theory regarded the citizenship clause of the Amendment not as a grant of right but only as a definition of citizenship, and construed the negative clauses "as restrictive only of discrimination directed against colored citizens *as such*." But in *Strauder v. West Virginia* (1880), the federal Supreme Court had clarified the earlier interpretation, reading the negative guarantees themselves as conferring on the colored man a positive immunity from discrimination—"the right to exemption . . . from legal discrimination *implying inferiority* in civil society, lessening the enjoyment of the rights which others enjoy, and *discriminations which are steps toward reducing them to the condition of a subject race*." Rightly understood, in other words, even the *Slaughter-House* theory of the Amendment allowed the Court to examine the Louisiana separate car law.[24]

2. But the *Slaughter-House* theory, "viewed analytically, [was] a strange one." The Court had perverted the rule that purpose and intent should be

resorted to in order to explain ambiguities, using the rule instead "to create ambiguities." Despite the clear wording of the Amendment—"every person," "no State," "any law," and "any person"—"the Court arrive[d] at the conclusion that this section was intended *only to protect the rights of the colored* citizen from infringement from State *enactment!*" Yet this interpretation would leave whites at the mercy of blacks should the latter "secure control of certain states as they ultimately will, for ten cannot always chase a thousand no matter how white the ten or how black the thousand may be . . . ." In fact, injuries to southern blacks having "call[ed] attention to possible kindred offenses," the Amendment banned *all* racially discriminatory action, "for one thing is certain, the language used is not particular but universal."

Also, the notion that the Amendment was intended to protect the colored race was "at best only half-true." The idea that states previously held complete control over persons within them—an accurate assessment—had become "the nurse and secure defence of slavery and the excuse and justification of rebellion." Accordingly, the Fourteenth Amendment was aimed at destroying the constitutional base for both rebellion and racial discrimination, and so it was doubly intended to overturn exclusive state control over persons within the states. Finally, "The people of the United States were not building for to-day and its prejudices alone, but for justice, liberty, and a nationality secure for all time." Altogether, then, the correct theory of the Fourteenth Amendment struck at any legislation that "discriminate[d] in the enjoyment of a public right *solely* on the ground of race," whatever the race of the parties against whom the legislation was directed.[25]

3. The decision in *United States v. Cruikshank* (1876), that the Fourteenth Amendment gave no new federal protection to rights associated with state citizenship, ran "squarely against" Plessy's case, but *Cruikshank* proceeded on the same mistaken view of the Amendment. The opinion in the case allowed that it is "the duty of the States to protect all persons within their boundaries in the enjoyment of those inalienable rights with which they were endowed by their creator"; but if the Amendment's first section truly gave no new federal protection against state failure to perform this duty, then the section was "the absurdest piece of legislation ever written in the statute book." After all, apprehension that states in the future might fail to protect the rights of their inhabitants was "the sole reason for the adoption of [Section One of] the XIVth Amendment." If Americans, in adopting the Amendment after a bloody war, intended to leave state sovereignty untouched, "then Carlyle's grim designation of the people of Great Britain as 'thirty millions of people—chiefly fools,' should, when applied to the American people, be amended by leaving out the 'chiefly' and saying 'every last one a fool.'"

Again *Strauder* provided clarification. In it, the Court recognized that the Fourteenth Amendment "prohibit[ed] legislation prejudicial to *any* class of citizenship whether colored or not," and "it [was] but a step farther" to the Amendment's "true construction": equal protection of the laws is not merely "a *comparative* equality . . . , but a just and universal equality whereby the rights of life, liberty, and property are secured to all—the rights which belong to a citizen in every free country and every republican government." The Amendment created "a *new citizenship*" which carried federal protection for the rights associated with it, as became particularly evident when the citizenship clause was construed using the argument of Justice Story in *Prigg v. Pennsylvania*.[26]

4. The *Civil Rights Cases* posed no barrier to review of the Louisiana separate car law. A close reading of Justice Bradley's opinion for the Court revealed that he did not address the issue of the citizenship clause of the Fourteenth Amendment as a grant of right; and regarding the negative or prohibitive clauses he expressly limited his discussion to individual acts, whereas a state law was at issue in the Plessy case. The *Civil Rights Cases* were also noteworthy because Justice Harlan's dissent "formally and distinctly set forth," for the first time, the view that national jurisdiction arises from the rights granted by the citizenship clause.[27]

E. To maintain that the Fourteenth Amendment mandates equality of right did "not impair the 'exclusive jurisdiction' of the State, except as to the *personal rights* of citizens," nor was the construction "open to the common objection that it would require" a national code of police regulations. Rather, this position "merely assert[ed] the right of the Federal Courts to pass upon legislative acts of the States touching such rights and the power of Congress to legislate in regard thereto, whenever it becomes necessary." Similar relationships between national and state authority arose in connection with the Constitution's provisions on bankruptcy, the obligation of contracts, and interstate commerce.[28]

F. Rather than establishing the Louisiana separate car law as a police regulation, the law's true purpose and effect infringed Fourteenth Amendment rights of citizenship.

1. While the police power defied exact definition, no one denied its existence. As the Court stated in the *Slaughter-House Cases*, borrowing language from Vermont Chief Justice Isaac F. Redfield in *Thorpe v. Rutland and Burlington Railroad* (1855), the power

> extends to the protection of the lives, limbs, health, comfort, and quiet of all persons, and the protection of all property . . . [and] persons and property are subjected to all kinds of restraints and burdens, in order to secure the general comfort, health, and prosperity . . . . [O]f the perfect right in the legislature to do which[,] no question was, or, upon acknowledged general principles, ever can be made, so far as natural persons are concerned.

Police regulations would necessarily "to a limited extent affect personal liberty," Tourgée explained, but "[e]very man must surrender something of this liberty for the well-being of the community of which he is a part." Yet, if the Fourteenth Amendment's first "section means anything," it gave the Court authority to review police regulations in order "to determine whether they unduly or unnecessarily interfere with the individual rights of the citizen or make unjust discrimination against any class . . . ." The Court, that is, had to test the true purpose and effect of a contested regulation: did it actually promote "the general health and morals of the whole community . . . [or] merely . . . minister to the wishes of one class or another"?[29]

2. For at least three reasons the Act failed as a valid police regulation under the foregoing test.

First and most obviously, its scope and provisions demonstrated it was not directed toward general public health, welfare, and morals. The statute applied only to railways, but was interracial contact on railway trains more contaminating than in houses, or on streets, or on street railways where contacts were closer and more frequent than on other railways? "And if color breeds contagion in a railway coach, why exempt nurses from the operation of the Act?" The exemption revealed the Act's real goal, which was not "to promote *general* comfort and moral well-being" but "to promote the happiness of one class by asserting its supremacy and the inferiority of another class." Nor could the purpose of the law have been to promote equality of accommodations, because by its plain wording, it attached criminal liability to a passenger's failure to obey a conductor's assignment, whether or not the assignment was to accommodations equal to those the passenger was ordered to leave. Then, too, the Act created *two* crimes, each of which, purely and simply, had race as an essential element: only a black could be convicted of taking a seat in a white car, and only a white could be convicted of taking a seat in a black car.[30]

Second, "[i]n the history of English jurisprudence only slavery ha[d] demanded that distinctions in civil rights or the enjoyment of public privilege be marked by race distinctions." The law's purpose, contended Tourgée, had to be interpreted in light of that history.[31]

Finally, the Court could not ignore "a fact inseparable from human nature, that, when the law distinguishes between the civil rights or privileges of two classes, it always is and always must be, to the detriment of the weaker class or race. A dominant race or class does not demand or enact class-distinctions for the sake of the weaker but for their own pleasure or enjoyment." The separate car law could not have been "an act to secure *equal* privileges . . . [for] these were already enjoyed under the law as it previously existed." The Act's real purpose—"simply to debase and distinguish against the inferior race"—was easily discerned in the label of "Jim Crow car." It was "to separate the Negroes from the whites in public conveyances for the gratification and recognition of the sentiment of white superiority and white supremacy of right and power."[32]

G. The Louisiana law was also void because it conflicted with the

Thirteenth Amendment. By the wording of the Thirteenth, the "slavery" it outlawed was "intended to embrace something more than a state of mere 'involuntary servitude,'" since it used both "slavery" and "involuntary servitude." Slavery had other incidents attached to it besides chattel bondage. Most basically, a slave was a person without rights, whose bondage was to "the dominant class individually and collectively." He had to display not only respect but also submissiveness. The Thirteenth Amendment's purpose "was not merely to destroy chattelism and involuntary servitude but the estate and condition of subjection and inferiority of personal right and privilege, which was the result and essential concomitant of slavery."[33]

An Evaluation

Tourgée's affirmative rights position, based on both the Thirteenth and Fourteenth Amendments, unquestionably struck at the heart of the Louisiana law. Explicating what he and Walker had perhaps intentionally left underdeveloped three years earlier in the Louisiana courts, it transcended technical contentions about rights of action and statutory arbitrariness that largely underlay the negative-rights attack on the measure. If Section One of the Fourteenth Amendment, bolstered by the Thirteenth and the Declaration of Independence, forbade legally mandated racial assortment, then the law *was* invalid; neither strained constructions of its language nor theories about the police power and related "facts" about interracial contact would rescue it. By the mid-1890s, however, existing case law made the affirmative-rights position difficult to maintain; and Tourgée backed away from the position just enough to open his presentation of it to difficulties.

Tourgée had understated the problem when he allowed that courts had shown "an inclination to overlook the force and effect" of the citizenship clause of the Fourteenth Amendment. More accurately, in practical terms the Supreme Court had rejected his interpretation of it. Justice Miller in the *Slaughter-House Cases* had read the clause not as conferring rights but as defining categories of citizenship. While his opinion focused mainly on the rights protected against state infringement under the privileges-or-immunities clause, his conclusion—that the latter clause did not give federal protection to rights associated with state citizenship—was not easily reconcilable with Tourgée's broad claim. Also, a citizenship argument nearly identical to Tourgée's had failed to persuade the Court in the *Civil Rights Cases*. There, it had been Justice Harlan who had advanced it, *in dissent*. Although each set of cases could be factually distinguished from *Plessy*, the result lacked persuasiveness. After all, Tourgée's affirmative-rights position eschewed fine distinctions.

Nor did Tourgée put his affirmative-rights argument on much sounder footing when he suggested that, properly construed, the prohibitive clauses of the Fourteenth Amendment together conveyed an *encompassing* body of affirmative rights. In both the *Slaughter-House Cases* and *Cruikshank*, the Court had construed the prohibitive clauses contrary to Tourgée's interpretation. The twist in *Slaughter-House* that ostensibly saved the Amendment as a protection *for blacks* was of little immediate help, either, for in *Plessy* the record was arguably silent as to the defendant's color. Further, the Court had *never* employed the prewar *Prigg* approach to interpreting the fugitive slave clause as a model for broadly interpreting either the prohibitive clauses collectively or all of Section One. The only colorably apposite use of *Prigg* since the war *in an opinion of the Court* had been in *Strauder v. West Virginia*, to elaborate the basis for the remedial authority of *Congress* with respect specifically to the equal protection clause. The most extensive review of *Prigg* had come from Harlan in the *Civil Rights Cases*—but, to repeat, Harlan wrote in dissent.[34]

Yet a bold application of *Prigg* to the Fourteenth Amendment might have supported Tourgée's position. In the 1842 case, Justice Story had written:

> If by one mode of interpretation [of constitutional language,] the right must become shadowy and unsubstantial, and without any remedial power adequate to the end, and by another mode it will attain its just end and secure its manifest purpose, it would seem upon principles of reasoning absolutely irresistible that the latter ought to prevail.[35]

Attention needed to focus on the source of the Fourteenth Amendment, which came from a people determined to eradicate the inequality of legal right and the caste distinctions that formed the basis of both slavery and the rebellion—inequality and distinctions that threatened to persist even after the formal abolition of slavery. Within such an approach, Section One could plausibly be interpreted to prohibit *all* discrimination based on color.

However, even granting the propriety of applying Justice Story's interpretive mode in *Prigg* to the Fourteenth Amendment, the conclusion that Section One outlawed all racial classification remained no more than *plausible* in the absence of adequate evidence. It was in this regard that Tourgée's broad affirmative-rights argument, *as he developed it*, proved especially weak. He simply did not amass the direct evidence necessary to show that the specific rights created by the Amendment's broad purpose of promoting legal equality and eliminating caste distinctions included a categorical right to freedom from racial assortments.

Perhaps the closest Tourgée came to offering authoritative support for the proposition was in repeating the language of *Strauder v. West Virginia*, that the Fourteenth Amendment conferred on blacks

> the right to exemption from unfriendly legislation against them distinctively as colored; exemption from legal discriminations, implying inferiority in civil society, lessening the security of their enjoyment of the

rights which others enjoy, and discriminations which are steps towards reducing them to the condition of a subject race.[36]

But what constituted "unfriendly legislation" or "legal discriminations, implying inferiority in civil society"?

Answering these questions finally required Tourgée to show that, in its purpose and effect, the Louisiana law degraded blacks. And asking whether it had that characteristic was in effect the converse of another question: Was the law a reasonable police regulation? Did it, that is, promote the health, welfare, and morals of the public? Accordingly, Tourgée went on to argue explicitly that the Act's mandate of racial separation *both* had the real purpose and effect of reducing Negroes to a subservient state *and* could not have been intended to promote legitimate police objectives. He did so by developing internal evidence from the law itself and by citing recent history and human nature, of which, he asserted, the Court must have knowledge. Yet, *having opened the issue*, neither he nor his colleagues examined, in order to discredit, the legal sources and purported empirical evidence that pointed to a contrary conclusion regarding the reasonableness of separation.

III

Samuel F. Phillips put together his brief shortly before oral argument in *Plessy*. After clarifying the procedural status of the case before the Supreme Court and noting that the Tourgée-Walker brief had already treated the case in its "large and very interesting" scope, Phillips's effort addressed a single Fourteenth Amendment issue.

Phillips contended that the separate car law abridged Homer Plessy's privileges or immunities as a citizen of the United States. This resembled Tourgée's argument that the law violated Plessy's affirmative rights of citizenship, but was more focused and examined the clause of Section One that neither Tourgée nor Walker had emphasized. A citizen's privileges or immunities, asserted Phillips, included "making use of the accommodations of even mere intra-state common carriers of passengers without being amenable to police on account of Color," and especially to do so "when such carriers do business to or from places at which the United States has permanent public offices for transacting business with its citizens."[37]

Although his claim rested solely on the privileges-or-immunities clause, the Washington attorney's argument was expansive and even abstruse, but not because of its legal complexity. His presentation largely omitted the legal niceties of case law. Phillips instead focused mainly on three broad propositions: (1) The arguable silence of the record regarding Plessy's color did not bar a constitutional challenge to the law as discriminating against blacks; (2) legally mandated separation constituted legal injury; and (3) among the rights thereby abridged were federally protected privileges or immunities. His development of these rested on allusive bases and used florid prose sprinkled with italics; and overall the brief had a reflexive and perplexing logical structure.

Phillips's initial contention responded to the arguable failure of the record in *Plessy* to establish whether Homer Plessy was white or colored. Assuming for the sake of argument that the Louisiana law abridged the right of a black citizen of the United States by enforcing "an inequality betwixt White and Colored citizens that otherwise is *at most* only a social matter, if at all," Phillips asked whether the law injured Plessy if he were not black but white. Unless it did, there would be no way, prior to Plessy's actual trial (which, it will be recalled, was halted by the appeals procedure), to determine whether Plessy could advance a privileges-or-immunities claim, because if he were in fact white, he would not be convicted under the law for taking a seat in a white car. But even if Plessy were white, Phillips contended, his "constitutional liberty" was "as much offended" as if he were black, for *"it is as much a constitutional privilege and duty of a White citizen to resist any attempt to make him an instrument for enforcing such legal inequality as it is for a Colored citizen to resist being made a victim thereof."* This was a "point requir[ing] no elaboration."[38]

Having disposed of the threshold issue, Phillips proceeded to the second step in his argument, which required establishing that the law created a legal inequality. This, he wrote, was "another proposition that may well be treated *briefly* under the light of those public matters of which a court takes notice." But his treatment of the point nonetheless occupied over a quarter of the space he gave to the privileges-or-immunities question and ranged from an examination of slavery and its legacy to an assertion about human nature and a delineation of the police power.

Slavery, he held, established a base from which to view legally enforced racial separation. The separate car law worked "a distinct disparagement" of a group whose members, because of their color, had mostly been within "the line of the late institution of slavery." The statute "amount[ed] to a *taunt by law* of that previous condition of their class—a taunt by the State, to be administered with perpetually repeated like taunts *in word* by railroad employees . . . ." "Everyone must concede," he wrote, that within society whites as a class occupied the position of Sir Walter Scott's Rob Roy: *"wherever he sate {sic}, was the head of the table."* But when law confirmed "social usage," it established "a pernicious *down-grade*." Nor was the tendency mitigated by the physical equality of accommodations, for "[w]hatever legally disparages and whatever is incident to legal disparagement is offensive to a properly constituted mind." This result flowed from "the most unchanging and most honorable principles of human nature . . . [which] agitate and, when occasion arises, *determine* all bosoms, from Saxon to Sepoy."[39]

Nor did classifying the statute as a police measure rescue it from the charge of inflicting legal injury. Like "fraud," "police" was "not susceptible of exact definition," but it was "certain that Color no more brings men within the operation of the laws of *police* than of those of *fraud.*" As for common carriers, existing law embodied a community judgment that "All men who comply with reasonable police and certain conditions arising from more or less expensive accommodations [shall] travel together . . . ." As an extension of the community, that is, common carriers put the traveler in the position of "a social being."

As a result, in their amenability to police regulations, carriers *differed* from the institutions of marriage and the family. The fate of future generations rested with these latter institutions, which meant that "[w]hether therefore [the] two races shall intermarry, and thus destroy both, is a question of police, and being such, the *bona fide* details thereof must be left to the legislature." Similarly, education was a task associated with the upbringing of children by parents; if "government steps in and takes the matter into its own hands, no constitutional objection upon mere general grounds can be made to provisions by law which respect, so far as may be, a prevailing parental sentiment of the community upon this interesting and delicate subject." These distinctions led to Phillips's conclusion: "*Separate cars*, and *separate schools*, therefore come under different orders of consideration." The permissibility of the separation in the second area did not establish the case for it in the first.[40]

In thus arguing that statutory separation of the races legally injured the black race, what had Phillips offered in proof? In reality, not much. Instead, he had asked the Court itself to supply the warrant for his assertions, by taking judicial notice both of the association between separate car laws and slavery and of tendencies in human nature.

His approach to denying that race was a legitimate classification in police regulations relating to common carriers was also problematic. For one thing, his description of the duties of carriers rested on their alleged common-law obligations and did not address the objection that common law was open to statutory modification. Beyond that, it may have made argumentative sense to concede that racial separation in schools was perhaps legitimate and then to contend that schools were institutionally distinguishable from carriers. Yet regarding his description of the common-law duties of carriers themselves, Phillips made no attempt to distinguish or criticize the substantial body of contrary case law, except for this elliptical comment (which had appeared before he even reached the police issue):

> We submit that there are opinions in some courts which go utterly astray in reckoning the "conveniences" of Colored cars as compensation for injury to that spirit of the free citizen which "THE PEOPLE OF THE UNITED STATES" must have anticipated as to arise and to be fostered in the breasts of those whom they generously associated with themselves by the late Amendments . . . .[41]

And that comment created an additional difficulty: in the course of attempting to show that a separate car law injured blacks, he assumed, without arguing the issue, that such an injury implicated *federally* protected rights.

Not until the third section of his argument did he explicitly explain why the right for which he contended fell within the privileges or immunities of citizens of the United States. Here his point of departure was the *Slaughter-House* doctrine of citizenship, which he accepted (without actually mentioning *Slaughter-House*) as sufficient to cover Plessy's case. He admitted, that is, that for the protection of certain civil rights "citizens even of the United States must ordinarily resort to the states," while other rights received federal protection.[42] Among the latter was a right of intrastate travel, so "that for citizens of the United States any State statute is unconstitutional that attempts, because of personal Color[,] to hinder, even if by insult alone, travel along highways, between any points whatever."[43] But what was the basis of this right?

Initially the Court had to recall the broad purpose of the Fourteenth Amendment and, specifically, "what the expression, '*We, the People of the United States*,' signifies, for all persons therein included . . . ." Put differently, the Plessy case required "certain high officers of the Government created by the 'People of the United States' . . . to '*sight back*,' as it were, upon such creators, and determine judicially their [the creators'] position within *the survey*: their 'privileges and immunities,' one or both." Without *explaining* how the assertion followed from such a "sighting back," Phillips then averred that the United States could not permit race "to become a ground of legal disparagement . . . unless with a disparagement of itself."[44]

Phillips next analyzed the two cases sanctioning "constitutional principles . . . that perhaps [came] nearest to the one in question" in *Plessy*. The first was *Washington, Alexandria, and Georgetown Railroad Company v. Brown* (1873). In early 1868, as elaborated in Chapter Six, Mrs. Catherine Brown had successfully sued the railway company for having been assigned to a separate-but-equal coach for blacks, and the Supreme Court affirmed the award in her favor on grounds that the company's 1863 congressional charter prohibited the exclusion of blacks from its cars. To interpret racial separation as falling within the statutory ban on exclusion, the Court in *Brown* drew on "the temper of Congress" in 1863. It thereby eschewed a "plodding," technical approach to statutory interpretation, argued Phillips. The Supreme Court in 1896 should similarly note that the Reconstruction Amendments "embodied and rendered permanent the public temper of that day, . . . amply replacing that 'temper of Congress' discernible, as the Court said, in the statute of 1863." By this extension, then, the *Brown* case supported the conclusion that Louisiana's law constituted a legal injury forbidden by the Fourteenth Amendment.[45]

The other case was *Crandall v. Nevada* (1868), which had invalidated a Nevada state tax of one dollar on each person leaving the state. This impermissibly infringed the right to travel that a citizen necessarily held in order to avail himself of the protection and services of the federal government, a "right [which] is in its nature independent of the will of any State over whose soil he must pass in its exercise." Although *Crandall* involved *inter*state travel, Phillips read its reasoning as applying to *intra*state travel as well: not only did both its wording and Justice Clifford's concurrence verify this, but also it was "impossible to hold that the United States protects ([*e.g.*]) a citizen of the United States resident in Mississippi during transit to their [*sic*] court-house, post-office, etc., in New Orleans, but does not protect a like citizen resident in Louisiana during similar transit." Pursuing the argument, Phillips reminded the Court that there were federal offices in New Orleans and a United States post office in Plessy's intended destination of Covington, Louisiana. The record did not reveal if Plessy had stated he was journeying to a federal office, but because the separate car law extended to *all* intrastate travel, it necessarily impinged on the federal right in question. The Supreme Court had held in analogous cases that it could not cure defects in criminal laws by adding words of limitation through judicial construction.[46]

If a separate car statute in fact hindered intrastate travel of persons in their capacities as United States citizens, Phillips's discussion of *Crandall* advanced his argument, but neither *Crandall* itself nor Phillips's discussion of it addressed this key issue. His argument about *Crandall* instead drew implicitly on his discussion of what constituted legal injury as established by *Brown*. Yet when he had said that the principle of *Brown* "c[a]me nearest to the one now in question," he in effect admitted that *Brown* did not quite fit *Plessy*. Rather, the Court itself would have to expand on or infer from *Brown* in order to conclude that the statutory requirement of separation equated with constitutional injury under the privilege-or-immunities clause.

In praising the Court in *Brown* for avoiding a "plodding" approach and instead deciding the case in keeping with Edmund Burke's "celebrated aphorism" that "[a] great empire and little minds go ill together," Phillips was clearly asking the present justices to do the same in *Plessy*. He reiterated the call to statesmanship when, in closing, he urged that a solution "place[d] . . . upon the broadest ground" was preferable to a resort to technical analysis of prior cases (as he had just done in discussing *Crandall*, for the first and only time in the brief). Just as the second step in his argument, exploring how legal separation equated with legal injury, had employed little actual evidence and avoided a discussion of case law, so his analysis of *Brown* largely avoided a positive attempt to deny contrary interpretations. Detailed analysis, Phillips seemed to join Tourgée in saying, would trivialize the great privilege of United States citizenship to which Plessy laid claim. But to a mind inclined toward technical legal argument, Phillips could be seen as simply assuming what he had to prove, in order to avoid issues whose investigation would not help his case.[47]

In the end, after three less-than-distinct stages, Phillips had reached a conclusion that, as presented, was mainly self-evident, with the attendant difficulty: it carried little or no persuasiveness unless one perceived its self-evident truth.

IV

The main argument on behalf of the separate car law—and formally in support of Judge Ferguson—came in the brief by Louisiana Attorney General Cunningham. This duplicated verbatim the brief that Lionel Adams had filed in 1892 before the Louisiana Supreme Court, with two additions. One was the opinion in *Ex parte Plessy*. Cunningham explained its inclusion by observing, perhaps accurately, that the unexpected notice that the Supreme Court was about to reach *Plessy* had not permitted him to prepare a separate defense of Judge Ferguson's denial of Plessy's plea to the jurisdiction. But fortunately, Cunningham advised the Court, the state Supreme Court's opinion "thoroughly cover[ed] the grounds presented in the case." The only original addition to the brief was a short discussion, little over a page in length, of the problems of classifying persons by race.[48] Because Cunningham's presentation took this form, only a few aspects of its thrust and specific details need highlighting here.

To defend the broad scheme of the separate car law, Cunningham relied on the authority of the *Civil Rights Cases* to deny almost summarily any Thirteenth Amendment violations. He made no concession to the claim that Louisiana relied on a portion of Justice Bradley's discussion which focused on individual actions rather than on legislative enactments. Giving more attention to the Fourteenth Amendment, the brief contended that it required only that states not legislate inequalities in right, but consistent with this restriction they could assort individuals by race pursuant to the police power. Some sixteen cases, plus references to legal encyclopedias and treatises, bolstered the argument. In this regard, the brief was imprecise, if not actually misleading, for it did not examine whether the cited sources involved *constitutional* challenges to racial classifications, nor did it specify if the classifications in question had been made pursuant to statutes or non-statutory regulations. In any event, the brief employed the material in order to indicate that at least some evidence existed to support the conclusion that racial classification in public facilities promoted public health and morals. Cunningham allowed, though, that the United States Supreme Court had never answered the precise question posed by *Plessy v. Ferguson*.[49]

To deflect specific equal protection and due process challenges, the brief relied on the Louisiana Supreme Court's construction of the law. Because, as thus construed, the law did not exempt railways or train officials from liability for civil damages in cases of incorrect assignment, the exemption provision did not deny equal protection through restricting a right of action available to other parties. Because of this same construction, plus the state high court's conclusion that criminal liability did not attach to a passenger's violation of an incorrect seat assignment, the law did not deprive a passenger of liberty or property without due process. Overall, then, the state denied Tourgée and Walker's argument that subsequent legal exoneration or a damage award could not rectify a non-complying passenger's initial loss of liberty and/or property.[50]

Also vitiating Homer Plessy's due process claims, according to the brief, was the consideration that a conductor's decision about a person's race was not arbitrary because, in most instances, race was readily apparent. And in those few instances in which "it would be hard to tell the difference between a negro and a white man," a form of judicial review was available. It was *only* in exploring the claim of arbitrariness that Cunningham incorporated new material. As we have seen, Tourgée and Walker had argued that the separate car law imposed a judicial duty on railway officers when it required them to assign passengers by race, for a decision as to a person's race involved a complex question of law and fact. But Cunningham countered that other parties "similarly situated" had maintained the opposite, "that every man must know the difference between a negro and a white man, [and] that the exercise of judgment is not necessary to determine the question . . . ." This contrary claim, he alleged, had come in several cases contesting state jury selection procedures, as part of an argument "that men must be put on juries because they are negroes."

The argument had the virtue of novelty, but otherwise had little to recommend it. To begin with, of the five jury-selection cases cited in the brief, in only one—*Virginia v. Rives* (1880)—did counsel for the Negro defendant claim that blacks had actually to sit on grand and petit juries in order to meet the requirements of the Fourteenth Amendment's equal protection clause. In other repects, the issue of who was a Negro simply did not arise in the cases. Although differing in factual detail and in the legal remedies sought, they involved the assertion that the *policy* of systematically excluding Negroes from jury service, whether by statutes or judicial practice, abridged the rights of Negro defendants. No need arose in them to determine whether a very few blacks had served as a result of mistaken racial identification. This hardly bolstered Louisiana's contention that, "as a rule, there is no question as to which race a man belongs, [and] it requires no exercise of judicial powers to determine that question . . . ."[51]

The second brief supporting the state's position came from Alexander Porter Morse and was filed two days *after* the oral argument. It responded specifically to the claim in Samuel Phillips's brief that the separate car law abridged Plessy's privileges or immunities as a United States citizen. Although no model of clarity, Morse's brief was less convoluted than Phillips's, and its specific assertions were more identifiable and more clearly and conventionally tied to standard legal authorities, with the exception of one foray into contemporary history and sociology.

As his basic premise, Morse maintained that the Fourteenth Amendment did not diminish the police powers of the states. He found this proposition in several Supreme Court decisions, beginning with the *Slaughter-House Cases*, and put especially well in *Barbier v. Connally* (1885): "[N]either the amendment—broad and comprehensive as it is—nor any other amendment, was designed to interfere with the power of the State, sometimes termed its police power, to prescribe regulations to promote the health, peace, morals, education, and good order of the people . . . ." In the process, he omitted the clear implication of the *Slaughter-House* majority that, if nothing else, the privileges-or-immunities clause did forbid police regulations that discriminated against blacks. But Morse could make the omission without too much violence to constitutional accuracy, because he allowed that *reasonable* police regulations must neither mandate inequality of treatment nor discriminate on the basis of color.[52]

Was classification by race a reasonable means of attaining police objectives, or did it constitute an impermissible act of discrimination? Morse admitted that the Court might not have full knowledge of "[w]hat considerations of public policy, or order, or well-being, or comfort of the travelling community may have led to the enactment of this statute," but it could take "judicial notice" of conditions in Louisiana and find "sufficient reason to presume that existing conditions justified the legislature in its enactment." One consideration was that the numerical imbalance of races in rural areas produced a "danger of friction from too intimate contact." The street-railway exemption offered corroboration of the legislature's sensitivity to the nuances of race-mixing, for in more heavily settled urban areas the races were more numerically equal, they "employ[ed] a more advanced civilization," and they were less likely to display a similar "danger of friction." In short, Morse contended (without quite saying so), racial prejudice created dangers that separation would mitigate.

The very terms of the law, the argument continued, met the tests of equal treatment and non-discrimination. On its face, the measure required equal accommodations, and "if discrimination there was, from the fact that separate cars were provided for white and colored persons, it applied [as] equally to white as to colored persons."[53]

As for Phillips's flat denial that color constituted a "ground for discipline or for police," Morse took two approaches. He first focused on the two cases which Phillips contended came closest to supporting his contention that the privileges-or-immunities clause banned racial separation on public carriers. Easily (if not adequately) distinguishing them, Morse observed that *Brown* turned on statutory construction and *Crandall* involved an interstate commerce issue. Actually, Phillips had cited *Brown* for the broader purpose of suggesting that the framers and ratifiers of the Fourteenth Amendment acted in an intellectual context that associated separation on racial grounds with the forbidden policy of exclusion. Admitting that the tax which had been contested in *Crandall* applied to interstate travel, Phillips had noted that in its opinion the Court had declined to rely on the interstate commerce clause, but instead had fashioned a constitutional right of personal travel for national purposes. Arguably more pertinent to defeating a claim based on *Crandall*, Morse contended that the Louisiana separate car law did not impede access to offices of the federal government.[54]

Morse's second approach was to misstate and then criticize one of Phillips's claims. As we have seen, Phillips portrayed the educational system as an extension of the institutions of marriage and the family, and hence perhaps amenable to racial assortment if parental sentiment ran in that direction, and then had written: "*Separate cars*, and *separate schools*, therefore come under different orders of consideration." Morse lifted this sentence out of context and construed it as juxtaposing (a) marital and family relationships against (b) both carriers *and* schools. With no difficulty he cited instances where Negro children were required to attend separate schools. Having thereby refuted Phillips's alleged (but non-existent) contention that assortment by color had never extended to schools, Morse had falsified Phillips's alleged (and again non-existent) conjunctive assertion about carriers *and* schools, and he could claim (however dubiously in point of logic) that the reasoning which warranted prohibition of interracial marriages seemed to apply as well to carriers.[55]

This attack prepared the way for extending the argument. Morse averred that in cases involving schools and other public facilities, including railways, courts had positively endorsed the principle that separation was "justified *on grounds of public policy and expediency*, whether this separation be provided for by legislative or municipal authority." Judges, he maintained, had found that authorities at the state or local level could more perceptively assess the need for a policy of separation. Moreover, in the anti-miscegenation case of *Pace v. Alabama* (1883), the United States Supreme Court had recognized the legitimacy of police legislation that took account of color; and in *Hall v. DeCuir* (1878), the Court had granted "that, to some extent at least and under some circumstances, such a separation is allowable at common law." As a capstone, Morse accurately observed that Congress had sanctioned separate schools in the District of Columbia in legislation passed in 1862, 1863, 1864, 1866, and 1873.

In the course of misconstruing and attacking Phillips's denial that the police power extended to racial separation on public carriers, Morse avoided the inaccurate claim that his own authorities had *all* reached Fourteenth Amendment issues in upholding separation, but he made no effort, either, to clarify that they had not all done so. Less artfully, he suggested that legislatively mandated separation had been upheld in several cases. Actually, he cited only one case—*Louisville, New Orleans and Texas Railway v. State,* decided by the Mississippi Supreme Court in 1889—that involved legislated separation; and, as we have seen, it dealt not with mandatory passenger assignments but only with requiring railways to provide separate cars. Still, however misleading and even wrong in detail, Morse's argument effectively punctured Phillips's implication that American law had never condoned racial separation on carriers as a means of promoting police objectives.[56]

Neither side's argument was free from difficulty. The core position advanced on behalf of Plessy, which substantially echoed Justice Harlan's dissent in the *Civil Rights Cases*, was a wide-ranging claim for national protection, under the Fourteenth Amendment, of all the rights protected prior to the Civil War by either state or federal governments, *plus* national protection of any other rights inferable from the Declaration of Independence and the Thirteenth Amendment. Resting their case ultimately on a color-blind Constitution and a radical understanding of the Reconstruction Amendments, Plessy's counsel also played on the ambiguity of scientific and legal definitions of race, but in the end argued that race itself was irrelevant to the determination of right, as a matter of law. Yet, by offering their own interpretations of human nature and by addressing the police power issue, they compromised their implicit denial of empirical "fact" as a relevant consideration for the Court. Further weakening their position, they relied on explicit and implicit rejection of prior Supreme Court decisions and widely accepted common-law doctrines; and their most conventional claims under the Fourteenth Amendment's restrictive clauses rested on a construction of the separate car law that the Louisiana Supreme Court had rejected.

Louisiana's case was flawed by a few strained interpretations of prior constitutional decisions, and it never grappled successfully with Albion Tourgée's challenging reading of the true meaning of the recent Amendments. By and large, however, it rested on existing case law—both constitutional and non-constitutional—and whatever legal deficiencies the non-constitutional cases had as precedent were mitigated by the consideration that within the state's argument they did not serve as precedent. The case benefitted, too, from the Louisiana Supreme Court's construction of the statute. Overall, Judge Ferguson's side of the argument possessed the persuasiveness of orthodoxy.

CHAPTER EIGHT

The Court Decides:
Jim Crow Affirmed

I

On May 18, five weeks after oral argument, the Supreme Court handed down its decision, voting seven-one to uphold the Louisiana's separate car law. The majority opinion came from Justice Henry Billings Brown, a native of Massachusetts who had been appointed to the Court in 1890 by Benjamin Harrison after a career as lawyer, Republican politician, and federal District Court judge in Michigan. Justice John Marshall Harlan provided the lone negative vote and filed a dissenting opinion.[1]

Brown was "preeminently a pragmatist," observes Robert J. Glennon, the most incisive analyst of his judicial philosophy, and he generally supported state police legislation. In 1898, for example, two years after the *Plessy* decision, he received national attention for his majority opinion in *Holden v. Hardy*, which upheld Utah's eight-hour law for miners as a reasonable police measure. There Brown described law, including the constitutional law of the Fourteenth Amendment, as "to a certain extent a progressive science." The Court, he advised, should keep this consideration in mind in order to avoid construing the Constitution in ways that "deprive the states of the power to so amend their laws as to make them conform to the wishes of the citizens as they may deem best for the public welfare without bringing them into conflict with the supreme law of the land."

Although historians properly look with suspicion upon after-the-fact pronouncements, Brown's comments in *Holden* fairly represent his earlier commitments. In Chapter Four, we saw him accord a strong presumption of constitutionality to the New York police measure involved in *Lawton v. Steele* (1894). On other occasions he had accepted limits on corporate power and even supported municipal ownership of utilities. When the Court invalidated a 2 percent income tax in the *Pollock* case (1895), Justice Field railed against the measure's socialistic implications, but Brown was one of the dissenters who voted to uphold it.

His pragmatism also emcompassed a ready acceptance of the dominant predilections of the late nineteenth century. Women, Indians, blacks, and Jews had slight standing in his universe. When Brown used the phrase "blood will tell" in his address to the American Bar Association's annual meeting in 1893, it was not just a convenient cliché. Not least as background to *Plessy*, he had participated in the reform-minded American Social Science Association and evidently took more than a passing interest in current scientific and other intellectual developments.[2]

Although usually a solid if unimaginative legal craftsman, Brown wrote an opinion in *Plessy* which was, to put it charitably, obscure. With ample reason, Robert Glennon has called it "remarkably obtuse."[3] But Brown's own intellectual orientation, along with the broader legal and intellectual context of *Plessy* developed in the preceding chapters, offers a point of departure in deciphering his handiwork—an effort which requires a rearrangement and reconstruction of segments of his opinion. The sympathetic reading which results does not equate with ultimate acceptance of Brown's position, yet it offers an alternative to simply recounting his obscurities. The approach is warranted, moreover, because Brown's most obvious failings in *Plessy* turn out to be fairly easily rectified into an exposition that legally was largely unexceptionable within the context of 1890s. And when his opaqueness is clarified, fundamental difficulties become more apparent.

II

Brown's statement of the case was direct. If not so favorable as Plessy's counsel could have wished, it did not ignore the "fact" that was central to part of their argument. Neither the information against Plessy nor his plea in Criminal District Court averred his color, Brown related, and the information only charged him with "going into a coach used by the race to which he did not belong." Nonetheless, Brown acknowledged, Plessy's petition for a writ of prohibition had asserted that the defendant was an octoroon in whom "the mixture of colored blood was not discernible." Brown also recounted the version of Plessy's arrest and incarceration that Tourgée and Walker had included in the petition to Louisiana's high court.[4]

As for the claim that the Louisiana law violated the Thirteenth Amendment, Brown responded tersely. The absence of constitutional conflict, he wrote, was "too clear for argument." Although on its face this seemed but a capsule summary of his subsequent discussion, the statement was actually more of a premise, for his ensuing comments skirted any serious attempt to grapple either with Tourgée's argument based on the Thirteenth Amendment or with Justice Harlan's similar contention in dissent. Brown equated "slavery" with "involuntary servitude," which entailed "a state of bondage [,] the ownership of mankind as a chattel, or at least the control of the labor and services of one man for the benefit of another, and the absence of a legal right to the disposal of his own person, property and services." Its abolition, then, presumably conveyed a legal right to the disposal of one's own person, but Brown did not extend the right to include freedom from badges of servitude. Quite the contrary, on the authority of the *Slaughter-House Cases*, he found that the need for passage of the Fourteenth Amendment was evidence of the Thirteenth's limited scope. Similarly, he wrote, the *Civil Rights Cases* ruled out refusal of accommodations as falling within the Thirteenth Amendment's ban—despite the fact that the section of Justice Bradley's 1883 opinion which he paraphrased and quoted pertained to *individual* acts of discrimination, not to legislatively mandated separation.

References to *Slaughter-House* and the *Civil Rights Cases* were ultimately less important to Brown's disposal of the Thirteenth Amendment than was the difference between a *distinction* and a *discrimination*:

> A statute which implies merely a legal distinction between the white and colored races—a distinction which is founded in the color of the two races, and must always exist so long as white men are distinguished from the other race by color—has no tendency to destroy the legal equality of the two races, or to reestablish a state of involuntary servitude.

The legal distinction embodied in the Louisiana law hence created no inequality, because, in view of the undeniable difference in color between the races, it was not an unreasonable distinction—or such is the implicit conclusion that gives sense to the argument.[5]

Brown's Thirteenth Amendment presentation emerges as incomplete in itself, for it stopped short of *explaining* the permissibility or reasonableness of "mere" legal distinctions based on color. This came only later, in the discussion of Homer Plessy's Fourteenth Amendment claims. Brown put off the issue by remarking: "Indeed, we do not understand that the Thirteenth Amendment is strenuously relied on by . . . [Plessy] in this connection"—which was only partly true. To be sure, Phillips had pushed the Amendment aside in his brief; but *his* explicit concern had been the Fourteenth Amendment's privileges-or-immunities clause, and he referred the Court to the arguments of Tourgée and Walker on other issues. It was Tourgée who had elaborated the Thirteenth Amendment claim, giving it a little over two pages out of thirty-one. If such attention hardly constituted an *emphasis*, nothing in Tourgée's comments indicated the Thirteenth Amendment was peripheral in importance. Rather, its guarantee merged with and was cognate to the freedom affirmatively guaranteed by the Fourteenth's citizenship clause.[6]

III

The bulk of Justice Brown's opinion addressed Plessy's Fourteenth Amendment claims, with a passing and brief exploration of an interstate commerce issue. Because the presentation was convoluted, an initial overview is useful.

The argument had this sequence:

(1) Brown began by considering the broad objectives of the Fourteenth Amendment and asked whether separation by race, on terms of equal-but-separate, was generally consistent with them. He found it was, but his explanation depended crucially on claims he did not elaborate until nearly the end of his opinion, in step five. Within step one itself, Brown delved into case and statutory law on school segregation.

(2) Next, he detoured to determine limits that other decisions (including a commerce case) placed on the application of separate-but-equal, and concluded that Louisiana's law fell within the limits.

(3) Brown then returned briefly to his main line of argument by asserting—quite inaccurately—that existing case law affirmed the *constitutionality* of legislatively mandated transportation segregation.

(4) He detoured a second time, to explore and dismiss several charges against the details of Louisiana's separate car law.

(5) Returning again to his main argument, he elaborated his broad conclusion that separation by race on railways was a valid exercise of the police power, consistent with the Fourteenth Amendment, and defended it against the charge that racial segregation was an arbitrary or unreasonable exercise of legislative authority contrary to the Amendment. This fifth step depended partly on evidence presented at the end of step four, his second detour. Step five also contained material crucial to his argument in step one that separation was generally consistent with the Fourteenth Amendment.

(6) Finally, Brown noted that although final resolution of Plessy's case *in Louisiana* might require determination of Plessy's race, definition of race was an issue of state law that was not before the Supreme Court.[7]

These meanderings are best examined by first following out Brown's main argument. We can then deal separately with his two detours (steps two and four). But because the second detour bears on the conclusion of his main argument, we need to return to the latter after reviewing the detours. We begin with the meaning of the Fourteenth Amendment.

After closely paraphrasing the Amendment, Brown turned to the *Slaughter-House Cases* in order to find its "proper construction." The Court in 1873 had not needed to define the colored race's "exact rights,"

but it was said generally that its [the Amendment's] main purpose was to establish the citizenship of the negro; to give definitions of citizenship

of the United States and of the States[;] and to protect from the hostile
legislation of the States the privileges and immunities of citizens of the
United States, as distinguished from those of citizens of the States.

If this formulation did not explicitly deny that the grant of citizenship
conveyed the positive right to be free of any distinction based on color,
neither did it entail recognition of the claim. Instead, Brown immediately
linked the Fourteenth Amendment to the case at hand in a way that flatly
rejected Tourgée's affirmative rights argument:

> The object of the amendment was undoubtedly to enforce the absolute
> equality of the two races before the law, but in the nature of things it
> could not have been intended to abolish distinctions based upon color, or
> to enforce social, as distinguished from political equality, or a commin-
> gling of the two races upon terms unsatisfactory to either.

An explanation of why "the nature of things" dictated that the
Fourteenth Amendment "could not have been intended to abolish distinctions based upon color" only appeared in step five of Brown's argument. It
came when he explored "the underlying fallacy" of Homer Plessy's position,
which he linked to two erroneous assumptions. The first was "that the
enforced separation of the two races stamps the colored race with a badge of
inferiority." To illustrate that this view was incorrect, Brown hypothesized
that if blacks were to dominate the Louisiana legislature at some future date,
and to pass a similar law, the white race assuredly would not regard itself as
having been marked as inferior. Mere legal distinctions, that is, did not
establish a feeling of inequality; the source of the feeling instead lay outside
of legal arrangements.[8]

Still more revealing was Brown's exploration of the second allegedly
erroneous assumption in Plessy's argument, "that social prejudices may be
overcome by legislation, and that equal rights cannot be secured to the negro
except by an enforced commingling of the two races." An initial problem
here is Brown's very meaning. The Louisiana law assuredly did *not* enforce
interracial "commingling." It seems likely, though, that by "legislation" he
meant law in the broad sense, encompassing the law of the Constitution.
This reading at least harmonizes his usage with what he certainly knew were
the dictates of the statute in question. In addition, toward the end of the
same paragraph, he employed "legislation" and "the Constitution" in a
fashion indicating that he intended the first term to encompass the second.
The passage is crucial and reads as follows:

> Legislation is powerless to eradicate racial instincts or to abolish
> distinctions based upon physical differences, and the attempt to do so can
> only result in accentuating the difficulties of the present situation. If the
> civil and political rights of both races be equal one cannot be inferior to
> the other civilly or politically. If one race be inferior to the other socially,

the Constitution of the United States cannot put them upon the same plane.

The same passage reveals Brown's own assumption—or, better, conclusion: racial instincts exist, and they, like physical distinctions themselves, are sufficiently rooted in man's nature as to be impervious to alteration through legal schemes. Much the same thought emerges, too, from the preceding several sentences, in which Brown described how social equality depended on "natural affinities." Quoting the New York school segregation case of *King v. Gallagher* (1883), he denied the efficacy of seeking such equality through "laws which conflict with the general sentiment of the community upon which they are designed to operate." In fact, *King v. Gallagher* may have directly and more generally informed Brown's thinking as he wrote this portion of his opinion. On the same page of the report from which he took the quotation, the New York Court of Appeals had described how, "[i]n the nature of things," many social distinctions lay beyond the reach of law, and how "attempt[ing] to enforce social intimacy and intercourse between races, by legal enactments, would probably tend only to embitter the prejudices, if any there are, which exist between them, and produce an evil instead of a good result." Two pages later, the New York Court added: "A natural distinction exists between these [white and black] races which was not created[,] neither can it be abrogated[,] by law . . . ."[9]

The view that race instincts, distinctions, and classifications inhered in the nature of man, and were not amenable to legal alteration, had constitutional significance. Since law *could* not alter such scientifically and naturally rooted "facts," the Reconstruction Amendments had not been intended to do so. Their framers and ratifiers, that is, would not have sought and intended the impossible. Brown may be criticized, of course, for giving no indication that this view of race and "the nature of things" was not universally accepted by the scientific and social science communities. Within his overall argument, however, the omission was not particularly damaging, as becomes apparent once we scrutinize the remainder of his exploration of whether separation was consistent with the Fourteenth Amendment's objects.

Well before fully expounding his nature-of-things premise about the Fourteenth Amendment, Brown had already explored its application in and confirmation by case and statutory law. "Laws permitting, and even requiring, their [that is, the two races'] separation in places where they are liable to be brought into contact," he claimed, "do not necessarily imply the inferiority of either race to the other, and have been generally, if not universally, recognized as within the competency of the state legislatures in the exercise of their police power." Separate schools provided the most common instance.

The pre-Civil War *Roberts* case, decided by the Massachusetts Supreme Judicial Court speaking through Chief Justice Lemuel Shaw, drew Brown's primary attention. Charles Sumner, as counsel for the black children seeking admission to Boston's racially segregated schools, had advanced "[t]he great principle . . . that by the constitution and laws of Massachusetts, all persons without distinction of age or sex, birth or color, origin or condition, are equal before the law." Shaw agreed, but then went on to contend that application of the principle did not prohibit the Boston school committee from using race, along with age and sex, as a basis for classifying students. The requirement, according to Shaw, was "only that the rights of all, as they are settled and regulated by law, are equally entitled to the paternal consideration and protection of law for their maintenance and security." Brown added that under several statutes, Congress had authorized separate schools in the District of Columbia, as had "many" state legislatures. He did not itemize these state statutes, but cited seven cases allegedly upholding such measures in Ohio, Missouri, California, Louisiana, New York, Indiana, and Kentucky.[10]

Brown's use of school legislation and related case law was problematic. An initial difficulty arose from *Roberts*, which in turn had been cited in Brown's New York, Missouri, and California cases. Because the case *preceded* the Fourteenth Amendment by nearly two decades, Shaw's opinion in it did not address the restrictions the Amendment placed on state authorities. But the difficulty on this front was more apparent than real. As the Louisiana Supreme Court observed when it used *Roberts*, the case—although dating from 1849—came from a "state[] where the civil rights of the colored race were fully recognized." The Massachusetts Constitution declared that "All men are born free and equal"; another article prohibited grants of exclusive privileges. Shaw read these provisions to mean "that colored persons . . . are entitled by law, in this commonwealth, to equal rights, constitutional and political, civil and social . . . ." So while Brown failed to elaborate the point, *Roberts* had been decided in the face of constitutional provisions which could be interpreted as providing an equivalent of the Fourteenth Amendment's protections.[11]

There were additional problems with the school cases. One arose out of the immediate reaction to *Roberts*. By upholding the separate-school regulation of the Boston school committee, the decision so inflamed equal-rights advocates in Massachusetts that in 1855 the legislature outlawed segregated schools. This sequence hardly indicated a community sentiment that separation was "reasonable." Brown's Louisiana school case, which was heard before the federal Circuit Court in New Orleans, posed another difficulty. The regulation at issue—a segregation order of the board of directors of the city's schools—almost certainly violated the legally superior mandate of the Louisiana Constitution, which provided: "There shall be no separate schools or institutions of learning established exclusively for any race by the state of Louisiana." (The federal judge had ruled that this issue was one of state law and not properly before him.) As for Brown's Kentucky case, it simply did not involve that state's separate school law, but rather invalidated the particular funding arrangements for separate schools.[12]

Finally, Brown failed to note decisions in which state courts had overturned separate-but-equal schooling, particularly *Clark v. Board of Directors*, the Iowa case from 1868. There, in diametric opposition to the *Roberts* doctrine, the state Supreme Court had persuasively argued that "the principle of equal rights to all, upon which our government is founded," created a presumption *against* racially segregated schools. That being so, ruled the Iowa court, then the state's existing school law, which was silent on the subject of separate schools, must be construed as denying to local school boards the option of establishing them. For a court to uphold a school board decision for separation not only "would be to sanction a plain violation of the spirit of our laws . . . but would tend to perpetuate the national differences of our people and stimulate a constant strife, if not a war of the races."[13]

But just as the difficulty posed by *Roberts*'s antebellum date proved minor, these additional problems with Brown's school materials were not especially troublesome, for two reasons. First, Brown had chosen his words carefully, writing that regulations for racial separation in schools "have been generally, *if not uniformly*, sustained by the courts"; and in that assertion he was undoubtedly correct. In 1895, Thomas M. Cooley summarized current doctrine in this fashion: "no [Fourteenth Amendment] right is violated when colored pupils are merely placed in different schools, provided the schools are equal, and the same measure of privilege and justice is given to each." As reviewed in Chapter Four, J. Morgan Kousser, the most thorough modern student of late nineteenth-century school discrimination decisions, has shown that blacks in fact won many suits, but allows that these favorable outcomes did not always entail formal rejection of separate-but-equal. Brown's statements in *Plessy*, Kousser writes, "were precise, if rather obviously disingenuous."[14]

If anything, Brown might have strengthened his presentation by emulating the more thorough approach of the New York Court of Appeals thirteen years earlier in *King v. Gallagher*. There, after noting arguably contrary cases, the court had distinguished them as arising "under statutes which either expressly forb[ade] or did not authorize the school authorities to separate the races . . . ."[15] Despite its fundamental anti-separatist premise, for example, *Clark* had formally turned on a point of *statutory* construction: as interpreted, Iowa's existing school law acted as a bar to separation.

The second reason for discounting Brown's lapses concerning his school evidence relates to the use he made of it. He did not rely on the cases as "authority" for his *Plessy* decision: they did not enter into his argument as precedent in a legally binding sense. As indicated by a careful reading of language already quoted, he only averred that the cases showed that other competent tribunals had *recognized* the validity as police measures of school laws which distinguished on the basis of color. So, too, he briefly mentioned state anti-miscegenation laws, which "may be said in a technical sense to interfere with the freedom of contract, and yet have been universally recognized as within the police power of the state."[16]

Brown did not immediately clarify why "recognition" of the legality of separation, in inferior courts and in cases not in point, bore on the question of the Louisiana law's constitutionality. Instead, he took his first detour, examining possible limitations on legislative action that arose out of prior cases. Not until three pages later did he return to his major argument, abruptly in mid-paragraph. He did so with a startling sentence: "Similar statutes for the separation of the two races upon public conveyances were held to be *constitutional* in *West Chester . . . v. Miles* . . . [and ten other state and federal cases]." This led to Brown's conclusion that "the enforced separation of the races, as applied to the internal commerce of the State" violated neither the privileges-or-immunities, due process, nor equal protection requirements of the Fourteenth Amendment.[17]

Whether or not his conclusion flowed either from what he had already discussed regarding the police power, or from arguments advanced later in the opinion, it unquestionably did not follow from *West Chester v. Miles* and the other cases he now cited as upholding the constitutionality of race-separation statutes—because the cases did *not* uphold the *constitutionality* of *legislatively* mandated separation. As Barton Bernstein has observed, "only one case even involved the constitutionality of a state statute," and the law at issue in it was an equal-accommodation act![18] One could quibble further that the case had involved a *state* constitutional provision, but at least the requirement duplicated a Fourteenth Amendment restriction.

This lone constitutional case—*People v. King* (New York, 1888)—turns out, however, to provide *some* support for Brown. It originated after the New York state legislature had mandated that no state citizen could, "by reason of race, color, or previous condition of servitude, be excluded from the equal enjoyment of any accommodation, facility, or privilege furnished by . . . owners, managers or lessees of theaters or other places of amusement . . . ." Convicted of excluding three black men, the owner of a skating rink appealed on grounds that the law violated the state constitution's prohibition against deprivation of life, liberty, or property without due process of law.

Although New York courts had helped pioneer a "substantive" meaning for due process, the state Court of Appeals noted that the language of the due process clause itself implied that "life, liberty and property may be justly affected by law," and that the prohibition did not deny exercise of "the police power[,] [which] covers a wide range of particular unexpressed powers reserved to the State affecting freedom of action, personal conduct and the use and control of property." As Lemuel Shaw had written (and the Court of Appeals quoted), "All property is held subject to those general regulations which are necessary to the common good and general welfare."

For the New York court, a variety of expressions—in constitutions, statute law, and judicial opinions—confirmed the public's interest in

> a policy which shall elevate them [the blacks] as individuals and relieve them from oppressive or degrading discrimination, and which shall encourage and cultivate a spirit which shall make them self-respecting, contented and loyal citizens, and give them a fair chance in the struggle of life, weighted, as they are at best, with so many disadvantages.

True, it was "impossible to enforce social equality by law," but the court could not say the law "ha[d] no basis in the public interest . . . ." Questions of the law's expediency or wisdom being no concern of judges, the Court of Appeals thus upheld the equal access law as a valid police measure.[19]

In form, the New York opinion contained clear parallels to the Louisiana opinion in *Ex parte Plessy*, as well as to Brown's own opinion in *Plessy v. Ferguson*. The outcome turned on the court's inability to find that the legislative judgment completely lacked support. The court's allowance that law could not enforce *social* equality also anticipated one of Brown's themes. But by no stretch of the imagination did the case uphold the constitutionality of a "statute[] for the *separation* of the two races upon public conveyances," as Brown claimed.

For accuracy, Brown should have written that the cases he cited had upheld not the *constitutionality* but the *reasonableness* of police regulations respecting racial mixing, for this they did. Even the New York case contained language interpretable as meaning race was a legitimate subject for police legislation. More important, the other ten cases, which involved transportation, on balance conveyed the current common-law doctrine, although Brown again omitted contrary holdings. Early cross-currents in case law had given way, in the late 1870s and beyond, to nearly uniform agreement among state appellate and lower federal courts that considerations of public comfort and welfare allowed common carriers to separate passengers by race so long as equal facilities were provided to those paying equal fares.[20]

Brown still postponed a clear statement of the reasonableness doctrine on which his constitutional argument rested, and instead examined several fairly focused objections to the Louisiana law. As with his first detour, we shall put off examining this second excursion in order to follow the main line of his argument.

The key paragraph came two pages later, and needs quotation in full:

> So far, then, as a conflict with the Fourteenth Amendment is concerned, the case reduces itself to the question whether the statute of Louisiana is a reasonable regulation, and with respect to this there must necessarily be a large discretion on the part of the legislature. In determining the question of reasonableness it is at liberty to act with reference to the established usages, customs and traditions of the people, and with a view to the promotion of their comfort, and the preservation of the public peace and good order. Gauged by this standard, we cannot

say that a law which authorizes or even requires the separation of the races is unreasonable, or more obnoxious to the Fourteenth Amendment than the acts of Congress requiring separate schools for colored children in the District of Columbia, the constitutionality of which does not seem to have been questioned, or the corresponding acts of state legislatures.[21]

In three respects, the paragraph requires comment.

For one thing, it seems irrelevant for Brown to have observed toward the end that no Fourteenth Amendment objections had been lodged against congressional action mandating racial separation in the District of Columbia's schools. The *prohibitive* clauses of the Amendment's first section apply only to the states, *not* to Congress. In reality, though, Brown's comment reflects passing recognition of the core of Plessy's case. The argument that Albion Tourgée fashioned around the Amendment's *affirmative* citizenship clause applied also to congressional action.

More important to the development of Brown's own argument is an implication of the paragraph. While Brown said the state legislature might act "with reference to the established usages customs and traditions," he implied that the Court, too, had at least *some* knowledge of those usages, customs, and traditions. Otherwise, it is difficult to see how application of the standard he used could produce the result he reached. In short, if other sections of his opinion revealed his recognition of contemporary scientific and legal views of race, this paragraph brought popular opinion and practice into the equation. It is true that Brown did not state that the Court agreed with popular sentiments, just as he avoided endorsing the views on racial separation embodied in the legal pronouncements—both judicial and legislative—that he cited. (By contrast, he had essentially endorsed as correct the scientific view that race differences inhere in the nature of things.) But at minimum he established popular sentiment and practice, along with legal and scientific testimony on race, as a link in his train of reasoning.

Finally, Brown's key paragraph cited no judicial authorities for the reasonableness standard—although here case law provided clear *precedent*. Partly, perhaps, the school and transportation cases he had already cited obviated the need, because, along with their endorsements of separation, they abounded with language about reasonableness (but largely not in the context of constitutional arguments). Mainly, though, the omission related to the conclusion of the detour that Brown had completed immediately prior to the key paragraph. It therefore becomes necessary to return to the departures he took from his main line of argument.

IV

In the midst of defending the overall constitutionality of racial separation on intrastate railways, Brown took the two detours already noted. The first of these, which for convenience can be labeled his "limitations excursion," explored four restrictions on racial regulations that the Supreme Court itself had developed.

The first limitation, on political and civil infringements, rested on a "distinction between laws interfering with the political equality of the negro and those requiring separation of the two races in schools, theatres and railway carriages . . . ." Here, citing major cases, Brown described how discriminatory jury selection laws and practices had been held unconstitutional as diminishing the legal security of blacks. In truth, the cases he mentioned drew no distinction between interferences with political equality and separation in public accommodations and facilities, for they did not discuss racial separation. Brown's language hence was shamefully misleading.[22] It was also inexact to the extent that common usage classified jury service as a civil, not political, right.

A second restriction forbade separate-car regulations contrary to congressional statute, as illustrated in *Washington, Alexandria, and Georgetown Railroad Company v. Brown*, the case from 1873 whose meaning Samuel F. Phillips and Alexander Porter Morse had debated. Arguably, the case had broader significance, but its principle extended at least as far as Brown asserted.[23]

Another limit ran against state legislation affecting commerce among the states. *Hall v. DeCuir* (1878) had struck down Louisiana's Reconstruction-era equal accommodation law as it applied to passengers within the state on interstate carriers. But this limitation itself was limited. Brown noted that in *DeCuir* the Court "expressly disclaimed" that the decision applied to "the statute as a regulation of internal commerce."[24] And the limitation was perhaps still narrower. In this regard, Brown could have strengthened his argument through a careful explication of how, in *DeCuir*, the Court had construed congressional inaction as an affirmative congressional mandate that the common law of carriers was to remain in effect for interstate carriers. Louisiana's law, as we observed in Chapter Six, therefore flew in the face of an implied and contrary congressional regulation; the conflict was not merely between a state law and an *un*exercised congressional power. So where Congress had not explicitly or implicitly spoken, the commerce limitation had less force; and in the aftermath of *DeCuir*, state equal accomodation legislation more clearly ran against *imputed* congressional intent than did laws mandating separation.

The final limitation emerged from the *Civil Rights Cases*. Congress could not directly legislate against the activities of individuals that infringed private rights, but could only, in Justice Joseph Bradley's language, "provide modes of redress against the operation of state laws and the action of state officers, executive or judicial, when these are subversive of the fundamental rights specified in the amendment."[25]

None of these four restrictions applied to the Louisiana separate car law, a point so obvious that Brown left it unstated with regard to three of them.

The only limitation that he explicitly related to Plessy's case was the *DeCuir* requirement of non-interference with interstate commerce (or, more strictly, non-interference with actual or implied congressional rules respecting interstate commerce). He did so by examining *Louisville, New Orleans and Texas Railway v. Mississippi* (1890), which he initially portrayed as "almost directly in point" with *Plessy*. On the contrary, the case was not at all "in point," for the action challenged in it was the conviction not of an intrastate traveler but of an interstate railway for failure to meet the Mississippi requirement of providing a separate car for blacks within the state. The Supreme Court in Washington had accepted the Mississippi Supreme Court's interpretation that the law applied only to traffic within the state, and agreed with the latter court that the law, thus construed, did not unconstitutionally burden interstate commerce. Because the case did not involve prosecution of a passenger for failing to go to an assigned car, the federal Supereme Court had stressed that its ruling left open the question of whether or not passengers themselves could be compelled by statute to abide by assignments to separate cars.[26]

Through deft quotation, however, Brown implied that in *Louisville, New Orleans and Texas* the Court had endorsed passenger separation. This he accomplished by pulling a statement out of the Court's opinion: "No question arises under this section, as to the power of the State to separate in different compartments interstate passengers, or affect, in any manner, the privileges and rights of such passengers." The words "this section" actually referred to the section of the Mississippi statute under which the railway had been prosecuted; but without any indication of the referent for the phrase (and Brown included none), the quoted excerpt remained at best ambiguous. Worse, however, in the context of Brown's comments the excerpt suggested positive acceptance of separation, for Brown had already written: "The [Mississippi] case was presented in a different aspect from the one under consideration [that is, *Plessy*], inasmuch as it was an indictment against the railway company for failing to provide separate accommodations, *but the question considered was the constitutionality of the law.*" Whether intentional or not, his language insinuated that the Mississippi case decided more than it did.[27]

Yet, viewed closely, the misleading details in Brown's comments on the Mississippi case were unimportant, for his discussion only introduced the question of whether Louisiana's mandatory separation of races violated the *DeCuir* restriction. As to the substance of that issue, because the state Supreme Court had already construed the Louisiana separate car law as applying only to intrastate passengers, the answer seemed obvious, given the Mississippi case. If the Mississippi law, construed to impose a separate car requirement on interstate railways, but only within the state, did not impermissibly burden commerce, then surely the Louisiana law did not impose a burden on interstate commerce. But rather than go into extensive detail, Brown brought the discussion to a halt by noting that "no question of interference with interstate commerce [could] possibly arise," because the

East Louisiana Railway, on which Plessy had sought carriage, was "purely a local line." With that observation about the factual basis of the Plessy case, the *DeCuir* restriction simply became irrelevant.[28]

Brown's second detour prior to clarifying the reasonableness standard—a "defensive excursion"—took him into several specific objections raised by Plessy's counsel. One was the claim of Tourgée and Walker that because the law exempted railways and train officials from damage suits arising out of its enforcement, it violated the equal protection clause. Brown indirectly admitted the point; he was "not prepared to say" that the exemption was "a valid exercise of the legislative power." Of course, the state Supreme Court had interpreted the provision as not conferring the immunity that its plain words did confer; and Judge Ferguson, in his earlier opinion on Plessy's initial plea to the jurisdiction of the trial court, found the exemption unconstitutional. In oral argument, Alexander Porter Morse may have taken Ferguson's approach. At least Brown wrote that he understood the state as conceding "that such part of the act as exempts from liability the railway company and its officers is unconstitutional." But Brown did not follow Tourgée and Walker to their conclusion, for he declined to hold that the liability-exemption clause was so central to the law's scheme that the whole law fell if the clause failed. Rather, he ignored the issue and hence skirted an essential part of Homer Plessy's major equal protection argument.[29]

In a parallel fashion, Brown agreed with Plessy's counsel that a conductor's authority to make seat assignments by race "obviously implies the power to determine to which race the passenger belongs," but then, taking two approaches, he rejected their conclusion that the arrangement resulted in a due process deprivation. Initially he addressed the contention that the law deprived a passenger of the right to a judicial determination regarding the complex question of his race—that is, that it lacked provision for the judicial process entailed in due process. The issue of Plessy's race, Brown asserted, did "not properly arise upon the record." His wording was murky, but he seems to have meant that because nothing in the record indicated Plessy had been wrongly assigned under whatever might be Louisiana's definition of who was white and who was black, there was no basis to conclude that Plessy had been deprived of liberty or property. The lack of judicial process thus was a moot issue.

But Brown quickly abandoned his reluctance and used a different route to explore the due process question. Conceding "for the purposes of this case" that a person's reputation as a member of the dominant race might be considered property "in the same sense that a right of action, or of inheritance, is property," he turned to Tourgée's claim that the law deprived Plessy of property in the form of reputation. Brown found no deprivation:

> If he [Plessy] be a white man and assigned to a colored coach, he may
> have his action for damages against the company for being deprived of his

so called property. Upon the other hand, if he be a colored man and be so assigned, he has been deprived of no property, since he is not lawfully entitled to the reputation of being a white man.

In short, once the statute was stripped of its liability-exemption provision, there existed a process for judicial review of seat assignments. It took the form of a damage suit, which would provide adequate remedy for any improper assignment.[30]

Why did Brown reach the due process/property issue, after just concluding that the cognate issue of adequacy of judicial process during seat assignment did not arise in the record before the Court? The reason may be that, along with the claim that the separate car law's liability-exemption provision violated the equal protection clause, the contention that the law deprived Plessy of property was the most legally orthodox and easily grasped of the Fourteenth Amendment arguments. Then, too, the issue provided an avenue for Brown to argue, in effect, that even if he had erred in concluding that the question of adequate judicial process in the course of seat assignment was not before the Court, it made no difference, for an assignment pursuant to the statute worked no deprivation. But whatever his reason for addressing the issue, Brown handled it in a cavalier fashion. As Tourgée had argued on brief, monetary damages were scant compensation for the criminal prosecution that could follow a passenger's refusal to abide by a conductor's incorrect seat assignment.

Brown next turned to Tourgée's reductio ad absurdum argument. Would not the reasoning that justified racial separation in public carriers similarly justify such regulations as the separation of people according to hair color and the identification of homes with different colors of paint? No, said Brown; and here he returned to his main Fourteenth Amendment argument, explicitly introducing the principle central to it. "[E]very exercise of the police power must be reasonable," he explained, "and extend only to such laws as are enacted in good faith for the promotion [of] the public good, and not for the annoyance or oppression of a particular class." As an example, in *Yick Wo v. Hopkins* (1886), the Court had struck down a San Francisco ordinance that regulated laundries by giving municipal authorities unbounded discretion to limit the persons engaged in the business and the sites they could use. This regulation, Brown correctly related, "was held to be a covert attempt on the part of the municipality to make an arbitrary and unjust discrimination against the Chinese race." State and federal courts had applied the same principle to the acts of state legislatures, he contended, citing sixteen cases either directly or by reference.[31]

V

Responding to one of Tourgée's focused attacks, Brown had finally begun to elaborate the concept that was crucial to his own defense of the separate car law. He then promptly left his "defensive excursion" and proceeded to complete his affirmative argument for the law as a justifiable police measure. This he accomplished by including his key paragraph on the reasonableness principle, which was quoted earlier. Yet, as already noted, the reasonableness paragraph itself included no judicial authorities. It implicitly rested instead on *Yick Wo* and the other sixteen cases that Brown had just cited in conjunction with his refutation of Tourgée's reductio ad absurdum argument.

Two of the additional sixteen cases turned on technical issues of evidence and selection of remedies and added only padding to the list, but the other fourteen prove revealing. Of these, four were state cases involving voter registration or balloting; ten were federal Supreme Court cases on alleged state discriminations against interstate or foreign commerce, with an additional issue figuring prominently in one of them. None of the cases raised a Fourteenth Amendment issue.

In ruling on access to the ballot, the state courts had held that registration laws and other regulations for establishing voter eligibility must be reasonable in the sense of facilitating rather than hindering exercise of state guaranteed rights to vote. In two of the cases courts struck down voting legislation and in two upheld it. The most recent case cited by Brown, from Ohio in 1885, invalidated a registration law establishing an annual seven-day period for registration with no alternative means of qualifying. To gain insight as to the parameters of what constituted a reasonable measure, the Ohio Supreme Court had turned to decisions in fourteen other states that had upheld registration schemes; it used these decisions not as direct precedent, but to indicate what other courts had accepted as reasonable regulations.[32]

To the extent the federal cases cited by Brown involved the commerce clause, they did not turn on the reasonableness of police regulations. In them, the Supreme Court uniformly held that otherwise valid police regulations were void if they conflicted with federal commerce regulations or infringed on the federal power over interstate and foreign commerce.

The most recent of the federal cases—*Louisville and Nashville Railroad Company v. Kentucky*, decided in March 1896 with the Court's opinion written by Justice Brown himself—also raised an obligation-of-contracts issue, for the railway claimed that a state constitutional provision restricting railway mergers impaired the line's charter grant. In the related portion of his opinion in this case, Brown used the reasonableness doctrine in the course of upholding the state restriction. In making charter grants, he explained, legislatures must be presumed to have reserved the authority to impose regulations reasonably calculated to further the public interest. To assess what constituted reasonableness in this sense, Brown looked to practice in other states, which he found accorded with Kentucky's policy against consolidation. "Indeed," he wrote, "the unanimity with which the states have legislated against the consolidation of competing lines shows that it is not the result of a local prejudice, but of a general sentiment that such monopolies are reprehensible." He then mentioned nine cases in which the Court had drawn limits around state authority when it burdened or interfered with interstate or foreign commerce. (These were the same additional nine commerce cases he cited in *Plessy*, where his citation of eight of them was through reference to their listing in *Louisville and Nashville*.) But his purpose was only to indicate some exceptions that helped delineate a "general rule," which he stated thus: "whatever is contrary to public policy or inimical to the public interests is subject to the police power of the state, and within legislative control, and in the exertion of such power the legislature is vested with a large discretion, which, if exercised bona fide for the protection of the public, is beyond the reach of judicial authority."[33]

On balance, then, there was a curious and significant dimension to Brown's claim in *Plessy* that the reasonableness principle guarded against the sort of further legal distinctions that Tourgée had envisioned in his reductio ad absurdum argument. His case citations, while not all relevant, pointed toward reasonableness not as a restrictive concept but rather as a doctrine of *empowerment*, or at least as a vehicle for importing broad public sentiment and existing legislative and judicial inclination into definitions of constitutional limitations. In a real sense, that is, the conclusion of Brown's "defensive excursion" provided some of the available support in case law that he failed to cite in his immediately forthcoming paragraph on reasonableness as an explicitly legitimating doctrine.

Quite aside from Brown's indirect means of documenting his key paragraph on reasonableness, it is also curious that he by no means fully indicated the available judicial support for it. In fact, he almost entirely ignored the highly pertinent line of state and federal cases involving police power issues under the Fourteenth Amendment that we explored in Chapter Four—including, interestingly, *Lawton v. Steele*, in which he himself had spoken for the Court two years earlier, using language anticipating his *Plessy* opinion.

Despite the missed opportunity, Brown easily concluded that Louisiana's separate car law constituted a reasonable exercise of the state's police power. For him and the Court's majority, it was simply not true that the Fourteenth Amendment categorically prohibited states from establishing race distinctions in statute law. Instead, the Amendment's meaning with respect to race-related regulations took shape from a doctrine that judges had fashioned in the course of applying the Amendment to other areas of American life. The *arguable* reality of racial traits and differences empowered legislatures to take them into account. There was enough evidence, that is, to prevent the Court from finding that the Louisiana legislature had no basis in reason to conclude that separation promoted public welfare. Part of the evidence came from the common-law acceptability of racial separation. Part of it came from common and expert opinion. The existence of contrary evidence was legally irrelevant.

All that remained open was whether Plessy qualified legally as a member of the white race or of the colored race. This, concluded Brown, "[might] undoubtedly become an issue of importance" when Homer Plessy went to trial in Louisiana. But in this area, state law would be controlling.[34]

If one ignores Brown's convoluted, clouded, and underdeveloped presentation, it was all simple and routine.

VI

Or was it? Justice Harlan thought not. In a dissent approximately equal in length to Brown's opinion for the Court, the Kentuckian lambasted the statute, endorsed the view that the Reconstruction Amendments categorically outlaw race distinctions, and criticized a few specifics in the majority opinion. Misleadingly free flowing on initial reading, Harlan's opinion on close inspection reveals a more rigorous structure; but in it he failed to grapple fully with Brown's approach—just as Brown systematically confronted neither Harlan's opinion nor the core argument of Plessy's counsel.

Harlan began in an unfortunately weak fashion. In the course of summarizing the Louisiana law, he ridiculed the narrow reach of its provision exempting "nurses attending children of the other race." Colored manservants or maids attending white *adults*, he noted, risked criminal prosecution if they exhibited zeal in serving their employers. The remark suggested on balance that Harlan would stress points of unwise policy and deleterious impact, an approach that his continuing tone of indignation *seemed* to confirm. His prompt concession that it was not the wisdom but the constitutionality of legislation that properly concerned the Court did not remedy the distraction.[35] And he never returned to dwell on the specific problems created by the nurse-exemption provision. As Tourgée and Walker had suggested on brief, the narrow scope of the exemption raised an equal protection issue—and one that Harlan might profitably have exploited, especially because Brown had nowhere addressed it in his opinion.

Moving explicitly to the question of constitutionality, Harlan satisfactorily established that in American law railways had a public character. They typically held powers of eminent domain, for example, which meant they could acquire private property through legal process (in return for compensation), even though owners might be unwilling to sell. Accordingly, Louisiana had acted unconstitutionally in conditioning access to a public service on the basis of race, because, observed Harlan, "[i]n respect of civil rights, common to all citizens, the Constitution of the United States does not . . . permit any public authority to know the race of those entitled to be protected in the enjoyment of such rights." No legislative or judicial body, he declared, "may have regard to the race of citizens when the civil rights of those citizens are involved," for such action was "inconsistent not only with that equality of rights which pertains to citizenship, National and State, but with the personal liberty enjoyed by every one within the United States."[36]

As for the source of this equality of right and personal liberty, Harlan looked to the Thirteenth Amendment's elimination of badges of servitude and the Fourteenth's grant of citizenship and prohibitions on state infringement. Without attempting to delineate the independent effects of each Amendment, he found that together "[t]hese notable additions to the fundamental law . . . removed the race line from our governmental systems." This interpretation he defended by quoting language from the Court's leading jury-service cases in order to affirm that whatever else the two Amendments together (or the Fourteenth alone) accomplished, they declared an equality of civil rights between the races and outlawed discriminations either based on color or tending to reduce blacks to servitude. If this gloss mirrored Tourgée's description (and, in turn, his own 1883 dissent), Harlan added the consideration that earlier in its current term the Court had offered yet another endorsement of the same view. *Gibson v. Mississippi*, decided on the same day that *Plessy* had been argued, held that "underlying all of those [earlier] decisions is the principle that the Constitution of the United States, in its present form, forbids, so far as civil and political rights are concerned, discrimination by the General Government or the States against any citizen because of his race. All citizens are equal before the law."[37]

Still, in Louisiana's view, the *distinction* required by the law did not equate with a legal *discrimination*. In oral argument, Harlan noted, Alexander Porter Morse had contended that the law "prescribes a rule applicable alike to white and colored citizens." But judges could not ignore the obvious. "Every one knows," the Justice exclaimed, "that the statute in question had its origin in the purpose, not so much to exclude white persons from railroad cars occupied by blacks, as to exclude colored people from coaches occupied by or assigned to white persons." The importance of establishing the character of railways as public highways now became clear, for Harlan explained that the law prohibited blacks and whites from voluntarily "choos[ing] to occupy the same public conveyance on a public highway." This infringed the liberty of each, for William Blackstone, the English jurist whose *Commentaries* had proved so influential in America, had defined "personal liberty" as "the power of locomotion, of changing situation, or removing one's person to whatsoever places one's own inclination may direct; without imprisonment or restraint, unless in due course of law." Drawing on Tourgée's reductio ad absurdum argument, Harlan further scored the "distinction" by observing that if it were not an infringement of personal liberty, then the state could as well mandate separate sides of streets for the two races, forbid interracial travel in streetcars or open private vehicles, segregate courtrooms, or extend the separate car law to isolate naturalized from native-born citizens or Protestants from Roman Catholics.[38]

But Louisiana and the Court's majority had a ready answer: as Harlan stated it, hypothetical regulations such as these "would be unreasonable, and could not, therefore, stand before the law." Here, finally, he reached the argument that lay at the core not only of Brown's opinion but also of the defenses of the law by the lower courts and the state. His statement of the central question was undeniably on target. "Is it meant," he asked, "that the determination of questions of legislative power depends upon the inquiry whether the statute whose validity is questioned is, in the judgment of the courts, a reasonable one, taking all the circumstances into consideration?"

He then undermined his own attack. In effect defining "reasonableness" as "in accord with sound public policy"—an oversimplification of the concept as it inhered in Brown's opinion and the body of case law surveyed in Chapter Four—he proceeded to rely on Theodore Sedgwick's treatise on statutory and constitutional interpretation as authority for the proposition that judges have no legitimate concern with "the wisdom or justice of the particular enactment." "If the power exists to enact a statute," concluded Harlan, "that ends the matter so far as the courts are concerned." But the material he used from Sedgwick came from a section that discussed *statutory* construction. The sole object of courts in construing legislation, declared Sedgwick, was to give effect to legislative intention. In context, the comments simply had no bearing on the issue of reasonableness in constitutional adjudication—and even Harlan's own quotations and paraphrases of Sedgwick revealed the irrelevance of the material to the issue at hand.[39]

What is even stranger, Harlan then reversed himself, acknowledging that courts had found "statutes . . . to be void, because unreasonable." On this point, he derived from "the adjudged cases" (none of which he cited) the rule that a determination of unconstitutionality required a finding that "the means employed were not at all germane to the end to which the legislature was competent."[40] Perhaps he meant that courts had no business examining the *extent* to which a specific measure promoted a legitimate governmental purpose; the power to act either existed or it did not. To say a law was unconstitutional because unreasonable, that is, was simply to say that it lacked any constitutional warrant. Yet in its wording, the test advanced by Harlan accorded with the doctrine of reasonableness in existing case law, including some that he had helped create. It was a test *at least* as lenient toward legislative discretion as Brown's reasonableness test, if not more so.

Harlan's next step followed not from the reasonableness principle as he had actually stated it, but from what he had probably intended to write. "Our Constitution is color-blind," he posited, "and neither knows nor tolerates classes among citizens. . . . The law regards man as man, and takes no account of his surroundings or of his color when his civil rights as guaranteed by the supreme law of the land are involved." The *Dred Scott* case, Harlan observed, had endorsed contrary principles: blacks possessed no rights as citizens of the United States, and the Constitution rested on the

proposition that they might be treated as inferior beings. But the Reconstruction Amendments, "it was supposed, had eradicated these [racist]
principles from our institutions," and had conveyed "the clear, distinct,
unconditional recognition by our governments, National and State, of every
right that inheres in civil freedom, and of the equality before the law of all
citizens of the United States without regard to race." They accordingly
constituted "[t]he sure guarantee of the peace and security of each race."[41]

In the midst of developing his premise about the guarantee embodied
in the Thirteenth and Fourteenth Amendments, especially when interpreted
against the backdrop of *Dred Scott*, Harlan stressed how the *Plessy* decision
would promote interracial violence—that it would, "in time, prove to be
quite as pernicious" as the earlier decision. "The destinies of the two races"
were so linked that "the interests of both require that the common
government of all shall not permit the seeds of race hate to be planted under
the sanction of law." Surely intended as a deep condemnation of separate-car
legislation on policy grounds, Harlan's strictures in this regard seem to
depart from his own disclaimer that courts had anything to do with the
wisdom of legislative choices. Yet his language was not merely emotive, for
it displayed the Louisiana law as violating the strict and absolute meaning
that he, like Tourgée, read into the two Amendments.

Again Harlan acknowledged and confronted the counter-argument: the
law of the Constitution could not have been intended to promote a social
equality that was impossible in the nature of things. Traveling together no
more promoted social equality, Harlan responded, than did serving together
in a jury box, joining together in a political assembly, or using in common
a city's streets. Quite the contrary. The Louisiana separate car law itself
allowed even the Chinese—"a race so different from our own that we do not
permit those belonging to it to become citizens"—to ride in coaches with
whites. Social equality was a bogus issue which had no bearing on the
meaning of the Reconstruction Amendments. The real issue was the
"arbitrary separation of citizens, on the basis of race, while they are on a
public highway," which was "a badge of servitude wholly inconsistent with
the civil freedom and the equality before the law established by the
Constitution." In this respect, the law's requirement of equality of accommodations was but a "thin disguise." The principles underlying the decision
in *Plessy* would justify separation even of jurors in an effort to protect
integrity of the white race from corruption, yet the Court, most recently in
its current term, had struck down jury discrimination.[42]

Finally, Harlan dismissed the cases that Alexander Porter Morse had
presented to support racial separation as unworthy of review. With evident
reference to *Roberts*, he noted that the most important of them predated the
Reconstruction Amendments. Others came from periods marked by peaking
race prejudice, "when it would not have been safe to do justice to the black
man." "Those decisions," he concluded,

cannot be guides in the era introduced by the recent amendments of the supreme law, which established universal civil freedom, gave citizenship to all born or naturalized in the United States and residing here, obliterated the race line from our systems of governments, National and State, and placed our free institutions upon the broad and sure foundation of the equality of all men before the law.[43]

With that, Harlan dropped the issue. Consistent with his probably intended (but not literal) denial that the reasonableness of legislation affected its constitutionality, he thus avoided close examination of whether his generalizations applied to all the cases and other evidence on racial separation that Brown's opinion and the briefs and oral argument for Louisiana had laid out.

Overall, Harlan's tone obscured the tight structure of his argument, but despite some lapses a structure was there. Faithful to the requests of both Tourgée and Phillips that the Court eschew "legal refinement" in favor of giving weight to "the fundamental principle of our government," he avoided the more technical of the claims advanced on Plessy's behalf, especially under the due process and equal protection clauses. He instead developed the position that legally mandated racial separation was by itself unconstitutional; and in his conclusion he attached this view to a revealing constitutional base. The law that Louisiana had enacted was "inconsistent with the guarantee given by the Constitution to each State of a republican form of government"; it placed "in a condition of legal inferiority a large body of American citizens, now constituting a part of the political community called the People of the United States, for whom, and by whom through representatives, our government is administered." By implicating the Constitution's guarantee clause, Harlan evoked the aspirations of the Radical Republicans, three decades earlier, but he also turned to a source that the judiciary had refused to employ in fashioning and enforcing personal rights.[44]

Justice Harlan's concluding grasp at the guarantee clause was symptomatic. Brown's opinion, for all its sloppiness had a firmer grounding in current law; yet Harlan's was better rooted in republican truths and, at least arguably, in history. The two men had partially failed to join issues, but that is hardly surprising. They spoke to broader audiences—and for larger principles.

CHAPTER NINE

Speaking to the Future

I

Albion Tourgée arrived home tired from the oral argument in *Plessy* and likely awaited news of the outcome with little hope and some anxiety. When the decision came down, he must have been pleased with Justice Harlan's dissent. Just as surely, Harlan must have welcomed the support he received elsewhere. Among editors outside the South who judged the judges, hostility to the decision overshadowed approval by perhaps three to one. The Negro press and some religious publications more emphatically condemned it. "The spirit of Roger B. Taney seems to be the presiding genius of that tribunal," declared the Chicago *Inter Ocean*, picking up one of Harlan's themes. "Take all these cases together," the paper said of *Plessy* and earlier pro-segregation decisions, "and they complete the denial [of] the fourteenth amendment." Even Booker T. Washington complained mildly in print. Using the reductio ad absurdum argument that Harlan had borrowed from Tourgée, he asked, "[W]hy cannot the courts go further and decide that all men with bald heads must ride in one car and all with red hair still in another? Nature is responsible for all these conditions."[1]

But such reaction was atypical. Although hostility to the Court's decision predominated among newspapers offering an opinion, the most common press response was simply routine notice of the case, or no mention at all.[2] The *New York Times*'s coverage is revealing. The paper included the decision in its regular Tuesday column on railway news, on page three,

196

sandwiched between reports of another Supreme Court railway decision, which overturned an Illinois law ordering minor re-routing of interstate passenger trains, and a request by the receivers of the Baltimore and Ohio for authority to issue new improvement bonds. By contrast, three of the fifty-three decisions decided or otherwise disposed of by the Court on May 18 received coverage on the front page of the *Times*. In one, the Court held that a sugar plantation owner had not violated the federal contract labor law by bringing in a German chemist under contract; and in the second, it disallowed a challenge to a portion of an heiress's multi-million-dollar inheritance. The third case found the Court refusing to hear an appeal to vacate the lower-court injunction that playwright Augustin Daly had obtained against two other playwrights who, he claimed, had plagiarized the "railroad scene" from his own play *Under the Gaslight*. "In other words," quipped the *Times*, "not even a 'railroad scene' can be railroaded into the legal purview of the Supreme Court of the United States."[3]

Of course, it was more than the gripping content of other decisions that railroaded *Plessy* out of prominent view. As regards the judiciary itself, the Populist revolt had lent drama to different issues, so that to the extent the Supreme Court attracted public attention, focus centered on its handling of railway taxation and rate regulation, the Sherman Anti-Trust Act, the income tax, and labor injunctions. Also, the rush of current events must have been distracting. During the week preceding the separate car decision, the Spanish commander in Cuba, Captain-General Valeriano Weyler, had threatened to execute several Americans taken prisoner off the filibustering ship *Competitor*. When his home government interposed a moderating hand, Weyler announced he regretted that he had not simply ordered the men shot. Meanwhile, reports circulated of a new American filibustering expedition. At home, William McKinley had emerged as the clear front-runner for the Republican presidential nomination; but among proponents of the gold standard, speculation focused on whether McKinley's silence on the money question indicated that he harbored hidden silver sympathies. And in Texas and the Midwest, tornadoes ("cyclones" in the parlance of the day) had killed an estimated 200 or more people.[4]

The indifference greeting *Plessy* had a still more fundamental source. Benno Schmidt has labeled the majority opinion "an untroubled endorsement of racial separation"—and it was. It embodied conventional wisdom. There seems little reason to doubt Justice Brown's accuracy when he later recalled that in reaching its decision, the Court experienced "little difficulty." In point of clarity, Brown's opinion (which, it needs remembering, was the Court's opinion) was atrocious, and its obscurities have often hidden from later readers its commonplace strengths within the 1890s. Specifically, Brown's conclusions did not rest on bad logic, bad social science, bad history, or bad constitutional law, as later alleged. Once his incidental lapses and nods are rectified, his logic turns out to be passable—at least by judicial standards. The vision of social reality that he posited did not lack substantial support in contemporary expert opinion; nor was his history jarringly inaccurate. Not least, these elements along with recent trends in American law, some having nothing to do with race, made his constitutional law largely unexceptional. In truth, an early student of the Fourteenth Amendment offered an assessment less tinged with anachronism. "The opinion enunciates sound principles of political science," wrote Charles Collins in 1912, "and is justified by the logic of history and of fact."[5]

The decision was so routine that within two years Brown himself did not find it noteworthy. In 1898, when he spoke for the Court in *Holden v. Hardy*, which upheld Utah's eight-hour law for miners against a Fourteenth Amendment challenge, Brown not only stressed the legitimacy of reasonable state police regulations, but included a crucial passage about legislative deference that closely paralleled language in *Plessy*. In the course of his exposition, he broadly reviewed prior judicial applications of the Amendment, including all the major race-related decisions under it—save one. He omitted any mention of *Plessy*, despite its having clearer relevance to the case at hand than did the race-related decisions that he discussed.[6]

Yet there was another side to the case. Against the conventional doctrine that served as a bastion for the separate car law, Homer Plessy's counsel had launched a radical attack; and Justice Harlan wrote it into *United States Reports*. The lawyers and to some extent Harlan additionally developed more standard claims resting especially on the Fourteenth Amendment's due process and equal protection clauses.

Bowing to legal orthodoxy, Plessy's attorneys squarely confronted the due process issue, raising the question of reputation as property. It may be protested that this claim responded only to the interests of a small and perhaps elitist group of "blacks"—those who could pass for white. Yet it was a practical, lawyer-like claim with a base in decisions holding that to call a white man a Negro was actionable.[7] If accepted, it would have "impossibly complicate[d] the enforcement of segregation," as Tourgée's biographer notes.[8] Counsel also advanced equal protection arguments, the key assertion being a technical claim that the separate car law denied a right of legal action that was available to others. But the Louisiana Supreme Court had already obviated each of these conventional attacks by construing the law as not immunizing railways against suits for wrong assignments. Further blunting the conventional arguments against the law, counsel for the state conceded that the provision in question was unconstitutional. Because misassigned blacks could now get their day in court, they suffered neither deprivation of due process nor denial of equal protection. A privileges-or-immunities argument proved no more conclusive.

Harlan addressed the conventional Fourteenth Amendment arguments less directly, for good reason. As Tourgée had come close to admitting on brief, the case law ran against them. Yet Harlan did not avoid the issues entirely. By stressing the public character of the facilities that Louisiana sought to regulate, he underscored that the separate car law violated the prohibitive clauses of the Amendment. By joining Plessy's counsel (at least implicitly) in denying the reasonableness of the law, he in effect concurred that it lacked an element which under conventional doctrine was essential to the validity of any police regulation.

In the final analysis, Harlan's central contention was his declaration that the "Constitution is color-blind." For this, the due process and equal protection clauses were secondary (although not irrelevant). His view rested primarily and broadly on the Thirteenth Amendment and the national citizenship clause of the Fourteenth. Plessy's attorneys had read these provisions in light of the Declaration of Independence, and Harlan gave them the same interpretation, but without explicit mention of the Declaration. Both for Harlan and for Plessy's counsel, that is, legally mandated or endorsed separation was ultimately unreasonable *as a matter of law*—period. Although the attorneys arguably compromised the point and Harlan left it implicit, the "facts" of science made no difference to the claim. Nor was history particularly crucial, though Harlan surely accepted the version of Reconstruction that Albion Tourgée had proposed.[9] Instead, the position relied on a simple and complex truth that cut through more than two decades of judicial accretions. At its core, Homer Plessy's case before the Court, which Harlan accepted, affirmed that American constitutional law necessarily embodies the principles of republican government, categorically rejecting recognition of race.

II

Brown probably would not have objected to the observation that he and the majority for which he spoke only reflected dominant trends of the times. When, writing from retirement in 1912, he took on the task of surveying the many dissents of Justice Harlan (who had died a year and a half earlier), he declared: "He, who would put himself abreast of the current thought of any particular epoch in the history of this country[,] cannot do better than to familiarize himself with the opinions of its great judges . . . ." Not an inordinately ambitious man, Brown perhaps would have disclaimed for himself the label of "great judge"; but the hypothetical reader might still have looked at Brown's opinions. For the Court's work in its generality, Brown averred, while not always "altogether unbiased," disclosed "the same division of sentiment among the judges as among the people whom they are presumed to instruct."

By contrast, Brown intimated that Harlan was a "great judge," or at least a great dissenter; and so, by implication, Brown admitted that the Kentuckian in his civil rights dissents likewise conveyed a broader strand of contemporary thought. Brown evidently doubted, however, that much would result. Harlan's dissents, he predicted, "will probably share the general fate and will not result in many changes in the law . . . ." Good lawyer that he was, Brown covered himself by allowing that a few of the dissents "will doubtless become the basis for future legislation, and perhaps for a reversal by the Court itself "—but he gave no hint that Harlan's *Plessy* opinion would share this happy fate.[10]

The issue Brown thereby raised leads to the question of *Plessy*'s impact. What results flowed from the majority and minority positions? In a word, what difference did the case make?

Plessy planted the doctrine of separate-but-equal more firmly than before in American law and particularly in the Constitution. It is true that Brown's opinion gave no explicit attention to the requirement of equality itself, a silence which has led one commentator to deny that the case really had anything to do with the equality portion of the doctrine. By this analysis, the case embedded a still more pernicious principle into constitutional law: that separation without reference to equality met the test of the Reconstruction Amendments.[11] Had Brown actually endorsed this view, he would only have set the Court in line with the trend of practice. But the separate car law linked separation to equality; Louisiana had defended the act partly on that ground; the state courts had noted the requirement of equality; and the sources of transportation segregation in non-constitutional case law, on which Brown partly relied, required that equal facilities accompany separation. In this context, whatever shortcomings *Plessy* manifested, a failure to require the separate-but-equal variety of equality cannot be counted among them.

One cannot confidently maintain, though, that without *Plessy* separate-but-equal would have lacked legal legitimacy. For one thing, within a few years other cases would probably have given the Supreme Court the opportunity to reach the same result. Four years later, for example, Kentucky's separate car law came up for review. After accepting the Kentucky Supreme Court's construction of the law as applying only to intrastate commerce, the federal Supreme Court, on an eight-to-one vote, summarily upheld it against a Fourteenth Amendment challenge on the authority of *Plessy*. Justice Brown spoke for the Court and Justice Harlan dissented without opinion.[12] Absent the 1896 decision, a fuller discussion of the Fourteenth Amendment issues would probably have been forthcoming. But a different result? This seems unlikely, for the same reason that a different result in *Plessy* itself is difficult to imagine within the context of the period.

A more compelling reason for discounting (but not dismissing) *Plessy*'s importance in establishing separate-but equal is that *prior* to 1896 courts had already accepted the doctrine as part of the common law of common carriers. They had declined to give private parties legal remedies against separation properly established by company regulation, despite the quasi-public status of common carriers. From the standpoint of the individual passenger, that is, separation was already legally mandatory if a carrier elected to decree it and a state equal accommodations law did not forbid it. In 1878, in *Hall v. DeCuir*, the Supreme Court itself construed congressional inaction regarding separation on common carriers as an endorsement of the permissibility of separate-but-equal within the common law governing them. This federalized the doctrine.

As a result, the first wave of *legislated* transportation segregation, enacted between 1887 and 1892, represented not so much an initial resort to law, but a change in the place of segregation within the legal matrix. This is not to say that the switch to statutory law made no difference. Persons who attempted to gain access to accommodations assigned to the other race no longer faced only denial of service without legal remedy. They were additionally liable to criminal prosecution. Not least, the legislation deprived transportation companies of any choice regarding segregation, which meant that remaining variations disappeared from southern practice. But the legal difference is easily overstated. The arguments that previously upheld company-imposed separation within the common law of common carriers now meshed nicely with the jurisprudence that courts had developed as they grappled with a plethora of non-racial police regulations challenged under the Fourteenth Amendment. Having already accepted one variety of equal-but-separate, courts confronted only the task of adaptation in order to validate the new version.

The United States Supreme Court's decision in *Plessy* nonetheless removed all doubt: separate-but-equal was unambiguously a part of the law of the Constitution. The Court, Albion Tourgée wrote, had "virtually nullified the fourteenth amendment . . . and emasculated the thirteenth." The blow was only partial, however. The justices had not gone so far as to hold explicitly that the Constitution recognized two categories of citizenship, one for whites and the other for non-whites, analogous to the stance it soon would take toward the inhabitants of the new territories acquired in the imperialist binge at the end of the decade. Rather, whatever the realities of the hardening color line in America, the formula associated with *Plessy* could be invoked against the worst deprivations. Thus, in *McCabe v. Atchison, Topeka, and Santa Fe* (1914), the Supreme Court indicated that in properly developed cases it would indeed hold intrastate railways to the standard of equality of service.[13]

Because of this "promising" side to *Plessy*, if it may be so labeled, the 1896 decision proved eventually to be a useful tool in the attack on racial segregation. *McCabe* signaled the beginning of the "journey *from* jim crow." Blacks, both individually and especially through the National Association for the Advancement of Colored People, used legal action to complicate and make more costly the enforcement of separation, by holding common carriers to the standard of real equality in facilities. Similarly, *Plessy* proved serviceable in the NAACP's fight against segregated schooling. In 1938, in the first school case in which the Court directly endorsed application of separate-but-equal to education, the doctrine served to strike down Missouri's arrangement to send blacks out-of-state for legal education. Both these trends came to fruition in the 1950s, when *Brown v. Board of Education* (1954) invalidated legally mandated segregation in education and *Gayle v. Browder* (1956) extended the *Brown* ruling to cover intrastate transportation.[14]

But prior to the success of the campaign against Jim Crow—aptly described by Catherine Barnes as "black initiative and federal response"— segregation laws and ordinances proliferated in the South. From hospitals before birth to cemeteries after death, separate-but-equal set the legal status of blacks. Fifty-four years after *Plessy*, one commentator found laws and decisions extending the doctrine "to every type of transportation, education, and amusement; to public housing, restaurants, hotels, libraries, public parks and recreational facilities, fraternal associations, marriage, employment, and public welfare institutions. It ha[d] pursued the negro even into prisons, wash houses in coal mines, telephone booths, and the armed forces." The separation extended as well to inanimate objects, as in Florida where school textbooks which had been used by one race were to be stored separately from those used by the other race. As for the detail of the codes, South Carolina provided an example in its 1917 circus regulation:

> Tent shows are to maintain separate entrances for different races. Any circus or other such traveling show exhibiting under canvas or out of doors for gain shall maintain two main entrances to such exhibition, and one shall be for white people and the other entrance shall be for colored people, and such main entrances shall be plainly marked "For White People," and the other entrance shall be marked "For Colored People," and all white persons attending such show or traveling exhibition other than those connected with the said show shall pass in and out of the entrance provided for white persons, and all colored persons attending such show or traveling exhibition shall pass in and out of the entrance provided for colored persons.

Violators could be fined not more than $500.[15]

Of all the legislated separation, the "jim crowing" of transportation, which had been the immediate issue in *Plessy*, probably proved the most galling. At the beginning of the new century, in the course of discussing the democratizing influence of relatively classless railway travel, Walter Weyl remarked how "[t]he exclusion of negroes from the compartments for whites in many Southern railways is a striking exception . . . ." The point was not lost on blacks, as Ray Stannard Baker and Gunnar Myrdal found in 1908 and 1944, respectively, when they probed Negro attitudes toward the color line. It was partly that the equality half of the separate-but-equal formula was frequently ignored, and partly that drivers and railway conductors often spoke and behaved abusively. Especially, though, transportation segregation had, as W. E. B. DuBois put it, "a publicly insulting character" which rubbed its way into the grain of daily life.[16]

After 1896, *Plessy* provided judicial authority for this degradation. It is frequently asserted or implied, however, that the decision did more—that it triggered both the second wave of separate car legislation, between 1898 and 1907, and the extension of compulsory segregation into other areas.[17] Did it, or does this view of the case's impact involve the historical fallacy of *post hoc ergo propter hoc*?

It had not taken a *Plessy*-type decision to trigger the first wave of legislation, in the years around 1890, when disfranchisement campaigns and accompanying anti-black political rhetoric had contributed to the segregation movement, along with white perceptions of distressingly uppity behavior by a new generation of Negroes. Similar elements undoubtedly helped to prompt the new separate car measures. In South Carolina, the first of the states contributing to the new wave of legislation, *Plessy* may in some sense have been the "decision which unlocked the door of the Jim Crow railroad car with a constitutional key," but the state's separate car law, passed in 1898, was part of a broader racist movement in politics spearheaded by the demagogic Ben Tillman. Significantly, too, separate car bills had been introduced regularly since the early 1890s; but after *Plessy* came down, the legislation still failed to pass. It was only in the second legislative session following the decision that a measure became law, as racial tension heated in the face of labor competition and as white fears arose that a new generation of blacks was replacing the compliant "fore de War variety of Negro."[18]

Elsewhere, as well, the evidence of *Plessy*'s direct role is slight. In Virginia, increased "nigger baiting" in state politics provided more of the major impetus for the legislation of 1900. It is also noteworthy that legislative activity promoting segregation in Virginia peaked in the 1920s and 1930s, a period not only well removed in time from 1896 but coinciding with more black assertiveness. North Carolina's first Jim Crow railway measure (1899) was enacted in the midst of the drive within the state to disfranchise blacks, and Maryland's law (1904) emerged as a by-product of an unsuccessful disfranchisement campaign. Oklahoma's contribution to transportation segregation (1907) was part of an anti-black movement accompanying the scramble for office following statehood. For the region as a whole, not only did racist agitation flourish but race separation fitted conveniently with Progressive-era ideals of social efficiency and progress.[19]

To be sure, by removing whatever doubts remained about the constitutional acceptability of segregation under the separate-but-equal formula, *Plessy* permitted the new legislation. But even as a permissive factor the case hardly stood alone. End-of-the-century imperialism, which led to colonial rule over non-white people abroad, helped free the white South from whatever restraints national opinion had imposed. Within the South itself, the decline in some places of older conservative elements within the Democratic Party, combined with the conservatives' adoption of race-baiting tactics, removed another restraint.[20]

There were, then, additional causal elements. Some served to encourage or incite further official segregation; others were permissive in their effects. Overall, one may argue about their importance in relation to each other. As regards an evaluation of *Plessy*, however, their meaning is clear enough. Although the decision may aptly serve as a symbol for legally mandatory segregation, the evidence calls for a "not proved" verdict on a close relationship between the Supreme Court's 1896 handiwork and the passage of new legislation.

III

In 1912, Henry Billings Brown largely conceded that John Marshall Harlan had been correct in identifying the intention behind Louisiana's separate car legislation as the degradation of blacks. By the middle of the twentieth century, Harlan seemed a prophet of the blossoming civil rights revolution, with the overturn of state-mandated school segregation in *Brown v. Board of Education* completing his constitutional vindication. Noting Harlan's vision of a color-blind Constitution, the *New York Times* editorialized after the *Brown* decision in May 1954 that "the words he used in lonely dissent . . . have become in effect . . . a part of the law of the land. . . . [T]here was not one word in Chief Justice [Earl] Warren's opinion that was inconsistent with the earlier views of Justice Harlan."[21]

History is seldom so neat and often more cunning. A case may be made that it was Justice Brown and the *Plessy* majority who stood vindicated by the last decades of the twentieth century. At a formal level, Chief Justice Warren failed to announce in 1954 that *Brown* had overruled the 1896 decision. Court watchers noted the omission. If not in *Brown*, some said, then the 1896 decision was overruled two years later in *Gayle v. Browder*, which invalidated city-ordered segregation of buses in Montgomery, Alabama. But again the Court did not explicitly reject *Plessy*, filing only a short *per curiam* opinion that rested on *Brown*. As of mid-1986, *Shepard's Citations*, the standard "finding aid" used by lawyers to trace subsequent judicial treatment of decisions, listed no case as having overruled *Plessy*. By then, though, some judges took a different view, commenting almost in passing that the 1954 decision had overturned the earlier ruling.[22]

More important, courts did not reject reliance on racial "facts," a central if not entirely explicit feature of Justice Brown's reasoning in *Plessy*. Nor did judges wholeheartedly embrace Justice Harlan's color-blind Constitution. The *Brown* case itself hinted that the spirit of *Plessy* survived in these regards. In upholding the finding of the federal trial court in Kansas that state-mandated segregation harmed school children, Chief Justice

Warren used an argument structurally similar to the one Justice Brown had used in upholding Louisiana's conclusion that separation promoted the public's welfare. "Whatever may have been the extent of psychological knowledge at the time of *Plessy v. Ferguson*," Warren held, the trial court's factual finding was "amply supported by modern authority," a statement he then documented through his soon-controversial Footnote Eleven, which cited seven studies by social scientists.[23] In 1896, it is true, the Court had deferred to legislative judgment about the "facts" of race, while in 1954 it deferred to a lower court's judgment, but in each instance conclusions about such "facts" entered into the reasoning. For Warren, a later critic observed, *Plessy*'s deficiency was "not that it asked the wrong questions but that it gave the wrong answers." The Chief Justice himself saw his social science authorities as important because they rebutted Justice Brown's social science.[24]

In *Brown*, Warren focused on the Fourteenth Amendment's equal protection clause. Once he found that legally segregated schooling violated the clause, he had no need to address the issue of due process violations. But in *Bolling v. Sharpe*, the school desegregation case from the District of Columbia that the Court decided along with *Brown*, Warren necessarily reached the due process issue. (Because the Fourteenth Amendment's prohibitive clauses do not apply to the federal government, *Bolling* turned on the due process clause of the Fifth Amendment.) Here, too, Warren declined to reject *Plessy*'s major premise. Rather than flatly holding segregation unreasonable as a matter of law—that is, as inconsistent with the true color-blind character of the amended Constitution, as Harlan had urged in 1896—the Chief Justice in effect admitted that some classifications based on race might be legitimate. Only then did he conclude that "[s]egregation in public education is not reasonably related to any proper governmental objective" and thus violated the due process rights of black school children in the District of Columbia.[25]

Yet *Brown* and its progeny invalidated legislated segregation in a variety of settings and in that sense undeniably struck at the system which *Plessy* had allowed. And if the reasoning in the 1954 opinions showed similarities to the reasoning of 1896, Warren at least did not overtly deny the correctness of Justice Harlan's dissent. In this regard, an argument can be made that if it was legitimate after *Brown* for the Court to rely solely on the 1954 decision as its authority for striking down segregation in non-educational areas, then *Brown* must have turned on the unconstitutionality of *all* racial classification by state agencies.[26] But within a quarter-century, a rather different conclusion was possible.

By the 1970s, attention shifted to affirmative action programs involving preferential or "benign" quotas for members of racial minorities. Their advocates had to show that *Brown* did not mean that *all* racial classifications were per se unconstitutional. In the *Bakke* case (1977), the Supreme Court

finally faced the issue. It overturned an admissions program of the medical
school of the University of California at Davis that set aside sixteen places in
each entering class for minority applicants. The Court also held that
admissions officers could take account of the racial identity of applicants as
one of several non-academic characteristics that might contribute desirable
qualities to the overall educational environment. Justice Lewis F. Powell
announced the Court's judgment and filed an opinion which gained
considerable attention because Powell provided the deciding vote in shaping
the Court's two-pronged judgment. He had no good reply to the charge that
in some cases such an admissions scheme would in fact use race as the crucial
determinant. A court, he could only say, must not presume that university
officials would operate the program "as a cover for the functional equivalent
of a quota system."[27]

Justice John Paul Stevens, joined by three other members of the Court,
strongly objected to any use of race (and thus voted with Powell to overturn
the program at the University of California-Davis and to order Allen Bakke's
admission). Because Stevens focused on the arrangement at Davis as a
statutory violation of the Civil Rights Act of 1964, he avoided extensive
constitutional analysis. But lurking only slightly beneath the surface of his
opinion was the charge that the Court had rejected Justice Harlan's
color-blind Constitution.[28]

What gave real substance to the charge was not Stevens's passing
comments, but rather the position taken by the four justices who joined
Powell in agreeing that the medical school might still take *some* account of
race. These four, who would have preferred to go further and forthrightly
accept the university's quota system, spoke out against letting "color
blindness become myopia which masks the reality that many [of those]
'created equal' have been treated within our lifetimes as inferior both by the
law and by their fellow citizens." Regarding a "color-blind" interpretation of
the equal protection clause, they stressed that the Court had "expressly
rejected this proposition on a number of occasions."[29]

One of the four, Justice Thurgood Marshall, bore in deeper in a separate
opinion. From his review of the events surrounding the adoption of the
Fourteenth Amendment, he found it "inconceivable that the . . .
Amendment was intended to prohibit all race-conscious relief measures."
Reminding his brethren "that the principle that 'the Constitution is
color-blind' appeared only in the opinion of the lone dissenter [in *Plessy*]," he
left the clear implication that the Constitution should not now be regarded
as color-blind. As if to underscore the chasm between his analysis and the one
advanced in the 1890s by Albion Tourgée and Justice Harlan, Marshall
portrayed the Declaration of Independence itself as the founding statement of
a racist nation. Against this backdrop, racial classification was a requisite to
remedying social ills.[30]

The debate over the relation of affirmative action to *Plessy* did not stop

with the Court. In the course of defending preferential treatment of
minorities, one scholar went so far as to label Harlan's view "color-blind
racism" and cautioned, "The courage of Harlan's dissent should not blind us
to the moral and historical limitations of his argument." It was a position
calculated to ensure white supremacy under the facade of equal protection.
Another academician argued that Harlan's slogan about a color-blind
Constitution really meant the Constitution was highly sensitive to color.
From the other side, a critic of affirmative action charged that the very
reasoning used to support supposedly benign racial classifications can be used
to support the outcome in *Plessy*, and that Justice Brown's 1896 opinion
indeed anticipated the reasoning on behalf of such classifications. After all,
Brown had written that "every exercise of the police power must be
reasonable, and extend only to such laws as are enacted in good faith for the
promotion for the public good, *and not for the annoyance or oppression* of a
particular class." Preferential racial classifications were "*Plessy v. Ferguson* all
over again, in new and modish dress."[31]

By the mid-1980s, "counting by race" had received further judicial
approval.[32] A resulting problem recalled the *Plessy* era when, one day,
Booker T. Washington observed a man riding in a colored coach. The
passenger, as Washington subsequently related the story, "was well known
in his community as a Negro, but . . . was so white that even an expert
would have [had] hard work to classify him as a black man," and so the
train's conductor was in a quandary. "If the man was a Negro, the conductor
did not want to send him into the white people's coach," Washington
surmised; "at the same time, if he was a white man, the conductor did not
want to insult him by asking him if he was a Negro." Presumably without
being obvious, the train official looked over the passenger's "hair, eyes, nose,
and hands, but still seemed puzzled." There remained the feet, which next
came under attentive glance. (The man evidently was barefoot.) Observing
the process, Washington said to himself: "That will settle it." The man's feet
identified him as black, and the conductor left him in his seat. In late 1985,
several New York City policemen sought to have their racial classifications
changed from white to black or Hispanic, their apparent goal, according to
a police official, being qualification for promotion to sergeant under a racial
quota. But the nation had progressed beyond the foot test. Proof of ethnicity
now had to meet federal guidelines.[33]

IV

In September 1896, four months after the Citizens' Committee to Test the
Constitutionality of the Separate Car Law lost its case, Louisiana Attorney
General Cunningham dutifully requested the Clerk of the United States
Supreme Court to forward the Court's formal order affirming the state
decision in *Ex parte Plessy*. The Clerk complied, and nothing now blocked

Homer Plessy's trial. On January 11, 1897, over four and a half years after his arrest for attempting to board a white car on the East Louisiana Railway, Plessy entered a plea of "guilty" in Criminal District Court and paid a twenty-five-dollar fine. The case by then had cost $2762 of the $2982 that the Citizens' Committee had raised to support its challenge to Jim Crow. The Committee distributed $160 of the remainder to Louisiana charities and used the final sixty dollars to inscribe "a flattering testimonial" to Tourgée, as the old carpetbagger publicly described it.[34]

Of the main characters in the case, James Walker died in July 1898, his role sufficiently obscured that obituaries praised him for his successful fight on behalf of Jim Crow. Albion Tourgée died in France in 1905, having received a consular appointment from President William McKinley the year after *Plessy* came down. Louis Martinet continued on in New Orleans as a lawyer and physician, dying in 1917. Homer Plessy, who lived to 1925, was largely lost to history.[35]

The *Plessy* case turns out finally as a story about losers, albeit dedicated losers. Quite at odds with the initial hopes of the Citizens' Committee, the federal Supreme Court's action ratified classification by race. The outcome came not from startling recent shifts in doctrine, nor from the Court's setting off boldly in a new direction in the case itself. Rather, it turned, almost inexorably, on incremental change. Acceptable law and passable social science—by the lights of the day—together denied the self-evident truth of the Declaration of Independence, a point the Committee underscored in its final report. "As the purpose of the Dred Scott decision was to secure and perpetuate slavery," Tourgée reflected after receiving the report, "so the effect of this decision is to establish that most degrading and inhuman form of oppression—legalized caste, based on race and color."

Yet the case is more than a tale of losers. Besides having their years in court, Martinet and his associates had their arguments displayed on the record—indeed, memorialized in Justice Harlan's dissent—to instruct later generations. "In defending the cause of liberty," declared the Citizens' Committee, "we met with defeat, but not with ignominy."[36] *Plessy v. Ferguson* made a difference, then, not so much for what it did, as for what it symbolized, negatively and positively, and for the sobering and nagging questions about citizenship in a scientific age that it posed—and poses—to anyone paying attention.

NOTES

INTRODUCTION "The *Plessy* Prison"

1. *Plessy v. Ferguson*, 163 U.S. 537, 550–51, 562, 559 (1896). The irony of Brown and Harlan's positions, when viewed in light of the origins of the two men, is suggested in C. Vann Woodward, "The National Decision Against Equality," in Woodward, *American Counterpoint: Slavery and Racism in the North/South Dialogue* (1971; New York, 1983), 229.

2. In order of quoted phrases: Herbert Storing, "The School of Slavery: A Reconsideration of Booker T. Washington," in *100 Years of Emancipation*, Robert A. Goldwin, ed. (Chicago, 1964), 66; Loren Miller, *The Petitioners: The Story of the Supreme Court of the United States and the Negro* (New York, 1966), 169; Justice Thurgood Marshall, dissenting and concurring in *Regents of the University of California v. Bakke*, 438 U.S. 265, 392 (1978); J. R. Pole, *The Pursuit of Equality in American History* (Berkeley, 1978), 197; Morton Keller, *Affairs of State: Public Life in Late Nineteenth Century America* (Cambridge, Mass., 1977), 453–54; Ralph T. Jans, "Negro Civil Rights and the Supreme Court, 1865–1949" (Ph.D. diss., Univ. of Chicago, 1951), 199; Benno C. Schmidt, Jr., "Principle and Prejudice: The Supreme Court and Race in the Progressive Era; Part I: The Heyday of Jim Crow," 82 *Colum. Law Rev.* (1982), 467; Miller, *Petitioners*, 170.

3. Keller, *Affairs of State*, 453; Loren P. Beth, *The Development of the American Constitution, 1877–1917* (New York, 1971), 197; Roy Wilkins, "Emancipation and Militant Leadership," in Goldwin, ed., *100 Years*, 26; Judge A. Leon Higginbotham, Book Review of Derrick A. Bell, *Race, Racism, and American Law*, in 122 *Univ. of Pa. Law Rev.* (1974), 1053–65 (Higginbotham's brackets); Woodward, "National Decision Against Equality," 212.

4. Robert J. Harris, *The Quest for Equality: The Constitution, Congress, and the Supreme Court* (Baton Rouge, 1960), 101; Beth, *Development of the American Constitution*, 197. Harris's remark about bad logic, etc., has been a favorite for subsequent quotation; see, for example, Otto H. Olsen, "Introduction," in *The Thin Disguise . . . Plessy v. Ferguson: A Documentary Presentation*, Olsen, ed. (New York, 1967), 17; Paul Oberst, "The Strange Career of *Plessy v. Ferguson*," 15 *Ariz. Law Rev.* (1973), 390; David W. Bishop, "*Plessy v. Ferguson*: A Reinterpretation," 62 *J. of Negro Hist.* (1977), 125.

5. For assertions that *Plessy* involved a conviction, see, for example, Sidney Kaplan, "Albion W. Tourgee: Attorney for the Segregated," 49 *J. of Negro Hist.* (1964), 129; Oberst, "Strange Career," 393. The claim that equal protection was the core issue has been widely stated or implied, as, for example, in Charles W. Collins, *The Fourteenth Amendment and the States* (1912; New York, 1974), 55; Leonard W. Levy, "'Separate But Equal': The History of a Noxious Doctrine," *The New Leader*, 2 Feb. 1953, at 8; Jack Greenberg, *Cases and Materials on Judicial Process and Social Change: Constitutional Litigation* (St. Paul, Minn., 1977), 20; Richard A. Maidment, "*Plessy v. Ferguson* Reexamined," 7 *J. of Amer. Studies* (1973), 125.

6. See, for example, Maidment, "*Plessy v. Ferguson* Reexamined," 126 (suggesting the Thirteenth Amendment argument was ill-advised); Woodward, "National Decision Against Equality," 224 (implicitly questioning the due process/ reputation argument); Greenberg, *Judicial Process*, 585–86 (questioning the case's timing).

7. Paul Oberst, "The Supreme Court and States Rights," 48 *Ky. Law J.* (1959), 78; Paul G. Kauper, "Segregation in Public Education: The Decline of *Plessy v. Ferguson*," 52 *Mich. Law Rev.* (1954), 1137; Schmidt, "Principle and Prejudice," 467; G. Edward White, *The American Judicial Tradition: Profiles of Leading American Judges* (New York, 1976), 143; *Univ. of California v. Bakke*, 438 U.S. at 392 (Marshall, concurring and dissenting); Richard F. Watt and Richard M. Orlikoff, "The Coming Vindication of Mr. Justice Harlan," 44 *Ill. Law Rev.* (1949), 13.

8. See, for example, *Los Angeles Times*, 4 Feb. 1980, pt. I, at 3, describing the reaction to Professor Derrick Bell of Harvard Law School, formerly an attorney with the NAACP Legal Defense and Education Fund, when he testified against the efficacy of racial balancing as a means to equal educational opportunity.

9. See Chapter Nine, *infra* (on press reaction); Carter G. Woodson, "Fifty Years of Negro Citizenship as Qualified by the United States Supreme Court," 6 *J. of Negro Hist.* (1921), 26–29; Charles Warren, 3 *The Supreme Court in United States History* (Boston, 1922); 2 *ibid.* (rev. ed., Boston, 1926), 621 n. 1; Carl Brent Swisher, *American Constitutional Development* (Boston, 1943) (Swisher's second edition [1954] mentioned *Plessy* briefly, at 1047); 2 *Documents of American History*, Henry Steele Commager, ed. (4th ed., New York, 1948). Later editions of Commager's *Documents* included *Plessy* as Document Number 343, in place of the Democratic Party Platform of 1896. (I am grateful to Professor Arthur Bestor for calling Commager's omission to my attention.) See also Higginbotham, Book Review, 122 *Univ. of Pa. Law Rev.* (1974), 1054–56, 1064, on the omission of *Plessy* from law school casebooks.

10. This analysis of the term is suggested by several authors; see, for example, Don E. Fehrenbacher, "Only His Stepchildren: Lincoln and the Negro," 20 *Civil War Hist.* (1974), 299–300, and Fehrenbacher's accompanying citations.

CHAPTER ONE   *De Facto* to *De Jure*: Transportation Segregation
in the South from the Civil War to the 1890s

1. *Century Dictionary and Cyclopedia* (New York, 1902), 4, 3233; Hugh M. Smythe, "The Concept 'Jim Crow,'" 27 *Social Forces* (1948), 45. On early Anglo-American racial stereotypes and their relation to the origins of slavery, see, for example, Winthrop D. Jordan, *White Over Black: American Attitudes Toward the Negro, 1550–1812* (Chapel Hill, 1968), 3–98: George M. Fredrickson, *White Supremacy: A Comparative Study in American and South African Slavery* (New York, 1981), 54–85.

2. Emile E. Delseriez to Marguerite Williams, 6 May, 20 June 1865, in John W. Blassingame, *Black New Orleans, 1860–1880* (Chicago, 1973), 174; *Journal of the Senate of the State of Delaware* (1866), 33, quoted in Harold B. Hancock, "Reconstruction in Delaware," *Radicalism, Racism, and Party Realignment: The Border States During Reconstruction*, Richard O. Curry, ed. (Baltimore, 1969), 197; George M. Fredrickson, *The Black Image in the White Mind: The Debate on Afro-American Character and Destiny, 1817–1914* (New York, 1971), esp. 165–97; Harold M. Hyman and William M. Wiecek, *Equal Justice Under Law: Constitutional Development, 1835–1875* (New York, 1982), 327–34. (Chapter Five, *infra*, offers a fuller account of American racist thought in the late nineteenth century.)

3. C. Vann Woodward, *The Strange Career of Jim Crow* (1955; 3rd rev. ed., New York, 1974), esp. 31–109; Woodward, "The Strange Career of a Historical Controversy," in Woodward, *American Counterpoint: Slavery and Racism in the North/South Dialogue* (1971; New York, 1983), 234–60; Howard N. Rabinowitz, "From Exclusion to Segregation: Southern Race Relations, 1865–1890," 63 *J. of Amer. Hist.* (1976), 330. To describe Woodward's focus and argument, two of his former students have suggested an apt analogy to three common statistical concepts: the mode, the mean, and the variance. The first measures dominant tendency; the second, average circumstance; and the third, degree of divergence. They argue, convincingly I think, that Woodward's primary focus is the last of these, or, as Woodward himself has put it, the "crosscurrents and uncertainties" and the "forgotten alternatives." See J. Morgan Kousser and James M. McPherson, "Introduction," in *Region, Race, and Reconstruction: Essays in Honor of C. Vann Woodward*, Kousser and McPherson, eds. (New York, 1982), xxvi–xxvii.

4. James Bryce, "Thoughts on the Negro Problem," 153 *North Amer. Rev.* (1891), 644; [J. B. Harrison,] "Studies in the South—Part IX," 50 *Atlantic Mon.* (1882), 626–27; David Macrae, *The Americans at Home* (Edinburgh, 1870), 2, 219, quoted in Howard N. Rabinowitz, *Race Relations in the Urban South, 1865–1890* (New York, 1978), 183.

5. See, for example, Charles Wynes, *Race Relations in Virginia, 1870–1902* (Charlottesville, 1961), 76; Frenise A. Logan, *The Negro in North Carolina, 1876–1894* (Chapel Hill, 1964), 176–83; Henry Dethloff and Robert C. Jones, "Race Relations in Louisiana, 1877–1898," 9 *La. Hist.* (1968), 311–14; Lawrence D. Rice, *The Negro in Texas, 1874–1900* (Baton Rouge, 1971), 144–48.

6. Rabinowitz, *Race Relations*, 183–84, 192–94; Chapter Six, *infra*.

7. Rabinowitz, *Race Relations*, 191; *The Sue*, 22 Fed. Rep. 843, 846–47 (1885); transcript of testimony in *DeCuir v. Benson*, Case No. 7800, 8th District

Court for the Parish of Orleans (1872–73); included in case file for *DeCuir v. Benson*, 27 La. Ann. 1 (1875), Docket No. 4829, Louisiana Supreme Court Archives, Earl K. Long Library, University of New Orleans; George Washington Cable, "The Negro Question" (1888), reprinted in *The Negro Question: A Selection of Writings on Civil Rights in the South*, Arlin Turner, ed. (New York, 1968), 129. See also Blassingame, *Black New Orleans*, 193. Testimony in *DeCuir v. Benson* indicates that assignment of blacks to the "Freedmen's Bureau" was not customary before the war, when exclusion from inside quarters was the rule.

8. This description draws on the evidence reviewed in the court cases discussed in Chapter Six, *infra*, with additional and corroborating detail provided by Emory R. Johnson, *American Railway Transportation* (2nd rev. ed., New York and London, 1910), 141–44; John R. White, Jr., *The American Railroad Passenger Car* (Baltimore, 1978), 462–66 and *passim*; Maury Klein, *History of the Louisville and Nashville Railroad* (New York, 1972), 56. On longer runs, other higher-fare accommodations such as sleeping cars were also available. For the legal consequences of denying appropriate seating to white males with first-class tickets, see *Bass v. Chicago and Northwestern Railway Company*, 36 Wis. 450 (1874).

9. Quoted in Woodward, *Strange Career*, 38–40. Stewart was assigned a separate dining table on a North Carolina steamboat. *Ibid.*, 39.

10. Thomas Wentworth Higginson, "Some War Scenes Revisited," 42 *Atlantic Mon.* (1878), 6–7; George Washington Cable, "The Silent South," 30 *Century Mag.* (1885), 685; Sir George Campbell, *White and Black: The Outcome of a Visit to the United States* (New York, 1879), 195. For Woodward's discussion of these three observers, see *Strange Career*, 35–37. In 1888, based on a trip he took in 1887, Cable reiterated his observation about Virginia and extended it to South Carolina. See Cable, "The Negro Question," 129.

11. Woodward, *Strange Career*, 38, 34–35.

12. "A Speech Delivered before the Women's New England Club," 27 Jan. [1890,] 3 *The Booker T. Washington Papers*, Louis R. Harlan, ed. (Urbana, Ill., 1972–84), 27–28 and 32 n. 1.

13. *Ibid.*, 28–29.

14. Wynes, *Race Relations in Virginia*, 68–71.

15. *Ibid.*, 71–74.

16. Margaret Law Callcott, *The Negro in Maryland Politics, 1870–1912* (Baltimore, 1969), 133–36; Logan, *Negro in North Carolina*, 177–80.

17. Joel Williamson, *After Slavery: The Negro in South Carolina During Reconstruction, 1861–1877* (Chapel Hill, 1965), 280–85; George B. Tindall, *South Carolina Negroes, 1877–1890* (Columbia, 1952), 299–300.

18. "A South Carolinian" [Belton O'Neall Townsend], "South Carolina Society," 39 *Atlantic Mon.* (1877), 676; Williamson, *After Slavery*, 284; Iza Duffus Hardy, *Between Two Oceans: or, Sketches of American Travel* (London, 1884), 305–8; *Heard v. Georgia Railway Company*, 1 Interstate Commerce Reports 719, 720 (1888). (See also *ibid.*, 722, where the I.C.C. specifically mentioned South Carolina again, along with Virginia and North Carolina.)

19. Woodward, *Strange Career*, 40 (quoting Stewart); Higginson, "Some War Scenes Revisited," 7; Duffus Hardy, *Between Two Oceans*, 306–7; *Cong. Rec.* 48 Cong., 2d sess., 316 (17 Dec. 1884).

20. Henry W. Grady, "In Plain Black and White," 29 *Century Mag.* (1885),

914–15; *Councill v. Western and Atlantic Railroad Company*, 1 Interstate Commerce Reports 638, 640 (1887).

21. Rabinowitz, *Race Relations*, 183, 196–97; *Cong. Globe*, 42 Cong., 2d sess., 3264 (9 May 1872); *Cong. Rec.*, 43 Cong., 2d sess., 946–47, 998 (4 Feb. 1875); Wharton, *The Negro in Mississippi*, 230–31; Blassingame, *Black New Orleans*, 194–95; Cable, "The Freedman's Case in Equity," 29 *Century Mag.* (1885), 415–16; Rice, *The Negro in Texas*, 140–47; Joseph H. Cartwright, *The Triumph of Jim Crow: Tennessee Race Relations in the 1880s* (Knoxville, 1976), 102–7, 183–91; Cable, "The Silent South," 685–86; David Key, "Civil and Political Status of the Negro," *Proc. . . . of the Bar Assoc. of Tenn. . . . 1885* (Nashville, 1886), 141–43; Grady, "In Plain Black and White," 915. Significantly, the I.C.C. bracketed Tennessee with Georgia. See *Councill v. Western and Atlantic Railroad Company*, 1 Interstate Commerce Reports 638, 640 (1887). Florida's practices seem to have escaped the attention of contemporaries and later historians and so remain a question mark.

22. Washington to the Editor of the Montgomery, Ala., *Advertiser*, 24 April 1885, in 2 *Booker T. Washington Papers*, 270–71. For similar descriptions, see the cases cited in Chapter Six, *infra*.

23. Blassingame, *Black New Orleans*, 190–92; Cable, "The Negro Question," 129; Dethloff and Jones, "Race Relations in Louisiana," 314; Dale A. Somers, "Black and White in New Orleans: A Study in Urban Race Relations, 1865–1900," 40 *J. of So. Hist.* (1974), 38; John William Graves, "Town and Country: Race Relations and Urban Development in Arkansas, 1874–1905" (Ph.D. diss., Univ. of Virginia, 1978), 109–41.

24. Cf. Franklin Johnson, *The Development of State Legislation Concerning the Free Negro* (New York, 1910), 14–15.

25. Laws of Mississippi, 1865, at 231–32 (Ch. 74, sec. 6); Wharton, *The Negro in Mississippi*, 230; Laws of Florida, 1865–66, at 25 (Ch. 1466, sec. 14).

26. General Laws of Texas, 1866, at 97 (Ch. 52); Rice, *The Negro in Texas*, 142, 145–46.

27. See Laws of Tennessee, 1867–68, at 84–85 (Ch. 66); Laws of Arkansas, 1868, at 39 (No. 15); *ibid.*, 1873, at 15–19 (No. 12); Laws of South Carolina, 1868–69, at 179 (No. 98); *ibid.*, at 337–38 (No. 233); *ibid.*, 1869–70, at 386–88 (No. 279); Laws of Louisiana, 1869, at 37 (No. 38); *ibid.*, 1870, Extra Session, 93 (No. 39); *ibid.*, 1873, at 156–57 (No. 84); Public Laws of Georgia, 1870, at 398 (No. 258); *ibid.*, 427 (No. 289); General Laws of Texas, 1871, at 16 (Ch. 21); Laws of Florida, 1873, at 25–26 (Ch. 1947); Laws of Mississippi, 1873, at 66–69 (Ch. 63). On the sequence of laws in Georgia, see Edmund L. Drago, *Black Politicians and Reconstruction in Georgia: A Splendid Failure* (Baton Rouge, 1982), 99–100. See generally Gilbert T. Stephenson, *Race Distinctions in American Law* (New York, 1910), 115–20.

28. Cable, "The Freedman's Case in Equity," 415; Williamson, *After Slavery*, 282–87; Elizabeth Hyde Botume, *First Days Among the Contrabands* (1893; reprint ed., New York, 1968), 267–69.

29. Tindall, *South Carolina Negroes*, 291–93; Blassingame, *Black New Orleans*, 183–85; *DeCuir v. Benson*, 27 La. Ann. 1 (1875); Roger A. Fischer, *The Segregation Struggle in Louisiana, 1862–77* (Urbana, Ill., 1974), 69–80. See also Germaine A. Reed, "Race Legislation in Louisiana, 1864–1920," 6 *La. Hist.* (1965), 386–89; Paul A. Kunkel, "Modifications in Louisiana Negro Legal Status under Louisiana

Constitutions, 1812–1957," 44 *J. of Negro Hist.* (1959), 13–15. In Mrs. DeCuir's case, the owners eventually gained reversal on appeal to the United States Supreme Court, in *Hall v. DeCuir*, 95 U.S. 485 (1878) (see Chapter Six, *infra*), but this does not detract from the case's significance as one indicator of the local judicial climate.

30. *Cong. Rec.*, 43 Cong., 1st sess., 425, App. 303 (6 Jan., 22 May 1874); *ibid.*, 43 Cong., 2d sess., 946–47, 998 (3, 4 Feb. 1875); Wharton, *Negro in Mississippi*, 231; Graves, "Town and Country . . . in Arkansas," 56–61; Rice, *Negro in Texas*, 146; Rabinowitz, *Race Relations*, 183.

31. Ernst Freund, *The Police Power: Public Policy and Constitutional Rights* (Chicago, 1904), 716–17; *Cong. Rec.*, 48 Cong., 2d sess., 316 (17 Dec. 1884); Isaac DuBose Seabrook, *Before and After, or Relations of the Races at the South*, John H. Moore, ed. (Baton Rouge, 1967), 14–15 (editor's introduction); *Heard v. Georgia Railway Company*, 2 Interstate Commerce Reports 508, 510 (1889) (citing the Georgia Railroad Commission case of *Gaines v. Defendant* [1888]). See also Albert N. Sanders, "Jim Crow Comes to South Carolina," *Proc. of the South Carolina Hist. Assoc.*, 1966, at 29–34; John H. Moore, "Jim Crow in Georgia," 66 *So. Atlantic Q.* (1967), 556–57.

32. Stanley J. Folmsbee, "The Origin of the First 'Jim Crow' Law," 15 *J. of So. Hist.* (1949), 235–40; Laws of Tennessee, 1875, at 216–17 (Ch. 130).

33. Laws of Tennessee, 1881, at 211–12 (Ch. 155); *ibid.*, 1891, at 135–36 (Ch. 52); Folmsbee, "Origins of the First 'Jim Crow' Law," 242–46; Cartwright, *Triumph of Jim Crow*, 104–7.

34. Laws of Florida, 1887, at 116 (Ch. 3743); Laws of Mississippi, 1888, at 48–49 (Ch. 27); *ibid.*, 45 (Ch. 26, sec. 2) (waiting rooms); General Laws of Texas, 1889, at 132–33 (Ch. 108); *ibid.*, 1891, at 44–45 (Ch. 41); *ibid.*, 165 (Ch. 103) (clarifying the street railway exemption); Laws of Louisiana, 1890, at 152–54 (No. 111); *ibid.*, 1894, at 133–34 (No. 98); Laws of Alabama, 1890–91, at 412–13 (Ch. 185); Laws of Arkansas, 1891, at 15–17 (Act 17); *ibid.*, 1893, at 200–201 (Act 114); Laws of Tennessee, 1891, at 135–36 (Ch. 52); Laws of Georgia, 1890–91, pt. I, 157–58 (No. 751); *ibid.*, 1899, pt. I, 66–67 (No. 369) (extending coverage to sleeping cars); Laws of Kentucky, 1891–93, at 63–64 (Ch. 40); Laws of South Carolina, 1898, at 777–78 (No. 483); *ibid.*, 1903, at 84 (No. 53) (clarifying freight train exemption); *ibid.*, 1904, at 438–39 (No. 249) (extending coverage to steam ferries); *ibid.*, 1906, at 76 (No. 52) (separate station dining rooms); Public Laws of North Carolina, 1899, at 539–40 (Ch. 384); *ibid.*, 1907, at 1238–39 (Ch. 850) (extending coverage to street cars); Laws of Virginia, 1899–1900, at 236–37 (Ch. 226); *ibid.*, 340 (Ch. 312) (steamboats); *ibid.*, 1901, at 329–30 (Ch. 300) (strengthening the steamboat regulation); Laws of Maryland, 1904, at 186–87 (Ch. 109); *ibid.*, 188–89 (Ch. 110) (steamboats); Laws of Oklahoma, 1907–08, at 201–4 (Ch. 15). See generally Stephenson, *Race Distinctions*, 207–36. Except where necessary to avoid ambiguity, full citations of state measures are omitted in the following footnotes.

35. PASSENGER CRIMINAL PENALTIES: Texas (1889, 1891), Louisana (1890, 1894), Alabama (1891), Arkansas (1891), Georgia (1891).

36. NURSE EXEMPTIONS: Florida (1887), Texas (1891), Louisiana (1890, 1894), Tennessee (1891), Georgia (1891), Kentucky (1892). PEACE OFFICER EXEMPTIONS: Arkansas (1891, 1894), Louisiana (1894), Kentucky (1892). EMPLOYEE EXEMPTIONS: Texas (1891), Arkansas (1891), Kentucky (1892). STREET

RAILWAY EXEMPTIONS: Louisiana (1890), Texas (1891), Arkansas (1891, 1893), Tennessee (1891). SLEEPING OR CHAIR CAR EXEMPTIONS: Texas (1889) [implied], 1891), Alabama (1891 [implied]), Arkansas (1893). Georgia, one of the nine states in the initial group, added a sleeping car exemption after *Plessy*, in 1899.

37. A possible exception might be the case of Louisiana, where perhaps a few white nurses were employed by blacks in the well-established Creole community, but this is simply conjecture.

38. John W. Graves, "The Arkansas Negro and Segregation, 1890–1903" (M.A. thesis, Univ. of Arkansas, 1967), 29.

39. W. J. Cash, *The Mind of the South* (1941; New York, 1960), 117–19 and *passim*. For a refinement of Cash's view, see Joel Williamson, *The Crucible of Race: Black-White Relations in the American South Since Emancipation* (New York, 1984), esp. 111–24, 253–54, on which I draw later in this chapter.

40. Joel Williamson, *New People: Miscegenation and Mulattoes in the United States* (New York, 1980), 77–78.

41. Woodward, *Strange Career*, 74–83. See also Lawrence Goodwyn, *Democratic Promise: The Populist Movement in America* (New York, 1976), esp. 244–306.

42. See, for example, Clarence A. Bacote, "The Negro in Georgia Politics, 1880–1908" (Ph.D. diss., Univ. of Chicago, 1955), 159–63; Charles L. Flynn, Jr., *White Land, Black Labor: Caste and Class in Late Nineteenth Century Georgia* (Baton Rouge, La., 1983), 180–82; Sheldon Hackney, *Populism to Progressivism in Alabama* (Princeton, 1969), 43–47; Wharton, *Negro in Mississippi*, 231–32; John W. Graves, "The Arkansas Separate Coach Law of 1891," 7 *J. of the West* (1968), 534–35; Graves, "Town and Country . . . in Arkansas," 287 n. 45. On the role of lower-class resentment, see also Fredrickson, *White Supremacy*, 269–70; C. Vann Woodwood, *Origins of the New South, 1877–1913* (Baton Rouge, 1951), 211–12.

43. Charlton W. Tebeau, *A History of Florida* (Coral Gables, Fla., 1971), 296; New Orleans *Daily Picayune*, 5 June 1890 at 4; *ibid.*, 10 July 1891 at 10; Laws of Mississippi, 1888, at 44–48 (Ch. 26); Laws of Arkansas, 1891, at 15–17 (Act 17); Robert C. Cotner, *James Stephen Hogg: A Biography* (Austin, Tex., 1959), 223–43; Daniel M. Robison, *Bob Taylor and the Agrarian Revolt in Tennessee* (Chapel Hill, 1935), 144–53. For further suggestive evidence of the association in Arkansas between support for segregation legislation and railway and other reform legislation, see Graves, "Town and Country . . . in Arkansas," 269–70. See also W. Ernest Douglas, "Retreat from Conservatism: The Old Lady of Broad Street [the Charleston *News and Courier*] Embraces Jim Crow," *Proc. of the South Carolina Hist. Assoc.*, 1958, at 3–11. When he first called for the Texas law (in an address proposing railway reform), Governor Hogg suggested its administration be assigned to the state railway commission. See "Message of Governor . . . ," Austin *Daily Statesman*, 22 Jan. 1891 at 12.

44. On the disfranchisement controversy, see J. Morgan Kousser, *The Shaping of Southern Politics: Suffrage Restriction and the Establishment of the One-Party South* (New Haven, 1974), 97–98, 109–16, 123–26, 132, 140–42, 154–55, 203, 210–14. The association of the disfranchisement debates with the advent of Jim Crow legislation, I should caution, is mine, not Kousser's.

45. Rabinowitz, *Race Relations*, 333–39; Hackney, *Populism to Progressivism*, 44–45; Rice, *Negro in Texas*, 147; Bacote, "The Negro in Georgia Politics," 159.

46. Bryce, "Thoughts on the Negro Problem," 650–51 (emphasis added).

47. For late nineteenth-century assessments of the Negro's alleged patholo-gies, see Chapter Five, *infra*. Joel Williamson, in *The Crucible of Race*, 253–54, 111–24, persuasively suggests the complex association between the drive for legislated segregation and white sexual phobias, Victorian morality, scientific thought, and black assertiveness. His use of the term "Radical," however, is needlessly unconventional. On white southern fears generally, see Lawrence J. Friedman, *The White Savage: Racial Fantasies in the Postbellum South* (Englewood Cliffs, N.J., 1971). The fear of miscegenation was increasing, it should be noted, even as its actual incidence was falling. See Williamson, *New People*, 61–109.

48. Richard C. Wade, *Slavery in the Cities: The South, 1820–1860* (New York, 1964), 243–61; John W. Cell, *The Highest Stage of White Supremacy: The Origins of Segregation in South Africa and the American South* (Cambridge, Eng., 1982), 131–70.

49. Paul Gaston, *The New South Creed: A Study in Southern Mythmaking* (New York, 1970), 136–50; Grady, "In Plain Black and White," 914–15; *Cong. Rec.*, 48 Cong., 2d sess., 317 (17 Dec. 1884). The five states using the phrase "equal but separate" were Mississippi (1888), Louisiana (1890), Alabama (1891), Arkansas (1891), and Tennessee (1891). Other phrases were "equally as good, and provided with the same facilities for comfort" (Florida, 1887), "of equal character as to comfort, etc." (Texas, 1889), "separate coaches . . . equal in all points of comfort and convenience" (Texas, 1891), "equal accommodations, in separate cars" (Geor-gia, 1891), and "no difference or discrimination in the quality, convenience, or accommodations in the [separate] cars or coaches or partitions" (Kentucky, 1892).

50. *Thompson v. Baltimore City Railway Company*, 23 Fed. Cases 1023 (C.C.D.Md., 1870) (No. 13,941); *Baltimore American*, 30 April 1870 at 1; *Civil Rights Cases*, 109 U.S. 3 (1883); Hackney, *Populism to Progressivism*, 45–46. The full report of *Thompson* (in the *American*) shows that, narrowly interpreted, the court's holding was only that the Fourteenth Amendment established the plaintiff's right to sue under the Circuit Court's diversity jurisdiction, but in language that closely associated the right to sue with the right to carriage. In the *Civil Rights Cases*, the Supreme Court "conced[ed], for the sake of the argument, that the admission to . . . a public conveyance . . . , on equal terms with all other citizens, is the right of every man and all classes of men . . . ." 109 U.S. at 24; see generally *ibid.* at 24–25.

51. Rabinowitz, *Race Relations*, 195–97; Rice, *Negro in Texas*, 148; Cell, *Highest Stage*, 173–80.

CHAPTER TWO   *Plessy* in Louisiana: The Test Cases

1. For the organizational effort behind the legal challenge to the law, I am heavily indebted to careful studies by Otto H. Olsen and C. Vann Woodward. See *The Thin Disguise: Turning Point in Negro History*, Plessy v. Ferguson, *A Documentary Presentation (1864–1896)*, Otto H. Olsen, ed. (New York, 1967); Otto H. Olsen, "Reflections on the *Plessy v. Ferguson* Decision of 1896," in *Louisiana's Legal Heritage*, Edward F. Haas, ed. (Pensacola, 1983), 163–87; C. Vann Woodward, "The National Decision Against Equality," in Woodward, *American Counterpoint: Slavery and Racism in the North-South Dialogue* (1971; New York, 1983), 212–33. Useful detail also appears in a paper by Nils R. Douglas, a New Orleans attorney, entitled "Who Was Louis A. Martinet?" (typescript, [New Orleans, ca. 1966]), and in

Citizens' Committee [to Test the Constitutionality of the Separate Car Law], *Report of Proceedings for the Annulment of Act 111 of 1890* (New Orleans, [1897]). Copies of the last two items are in The Amistad Research Center, New Orleans.

2. New Orleans *Daily Picayune*, 12 May 1890 at 3; 15 May 1890 at 8; 9 July 1891 at 8; 11 July 1891 at 8; Memorial of the American Citizens' Equal Rights Association, in Olsen, ed., *Thin Disguise*, 47–50; Woodward, "National Decision Against Equality," 215–16. The lottery "bill" was actually a proposed constitutional amendment; as such, it required an absolute two-thirds vote in each house and approval by the people. After it had secured the required legislative votes, Governor Nicholls vetoed it. The house of representatives overrode the veto by the required two-thirds, but lottery supporters in the senate fell one vote short of the necessary two-thirds. Thereupon the senate resolved that as a constitutional amendment, the recharter bill did not require the governor's signature and the house concurred. After the secretary of state refused to submit the measure to popular vote, the lottery's supporters obtained a court injunction ordering him to act. But in the face of changing public sentiment and hostile federal legislation, the lottery company announced it would not accept a charter renewal, and the recharter amendment was soundly defeated in 1892. See Berthold C. Alwes, "The History of the Louisiana State Lottery," 27 *La. Hist. Q.* (1949), 1029–97.

3. Laws of Louisiana, 1890, at 152–54 (No. 111). The law's concluding section was a customary provision repealing any contrary or inconsistent laws.

4. R.-L. Desdunes, *Nos Hommes et notre histoire* (Montreal, 1911), 184–86; Douglas, "Who Was Martinet?" *passim*; Editorial, New Orleans *Crusader*, 19 July 1890, in Olsen, ed., *Thin Disguise*, 55; Citizens' Committee, *Report of Proceedings*, 1–3, 8; Martinet to Albion W. Tourgée, 5, 11, 25, 28 Oct., 7 Dec. 1891; Eli C. Freeman to Tourgée, 4 Aug. 1890, Albion W. Tourgée Papers, Chautauqua County Historical Society, Westfield, New York (microfilm ed., Kent State University). Unless otherwise indicated, all manuscript correspondence to and from Tourgée is from the Tourgée Papers. Most of the items *from* Tourgée are hand-written copies and some are undated. Dates in brackets indicate items I have dated on the basis of internal evidence or references in other correspondence.

5. Martinet to Tourgée, 25, 28 Oct., 7, 28 Dec. 1891; Walker to Tourgée, 2 Jan. 1892; *Report of the Thirty-third Annual Meeting of the Amer. Bar Assoc. . . . 1910* (Baltimore, 1910), 124.

6. Martinet to Tourgée, 5 Oct. 1891. This long letter, which refers to Tourgée's views as well, was a response to a letter from Tourgée now missing.

7. Martinet to Tourgée, 7, 28 Dec. 1891.

8. Walker to Tourgée, 2, 21 Jan., 25 Feb., 14 March 1892; Tourgée to Walker, [14 Jan. 1892]; New Orleans *Daily Picayune*, 25 Feb. 1892 at 8; Information against Daniel F. Desdunes, 14 March 1892, (hereafter cited as "Desdunes Information"); Defendant's Plea, sworn out 19 March 1892, filed 21 March 1892 (hereafter cited as "Desdunes Plea"), both in Case File for *State v. Desdunes* (Case No. 18,685, Section A, Criminal District Court, Parish of Orleans, 1892) (hereafter cited as "Desdunes Case File"). A photocopy of the Desdunes Case File is in the Archives and Manuscripts Department, Earl K. Long Library, University of New Orleans.

9. *Louisville, New Orleans and Texas Railway Company v. State*, 66 Miss. 662, 674–75 (1889); *Hall v. DeCuir*, 95 U.S. 485 (1878); *Wabash, St. Louis, and Pacific*

Railway Company v. Illinois, 118 U.S. 557 (1886); *Louisville, New Orleans and Texas Railway Company v. Mississippi*, 133 U.S. 587, 591 (1890). *Hall v. DeCuir* is discussed more extensively in Chapter Six, *infra*, in connection with its influence on equal-but-separate as a common-law doctrine. Dissenting in the *Louisville* case, Justices Harlan and Bradley penetrated to the reality of the Mississippi statute, arguing it necessarily applied to passenger arrangements on trains *in* interstate commerce and thus fell under the prohibition of the *DeCuir* doctrine. See 133 U.S. at 592–95.

10. Walker to Tourgée, 2, 9 Jan., 25 Feb., 14 March 1892; Martinet to Tourgée, 3 Feb. 1892; Tourgée to Walker, [14 Jan.], 1, 12 March 1892; fragment from Tourgée to Walker, [ca. 18 March 1892]; Desdunes Information; Desdunes Plea. What Tourgée did reject was use of the new Interstate Commerce Act, which Walker had initially mentioned. Perhaps as a result, Walker in effect argued before the trial court that the Interstate Commerce Act did not apply. (See Tourgée to Walker, [14 Jan. 1892]; Brief of Points and Authorities for the Defendant, 21 March 1892, Desdunes Case File.) In "The National Decision Against Equality," Professor Woodward portrays Tourgée as "doubtful" regarding the interstate commerce issue, but incorrectly links a comment by Tourgée rejecting the issue of "multifarious" subject matter, which is discussed below, to Tourgée's opinion on the usefulness of the commerce issue. Actually, Tourgée only left it to Walker to flesh out the commerce argument, commenting at one point: "Let me say that I had no idea of ignoring the interstate commerce phase of the controversy. I simply did not formulate that specifically, that is[,] with reference to the statute, because I saw you were interested in it and did not doubt [you] could do it better than I." Tourgée to Walker, [ca. 10 March 1892].

11. *Louisville, New Orleans and Texas*, 133 U.S. at 589; Walker to Tourgée, 25 Feb. 1892.

12. Tourgée to Walker, 1 March 1892; Desdunes Plea. See also Tourgée to Walker, [14 Jan. 1892]. In his draft plea, Tourgée referred consistently to "indictment"; Walker changed this to "information" after the prosecutor proceeded via the latter route. The fourteenth averment may have been added by Tourgée to the copy of the draft plea that he mailed to Walker, although it does not appear in the draft manuscript copy of Tourgée's letter to Walker of 1 March. If it was not added at that point, Tourgée may have added it when Walker sent Tourgée, for the latter's approval, the plea Walker intended to file, or Walker may have added it himself to the plea. (See Walker to Tourgée, 8 March 1892; Tourgée to Walker, 12 March 1892.) But since the fourteenth point omits any mention of the commerce argument, it was probably Tourgée's contribution, not Walker's, in view of the division of labor between the two.

13. Walker to Tourgée, 9, 21 Jan., 6 March 1892; Tourgée to Walker, 1 March 1892; Tourgée to Walker, [ca. 10 March 1892].

14. Walker to Tourgée, 2, 21 Jan. 1892; *Ex parte Royall*, 117 U.S. 241 (1886). Walker also mentioned *Ex parte Fonda*, 117 U.S. 516 (1886), which had been decided on the authority of *Royall*. A reading of U.S. Supreme Court decisions from the early 1890s indicates that attorneys and lower courts were often confused regarding the exact appellate functions of the new Circuit Courts of Appeals.

15. Tourgée to Walker, [14 Jan.], 1 March, [ca. 10 March] 1892; Walker to Tourgée, 9, 21 Jan., 6 March 1892.

16. Walker to Tourgée, 25 Feb., 6 March 1892; Tourgée to Walker, 1 March, [ca. 10 March], 12 March 1892.

17. Tourgée to Walker, [18 March 1892].

18. Tourgée to Walker, 1 March, [ca. 10 March], 1892; Walker to Tourgée, 9, 21 Jan., 25 Feb., 6 March 1892; Desdunes Information. See also Martinet to Tourgée, 3 Feb. 1892.

19. Notice of Arraignment, 18 March 1892, Desdunes Case File; Walker to Tourgée, 18 March 1892; Brief of Points and Authorities for the Defendant, filed 21 March 1892; Demurrer to Plea [undated], Desdunes Case File. Judge Marr disappeared on his way home from voting in an election. A seventy-three-year-old who had been in "feeble health" for several years and suffered from vertigo, he probably fell off a levee and drowned. Within a week his family assumed he was dead, but his successor in Section A, John H. Ferguson, was not sworn in until July 5. See New Orleans *Daily Picayune*, 20 April 1892 at 2; 21 April 1892 at 2; 22 April 1892 at 3; 26 April at 3; 6 July 1892 at 3. For the impact of the disappearance on the case, see Citizens' Committee, *The Violation of Constitutional Right* (New Orleans, 1893), 2, a copy of which is in The Amistad Research Center, New Orleans.

20. *State ex rel. Abbott v. Hicks, Judge*, 44 La. Ann. 583, 11 So. 74, 76 (1892).

21. Notation of disposition, dated 9 July 1892, on Desdunes Information; Editorial, New Orleans *Crusader*, quoted in Olsen, "Reflections on the *Plessy v. Ferguson* Decision of 1896," 174. After Walker's plea was sustained, the District Attorney's office filed a *nolle prosequi*. See notation on Information and also Martinet to Tourgée, 4 July 1892 [*sic*; the letter is so dated but its composition continued in stages through 29 August]. Evidently responding to a now-missing letter, Martinet wrote Tourgée: "Of course, I do not entertain the same favorable results [in a new case] as hopefully as in the Desdunes [case]. But perhaps it is best that the battle be fought. I rely, however, more on the fact that the Negro's right to travel interstate being recognized, & if maintained by him[,] it will throw the 'Jim Crow' car into disuse, *as you say*." *Ibid.*, emphasis added.

22. Tourgée to Walker, [14 Jan. 1892]. Tourgée had added, with reference to himself, "A man who has been substantially out of practice for half a dozen years has no right to an opinion on such points beside one who has been in the traces right along."

23. Tourgée's proposed denial that Desdunes was a Negro did not go into the jurisdictional plea; but an averment about the scientific and legal difficulty of a conductor's classifying by race was included, and it pointed to a comparable vulnerability in any information alleging a defendant's race.

24. Telegrams, Martinet to Tourgée, 26 May, 1 June 1892; telegram, Tourgée to Martinet, [2 June 1892], emphasis added; affidavit by Detective C. C. Cain, 8 June 1892, before Second Recorder's Court of the City of New Orleans; Petition for Writs of Prohibition and Certiorari, *Ex parte Plessy*, 45 La. Ann. 80, 11 So. 948 (1892), in Plessy La. Case File (see below); Charles E. O'Neil, S. J., "Foreword" to Rodolphe L. Desdunes, *Our People and Our History*, Dorothea O. McCants, trans. (Baton Rouge, 1973), xiii; Woodward, "National Decision Against Equality," 221–22. The Criminal District Court, Parish of Orleans, is now unable to locate its case file for *State v. Plessy*, No. 19,117 (1892), but a photocopy is available at The Amistad Research Center, New Orleans, in items collected by Nils R. Douglas, the New Orleans attorney who examined the Plessy case in the

mid-1960s and then had access to the file. A full manuscript copy (except for a crucial notation from 1897), along with excerpts of pertinent Criminal District Court proceedings, is in the Louisiana Supreme Court's case file for *Ex parte Plessy*, No. 11,134 (1892), Louisiana Supreme Court Archives, Archives and Manuscripts Division, Earl K. Long Library, University of New Orleans (hereafter cited as "Plessy La. Case File"). The material also appears in the printed *Record, Case No. 15248*, United States Supreme Court, No. 880, October Term, 1893 (Washington, 1893) (hereafter cited as "Plessy Appellate Record"), a copy of which is in the Tourgée Papers. Unless otherwise indicated, Criminal District Court documents in *State v. Plessy* may be found in any of these sources. Most are also reprinted (and more readily available) in Louisiana's eventual brief before the United States Supreme Court, described in Chapter Seven, *infra*.

25. Information against Plessy, filed 20 July 1892 (hereafter "Plessy Information"); Martinet to Tourgée, 4 July 1892 [that is, the letter which was continued in sections until 29 Aug.]; Defendant's Plea to the Jurisdiction, filed 13 Oct. 1892 (hereafter "Plessy Plea"); Demurrer to Plea, filed 28 Oct. 1892; Judge Ferguson's Opinion, filed 18 Nov. 1892 (hereafter "Ferguson Opinion"); certified copies of proceedings, Section A, Criminal District Court, Parish of Orleans, 13, 28 Oct., 18 Nov. 1892, in Plessy La. Case File. On the oral arguments, see Rodolphe Desdunes's later recollections (*Nos Hommes et notre histoire*, 188–89); New Orleans *Daily Picayune*, 29 Oct. 1892 at 9; and, specifically regarding Walker's presentation, Judge Ferguson's comment in his opinion on the plea: "The argument . . . by the counsel for the defendant displayed great research, learning, and ability."

26. Answer of John H. Ferguson, filed 26 Nov. 1892; Brief for Respondent [Ferguson], filed 1 Dec. 1892, at 21–22 (hereafter "Ferguson La. Brief"), both in Plessy La. Case File; Walker to Tourgée, 28 Oct. 1893. As for Martinet's ongoing involvement, it bears mention that he acted as notary for the several filings in *Ex parte Plessy*.

27. 11 So. at 74–75.

28. Certified copy of proceedings, Criminal District Court, 13, 28 Oct., 18 Nov. 1892; Petition for Writs of Prohibition and Certiorari, filed 22 Nov. 1892 (hereafter "Plessy Petition"); Brief for Relator [Plessy], filed 1 Dec. 1892 (hereafter "Plessy La. Brief"), both in Plessy La. Case File; Ferguson La. Brief. Miscellaneous documents relating to *Ex parte Plessy* were also filed in the same period; see Plessy La. Case File.

29. Prohibition and Certiorari to John H. Ferguson, filed 22 Nov. 1892; sheriff's return on same, filed 23 Nov. 1892; Relator's Application for Rehearing, filed 26 Dec. 1892 (hereafter "Plessy Rehearing Application"), all in Plessy La. Case File; *Ex parte Plessy*, 11 So. at 948–51.

30. See Plessy Appellate Record, 33–51, for the various writ of error filings.

CHAPTER THREE   *Plessy* in Louisiana: The Constitutional Clash

1. Assignment of Errors, Plessy Appellate Record, 48, 51. The Assignment of Errors also appears in the brief that Tourgée and Walker eventually filed with the Federal Supreme Court and is readily available in 13 *Landmark Briefs and Arguments of the Supreme Court of the United States*, Philip B. Kurland and Gerhard Casper, eds.

(Arlington, Va., 1975), 30–32. Except where a reference is not readily identifiable from the text, this chapter omits further citations to the Assignment of Errors.

2. For late nineteenth-century practice, see "Writs of Error," 6 *American and English Encyclopedia of Law*, John H. Merrill, *et al.*, comps. (Northport, Long Island, N.Y., 1888), 810–83; W. Calvin Chesnut, "Assignment of Errors," 2 *Encyclopedia of Pleading and Practice . . .* , William M. McKinney, comp. (Northport, Long Island, N.Y., 1895), 926–39,

3. The two obvious exceptions are paragraph one, which refers to "the rights, privileges, and immunities of citizens," and paragraph four, which mentions "equal protection" and "due process." A possible third exception is paragraph twelve, which uses the phrase "the rights and privileges of citizens," arguably a reference to the privileges-or-immunities clause, but just as reasonably a shorthand reference to the sum of Thirteenth and Fourteenth Amendment protections.

4. Plea to the Jurisdiction, averment 14; Plessy La. Brief, 21, 9–10.

5. Ferguson La. Brief, 26; *Ex parte Plessy*, 45 La. Ann. 80, 11 So. 948, 949 (1892).

6. New Orleans *Daily Picayune*, 29 Oct. 1892 at 9; Plea to the Jurisdiction, averments 11, 12, 13; Ferguson Opinion; Plessy La. Brief, for example, at 1, 17, 22; *Ex parte Plessy*, 11 So. at 949. The lower federal cases on which Ferguson relied were *The Sue*, 22 Fed. 843 (D.Md., 1885), *Logwood and Wife v. Memphis and Cincinnati Railroad Company*, 23 Fed. 318 (C.C.W.D.Tenn., 1885), and *Murphy v. Western and Atlantic Railroad Company*, 23 Fed. 637 (C.C.E.D.Tenn., 1885).

7. Plea to the Jurisdiction, averment 8; *Daily Picayune*, 29 Oct. 1892 at 9; Ferguson Opinion; Ferguson La. Brief, 29–30; Plessy La. Brief, 16–18; *Ex parte Plessy*, 11 So. at 950–51.

8. Plea to the Jurisdiction, averments 9, 14. The plea to the jurisdiction is copied several times in the appellate documents, in places with the wording "invidious distinction," and elsewhere with "insidious distinction." As originally filed, it used "invidious distinction."

9. Ferguson Opinion, emphasis added.

10. Ferguson La. Brief, 26–28. Although the purpose of this chapter is not to evaluate the arguments made during the Louisiana phase of *Plessy*, it needs underscoring that Adams omitted to note that Justice Bradley, in the portion of his opinion in the *Civil Rights Cases* on which Adams relied, had explicitly restricted his remarks to *private* acts denying admission and had suggested that legislatively mandated denial might indeed constitute a badge of servitude. In addition to the *Civil Rights Cases* and the three lower federal court cases previously used by Judge Ferguson, Adams also relied on 18 *American and English Encyclopedia of Law* (1892), 753–54, and Christopher G. Tiedeman, *A Treatise on the Limitations of Police Power in the United States* (St. Louis, 1886), 614 (sec. 201). Adams's use of the *American and English Encyclopedia*, vol. 18 of which had just appeared, may indicate access to an up-to-date library, but it more significantly reveals looseness with legal authorities, for the section from which he quoted (without actually indicating it as a quotation) also asserted the legitimacy of equal accommodations laws under the police power. This at least gave a different tone to the section than Adams conveyed. On the other hand, the same section of the encyclopedia cited some fourteen cases (the three Adams cited in his brief plus eleven others) that purportedly supported the

permissibility of racial separation in schools or public conveyances. (See 18 *Amer. and Eng. Encyclopedia*, 754n–755n.)

11. Plessy La. Brief, 4–5, 11, 22. To be sure, Tourgée and Walker recognized the possibility of white nurses traveling with black children, but in effect dismissed it. (*Ibid.* at 5.) It is not clear from the published report whether *Logwood*, one of the cases cited by Ferguson, actually resulted in a damage award. See 23 Fed. at 318–19 (jury charge).

12. Plessy La. Brief, 21–22, emphasis added.

13. *Ex parte Plessy*, 11 So. at 949, 950. See *Louisville, New Orleans and Texas Railway Company v. Mississippi*, 133 U.S. 587, esp. at 589, 591 (1890). Before the Mississippi Supreme Court, the railway had implicitly argued that the act violated the Fourteenth Amendment and the state denied the claim, but in upholding the act the state court never addressed the Fourteenth Amendment issue. See *Louisville, New Orleans and Texas Railway Company v. State*, 66 Miss. 662, esp. at 664, 670 (1889) (summaries of briefs).

14. *Ex parte Plessy*, 11 So. at 950–51; *Roberts v. City of Boston*, 5 Cushing 198, 209 (Mass., 1849); *West Chester and Philadelphia Railroad Company v. Miles*, 55 Pa. 209, 215 (1867), both quoted in 11 So. at 950. Fenner dropped the qualifier "probably" from the *Roberts* quotation.

15. 11 So. at 950–51.

16. This is the language in question: "[S]hould any passenger refuse to occupy the coach or compartment to which he or she is assigned by the officer of such railway, said officer shall have power to refuse to carry such passenger on his train, and for such refusal neither he nor the railway company which he represents shall be liable for damages in any of the courts of this State." Laws of Louisiana, 1890, at 153 (No. 111) (sec. 2).

17. Plea to the Jurisdiction, esp. averments 6, 14; Ferguson Opinion; Plessy La. Brief, 7–8. See also Petition for Rehearing, filed 26 Dec. 1892, Plessy La. Case File (hereafter "Plessy Rehearing Petition"); Relator's [i.e., Plessy's] Brief for Rehearing, 2–3, Plessy La. Case File (hereafter "Plessy Rehearing Brief").

18. Ferguson La. Brief, 30; *Ex parte Plessy*, 11 So. at 951.

19. *Daily Picayune*, 29 Oct. 1892 at 9; Ferguson Opinion; Plessy Petition.

20. Cain's affidavit had been sworn out before a lower court, the First Recorder's Court of the City of New Orleans. See Affidavit of C. C. Cain, 8 June 1892, Plessy La. Case File.

21. Answer of Respondent [Ferguson], filed 26 Nov. 1892, Plessy La. Case File; Ferguson La. Brief, 22–23; Plessy La. Brief, 15–16.

22. Plessy La. Brief, 12, and see also 8–9; *Ex parte Plessy*, 11 So. at 951. As for the remedy that Fenner held the law allowed, see the discussion of paragraph nine, *infra*.

23. Plessy La. Brief, 5–6. See also *ibid.*, 20–21; Plessy Rehearing Petition; Plessy Rehearing Brief, 3.

24. Plessy La. Brief, 9–11; Plessy Rehearing Brief, 3.

25. Plea to the Jurisdiction, averment 12; Plessy La. Brief, 3–4, 19; Ferguson Opinion; *Ex parte Plessy*, 11 So. at 951. See also Plessy Rehearing Brief, 2–3.

26. Plea to the Jurisdiction, averments 3, 7, 10; Ferguson Opinion.

27. Plessy La. Brief, 11–14, 20. Actually none of the quoted authorities advanced the proposition about delegation of power, but from the statement "It is

not regarded as a delegation of power to confer the right of local government on municipal corporations" (3 *Amer. and Eng. Encyclopedia of Law* [1887], 681), the brief extrapolated this rule: "It is otherwise as to private corporations and common carriers," although the cited source contains no reference to the rule.

28. Ferguson La. Brief, 29, citing *Century Dictionary*, 1111, and *Anderson's Law Dictionary*, 195; *Ex parte Plessy*, 11 So. at 951.

29. Plessy Rehearing Brief, 2.

30. *State v. McCrystol*, 43 La. Ann. 907, 9 So. 922, 924 (1891), quoting *United States v. Hartwell*, 6 Wallace 385, 396 (1868).

31. See Charles C. Moore, "United States Courts," in 22 *Encyclopedia of Pleading and Practice . . .* , William M. McKinney, comp. (Northport, Long Island, N.Y., 1902), 327–33 and nn. for relevant cases.

32. The jurisdictional statute remained essentially sec. 25 of the Judiciary Act of 1789, incorporated into Revised Statutes, sec. 709 (1874), as amended by 18 Stat. 318 (Act of 18 Feb. 1875, Ch. 80).

CHAPTER FOUR   The Constitutional Environment: Lost Origins and Judicial Deference

1. Herman Belz, *A New Birth of Freedom: The Republican Party and Freedmen's Rights, 1861 to 1866* (Westport, Conn., 1976), 113–23.

2. For a synopsis of the debates on the Freedmen's Bureau extension and the Civil Rights Bill, see Horace E. Flack, *The Adoption of the Fourteenth Amendment* (Baltimore, 1908), 11–54; for the final measures, see Act of 16 July 1866, 14 Stat. 173, and Act of 9 April 1866, *ibid.*, 27.

3. For a summary of congressional action on the Amendment, see Flack, *Adoption of the Fourteenth Amendment*, 11–139. For state action, see *ibid.*, 161–209.

4. Harold M. Hyman and William M. Wiecek, *Equal Justice Under Law: Constitutional Development 1835–1875* (New York, 1982), esp. 386–438.

5. Alfred H. Kelly, "The Fourteenth Amendment Reconsidered: The Segregation Question," 54 *Mich. Law Rev.* (1956), 1077–86; *Corfield v. Coryell*, 6 Fed. Cases 546, 551–52 (C.C.E.D. Pa., 1823) (Case no. 3,230); *Cong. Globe*, 39 Cong., 1 sess., 2542 (10 May 1866); Hyman and Wiecek, *Equal Justice*, 393–419; Charles Fairman, *Reconstruction and Reunion, 1865–88, Part One*, [vol. 2 of the Holmes Devise, *History of the Supreme Court of the United States*] (New York, 1971), 1300.

6. Kelly, "The Fourteenth Amendment Reconsidered," 1050. Kelly posed the question specifically about the Fourteenth Amendment, at the time historians were again beginning to probe its origins in the aftermath of *Brown v. Board of Education*, but it can as well be applied to both Amendments. For views anticipating Hyman and Wiecek's, see Flack, *Adoption of the Fourteenth Amendment, passim*; Howard Jay Graham, "Our Declaratory Fourteenth Amendment," in Graham, *Everyman's Constitution* (Madison, 1968), 298–335; Jacobus tenBroek, *Equal Under Law* (1951; enlarged ed., New York, 1965), esp. 201–39. For more restrictive interpretations, see Fairman, *Reconstruction and Reunion*, 1117–1300; Herman Belz, *Emancipation and Equal Rights: Politics and Constitutionalism in the Civil War Era* (New York, 1978), 110–22; Belz, *New Birth*, 157–82; and for an example of history

narrowly written with lawyers' rules of evidence and interpretation, denying any breadth, see Raoul Berger, *Government by Judiciary: The Transformation of the Fourteenth Amendment* (Cambridge, Mass., 1977), pt. 1.

7. Flack, *Adoption of the Fourteenth Amendment*, 41–45, 52–54; Belz, *New Birth*, 147–48. See also Howard N. Rabinowitz, "From Exclusion to Segregation: Southern Race Relations, 1865–1890," 63 *J. of Amer. Hist.* (1976), 325–50.

8. *Cong. Globe*, 39 Cong., 1 sess., 318–19, 322, 505 (Trumbull, 19, 30 Jan. 1866), 1117 (Wilson, 1 March), 2765 (Howard, 23 May), 1063–64 (Stevens, 27 Feb.). Stevens did not explicitly cite race as an example of permissible classification (instead he used differential treatment of married and unmarried women), but Representative Robert Hale, a Conservative Republican from New York, to whom Stevens had been responding, immediately assimilated Stevens's comments to the permissibility of racial classification, with no response from Stevens. Stevens later offered a comparable view; see *ibid.*, 2459 (8 May). See generally Belz, *New Birth*, 147–53; Alexander M. Bickel, "The Original Understanding of the Segregation Decision," 69 *Harv. Law Rev.* (1955), 1–65.

9. *Cong. Globe*, 39 Cong., 1 sess., 2961 (5 June 1866); *Carr v. Corning*, 182 F.2d 14, 17–18 (D.C. Cir., 1950) (summarizing early District of Columbia school legislation); Appendix to Supplemental Brief for the United States on Reargument, *Brown v. Board of Education of Topeka*, 347 U.S. 483 (1954), 160–393 (summarizing state school and anti-miscegenation laws). On the issue of state legislation, the Supplemental Brief of the United States in *Brown* agrees factually with the respondent's brief; see Brief for State of Kansas on Reargument, *ibid.*, 70–92. (In counting states, I have omitted those that soon repealed separate-school and anti-miscegenation legislation.) These briefs may be found in *Landmark Briefs and Arguments of the Supreme Court of the United States*, Philip B. Kurland and Gerhard Caspar, eds. (Arlington, Va., 1975–   ), vols. 49 and 49A.

10. Fairman, *Reconstruction and Reunion*, 1321–33.

11. The arguments are summarized in *ibid.*, 1343–49. For the full briefs and Campbell's oral argument, see 6 *Landmark Briefs*, 535–732. The quotations are from Campbell's initial brief, *ibid.*, 571–72.

12. *Slaughter-House Cases*, 16 Wallace 36, 68–72 (1873). Miller allowed that such comparable servitudes as peonage, Chinese coolie labor, or involuntary long-term apprenticeship also fell within the Thirteenth Amendment's ban.

13. *Ibid.*, 73–81.

14. *Ibid.*, 83–130. For a careful critique of Miller's opinion, see Robert J. Kaczorowski, "The Nationalization of Civil Rights: Constitutional Theory and Practice in a Racist Society, 1866–1883" (Ph.D. diss., Univ. of Minn., 1972), 257–67 and *passim*. On earlier use of due process, see Edward S. Corwin, "The Doctrine of Due Process of Law Before the Civil War," 24 *Harv. Law Rev.* (1911), 366–85, 460–79.

15. *Slaughter-House Cases*, 16 Wallace at 70–72; Act of 31 May 1870, 16 Stat. 140, 144 (sec. 18); Hyman and Wiecek, *Equal Justice*, 464–69. Justice Field's dissent in *Slaughter-House* explicitly made the point Miller hinted at, that the need for the Fourteenth demonstrated the limited scope of the Thirteenth; see 16 Wallace at 97.

16. Charles W. Collins, *The Fourteenth Amendment and the States* (1912; reprint ed., New York, 1974), 48–55, 183, plus two omissions from Collins's listing:

United States v. Harris, 106 U.S. 629 (1883), and *Wood v. Brush*, 140 U.S. 278 (1891).

17. Act of 31 May 1870, 16 Stat. 140, 141 (sec. 6); Act of 20 April 1871, 17 Stat. 13, 14 (sec. 2). For a brief history of the enforcement measures and subsequent constitutional challenges, see Eugene Gressman, "The Unhappy History of Civil Rights Legislation," 50 *Mich. Law Rev.* (1952), 1333–43. On their congressional context and enforcement history, see William Gillette, *Retreat from Reconstruction, 1869–79* (Baton Rouge, 1979), 25–55.

18. John S. Ezell, "The Civil Rights Act of 1875," 50 *Mid-America* (1968), 251–71; Gillette, *Retreat*, 196–210, 259–73; Act of 1 March 1875, 18 Stat. 335, 336.

19. Michael Les Benedict, "Preserving Federalism: Reconstruction and the Waite Court," *Supreme Court Rev.* (1978), 59.

20. *United States v. Cruikshank*, 92 U.S. 542, 551–59 (1876). Hearing the case on circuit in New Orleans, Justice Bradley had voted to uphold the indictments under the Thirteenth and Fifteenth Amendments, but he, too, now joined in the Court's opinion. See *United States v. Cruikshank*, 25 Fed. Cases 707 (C.C.D.La., 1874) (No. 14,897).

21. *Harris*, 106 U.S. at 637–40.

22. See Benedict, "Reconstruction and the Waite Court," esp. 66–75.

23. *Civil Rights Cases*, 109 U.S. 3, 9–19, 22, 25 (1883) (the quotations are at 13, emphasis added). The example of an exclusionary law came during Bradley's Thirteenth Amendment discussion. He did not reach the 1875 law's validity in federal territories or the District of Columbia, "which are subject to the plenary legislation of Congress in every branch of municipal legislation." *Ibid.*, 19.

24. *Ibid.*, 17 (emphasis added), 23–26.

25. *Ibid.*, 26, 32–37.

26. *Ibid.*, 36, 43–57.

27. *Ibid.*, 37–42, 57–62.

28. *Slaughter-House Cases*, 16 Wallace at 71; *Strauder v. West Virginia*, 100 U.S. 303 (1880) (allowing removal under Sec. 641 when a state law in effect limited jury service to white citizens); *Virginia v. Rives*, 100 U.S. 313 (1880) (disallowing removal when existing laws made no discrimination against jury service by blacks; also denying a black defendant a right to have a quota of blacks on his jury); *Ex parte Virginia*, 100 U.S. 339 (1880) (allowing prosecution of state judge, under Section 4 of the Civil Rights Act of 1875, for excluding blacks from juries); *Neal v. Delaware*, 103 U.S. 370 (1881) (denying removal but ordering new trial after a state court had refused to hear evidence on exclusion of blacks from juries on account of race); *Bush v. Kentucky*, 107 U.S. 110 (1883) (reversing state court refusal to set aside indictment in face of evidence in fact and law that blacks had been excluded from grand jury because of race). The section of the 1875 Civil Rights Act upheld in *Ex parte Virginia* was not subsequently involved in the *Civil Rights Cases*.

29. *Ex parte Virginia*, 100 U.S. at 367–68 (Field, J., dissenting); *Strauder*, 100 U.S. at 307–8.

30. *Wood v. Brush*, 140 U.S. 278 (1891); *Andrews v. Swartz*, 156 U.S. 272 (1895); *Gibson v. Mississippi*, 162 U.S. 565 (1896); *Smith v. Mississippi*, 162 U.S. 592 (1896); *Murray v. Louisiana*, 163 U.S. 101 (1896).

31. *Pace v. Alabama*, 106 U.S. 583 (1883). The remaining Fourteenth

Amendment case involving blacks that the federal Supreme Court decided prior to *Plessy* concerned the validity of an antebellum deed of property executed by a Negro, but was dismissed for lack of a federal question, the Court finding that the state decision was supported by independent state grounds. See *Beatty v. Benton*, 135 U.S. 244 (1890).

32. Revised Statutes, secs. 691–92, 697, 709. Sections 691–92 limited review in civil cases to instances where the matter in dispute exceeded $5000. This amount varied somewhat in cases arising in the federal territories and the District of Columbia. Section 697 restricted review of lower federal criminal cases to instances where the sitting circuit judges divided on a point of law (in which case, review was by certificate of division). A right of appeal from federal circuit courts in capital criminal cases was established in 1889. Section 709 allowed review in state cases (by writ of error) only when the highest court of a state in which a decision could be obtained had ruled *against* a claimed federal right. The Judiciary Act of 3 March 1891 broadened the Supreme Court's appellate jurisdiction over lower federal courts on writ of error to include cases involving "construction or application of the Constitution," "the constitutionality of any law of the United States," or the validity of a state law under the Constitution. 26 Stat. 826, 827–28 (sec. 5). See generally Felix Frankfurter and James M. Landis, *The Business of the Supreme Court: A Study in the Federal Judicial System* (New York, 1928), 56–85.

33. Kaczorowski, "Nationalization of Civil Rights," 210–52 (showing that initially under the Thirteenth and Fourteenth Amendments, lower federal and perhaps state courts took a less restrictive view); Jonathan Lurie, "The Fourteenth Amendment: Use and Application in Selected State Court Civil Liberties Cases, 1870–1890—A Preliminary Assessment," 28 *Amer. J. of Legal hist.* (1984), 297–99, 304–12; J. Morgan Kousser, *Dead End: The Development of Nineteenth-Century Litigation on Racial Discrimination in Schools* (Oxford, Eng., 1986), *passim* and esp. 9–12, 18–19, 21–22, 41 n. 38. The conclusion regarding the higher proportion of cases won by blacks during 1868–96 is not Kousser's but mine, based on inference from his data and from an earlier version of his study that focuses on fewer cases but allows different disaggregation of the data. (See Kousser, "Dead End . . . ," Social Science Working Paper 349, California Institute of Technology, 1980.) With respect specifically to the context of transportation segregation in the South and the Plessy case, it is noteworthy that Kousser found that southern jurisdictions remained the least open to black challenges to school discrimination. Regarding lower court cases, see also Stephen J. Riegel, "The Persistent Career of Jim Crow: Lower Federal Courts and the 'Separate But Equal' Doctrine, 1865–1896," 28 *Amer. J. of Legal Hist.* (1984), 17–40.

34. *Chicago, Milwaukee, and St. Paul Railway Company v. Minnesota*, 134 U.S. 418 (1890); *Reagan v. Farmers Loan and Trust Company*, 154 U.S. 362 (1894); *Munn v. Illinois*, 94 U.S. 113, 132 (1877).

35. See, for example, *Regents of the University of California v. Bakke*, 438 U.S. 265, 291–92 (1978); Robert G. McCloskey, *The American Supreme Court* (Chicago, 1960), 115–35; Louis H. Pollak, "Emancipation and the Law: A Century of Progress," in *100 Years of Emancipation*, Robert A. Goldwin, ed. (Chicago, 1964), 164–65, 169–70; Olsen, ed., *The Thin Disguise*, 19; J. Morgan Kousser, "Separate but *not* Equal: The Supreme Court's First Decision on Racial Discrimination in Schools," 46 *J. of So. Hist.* (1980), 36. For an influential sketch of early

comments allegedly foreshadowing substantive due process, see Rodney L. Mott, *Due Process of Law: A Historical and Analytical Treatise* . . . (Indianapolis, 1926), 334–42.

36. See, for example, Ernst Freund, *The Police Power: Public Policy and Constitutional Rights* (Chicago, 1904), 65–66; Frank J. Goodnow, *Social Reform and the Constitution* (New York, 1911), 329–30; J. Willard Hurst, *Law and the Conditions of Freedom in the Nineteenth Century United States* (Madison, Wisc., 1956), 104 and 129 n. 37; Charles W. McCurdy, "Justice Field and the Jurisprudence of Government-Business Relations: Some Parameters of Laissez Faire Constitutionalism, 1863–1897," 61 *J. of Amer. Hist.* (1975), 970–1005; *Allgeyer v. Louisiana*, 165 U.S. 578 (1897); Morton Keller, *Affairs of State: Public Life in Late Nineteenth Century America* (Cambridge, Mass., 1977), 366–69; John E. Semonche, *Charting the Future: The Supreme Court Responds to a Changing Society, 1890–1920* (Westport, Conn., 1978), 15–90.

37. *Slaughter-House Cases*, 16 Wallace at 62; Thomas M. Cooley, *A Treatise on . . . Constitutional Limitations* . . . (1868; 6th ed., Boston, 1890), 705–6; *Commonwealth v. Alger*, 7 Cushing 53, 84–85 (Mass., 1851); *Thorpe v. Rutland and Burlington Railroad Company*, 27 Vermont 140, 150 (1855). See generally Leonard W. Levy, *The Law of the Commonwealth and Chief Justice Shaw* (1957; New York, 1967), 229–65.

38. W. G. Hastings, "The Development of Law as Illustrated by the Decisions Relating to the Police Power of the State," 39 *Proc. of the Amer. Philosophical Soc.* (1900), esp. 418–39; Elmer E. Smead, "*Sic Utere Tuo ut Alienum Non Laedas*: A Basis of the State Police Power," 25 *Cornell Law Q.* (1935), 276–86; James Kent, 2 *Commentaries on American Law* (New York, 1827), 276; *Alger*, 7 Cushing at 85; Harry N. Scheiber, "The Road to *Munn*: Eminent Domain and the Concept of Public Purpose in the State Courts," in 5 *Perspectives in Amer. Hist.* (1971), 329–402 and esp. 373–75. For state activities, see, for example, Hurst, *Law and the Conditions of Freedom, passim*; Keller, *Affairs of State*, 162–81, 409–521.

39. *Slaughter-House Cases*, 16 Wallace at 61–62, 87–89, 114, 117, 119–20. Later in the same term, Bradley and Field offered glosses on their *Slaughter-House* dissents that stressed more explicitly how it was the duty of the judge himself to assess the real connection between a purported police regulation and the public welfare. *Bartemeyer v. Iowa*, 18 Wallace 129, 136–39 (1874).

40. *Bradwell v. Illinois*, 16 Wallace 130, 142–143 (1873). The fourth *Slaughter-House* dissenter, Chief Justice Salmon P. Chase, dissented in *Bradwell* without opinion. On *Bradwell* generally, see Fairman, *Reconstruction and Reunion*, 1364–68.

41. *Munn*, 94 U.S. at 132–33.

42. *Davidson v. Board of Administrators of the City of New Orleans*, 96 U.S. 97, 104 (1878); *Missouri Pacific Railroad Company v. Humes*, 115 U.S. 512, 519–21, 523 (1885). See also Field's opinion in *Minneapolis and St. Louis Railway Company v. Beckwith*, 129 U.S. 26 (1889).

43. *Mugler v. Kansas*, 123 U.S. 623, 653–57 (1887); *Powell v. Pennsylvania*, 127 U.S. 678, 679–81 (1888).

44. *Mugler*, 123 U.S. at 660–63; Ray A. Brown, "Due Process, Police Power, and the Supreme Court," 40 *Harv. Law Rev.* (1927), 947.

45. *Powell*, 127 U.S. at 683–87. Harlan partly quoted from *The Sinking Fund Cases*, 99 U.S. 700, 718 (1879), in which, however, the Supreme Court had extended the presumption of constitutionality to *federal* legislation.

46. *Powell*, 127 U.S. at 687–99 (Field, J., dissenting). Field also dissented in *Mugler*, but only to the portion of the Court's opinion relating to a companion case that involved the propriety of equity proceedings against offenders.

47. *Chicago, Milwaukee, and St. Paul Railway Company* 134 U.S. at 418–35, 456–59; *ibid.*, 461–66 (Bradley, J., dissenting).

48. *Budd v. New York*, 143 U.S. 517, esp. 545–48 (1892); *ibid.*, 548–52 (Brewer, J., dissenting).

49. *Reagan v. Farmers Loan and Trust Company*, 154 U.S. 362, 392, 394–96, 413 (1894).

50. *Brass v. North Dakota*, 153 U.S. 391, esp. 403–4 (1894).

51. *Lawton v. Steele*, 152 U.S. 133, 136–37, 142 (1894). Brown observed that under the law in question an individual whose nets were wrongly seized by authorities "may replevy his nets . . . or . . . may have his action for their value."

52. Scott M. Reznick, "Empiricism and the Principle of Conditions in the Evolution of the Police Power: A Model for Definitional Scrutiny," *Wash. Univ. Law Q.* (1978), esp. 1–40; Edward S. Corwin, *Liberty Against Government: The Rise, Flowering and Decline of a Famous Juridicial Concept* (Baton Rouge, 1948), 145. Corwin admittedly argued that the Court also squinted in the other direction, toward the position taken by Field and Bradley that the judges themselves must agree that the facts justified the law, but his evidence linked the acceptance of this approach by Supreme Court majorities to the post-*Plessy* period. *Ibid.*, 146–52.

53. *People v. Marx*, 99 N.Y. 377 (1885); *People v. Gillson*, 109 N.Y. 389, 407 (1888). Finally, after the New York Court of Appeals had voided a workmen's compensation law on Fourteenth Amendment grounds, Congress in 1914 amended the Judiciary Act to give the federal Supreme Court jurisdiction to review by writ of certiorari state decisions in *favor* of a claimed federal right. *Ives v. South Buffalo Railway Company*, 201 N.Y. 271 (1911); Act of 23 Dec. 1914, 38 Stat. 790. See Frankfurter and Landis, *The Business of the Supreme Court*, 190–98, for the history of the episode.

54. Mott, *Due Process of Law*, 268–99, 337–38 and n. 24; Joseph Tussman and Jacobus tenBroek, "Equal Protection of the Laws," 37 *Calif. Law Rev.* (1949), 341–81; Melvin I. Urofsky, "State Courts and Protective Legislation during the Progressive Era: A Reevaluation," 72 *J. of Amer. Hist.* (1985), 63–91; Lawrence M. Friedman, "Freedom of Contract and Occupational Licensing 1890–1910: A Legal and Social Study," 52 *Calif. Law Rev.* (1965), 487–534; Harry N. Scheiber, "Public Rights and the Rule of Law in American Legal History," 72 *Calif. Law Rev.* (1984), 217–51. Although less careful in distinguishing between publicized cases and the overall work of the state judiciaries, Arnold M. Paul, *Conservative Crisis and the Rule of Law: Attitudes of Bench and Bar, 1887–1895* (1960; New York, 1969), *passim*, and Loren P. Beth, *The Development of the American Constitution, 1877–1917* (New York, 1971), 218–30, also offer useful insights.

55. Keller, *Affairs of State*, 407; *In the Matter of Jacobs*, 98 N.Y. 98, 102–5 (1885).

56. *Ibid.*, 112–15 (emphasis added).

57. *Ibid.*, 105–7. The opinion also included quotations from other state and federal cases that suggested the same conclusion.

58. *Godcharles and Company v. Wigeman*, 113 Pa. 431, 436–37 (1886); *Ritchie v. People*, 155 Ill. 98, 103–13 (1895). *Ritchie* was decided in March, well before the

beginning of the federal Supreme Court's October 1895 term, during which *Plessy* was finally called and final briefs filed.

59. Urofsky, "State Courts and Protective Legislation," 88; Paul, *Conservative Crisis, passim.*

60. *Jacobs*, 98 N.Y. at 110; *Ritchie*, 155 Ill. at 106, 110.

61. See also entry for "Reasonableness," 16 *Amer. and Eng. Encyclopedia of Law* (1892), 1077 n. 1 (quoting *State v. Vandersluis*, 42 Minn. 129, 131 [1889]).

62. Charles Warren, "The Progressiveness of the United States Supreme Court," 13 *Colum. Law Rev.* (1913), 294–313; Brown, "Due Process of Law, Police Power, and the Supreme Court," 943–68.

CHAPTER FIVE   The Intellectual Environment: Racist Thought in the Late Nineteenth Century

1. Oliver Wendell Holmes, Jr., *The Common Law* (1881; reprint ed., Cambridge, Mass., 1963), 5. Barton J. Bernstein also notes the pertinence of Holmes's comment to *Plessy*; see his "*Plessy v. Ferguson*: Conservative Sociological Jurisprudence," 48 *J. of Negro Hist.* (1963), 196.

2. *Brown v. Board of Education of Topeka*, 347 U.S. 483, 494 n. 11 (1954); Lawrence M. Friedman, *et al.*, "State Supreme Courts: A Century of Style and Citation [1870–1970]," 33 *Stan. Law Rev.* (1981), 811–17 and *passim*. See also Karl N. Llewellyn, *The Common Law Tradition: Deciding Appeals* (Boston, 1940), 35–41. For perspective on Warren's footnote eleven, see Richard Kluger, *Simple Justice: The History of* Brown v. Board of Education *and Black America's Struggle for Equality* (New York, 1976), 705–7.

3. See, for example, Robert J. Harris, *The Quest for Equality: The Constitution, Congress, and the Supreme Court* (Baton Rouge, 1960), 98–102; Bernstein, "Conservative Sociological Jurisprudence," 196–205 and esp. 199. While characterizing the social science used in *Plessy* as "questionable" and "dubious," Professor Bernstein allows that it reflected dominant views of the period.

4. Although focusing on a very different substantive area, an informative introduction to the problem of deciphering "public opinion" in the late nineteenth century is in Ernest R. May, *American Imperialism: A Speculative Essay* (New York, 1968), 17–43.

5. For detailed accounts of nineteenth-century racial theorizing in America, see George M. Fredrickson, *The Black Image in the White Mind: The Debate on Afro-American Character and Destiny, 1817–1914* (New York, 1971); William Stanton, *The Leopard's Spots: Scientific Attitudes toward Race in America, 1815–59* (Chicago, 1960); John S. Haller, Jr., *Outcasts from Evolution: Scientific Attitudes of Racial Inferiority, 1859–1900* (Urbana, Ill., 1971). I have relied on these studies in identifying the major racist spokesmen. Shorter descriptions of the scientific racism of the period are in Paul F. Boller, Jr., *American Thought in Transition: The Impact of Evolutionary Naturalism, 1865–1900* (Chicago, 1969), 199–215; Thomas F. Gossett, *Race: The History of an Idea in America* (Dallas, 1963), 144–75; James W. VanderZanden, "The Ideology of White Supremacy," 20 *J. of the Hist. of Ideas* (1959), 385–402.

6. C. Vann Woodward, *The Strange Career of Jim Crow* (3rd rev. ed., New

York, 1974), 39–65; Guion Griffis Johnson, "Southern Paternalism toward Negroes After Emancipation," 28 *J. of So. Hist.* (1957), 483–509; Thomas N. Page, *The Old South: Essays Social and Political* (1892; reprint ed., New York, 1968), 314–15; Carl V. Harris, *Political Power in Birmingham, 1871–1921* (Knoxville, 1977), 186; Frenise A. Logan, *The Negro in North Carolina, 1876–1894* (Chapel Hill, 1964), 212; Howard N. Rabinowitz, *Race Relations in the Urban South, 1865–1890* (New York, 1978), 18–29, 334–39; Claude H. Nolen, *The Negro's Image in the South: The Anatomy of White Supremacy* (Lexington, Ky., 1967), 192; Lawrence J. Friedman, *The White Savage: Racial Fantasies in the Postbellum South* (Englewood Cliffs, N.J., 1971), 123–24, 127.

7. Henry M. Field, *Bright Skies and Dark Shadows* (New York, 1890), 115–17, 144–45, 167–75; Richard W. Gilder, Editorial, 23 *Century Mag.* (1883), 945–46; Alton Hornsby, Jr., "Retrospect," in *In the Cage: Eyewitness Accounts of the Freed Negro in Southern Society, 1877–1929*, Hornsby, ed. (Chicago, 1971), 260. On northern opinion generally, see Rayford W. Logan, *The Betrayal of the Negro from Rutherford B. Hayes to Woodrow Wilson* (New York, 1965), esp. 165–275. (But see note 9, *infra*.) Not surprisingly, Thomas Nelson Page approvingly quoted Field on Negro mediocrity. See Page, *The Old South*, 255.

8. J. Morgan Kousser, *The Shaping of Southern Politics: Suffrage Restriction and the Establishment of the One Party South, 1880–1910* (New Haven, 1974), *passim* and esp. 238–39 for a summary of the restrictive measures; Andrew McLaughlin, "Mississippi and the Negro Question," 70 *Atlantic Mon.* (1892), 829; Page, *The Old South*, 325. The timing of the widespread move for suffrage restriction is explained partly by the rise of the agrarian movement, partly by the possibility of a new federal election law. (Threatened federal enforcement of state requirements made it important to have restrictions written into law rather than rely on intimidation and fraud for control of dissident voting.) While Mississippi was the first state to use the convention device to embed suffrage restriction into its constitution, attempts to restrict voting by ordinary legislation, often ignored by historians, had dotted the 1880s. See Kousser's model study, chs. 4–5. As evidence of the dominant outlook on Reconstruction, it is significant that George Washington Cable, one of the few southerners actively to defend Negro rights, referred to "the dreadful episode of reconstruction." See Cable, "The Freedman's Case in Equity," 29 *Century Mag.* (1885), 412.

9. John A. Garraty, *Henry Cabot Lodge* (New York, 1953), 117–20; John T. Morgan, "The Race Question in the United States," 2 *Arena* (1890), reprinted in *The Development of Segregationist Thought*, Idus A. Newby, ed. (Homewood, Ill., 1968), 23; E. L. Godkin, "The Republican Party and the Negro," 7 *Forum* (1889), 252–57; James Bryce, "Thoughts on the Negro Problem," 153 *North Amer. Rev.* (1891), 654. See generally Stanley P. Hirshson, *Farewell to the Bloody Shirt: Northern Republicans and the Southern Negro, 1877–1893* (Bloomington, 1962), 200–235; Kousser, *Shaping of Southern Politics*, 20–31. It needs noting that during the debate on Lodge's bill, leading Republicans roundly attacked the idea of Negro inferiority.

10. Gerald H. Gaither, *Blacks and the Populist Revolt: Ballots and Bigotry in the "New South"* (University, Ala., 1977), 132–34 and *passim*; *Arkadelphia Siftings*, [1892], and Little Rock *Arkansas Gazette*, 9 Sept. 1892, both quoted in John W. Graves, "Negro Disfranchisement in Arkansas," 26 *Ark. Hist. Q.* (1967), 205, 212–13.

11. Henry W. Grady, "In Plain Black and White: A Reply to Mr. Cable," 29 *Century Mag.* (1885), 911–12; Morgan, "Race Question," in Newby, ed., *Segregationist Thought*, 23; Editorial, *Working Christian*, 22 April 1875, quoted in John W. Storey, "The Negro in Southern Baptist Thought, 1865–1900" (Ph.D. diss., Univ. of Kentucky, 1968), 195; Field, *Bright Skies*, 202.

12. *Cong. Rec.*, 54th Cong., 1 sess., 2817–20 (16 March 1896). See generally, Garraty, *Lodge*, 140–45; Richard Weiss, "Racism in the Era of Industrialism," in *The Great Fear: Race in the Mind of America*, Gary B. Nash and Richard Weiss, eds. (New York, 1970), 133–36.

13. Stanton, *Leopard's Spots*, 1–23; Cable, "The Negro Question in the United States," [1888], reprinted in *The Negro Question: A Selection of Writings on Civil Rights in the South*, Arlin Turner, ed. (New York, 1968), 126. Cable linked any existing Negro deficiencies to the race's having been both "under the iron yoke" of slavery in America and, before that, amidst an inhospitable African environment; he forecast rapid improvement if the race were given "a white man's chance"; but he held, too, that "[d]issimilar races are not inclined to mix spontaneously." *Ibid.*, 126, 146.

14. Stanton, *Leopard's Spots*, 24–144; Haller, *Outcasts from Evolution*, 3–18, 69–86. See also Stephen Jay Gould, *The Mismeasure of Man* (New York, 1981), 30–72 (which includes an analysis, at 50–69, of Morton's apparently unconscious errors in measurement and inference); and on the question of Nott's motives, compare Stanton, *Leopard's Spots*, 65–72, 158–60, with Fredrickson, *Black Image*, 78–80.

15. Haller, *Outcasts from Evolution*, 78–94, 155–83; Edward Pfeiffer, "United States," in *The Comparative Reception of Darwinism*, Thomas F. Glick, ed. (Austin, Tex., 1974), 168–96; George W. Stocking, Jr., *Race, Culture, and Evolution: Essays in the History of Anthropology* (New York, 1968), 44–68 and esp. 45–49. See also Fredrickson, *Black Image*, 228–55.

16. Compare Richard Hofstadter, *Social Darwinism in American Thought* (rev. ed., Boston, 1955), 31–122, with Robert C. Bannister, *Social Darwinism: Science and Myth in Anglo-American Social Thought* (Philadelphia, 1979), *passim*; and see Stocking, *Race, Culture, and Evolution*, 234–69; Pfeiffer, "United States," 198–202; *Evolutionary Thought in America*, Stow Persons, ed. (New York, 1956), chs. 4–6; Boller, *American Thought in Transition*, 47–93; James A. Rogers, "Darwinism and Social Darwinism" 33 *J. of the Hist. of Ideas* (1972), 265–80; Anthony Leeds, "Darwinian and 'Darwinian' Evolutionism in the Study of Society and Culture," in Glick, ed., *Comparative Reception*, esp. 438–48; Loren Eiseley, *Darwin's Century: Evolution and the Men Who Discovered It* (New York, 1958), 205–53; James R. Moore, *The Post-Darwinian Controversies . . . 1870–1900* (Cambridge, Eng. 1979), 125–90; and, for encyclopedic detail, Ernest Mayr, *The Growth of Biological Thought: Diversity, Evolution, and Inheritance* (Cambridge, Mass., 1982), parts II and III *passim*.

17. George W. Stocking, Jr., "American Social Scientists and Race Theory, 1890–1915" (Ph.D. diss., Univ. of Pennsylvania, 1960), esp. 334–45, 469–510; Gould, *Mismeasure*, 73–74, 82–107, 122–43.

18. Haller, *Outcasts from Evolution*, 19–39 (and see also *ibid.*, 40–68); Stocking, "American Social Scientists," appendix B, 601–17, interpreted through bibliographical entries at viii–xxxvii. Figures on articles appearing only in the period of 1896 and earlier cannot be separated out of Stocking's data, hence my use of figures for authors who *began publishing* in 1896 or earlier. This results in inclusion

of some articles published after 1896, but Stocking's discussion and my own reading of selected items indicate the figures in Table I accurately characterize the material published in the pre-*Plessy* period.

19. The hold of scientific racism is better appreciated when one recalls that not until just after the turn of the century did American social science begin significantly to break free from the biological-evolutionary analogy as an organizing principle and, concomitantly, from neo-Lamarckianism. That break, in turn, depended on the discrediting of neo-Lamarckianism in biology proper, as discussed earlier, which helped reorient interest toward the role of social process in the transmission of culture. In the twentieth century, "culture" has shifted in definition to include the totality of *learned* behavior, as opposed to behavior determined by evolutionary law. See, for example, Stocking, *Race, Culture, and Evolution*, 198–233 (which underscores the importance of Franz Boas's contributions); Hamilton Cravens, "The Abandonment of Evolutionary Social Theory in America: The Impact of Academic Professionalization upon American Sociological Theory, 1890–1920," 12 *Amer. Studies* (1971), 5–20.

20. David G. Brinton, "The Aims of Anthropology," 2 *Science* (New Series, 1895), 241–42, 248–49. These conclusions came under Brinton's discussion of the subfield of ethnology, "the natural science of social life"; they flowed, he said, from study of "the psychology of the individual; [for] in his personal feelings and thoughts will be discovered the final and only complete explanation of the forms of sociology and the events of history." *Ibid.*, 250. See also Brinton's remarks on applied anthropology, *ibid.*, 250–51. For an earlier statement, see Brinton, *Negroes* (Philadelphia, 1891), esp. 5–6, 11–12. On Brinton generally, see Haller, *Outcasts*, 100–120.

21. Franklin H. Giddings, *Principles of Sociology* (3rd ed., New York, 1896), 18–19; Nathaniel Shaler, "Race Prejudices," 58 *Atlantic Mon.* (1886), 510, 514, 516–18; Shaler, "Science and the African Problem," 66 *ibid.* (1890), 44; Shaler, "The Nature of the Negro," 3 *Arena* (1890), 25. On Shaler's influence, see Haller, *Outcasts from Evolution*, 167. While an undergraduate at Harvard from 1888 to 1890, W. E. B. DuBois had Shaler as a teacher and evidently held him in some respect. In his *Autobiography*, between mentioning his debts to various professors (including William James, Josiah Royce, George Santayana, and Albert Bushnell Hart), DuBois recalled, "Shaler invited a Southerner, who objected to sitting beside me, out of [*i.e.*, to leave] class; he said he wasn't doing very well, anyway." W. E. B. DuBois, *The Autobiography of W. E. B. DuBois* (New York, 1968), 132–33, 143.

22. Frederick Hoffman, *Race Traits and Tendencies of the American Negro*, Publications of the Amer. Econ. Assoc., no. 11 (Washington, D.C., 1896), v, 1, 310; Hoffman to J. W. Jenks, 4 Nov. 1895, in American Economic Association Archives, Special Collections Department, Northwestern University Library. *Race Traits* appeared in print several months *after* the United States Supreme Court handed down *Plessy*, and its preface is dated 28 July 1896, but correspondence between Hoffman and the AEA indicates it was largely completed during the year prior to the *Plessy* decision. In any event, it merely elaborated positions Hoffman had staked out in journals during the previous several years, and, as John Haller observes, it was "a summation of the century's medical and anthropological accumulations concerning race relations in America." *Outcasts from Evolution*, 60; see also Fredrickson, *Black Image*, 249. The questions raised initially by the AEA's editorial referees about the work had to do with statistical details and textual

development, not basic conclusions. See William A. Scott to J. W. Jenks, 30 Oct. 1895; Davis R. Dewey, undated memorandum, both in AEA Archives. For Hoffman's earlier publications, see "Vital Statistics of the Negro," 5 *Arena* (1892), 529–42; "Vital Statistics of the Negro," *Medical News*, 22 Sept. 1894, at 320–34; "The Negro in the West Indies," 3 *Publications of the Amer. Statistical Assoc.* (1895), 181–200.

23. Hoffman, *Race Traits*, 90–95, 229–41, 250–309; Philip A. Bruce, *The Plantation Negro as a Freeman* (1889; reprint ed., Williamstown, Mass., 1970), 83–88, 175–240; Shaler, "Nature of the Negro," 32–33; Haller, *Outcasts from Evolution*, 52–57.

24. Hoffman, *Race Traits*, 33–148, 217–39, 227–93; Bruce, *Plantation Negro*, 77–93, 249; Henry Gannet, *Statistics of the Negroes in the United States* (Baltimore, 1894), 24–25, 28; Friedman, *White Savage*, 122–24. See generally Haller, *Outcasts from Evolution*, 41–50.

25. Hoffman, *Race Traits*, 213–16, 236–38, 327–28; Bruce, *Plantation Negro*, 144, 160–74, 241. Attempting an explanation of the phenomenon, Daniel Brinton argued that black mental development was about equal to that of whites until puberty, "[b]ut after that important physical change, there supervenes a visible ascendancy of the appetites and emotions over the intellect, and an increasing indisposition to mental labor." Brinton, *Negroes*, 11.

26. Haller, *Outcasts from Evolution*, 58–59, 107, 118–19, 130–31, 177–78; Edward D. Cope, "Twin Perils of the Indo-European," 3 *Open Court* (1890), 2054; Hoffman, *Race Traits*, 202, 312; Haller, *Outcasts from Evolution*, 41–50; Fredrickson, *Black Image*, 238–51; Bruce, *Plantation Negro*, 242–46, 255–56. On Cope's background and evolutionary commitments, see also Moore, *Post-Darwinian Controversies*, 146–51, which describes Cope as "The intellectual force of [American] Neo-Lamarckianism."

27. Fredrickson, *Black Image*, 247 (emphasis added); Lester D. Stephens, *Joseph LeConte: Gentle Prophet of Evolution* (Baton Rouge, 1982), *passim* and esp. 196–242; Joseph LeConte, *The Race Problem in the South* (New York, 1892), 351–54, 373–82. See also Haller, *Outcasts from Evolution*, 205–10. Along with Shaler and Cope, according to Haller, LeConte "epitomized in many ways the most 'scientifically' acceptable attitudes of the late nineteenth century on the Negro, the immigrant, and the so-called 'inferior races.'" *Ibid.*, 153.

28. Hoffman, *Race Traits*, 226–28; Bannister, *Social Darwinism*, 114–36, 180–200.

29. Frederick Douglass, "The Claims of the Negro Ethnologically Considered," 1854, in *Negro Social and Political Thought, 1850–1920*, Howard Brotz, ed. (New York, 1966), 226–44; Douglas, "Oration in Memory of Abraham Lincoln . . . at the Unveiling of the Freedmen's Monument . . . ," 14 April 1876, in 4 *The Life and Writings of Frederick Douglass*, Philip S. Foner, ed. (New York, 1955), 309–19; Douglass, "The Color Line," 132 *North Amer. Rev.* (1881), in *ibid.*, 342–52; Douglass, Speech on the *Civil Rights Cases*, Washington, D.C., 22 Oct. 1883, in *ibid.*, 392–403; Douglass, *The Lesson of the Hour* [regarding lynching] (1894), in *ibid.*, 491–523; August Meier, *Negro Thought in America, 1880–1915: Racial Ideologies in the Age of Booker T. Washington* (Ann Arbor, Mich., 1963), 75–82; and see generally Waldo E. Martin, Jr., *The Mind of Frederick Douglass* (Chapel Hill, 1984), esp. 109–35, 219–50.

30. W. E. B. DuBois, *The Souls of Black Folk* (1903; reprint ed., Johnson Reprint Corp., 1968), 41–42; Atlanta Exposition Address, 18 Sept. 1895, in 3 *The Booker T. Washington Papers*, Louis R. Harlan, ed. (Urbana, Ill., 1972–84), 583–87; Louis R. Harlan, *Booker T. Washington: The Making of a Black Leader, 1856–1901* (New York, 1972), 218.

31. Washington, "The Educational Outlook of the South," 18 July 1884, in 2 *Washington Papers*, 255–62. The NEA published Washington's speech as a pamphlet in 1885; see *ibid.*, 262 (editor's note). I have altered the sequence of Washington's remarks.

32. Harlan, *Washington*, 218–28; Louis R. Harlan, "The Secret Life of Booker T. Washington," 37 *J. of So. Hist.* (1971) 395–403.

33. Meier, *Negro Thought*, 48–49, 209, and 121–247 *passim*. In his detailed and careful study of *Black Ohio and the Color Line* (Urbana, Ill., 1976), 190–208, David Gerber demonstrates that the segregationist stance represented a minority and not entirely disinterested view among Ohio's black educators, but nonetheless was "a coherent position, forged by a highly respected, articulate, and intellectual, if small, group" (201).

34. Elliott M. Rudwick, *W. E. B. DuBois: Propagandist of the Negro Protest* (2nd ed., Philadelphia, 1968), 20–27; New York *Age*, 13 June 1891, quoted in Meier, *Negro Thought*, 192; *ibid.*, 190–96, 204–5. DuBois, *The Philadelphia Negro: A Social Study* (Philadelphia, 1899), which reported work that DuBois had begun in 1896, arguably supported the same conclusion. Although denying the cause lay in innate traits, it documented the serious health and crime problems within the Philadelphia Negro community. See esp. 147–63, 235–68.

35. Robert Penn Warren, *Who Speaks for the Negro?* (New York, 1965), 52–53.

36. Fredrickson, *Black Image*, 321; Haller, *Outcasts from Evolution*, 210.

CHAPTER SIX   The Transportation Law Environment: Access by Leave, Not Right

1. J. Willard Hurst, *The Growth of American Law: The Law Makers* (Boston, 1950), 193. See generally *ibid.*, 170–95; Morton Keller, *Affairs of State: Public Life in Late Nineteenth Century America* (Cambridge, Mass., 1977), 343–62.

2. On the status of railway regulation, see Charles C. Savage, "State Legislation Affecting Railroad Traffic," 23 *Amer. Law Register* (new series, 1884), 81–93; William S. Ellis, "State Railroad Commissions," 32 *ibid.* (1893), 632–39, 709–21; Maxwell Ferguson, *State Regulation of Railroads in the South*, [Columbia Univ. Studies in History, Economics, and Public Law, vol. 67, no. 2] (New York, 1916).

3. In *Swift v. Tyson*, 16 Peters 1 (1842), a case involving negotiable instruments, the Supreme Court allowed federal courts in diversity cases to turn to (and in effect to fashion) "the general principles and doctrines of commercial jurisprudence" when the statutory law of the forum state (that is, the state in which the federal court was sitting), as interpreted by the state's own courts, did not provide a basis for decision. After the Civil War, federal courts used the *Swift* doctrine as a basis to develop federal common law broadly in non-criminal areas. See

Tony Freyer, *Harmony and Dissonance: The* Swift *and* Erie *Cases in American Federalism* (New York, 1981), esp. 55–75. As for the state cases, it deserves noting that Louisiana, where *Plessy* originated, was unique among American states in *not* being a common-law jurisdiction on the civil side, but as we have already seen in Chapter Three, the authors of the state court opinions in *Plessy*—a criminal case—did not hesitate to draw on decisions from common law jurisdictions.

4. On the common law of common carriers, see, for example, Joseph K. Angell, *A Treatise on the Law of Carriers of Goods and Passengers by Land and by Water* (5th ed., rev. by John Lathrop, Boston, 1877), esp. 465–77; Robert Hutchinson, *A Treatise on the Law of Carriers as Administered in the Courts of the United States and England* (Chicago, 1882), esp. 432–40, 470–75; H. G. Wood, 3 *A Treatise on the Law of Railroads* (3 vols., Boston, 1885), esp. 1436–37. For two early and seminal judicial statements, see the opinions by Joseph Story in *Jencks v. Coleman*, 13 Fed. Cases 442 (C.C.D.R.I., 1835) (No. 7,258), and Lemuel Shaw in *Commonwealth v. Power*, 7 Metcalf 588 (Mass., 1844). Also useful is the survey of case law, as it had developed through the mid-1880s, which is appended as an annotation to the report of *Power* found in 46 *American Decisions . . . to the Year 1869*, A. C. Freeman, comp. and annotator (San Francisco, 1886), 471–86.

5. *West Chester and Philadelphia Railroad Company v. Miles*, 55 Pa. 209, 210–11 (1867).

6. *Ibid.*, 212.

7. *Ibid.*, 212–14.

8. *Ibid.*, 214–15. The 1837 case was *Hobbs v. Fogg*, 6 Watts 533.

9. *Roberts v. City of Boston*, 5 Cushing 198 (Mass., 1849); *Day v. Owen*, 5 Mich. 520, 526–27 (1858). See also *Goines v. M'Candless*, 4 Philadelphia Reports 255, esp. 256–57 (Phila. Dist. Ct., 1861), upholding a Philadelphia street railway regulation assigning blacks to outside platforms. In *Goines*, the court stated that "there is much in the relation between them [blacks and whites] which must be left to the lessons of experience, and [to] the tribunal of public opinion, which cannot be arbitrarily forced or hastened, without producing or augmenting repulsion and antipathy, and endangering a collision, which must necessarily prove disastrous to the weaker party." *Ibid.*, 257.

10. *West Chester v. Miles*, 55 Pa. at 211, 213.

11. *Ibid.*, 215. Eleven years later, Agnew, by then Pennsylvania's Chief Justice, joined the court's opinion upholding a damage award in the leading Pennsylvania decision applying the state's civil rights law of 1867; see *Central Railroad of New Jersey v. Green and Wife*, 86 Pa. 421 (1878).

12. Perhaps *Miles*'s source—a northern court—also contributed to the decision's continuing attraction. This at least is suggested by the different fate of *Scott v. State*, 39 Ga. 321 (1869). Immediately at issue in *Scott* was the continued validity of antebellum miscegenation legislation, for a provision of the new 1868 Georgia constitution provided that "the social status of the citizen shall never be the subject of legislation." Construing the provision, state Chief Justice Joseph E. Brown frankly endorsed the doctrine of separate-but-equal as part of the common law of common carriers, which, like the challenged anti-miscegenation law, illustrated for him the area into which *new* legislation could never intrude. Brown's remarks on the dangers of racial amalgamation exceeded Justice Agnew's in their stridency and could have served nicely in the 1890s as a précis for Frederick Hoffman's *Race Traits*.

(See esp. 39 Ga. at 323–27.) But Brown barely concealed his contempt for the results of the recent war ("the late civil strife"), and *Scott* largely disappeared from judicial view. See also Edmund L. Drago, *Black Politicians and Reconstruction in Georgia: A Splendid Failure* (Baton Rouge, 1982), 41.

13. *Chicago and North Western Railroad Company v. Williams*, 55 Ill. 185, 186–89 (1870). The state Supreme Court's bow to separate-but-equal contrasted with the trial judge's simple denial of the company's right to exclude Mrs. Williams on the basis of color. See "Rights of Colored Persons on Railways," 2 *Chicago Legal News* (1869), 52 (summarizing the case in trial court).

14. *Thompson v. Baltimore City Passenger Railway Company*, 23 Fed. Cases 1023 (C.C.D.Md., 1870) (No. 13,941); *Baltimore American*, 30 April 1870 at 1–2. *Federal Cases* simply lists this and the *Fields* case (which is discussed in the following paragraph), without any further detail. The reports of the two cases in the *American* are especially full.

15. *Fields v. Baltimore City Passenger Railway Company*, 9 Fed. Cases 11 (C.C.D.Md., 1871) (No. 4,763); *Baltimore American*, 11 Nov. 1871 at 2, 4; 13 Nov. 1871 at 4; 14 Nov. 1871 at 4; 15 Nov. 1871 at 2. For a sketchier account, see *The Sun* (Baltimore), 10 Nov. 1871 at 4; 11 Nov. 1871 at 4; 13 Nov. 1871 at 4; 14 Nov. 1871 at 4.

16. *Bell v. Maryland*, 378 U.S. 226, 308 n. 26 (1964) (Goldberg, J., concurring); *Baltimore American*, 14 Nov. 1871 at 2. Justice Goldberg was perhaps misled by the federal government's brief, which neglected aspects of the first reports of the case and which (like Goldberg) omitted to note a correction that the *American* subsequently issued. See Supplemental Brief for the United States as Amicus Curiae, *Bell v. Maryland*, 378 U.S. 226 (1964), 51–52 and n. 91; *Baltimore American*, 15 Nov. 1871 at 2.

17. *Cully v. Baltimore and Ohio Railway Company*, 6 Fed. Cases 946, 946–47 (D.Md., 1876) (No. 3,466).

18. *Jennings v. Third Avenue Railroad Company* (Brooklyn, N.Y., 1855), summarized in *New York Daily Tribune*, 23 Feb. 1856, reprinted with additional commentary in *The Pacific Appeal* (San Francisco), 16 May 1863 at 3; *People v. Pond* (San Francisco, 1863), summarized in *The Pacific Appeal*, 6 June 1863 at 3. I am indebted to Professor J. Morgan Kousser for calling these two cases to my attention.

19. *Washington, Alexandria, and Georgetown Railroad Company v. Brown*, 17 Wallace 445, 447–49, 452–53 (1873). For context and background, see John P. Frank and Robert F. Munro, "The Original Understanding of Equal Protection of the Laws," in *One Hundred Years of the Fourteenth Amendment: Implications for the Future*, Jules B. Gerard, ed. (Buffalo, N.Y., 1973), 72–74. For brief summaries of *Brown* and most of the other federal cases discussed in this chapter, see Sarah H. Lemmon, "Transportation Segregation in the Federal Courts since 1865," 38 *J. of Negro Hist.* (1953), 175–83. In *Brown*, the railway company also defended by alleging faulty service of process and general absence of corporate liability while in receivership, but the Court allowed neither claim. As regards the issue of segregation, the Court also had to determine whether subsequent reorganization and charter grants affected the ban on exclusion on the basis of color, and held they did not. See 17 Wallace at 446–47, 451–52.

20. *Coger v. North Western Union Packet Company*, 37 Iowa 145, 146–49 (1873).

21. *Ibid.*, 149–51 (emphasis added), 147. As to the argument that Mrs. Coger's ticket for transportation was a voluntarily-entered contract limiting her meal privileges, the trial judge ruled that if the jury found the ticket pertained only to transportation, it had no effect on meal privileges. *Ibid.*, 147; see also 158–59.

22. *Ibid.*, 152–57; *Clark v. Board of Directors*, 24 Iowa 266 (1868). Although Beck referred to "the recent constitutional amendments" (37 Iowa at 155), he discussed only the Fourteenth.

23. *Coger*, 37 Iowa at 157–60.

24. *Heard v. Georgia Railroad Company*, 1 Interstate Commerce Reports 719, 722 (1888); *Brown*, 17 Wallace at 447.

25. For example: "If the negro must submit to *different* treatment, to accommodations *inferior* to those given to the white man, when transported by public carriers, he is deprived of the benefits of this very principle of equality. . . . She [Mrs. Coger] was refused accommodations equal to those enjoyed by white persons." *Coger*, 37 Iowa at 153 (emphasis added), 157.

26. Owen Wister, "A Note of the Line of Cases in Which the Discrimination Is Made Not Between the Sex but the Color of Citizens," 32 *Amer. Law Register* (new series, 1893), 754. See also annotation appended to *Summit v. State*, 76 Tenn. 413 (1881), in 9 *American and English Railroad Cases* . . . (Northport, Long Island, N.Y., 1882), 307: "It is clear, however, that the accommodations afforded her [Mrs. Coger] were not equal to those enjoyed by white passengers, so that the case has no great weight."

27. *DeCuir v. Benson*, 27 La. Ann. 1, 2–4 (1875); Laws of Louisiana, 1869, at 37 (Ch. 38); Louisiana Const. of 1868, in 1 *Federal and State Constitutions, Colonial Charters, and Other Organic Laws* . . . , Benjamin P. Poore, comp. (Washington, D.C., 1878), 756 (Art. 13); *DeCuir v. Benson*, 27 La. Ann. at 9–11 (Justice W. G. Wyly, dissenting) (summarizing trial evidence). The full trial proceedings in *DeCuir v. Benson*, No. 7,800, 8th District Court for the Parish of Orleans (1872–73), reveal a few exceptions to the general custom of segregation on the Mississippi River, but generally indicate that Justice Wyly's dissent accurately summarized the evidence. See case file for *DeCuir v. Benson*, No. 4,829, Louisiana Supreme Court Archives, Earl K. Long Library, University of New Orleans.

28. *DeCuir v. Benson*, 27 La. Ann. at 3–6 (emphasis added).

29. *Ibid.*, 2; *Hall v. DeCuir*, 95 U.S. 485, 486, 492 (1878); *Gibbons v. Ogden*, 9 Wheaton 1 (1824). For the federal statute, see 16 Stat. 453.

30. Eliza Jane Hall was administratrix of Benson's estate. See the report in 24 L.Ed. 547, which also gives the exact date of the decision (14 Jan. 1878), sometimes incorrectly cited as 1877.

31. *Hall v. DeCuir*, 95 U.S. at 487–89; *Cooley v. Board of Wardens of the Port of Philadelphia*, 12 Howard 299 (1851).

32. See *Gibbons*, 9 Wheaton at 209–11, for the shift in Marshall's line of argument from the exclusivity of congressional power to the supremacy of federal over state law.

33. *Hall v. DeCuir*, 95 U.S. at 490. Field's remark was from *Welton v. Missouri*, 91 U.S. 275, 282 (1875).

34. *Hall v. DeCuir*, 95 U.S. at 490, 486.

35. See J. R. Pole, *The Pursuit of Equality in American History* (Berkeley and Los Angeles, 1978), 183–85.

36. *Hall v. DeCuir*, 95 U.S., esp. at 501–9. The full dissent is at 491–517.

37. Louis H. Pollak, "Emancipation and Law: A Century of Progress," in *100 Years of Emancipation*, Robert Goldwin, ed. (Chicago, 1964), 166–67; 18 Stat. 335, 336. Loren Miller, *The Petitioners: The Story of the Supreme Court of the United States and the Negro* (New York, 1966), 442 n. 3, also notes that Congress had not been silent. Section One is quoted on p. 71, *supra*.

38. *Civil Rights Cases*, 109 U.S. 3 (1883).

39. *Louisville, New Orleans and Texas Railway Company v. Mississippi*, 133 U.S. 587, 592–95 (1890); *Plessy v. Ferguson*, 163 U.S. 537, 552–64 (1896); *Civil Rights Cases*, 109 U.S. at 60–61.

40. *Civil Rights Cases*, 109 U.S. at 27.

41. *Ibid.*, 10; Brief for Robinson and Wife, *Robinson and Wife v. Memphis and Charleston Railroad Company*, 109 U.S. 3 (1883), 34. Even the quoted wording from the brief was murky in context. Besides citing *Coger* for support, the brief turned to *Chicago and North Western v. Williams* and *Gray v. Cincinnati Railroad Company*, 11 Fed. 683 (C.C.S.D.Ohio, 1882) (discussed below), both of which admitted the possibility that separate-but-equal was a permissible standard. The brief also offered *West Chester v. Miles* to support the equality-means-identity formulation!

42. *Civil Rights Cases*, 109 U.S. at 21–25. After the last quoted sentence, Bradley added: "If the laws themselves make any unjust discrimination, amenable to the prohibitions of the Fourteenth Amendment, Congress has full power to afford a remedy under that amendment and in accordance with it." *Ibid.*, 25. But unless one interprets this as meaning "if *other* laws make any unjust discrimination . . . ," the whole passage is obscure.

43. John Hope Franklin, "The Enforcement of the Civil Rights Act of 1875," 6 *Prologue: The J. of the Nat. Archives* (1974), 225–35 and esp. 228–34.

44. Charge to Grand Jury—The Civil Rights Act, 30 Fed. Cases 999, 999–1002 (C.C.W.D.N.C., 1875) (No. 18,258).

45. *United States v. Dodge*, 25 Fed. Cases 882, 882–83 (W.D.Tex., 1877) (No. 14,976). For similar, if implicit, separate-but-equal interpretations of the Act's coverage, see Charge to Grand Jury, 4 May 1875, Dist. Ct., E. Dist., Texas, reported in *New York Times*, 5 May 1875 at 1; *Smoot v. Kentucky Central Railway Company*, 13 Fed. 337 (C.C.D.Ky., 1882); *United States v. Washington*, 20 Fed. 630 (C.C.W.D.Tex., 1883). Stephen J. Riegel goes so far as to state, "[T]he lower federal courts which addressed the meaning of 'full and equal enjoyment' of accommodations uniformly rejected this [the equality-means-identity] interpretation of the [Civil Rights] act," and finds "that the courts consistently understood 'separate but equal' to be synonymous with 'equal'." Riegel, "The Persistent Career of Jim Crow: Lower Federal Courts and the 'Separate but Equal' Doctrine, 1865–1896," 28 *Amer. J. of Legal Hist.* (1984), 32–33; see also 35. This may be a bit strong, because, as Riegel notes (*ibid.*, 21 n. 19), many cases went unreported, which makes assessment difficult. Also, some of the reported cases involved blatantly unequal accommodations or exclusion, in which instances judges did not have to reach the issue of separate-but-equal versus equality-means-identity. See, for example, *United States v. Newcomer*, 27 Fed. Cases 127 (E.D.Pa., 1876) (No. 15,868), which, however, involved inn accommodations, not transportation.

46. *Green v. City of Bridgeton*, 10 Fed. Cases 1090, 1091–93 (E.D.Ga., 1879)

(No. 5,754); *Bertonneau v. Board of Directors of the City Schools of New Orleans*, 3 Fed. Cases 294, 296 (C.C.D.La., 1878) (No. 1,361).

47. *Gray v. Cincinnati Railroad Company*, 11 Fed. 683, esp. 685–87 (C.C.S.D.Ohio, 1882). Regarding the smoking car accommodation to which Mrs. Gray had been assigned, Swing remarked: "It is very unpleasant for gentlemen, sometimes, to sit in a car of that character. Not every man likes to smoke; not every man likes tobacco. It is bad enough for them to force a gentleman who does not use tobacco, and who sickens at the scent of smoke or tobacco, into a car of that character, let alone forcing a lady there with a sick child." *Ibid.*, 687. Professor Franklin indicates that *Green* was decided under the Civil Rights Act (see Franklin, "Enforcement of the Civil Rights Act," 232), but Judge Swing evidently took the case under his court's diversity jurisdiction. (Mrs. Gray was a resident of Kentucky, and the railway, an Ohio corporation.)

48. Brief for Robinson and Wife, *Robinson and Wife v. Memphis and Charleston Railroad Company*, 103 U.S. 3 (1883), 33. Indeed, the trial judge did give a separate-but-equal interpretation to the Civil Rights Act, although his jury instruction was not as favorable as the one requested by the Robinsons. *Ibid.* (As noted earlier, however, the Robinsons also advanced—albeit ambiguously—the stronger equality-means-identity argument.) Complicating *Robinson and Wife* was the railway's allegation that Mrs. Robinson had been denied admission because of suspicions about her character and probable conduct. See *ibid.*, 14–32.

49. Franklin, "Enforcement of the Civil Rights Act," 232. Regarding the conclusion that Negroes should have prevailed under the separate-but-equal standard, see also the factual situations reviewed in *ibid.*, *passim*, and in Alan F. Westin, "The Case of the Prejudiced Doorkeeper," in *Quarrels That Shaped the Constitution*, John Garraty, ed. (New York, 1964), 128–35.

50. For the history of the act, see L. E. Murphy, "The Civil Rights Law of 1875," 12 *J. of Negro Hist.* (1927), 110–27; William Gillette, *Retreat from Reconstruction, 1869–1879* (Baton Rouge, 1979), 196–210, 259–75. Insights into the range of motives, in and out of Congress, emerge from *ibid.*, and also from Bertram Wyatt-Brown, "The Civil Rights Act of 1875," 18 *West. Pol. Q.* (1975), 763–75; Alfred H. Kelly, "The Congressional Controversy over School Segregation, 1867–1875," 64 *Amer. Hist. Rev.* (1959), 537–63. For a summary of the debates that focuses on statements arguably supporting a separate-but-equal intent, see Alfred Avins, "Racial Segregation in Public Accommodations: Some Reflected Light on the Fourteenth Amendment from the Civil Rights Act of 1875," 18 *West. Reserve Law Rev.* (1967), 1251–83. (But note that Professor Avins's attempt to infer the intent of the framers of the Fourteenth Amendment from the positions some of them took years later involves large and problematic conceptual leaps.) For a selective excerpting of evidence from the debates to show that Congress intended to mandate identity of accommodations, see Milton R. Konvitz and Theodore Leskes, *A Century of Civil Rights* (New York, 1961), 90–101.

51. Quoted in Joseph H. Cartwright, *The Triuph of Jim Crow: Tennessee Race Relations in the 1880s* (Knoxville, 1976), 185.

52. One might argue that a constitutionally validated Civil Rights Act would *at minimum* have laid a foundation for more vigorous federal enforcement of the equality requirement of the separate-but-equal principle than occurred through sporadic common-law suits, and that this outcome would have worked to the benefit

of blacks for whom first-class fares too often bought accommodations which were unquestionably inferior, whether integrated or segregated. But this hypothetical result seems quite unrealistic, for vigorous federal enforcement itself was unlikely in an era of truly limited government, low budgets, and a strong Democratic Party presence in Washington.

53. *The Sue*, 22 Fed. 843, 843–44, 846 (D.Md., 1885). For clarity of presentation, I have slightly rearranged the sequence of Morris's argument.

54. *Ibid.*, 845–48. For statements of the law comparable to Morris's, see the jury charges in *Logwood and Wife v. Memphis and Cincinnati Railroad Company*, 23 Fed. 318 (C.C.W.D.Tenn., 1885), and *Murphy v. Western and Atlantic Railroad Company*, *ibid.*, 637 (C.C.E.D.Tenn., 1885), both of which are put in context in Cartwright, *The Triumph of Jim Crow*, 187–89.

55. *Britton v. Atlantic and Charlotte Air-Line Railroad Company*, 88 N.C. 536 (1883). On the status of separate-but-equal, the court stated: "This right, as regards the separation of white and colored races in public places, has been expressly and fully recognized in many of the courts, both state and national. . . . [Citing *West Chester v. Miles, Day v. Owen*, and *Hall v. DeCuir*.] In some of the cases, it is said not to be barely a right appertaining to the carrier, *but a positive duty*, whenever its exercise may be necessary in order to prevent contacts and collisions arising from natural or well known antipathies, such as are likely to lead to disturbances from promiscuous intermingling." 88 N.C. at 542 (emphasis added).

56. *Houck v. Southern Pacific Railway Company*, 38 Fed. 226, 226–30 (C.C.W.D.Tex., 1888). Although agreeing that Mrs. Houck had been wrongfully excluded, Judge Boarman reduced her award from $5,000 to $2,500, finding the evidence insufficient to support the conclusion that her illness and miscarriage were the direct consequences of the acts of the railway's agents, as opposed to being the result of her own decision, after being denied admission to the ladies' car, to ride on the outside platform rather than in the colored car.

57. *Chesapeake, Ohio, and Southwestern Railroad Company v. Wells*, 85 Tenn. 613, 614–15 (1887); Laws of Tennessee, 1875, at 216–17 (Ch. 130); *ibid.*, 1881, at 211–12 (Ch. 155); Cartwright, *The Triumph of Jim Crow*, 189–91; *Chilton v. St. Louis and Iron Mountain Railroad Company*, 114 Mo. 88, 92 (1893). For the conclusion that the Tennessee Supreme Court equated the requirements of the 1881 Tennessee separate car law with the requirements inhering in the case law, see the gloss put on *Wells* only three days later, in *Memphis and Charleston Railway Company v. Benson*, 85 Tenn. 627, 631 (1887).

58. *McGuinn v. Forbes*, 37 Fed. 639, 639–40 (D.Md., 1889).

59. *Cong. Rec.*, 48th Cong., 2 sess., 296–97, 315–22 (16, 17 Dec. 1884). Breckinridge's amendment was a substitute for the first amendment offered after O'Hara's had passed, which would have provided: "Nothing in this act contained [*sic*] shall be so construed as to prevent any railroad company from providing separate accommodations for white and colored persons." *Ibid.*, 316, 320.

60. *Ibid.*, 323, 332–33 (17, 18 Dec. 1884); Act of 4 Feb. 1887, 24 Stat. 379, 380 (sec. 3).

61. *Councill v. Western and Atlantic Railroad Company*, 1 Interstate Commerce Reports 355 (1887) (preliminary hearing); same case, *ibid.*, 638 (1887) (report and opinion of the Commission); *Heard v. Georgia Railroad Company*, 1 Inters. Comm. Rep. 493 (1887) (pleadings); same case, *ibid.*, 719 (1888) (report and opinion);

Heard v. Georgia Railroad Company, 2 Inters. Comm. Rep. 392 (1889) (Heard's complaint); same case, *ibid.*, 508 (1889) (report and opinion). These cases are available in two different reports, the other being the *Interstate Commerce Commission Reports*, commonly cited "I.C.C.," in which the main opinions are found in vol. 1, at 339 (*Councill*), vol. 1, at 428 (*Heard I*), and vol. 3, at 111 (*Heard II*).

62. 1 Inters. Comm. Rep. at 355, 493–94; 2 *ibid.*, 392.

63. August Meier, *Negro Thought in America, 1880–1915: Racial Ideologies in the Age of Booker T. Washington* (Ann Arbor, Mich., 1963), 208–10; 1 Inters. Comm. Rep. at 355, 641, 722, 723; 2 *ibid.*, 514. Councill also asked monetary damages for the injuries and indignities he had suffered, but the Commission denied its own jurisdiction on this issue. See 1 *ibid.*, 640.

64. *Ibid.*, 640, 641, 721, 722. In *Councill* the Commission indicated that separation was common in all states with large black populations, but qualified this conclusion in *Heard I*: "In South Carolina, according to the evidence, and as was alleged in the argument, in the States of Virginia and North Carolina, where the colored population is large, no separation is made." *Ibid.*, 722. Councill's own trip through Tennessee had indeed disclosed variation in practice in that state.

65. *Ibid.*, 355, 640, 720; 2 *ibid.*, 509, 510–11.

66. 1 *ibid.*, 721; *Smith v. Chamberlain* 38 S.C. 529, 545–46 (1893); *Plessy v. Ferguson*, 163 U.S. at 548.

67. Isaac F. Redfield, 1 *The Law of Railways Embracing . . . Common Carriers . . .* (4th ed., Boston, 1869), 107; 1 *ibid.* (5th ed., Boston, 1873), 115; 1 *ibid.* (6th ed., rev. by J. Kendrick Kinney, Boston 1888), 101–2 n. (d); Thomas M. Cooley, *A Treatise on the Law of Torts, or the Wrongs Which Arise Independent of Contract* (Chicago, 1880), 284–85; Cooley, *The Elements of Torts* (Chicago, 1895), 103–4; *Heard v. Georgia Railway Company*, 1 Inters. Comm. Rep. 719 (1888). The second edition of Cooley's *Treatise on Torts* (Chicago, 1888), 335–36, added citations affirming the right of carriers to separate by race, but retained the qualification mentioned in the text. Cooley had toured the South in the spring of 1887 as a member of the new Interstate Commerce Commission. After the first *Heard* case, he confided his own sentiments to his diary: "Mr. Cromwell [Heard's counsel] said with great justice that the only way to have equal accommodations was to have identical accommodations." (Alan Jones, "Thomas M. Cooley and the Interstate Commerce Commission: Continuity and Change in the Doctrine of Equal Rights," 81 *Pol. Sci. Q.* [1966], 613, 614 n. 43.) This remark may not be all it seems, however, for it suggests the opinion that equal accommodations were not necessarily identical accommodations—but only that the latter would guarantee the former.

68. Robert Hutchinson, *A Treatise on the Law of Carriers as Administered in the Courts of the United States and England* (Chicago, 1882), 438–40 and 439 n. 1; *ibid.* (2nd ed., rev. by Floyd R. Mechem, Chicago, 1891), 618–22 and 619 n. 1 (adding detail to the 1882 edition); Owen Wister, "A Note of the Line of Cases in Which the Discrimination Is Made Not Between the Sex but the Color of Citizens," 32 *Amer. Law Register* (new series, 1893), 748–56 (annotating *Smith v. Chamberlain*, 38 S.C. 529 [1893], which upheld separate-but-equal facilities in railway stations). Wister rested his view on the following propositions, which he extracted from the case law:

"(1) A railroad company has the common law right as a carrier to make reasonable regulations regarding and controlling the management and transportation of its passengers; and whether any particular regulation so made is or is not a reasonable one, is a mixed question of law and fact.

"(2) A regulation providing separate and equal accommodations for whites and blacks is a reasonable one, if the social conditions of the district make separation in trains, boats, etc., advisable.

"(3)The accommodations must be equal in convenience and comfort.

"(4) The Four[teen]th Amendment and the Civil Rights Bill do not affect or concern this police power of common carriers."

See also Joseph K. Angell, *A Treatise on the Law of Carriers of Goods and Passengers by Land and by Water* (5th ed., rev. by John Lathrop, Boston, 1877), 467–68 and 468 n. (a); annotation appended to *United States v. Buntin*, 10 Fed. 730, 736–41 and esp. 739–41 (C.C.S.D.Ohio, 1882); annotation to *Gray v. Cincinnati Southern Railway Company*, 11 Fed. 683, 687–88 (C.C.S.D.Ohio, 1882); annotation to *Summit v. State*, 76 Tenn. 413 (1881), in 9 *American and English Railroad Cases* . . . (Northport, Long Island, N.Y., 1882), 306–7; H. G. Wood, 2 *A Treatise on the Law of Railroads* (Boston, 1885), 1034–35; annotation to *Commonwealth v. Power*, 7 Metcalf 596 (Mass., 1844), in 46 *American Decisions* . . . *to the Year 1869*, A. C. Freeman, comp. and annotator (San Francisco, 1886), 471–87 and esp. 482–83; annotation to *West Chester and Philadelphia Railroad Co. v. Miles*, 55 Pa. 209 (1867), in 93 *ibid.*, 750; 3 *American and English Encyclopedia of Law*, John H. Merrill, *et al.*, comps. (Northport, Long Island, N.Y., 1887), 728 [n. 2]; 18 *ibid.* (1892), 754–55 n. 2; Charles F. Beach, 2 *The Modern Law of Railways* (San Francisco, 1890), 1088–89 and nn. 5–7; D. H. Pingrey, "A Legal View of Racial Discrimination," 30 *Amer. Law Register* (new series, 1891), 60–105 and esp. 89–93; Henry C. Black. *Handbook of American Constitutional Law* (St. Paul, 1895), 410 and n. 54; Stewart Rapalje and William Mack, 3 *A Digest of Railway Decisions* . . . *in the United States, England, and Canada* (Northport, Long Island, N.Y., 1895), 25–31.

69. Valerie W. Weaver, "The Failure of Civil Rights, 1875–1883, and Its Consequences," 54 *J. of Negro Hist.* (1969), 373–81; Gilbert T. Stephenson, *Race Distinctions in American Law* (New York, 1910), 102–22. Kansas, Massachusetts, New York, and Pennsylvania had passed civil rights laws prior to 1875. Between 1883 and 1890, Massachusetts and Pennsylvania enacted further measures and were joined by Colorado, Connecticut, Illinois, Indiana, Iowa, Michigan, Minnesota, Nebraska, New Jersey, Ohio, Rhode Island, and Washington. Under the ruling in *Hall v. DeCuir*, these acts did not apply to interstate transportation, but Weaver describes public conveyances as the area in which voluntary compliance with the Acts was highest in the North. "Failure of Civil Rights," 377; see also Milton R. Konvitz, *The Constitution and Civil Rights* (New York, 1947), 109–23.

70. *Cong. Rec.*, 48th Cong., 2 sess., 316 (17 Dec. 1884); *Heard v. Georgia Railway Company*, 2 Inters. Comm. Rep. 508, 511 (1889); *Code of Georgia, Annotated*, Orville A. Black, *et al.*, eds. (Atlanta, 1936), bk. 6, at 101 (sec. 18–205); Laws of Florida, 1891, at 92 (Ch. 4055) (late repeal of equal accommodations law); Note, "The Matter of Racial Differences and Local Police Regulations," 5 *Loyola {of New Orleans} Law Rev.* (1949), 74 (continued force of Louisiana's equal accommodations Act); Laws of Arkansas, 1907, at 728 (Act 303) (late repeal of equal accommodations law).

71. Frederick Douglass, Speech at Lincoln Hall, Washington, D.C., 22 Oct. 1883, in 4 *The Life and Writings of Frederick Douglass*, Philip S. Foner, ed. (New

York, 1955), 396–97; George W. Cable, "The Negro Question," 1888, in *The Negro Question: A Selection of Writings on Civil Rights in the South*, Arlin Turner, ed. (New York, 1968), 129.

CHAPTER SEVEN   *Plessy* Before the United States Supreme Court

1. Revised Statutes, sec. 709, codifying Section 25, Judiciary Act of 1789, 1 Stat. 85; S. F. Phillips to Tourgée, 9 Feb., 1 May 1893, 20 Jan., 1, 28 April 1896. Unless otherwise indicated, manuscript correspondence cited in this chapter is found in the Tourgée Papers.

2. Revised Statutes, sec. 710; "Rules of the Supreme Court of the United States, Announced January 7, 1884," in 108 U.S. Reports at 589 (Rule 26); William W. DeHurst, *The Rules of Practice in the United States Courts, Annotated* (New York, 1907), 130–33; Martinet to Tourgée, 2 Feb., 30 May, 4 Aug. 1893; Phillips to Tourgée, 1 May 1893; Walker to Tourgée, 28 Oct. 1893. On early expectations, see also Citizens' Committee, *The Violation of a Constitutional Right* (New Orleans, 1893), 2. Published in Aug. 1893, this flatly stated (in a preface evidently written by Martinet): "It [the Plessy case] will be argued next fall."

3. Tourgée to Martinet, 31 Oct. 1893; Martinet to Tourgée, 2 Feb. 1893. The Court had in fact reversed itself on constitutional questions, with the legal tender issue probably the most notable example by the 1890s. On Tourgée's plans for a new paper, to be published by the National Citizens Rights Association (which he himself had organized through his weekly columns in the Chicago *Inter Ocean*), see Otto H. Olsen, *Carpetbagger's Crusade: The Life of Albion Winegar Tourgée* (Baltimore, 1965), 321–23.

4. Charles Warren, 2 *The Supreme Court in United States History* (rev. ed., Boston, 1926), 727 n.3, confirmed by a spot check of decided cases to determine typical delays; Walker to Tourgée, 5 Aug. 1895; Phillips to Tourgée, 20 Jan. 1896. On the impact of the 1891 legislation, see Felix Frankfurter and James M. Landis, *The Business of the Supreme Court: A Study in the Federal Judicial System* (New York, 1928), 102–45.

5. Martinet to Tourgée, 29 Jan. (telegram), 4 March 1896; Walker to Tourgée, 9 April 1896; Phillips to Tourgée, 20 Jan., 6 Feb. 1896; M. J. Cunningham to James H. McKenney, Clerk of the U.S. Supreme Court, 30 March 1896, in Clerk's File, *Plessy v. Ferguson*, file number 15,248, Supreme Court Case Files, Record Group 267, National Archives, Washington, D.C. (hereafter cited as "Clerk's File, Plessy"). Cunningham probably informed the Clerk of his plans not to attend the oral argument by way of his co-counsel in Washington, Alexander Porter Morse. No written communication from Cunningham appears in the Clerk's File, but reference to a local telephone call appears in other correspondence; see, for example, Phillips to Tourgée, 1 April 1896. Tourgée's letters to Reed dot his correspondence; see also Olsen, *Carpetbagger's Crusade*, 303–5, 320–21.

6. Phillips to Tourgée, 1 April 1896; Tourgée to Clerk of the Supreme Court, 3, 4 April 1896, Clerk's File, Plessy. I date the Clerk's telephoned notification to Phillips on the basis of his telegraphed notification to M. J. Cunningham, in New Orleans, 28 March 1896, Clerk's File, Plessy.

7. James H. McKenney to Tourgée, 6, 7 April 1896, Clerk's File, Plessy; Emma Tourgée's diary, 1895–98, entry for 10 April 1896, Tourgée Papers.

8. Counsel appearing for argument are listed in *Plessy v. Ferguson*, 163 U.S. 538, 540 (1896). The Supreme Court's Minute Book (National Archives) indicates that Tourgée went first, followed by Morse, with Phillips concluding. (Oct. 1895 term, entries for 13 April 1896, at 522–23.) On Walker's health, see Walker to Tourgée, 9 April 1896, Tourgée Papers. On Morse, see 2 *Who Was Who in America, 1897–1942* (Chicago, 1943), 870. The dates on which the attorneys filed as counsel of record are indicated on certificates in the Clerk's File, Plessy. (Tourgée and Phillips filed in Jan. 1893; Cunningham, in Aug. 1895.) The other civil rights-related case was *Murray v. Louisiana*, 163 U.S. 101 (1896), in which the Court upheld a murder conviction challenged on grounds that New Orleans authorities excluded blacks from juries. On the date of submission of Morse's brief, see the date stamp on the Supreme Court's file copy (microfilm edition).

9. Brief for Plaintiff in Error, submitted by Albion Tourgée and James C. Walker, *Plessy v. Ferguson*, 163 U.S. 537 (1896), 7 (hereafter cited as Tourgée-Walker U.S. Brief). Tourgée's section of the brief occupied pp. 5–36; Walker's, pp. 37–53. The briefs filed in *Plessy* before the U.S. Supreme Court are available in *Landmark Briefs and Arguments . . .* , Philip B. Kurland and Gerhard Casper, eds. (Arlington, Va., 1975), vol. 13. Tourgée's notes for the oral argument (hereafter cited as "Tourgée notes") are filed with his papers for 1892 (see Tourgée Papers, microfilm reel 31), but internal evidence indicates that they were written after Tourgée had available the printed version of his and Walker's brief. The notes are typed on numbered half-pages, with additions in Tourgée's own hand.

10. Tourgée-Walker U.S. Brief, 7–9. See also *ibid.*, 45–47; Tourgée notes, 1–7.

11. Tourgée-Walker U.S. Brief, 42–43. See also Tourgée notes, 6.

12. Tourgée-Walker U.S. Brief, 30, 48–49.

13. *Ibid.*, 4, 31, 45.

14. *Ibid.*, 10–11, 38–41, 43; Tourgee notes, 10, 16a–16b. The South Carolina case was *White v. Tax Collector*, 3 Richardson 136 (1846) (quotation at 140). See also Tourgée-Walker U.S. Brief, 48–53.

15. *Ibid.*, 41–43. It was also in this context that one of the equal protection claims arose. By restricting the access that certain passengers had to courts, the enactment denied equal protection of the laws.

16. *Ibid.*, 9. See also *ibid.*, 39; Tourgée notes, 20–21.

17. Tourgée-Walker U.S. Brief, 9–10; Tourgée notes, 18–19.

18. Tourgée-Walker U.S. Brief, 10, 43.

19. *Ibid.*, 48–51, 11; Tourgée notes, 16–17; The decisions upon which Tourgée drew in arguing that federal courts need not follow state court constructions of state laws actually held (1) that federal courts were not bound to follow *later* state court decisions when the rights at issue involved the interpretation placed on state law at an *earlier* time (*Gelpcke v. City of Dubuque*, 1 Wallace 175, 206 [1863]) and (2) that where local law was not settled, federal courts might exercise their own judgment as to its content (*Burgess v. Seligman*, 107 U.S. 20, 33–34 [1882]).

20. Tourgée-Walker U.S. Brief, 11–13; Tourgée notes, 23–39.

21. Tourgée-Walker U.S. Brief, 13–14, 27; Tourgée notes, 40–44.

22. Tourgée-Walker U.S. Brief, 14, 28–30; Tourgée notes, 8–9.

23. Tourgée-Walker U.S. Brief, 34–35.

24. *Ibid.*, 14–17, 25, partly quoting *Strauder v. West Virginia*, 100 U.S. 303, 308 (1880) (Tourgée's emphasis).

25. Tourgée-Walker U.S. Brief, 19–21, 23; Tourgée notes, 23–28, 7a–8.

26. Tourgée-Walker U.S. Brief, 21–23, 26–27.

27. *Ibid.*, 24–25.

28. *Ibid.*, 27–28.

29. *Ibid.*, 17–18; see also 46–47. I have corrected minor errors in Tourgée's quotation from *Thorpe v. Rutland and Burlington Railroad*, 27 Vermont 140, 149–50 (1855).

30. Tourgée-Walker U.S. Brief, 19, 30–31; Tourgée notes, 7a–11, 14–15. Tourgée observed that if there were any white nurses employed in Louisiana to care for colored children, the Court would note that they were too few to take into account in interpreting the significance of the nurse exemption.

31. Tourgée-Walker U.S. Brief, 25–26.

32. *Ibid.*, 26; Tourgée notes, 11–14.

33. Tourgée-Walker U.S. Brief, 31–33.

34. See *Strauder v. West Virginia*, 100 U.S. 303, 310 (1880); *Civil Rights Cases*, 109 U.S. 3, 28–35, 50 (1883).

35. *Prigg v. Pennsylvania*, 16 Peters 539, 612 (1842). While Story disclaimed that he was "laying down any rule of interpretation" for portions of the Constitution other than the fugitive slave clause, and suggested "that no uniform rule of interpretation can be applied to it [the Constitution]," he then wrote that

> "perhaps[] the safest rule of interpretation after all will be found to be, to look to the nature and objects of the particular powers, duties, and rights, with all the lights and aids of contemporary history; and to give to the words of each just such operation and force, consistent with their legitimate meaning, as may fairly secure and attain the ends proposed."

Ibid., 610–11.

36. Tourgée-Walker U.S. Brief, 17, quoting *Strauder v. West Virginia*, 100 U.S. at 308 (Tourgée's italics omitted).

37. Brief for Plaintiff in Error, submitted by S. F. Phillips and F. D. McKenney, *Plessy v. Ferguson*, 163 U.S. 537 (1896), 1–5, 6 (hereafter cited as Phillips Brief). Although the brief was also signed by his law partner, F. D. McKenney, it was apparently Phillips's own work. See Phillips to Tourgée, 4 Feb., 1 April 1896.

38. *Ibid.*, 6–7.

39. *Ibid.*, 6–9.

40. *Ibid.*, 9–12.

41. *Ibid.*, 8–9.

42. Phillips in effect put off further consideration of the content of the rights attaching to the two categories of citizenship with the comment: "Whether the line of distinction betwixt these classes, as heretofore sometimes indicated, may not cede too much territory that is really Federal, may be left to future consideration." *Ibid.*, 13.

43. *Ibid.*

44. *Ibid.*, 14–15.

45. *Ibid.*, 15–18.

46. *Crandall v. Nevada*, 6 Wallace 35, 44 (1868); Phillips Brief, 19–22. The rule against curing defects through construction came from *United States v. Reese*, 92 U.S. 214, 220–21 (1875), the *Trade-mark Cases*, 100 U.S. 82, 99 (1879), and *Baldwin v. Franks*, 120 U.S. 678, 685–86 (1887). The rule emerging from these cases applied to instances where statutory language was overly broad; it did not run counter to the rule that a statute might be held partially valid and partially invalid *if* by its terms its valid and invalid sections were separable without the aid of judicial construction. See *Baldwin*, 120 U.S. at 687.

47. Phillips Brief, 15, 17–18, 22–23.

48. Brief on Behalf of Defendant in Error, submitted by M. J. Cunningham, *Plessy v. Ferguson*, 163 U.S. 537 (1896), 39–41.

49. *Ibid., passim.*

50. *Ibid.*, esp. 39, 50–51.

51. *Ibid.*, 39–41. The five cases were *Strauder v. West Virginia*, 100 U.S. 303 (1880); *Virginia v. Rives*, 100 U.S. 313 (1880); *Ex parte Virginia*, 100 U.S. 339 (1880); *Neal v. Delaware*, 103 U.S. 370 (1881); *Murray v. Louisiana*, 163 U.S. 101 (1896). The decision in *Murray* was handed down on 18 May 1896, the same day as *Plessy*; Cunningham identified the case by its docket number.

52. Brief on Behalf of Defendant in Error, submitted by Alexander Porter Morse, *Plessy v. Ferguson*, 163 U.S. 537 (1896), 4–5, 7–9 (hereafter cited as Morse Brief); *Barbier v. Connally*, 113 U.S. 27, 31 (1885), slightly misquoted in Morse Brief, 5.

53. Morse Brief, 4–5, 8.

54. *Ibid.*, 11–12.

55. *Ibid.*, 12–13. See Phillips Brief, 10–11.

56. Morse Brief, 13–14.

CHAPTER EIGHT   The Court Decides: Jim Crow Affirmed

1. Justice David Brewer had missed the hearing and did not participate in the case; see Supreme Court Minute Book, entry for 13 April 1896, at 522. For Brown's background, see Charles A. Kent, *Memoir of Henry Billings Brown . . . Consisting of an Autobiographical Sketch with Additions to His Life* (New York, 1915), 20–29, 42–76. Brown still lacks a full-scale biography. My inquiries to librarians and archival searchers at the University of Michigan Library and the Detroit Public Library, which hold the major collections of Brown's papers, have disclosed no material on Brown's participation in *Plessy*; John Marshall Harlan's papers in the Library of Congress and the University of Louisville Law Library are similarly barren for Harlan's dissent.

2. Robert J. Glennon, Jr., "Justice Henry Billings Brown: Values in Tension," 44 *Univ. of Colo. Law Rev.* (1973), 603, 566, 584, 599–601, and *passim*; *Holden v. Hardy*, 169 U.S. 366, 386–87 (1898); Henry B. Brown, "The Distribution of Property," *Report of the Sixteenth Annual Meeting of the Amer. Bar Assoc. . . . 1893* (Philadelphia, 1893), 218; Kent, *Memoir*, 70–71, 81–83. See also Joel Goldfarb, "Henry Billings Brown," 2 *The Justices of the United States Supreme Court, 1789–1969*, Leon Friedman and Fred L. Israel, eds. (New York, 1970), 1553–63. On the broad base and reformist tendencies of the American Social Science Association, see Thomas

L. Haskell, *The Emergence of Professional Social Science: The American Social Science Association and the Nineteenth Century Crisis of Authority* (Urbana, Ill., 1977), 97–167; Mary O. Furner, *Advocacy and Objectivity: A Crisis in the Professionalization of American Social Science, 1865–1905* (Lexington, Ky., 1975), 10–34.

    3. Glennon, "Justice Henry Billings Brown," 589.

    4. *Plessy v. Ferguson*, 163 U.S. 537, 541 (1896).

    5. *Ibid.*, 542–43; *ibid.*, 555 (Harlan, dissenting).

    6. *Ibid.*, 543; Phillips Brief, 13; Tourgée-Walker U.S. Brief, 31–33.

    7. The corresponding pages in his opinion are as follows: step 1: 543–45; step 2: 545–48; step 3: 548; step 4: 548–50; step 5: 550–52; step 6: 552. The division of the opinion into "steps," I should stress, is mine, not Brown's.

    8. *Plessy*, 163 U.S. at 543–44, 551.

    9. *Ibid.*, 551–52; *People ex rel. King v. Gallagher*, 93 N.Y. 438, 448, 450 (1883).

    10. *Plessy*, 163 U.S. at 544–45; *Roberts v. City of Boston*, 5 Cushing 198, 206 (Mass., 1849).

    11. *Ex parte Plessy*, 45 La. 80, 11 So. 948, 950 (1892); *Roberts*, 5 Cushing at 206. On the objection that *Roberts* predated the Fourteenth Amendment, see Barton J. Bernstein, "Case Law in *Plessy v. Ferguson*, 47 *J. of Negro Hist.* (1962), 193–94; J. Morgan Kousser, *Dead End: The Development of Nineteenth-Century Litigation on Racial Discrimination in Schools* (Oxford, Eng., 1986), 4, 34–35 n. 15. Bernstein indicates that *People ex rel. King v. Gallagher*, 93 N.Y. 438 (1883), *Lehew v. Brummell*, 103 Mo. 546 (1890), and *Ward v. Flood*, 36 Cal. 37 (1874), all *relied* on *Roberts*. All three cited *Roberts*, but only in *Ward* was *Roberts* crucial to the line of argument, as opposed to being merely supportive in the sense of providing *additional* authority. See 93 N.Y. at 453–54; 103 Mo. at 553; 36 Cal. at 52–57 and esp. 56. Kousser finds the egalitarian provisions of the Massachusetts constitution vaguer than the Fourteenth Amendment's privileges-or-immunities and equal protection clauses. Given the vagaries of constitutional interpretation, I am not convinced the difference is significant, at least for Brown's argument, which did not crucially depend on the precise equivalence of the provisions.

    12. Leonard W. Levy and Douglas L. Jones, "Introduction," in *Jim Crow in Boston: The Origins of the Separate but Equal Doctrine*, Levy and Jones, eds. (New York, 1974), xxvi–xxix; *Bertonneau v. Board of Directors of City Schools of New Orleans*, 3 Fed. Cases 294, 295 (C.C.D.La., 1878) (No. 1,361) (quoting La. Const. of 1868, Art. 135); *Dawson v. Lee*, 83 Ky. 50, 55–57 (1885).

    13. *Clark v. Board of Directors*, 24 Iowa 266, 269, 276 (1868). See generally Kousser, *Dead End*, esp. 16–18.

    14. *Plessy*, 163 U.S. at 545 (emphasis added). Cooley, *The Elements of Torts* (Chicago, 1895), 105; Kousser, *Dead End*, 54 n. 87. See also *ibid.*, 26–27. In his earlier *Treatise on . . . Constitutional Limitations . . .* (6th ed., Boston, 1890), 481–82 n. 1, Cooley also recognized the acceptance of segregated schools and linked such prohibitions as existed against them to affirmative state action. (See also annotator's note to *United States v. Buntin*, 10 Fed. 730, 736–37 [1882].) Lest Cooley's credentials be suspect, notwithstanding his status as the era's leading constitutional commentator, in 1869 while Chief Justice of Michigan's Supreme Court, he had written the opinion in a case overturning Detroit's long-standing policy of school separation; but as was typical in such cases, the basis for the decision was statutory

construction. See *Workman v. Board of Education of Detroit*, 18 Mich. 399, 408–14 (1869); Kousser, *Dead End*, 10, 18–19.

15. *King v. Gallagher*, 93 N.Y. at 454–55.

16. *Plessy*, 163 U.S. at 545.

17. *Ibid.*, 548 (emphasis added). One source of difficulty in following Brown's exposition is his paragraphing. Here, for example, a distracting paragraph break falls between his brief discussion of the cases and the conclusion he drew from the cases.

18. Bernstein, "Case Law in *Plessy v. Ferguson*," 196.

19. *People v. King*, 110 N.Y. 418, 423–24, 426–27 (1888), in part quoting from *Commonwealth v. Alger*, 7 Cushing 53, 85 (Mass., 1851).

20. See Chapter Six, *supra*. Brown also omitted to mention that many northern states had abrogated the common law of common carriers in this respect through passage of equal accommodations legislation, also discussed in Chapter Six. Besides *West Chester v. Miles* and *People v. King*, Brown cited *Day v. Owen*, 5 Mich. 520 (1858) (which clearly was inapposite, owing to its endorsement of separate-and-*un*equal); *Chicago and North Western Railway Company v. Williams*, 55 Ill. 185 (1870); *The Sue*, 22 Fed. 843 (D.Md. 1885); *Logwood and Wife v. Memphis and Cincinnati Railroad Company*, 23 Fed. 318 (C.C.W.D.Tenn., 1885); *Chesapeake, Ohio, and Southwestern Railroad Company v. Wells*, 85 Tenn. 613 (1887), *Memphis and Charleston Railway Company v. Benson*, 85 Tenn. 627 (1887); *Heard v. Georgia Railroad Company*, 1 Inters. Comm. Rep. 719 (1888); *Heard v. Georgia Railroad Company*, 2 Inters. Comm. Rep. 508 (1889); *McGuinn v. Forbes*, 37 Fed. 639 (D.Md., 1889). Brown's lapse in referring to constitutionality is all the more surprising in view of his eventual unambiguous statement that the core question in *Plessy* was the reasonableness of the separate car law.

21. *Plessy*, 163, U.S. at 550–51.

22. *Ibid.*, 545. See *Strauder v. West Virginia*, 100 U.S. 303 (1880); *Virginia v. Rives*, 100 U.S. 313 (1880); *Neal v. Delaware*, 103 U.S. 370 (1881); *Bush v. Kentucky*, 107 U.S. 110 (1883); *Gibson v. Mississippi*, 162 U.S. 565 (1896).

23. *Plessy*, 163 U.S. at 545–46.

24. *Ibid.*, 546.

25. *Ibid.*, 546–47, quoting the *Civil Rights Cases*, 109 U.S. 3, 11 (1883).

26. See *Louisville, New Orleans and Texas Railway Company v. Mississippi*, 133 U.S. 587 (1890), as discussed in Chapter Two.

27. *Plessy*, 163 U.S. at 547–48 (emphasis added), partly quoting *Louisville, New Orleans and Texas Railway Company v. Mississippi*, 133 U.S. at 591.

28. *Plessy*, 163 U.S. at 548.

29. *Ibid.*, 548–49.

30. *Ibid.*, 549.

31. *Ibid.*, 549–50; *Yick Wo v. Hopkins*, 118 U.S. 356 (1886).

32. See *Daggett v. Hudson*, 43 Ohio 548, 563–65 (1885). The other voting cases Brown cited were *Capen v. Foster*, 12 Pickering 485 (Mass., 1832); *State ex rel. Wood v. Baker*, 38 Wis. 71 (1875) (both upholding registration laws as reasonable means of implementing the right to vote); and *Monroe v. Collins*, 17 Ohio 665 (1868) (overturning legislation that unreasonably burdened racially mixed voters who met the state's definition of who was white). The two irrelevant cases—*Orman v. Riley*, 15 Calif. 48 (1860), and *Hulseman v. Rems*, 41 Pa. 396 (1861)—involved the counting of soldier's votes.

33. *Louisville and Nashville Railroad Company v. Kentucky*, 161 U.S. 677, 696–701 (1896). See *ibid.*, 700, for a listing and description of the other commerce cases that Brown included by reference in *Plessy* at 550.

34. *Plessy*, 163 U.S. at 552.

35. *Ibid.*, 553.

36. *Ibid.*, 553–55. For confirmation of Harlan's description of nineteenth-century railways as quasi-public agencies by virtue of their eminent domain powers, see Harry N. Scheiber, "Property Law, Expropriation, and Resource Allocation by Government, 1789–1910," 33 *J. of Econ. Hist.* (1973), 232–51.

37. *Plessy*, 163 U.S. at 555–56, in part quoting from *Gibson v. Mississippi*, 162 U.S. 565, 591 (1896). Harlan, who had written the Court's opinion in *Gibson*, failed to add in *Plessy* that the black defendant in *Gibson* nonetheless had his murder conviction and death sentence upheld.

38. *Plessy*, 163 U.S. at 556–58, in part quoting William Blackstone, 1 *Commentaries on the Laws of England* (1765–69; facsimile reprint ed., Chicago, 1979), 130.

39. *Plessy*, 163 U.S. at 558–59; Theodore Sedgwick, *A Treatise on the Rules Which Govern the Interpretation and Construction of Statutory and Constitutional Law* (2nd ed., with additional notes by John Norton Pomeroy, New York, 1874), 324–27.

40. *Plessy*, 163 U.S. at 559.

41. *Ibid.*, 559–60.

42. *Ibid.*, 559–63.

43. *Ibid.*, 563.

44. Tourgée-Walker U.S. Brief, 36; Phillips Brief, 18, 22; *Plessy*, 163 U.S. at 563–64. For the guarantee clause, see U.S. Constitution, Art. IV, sec. 4; and for its salience during the early Reconstruction period, as well as the ongoing refusal of the judiciary to enforce it, see William M. Wiecek, *The Guarantee Clause of the U.S. Constitution* (Ithaca, N.Y.), 129, 171–209, 233–39, 292.

CHAPTER NINE   Speaking to the Future

1. Emma Tourgée's diary, entry for 16 April 1896, in Tourgée Papers; Otto H. Olsen, "Introduction," in *The Thin Disguise . . . Plessy v. Ferguson: A Documentary Presentation*, Olsen, ed. (New York, 1967), 25–27, 30 n. 4; Chicago *Inter Ocean*, 20 May 1896, quoted in James M. McPherson, *The Abolitionist Legacy from Reconstruction to the NAACP* (Princeton, 1975), 300; Washington, "Who Is Permanently Hurt?" 16 *Our Day* (June 1896), 311, in 4 *The Booker T. Washington Papers*, Louis R. Harlan, ed. (Urbana, Ill, 1972–84), 186.

2. See Rayford W. Logan, *The Betrayal of the Negro from Rutherford B. Hayes to Woodrow Wilson* (New York, 1965), 211–12; Olsen, *Thin Disguise*, 25–26. Both Logan and Olsen made careful surveys of press and periodical reaction, and while their arguments differ in emphasis regarding national response to *Plessy*, their figures indicate the preponderance of indifference.

3. *New York Times*, 19 May 1896 at 1, 3. The cases mentioned in the text are *Illinois Central Railroad Company v. Illinois ex rel. Butler*, 163 U.S. 142 (1896); *United States v. Laws*, 163 U.S. 258 (1896); *Cornell v. Green*, 163 U.S. 75 (1896); and *Webster v. Daly*, 163 U.S. 155 (1896).

4. Alan F. Westin, "The Supreme Court and the Populist Movement," 15 *J. of Politics* (1953), 3–41; John E. Semonche, *Charting the Future: The Supreme Court Responds to a Changing Society, 1890–1920* (Westport, Conn., 1978), 51–79; *New York Times*, 11–18 May 1896, *passim*.

5. Benno C. Schmidt, Jr., "Principle and Prejudice: The Supreme Court and Race in the Progressive Era; Part I: The Heyday of Jim Crow," 82 *Colum. Law Rev.* (1982), 466; Henry Billings Brown, "The Dissenting Opinions of Mr. Justice Harlan," 46 *Amer. Law Rev.* (1912), 337–38; Robert J. Harris, *The Quest for Equality: The Constitution, Congress, and the Supreme Court* (Baton Rouge, 1960), 101; Charles W. Collins, *The Fourteenth Amendment and the States* (1912; reprint ed., New York, 1974), 72.

6. *Holden v. Hardy*, 169 U.S. 366 (1898); for the language paralleling *Plessy*'s, see 398; for the discussion of race-related cases, see 383–84.

7. See Gilbert T. Stephenson, *Race Distinctions in American Law* (New York, 1910), 26–27. For example: "Under the social habits, customs, and prejudices prevailing in Louisiana, it cannot be disputed that charging a white man with being a Negro is calculated to inflict injury and damage." *Spotarno v. Fourichon*, 40 La. Ann. 423 (1888), quoted in *ibid.*, 27.

8. Otto H. Olsen, *Carpetbagger's Crusade: The Life of Albion Winegar Tourgée* (Baltimore, 1965), 329.

9. It may be significant that at the end of the Civil War and just afterward, Harlan campaigned in Kentucky *against* the Thirteenth and Fourteenth Amendments on grounds that they were revolutionary and pro-Negro. After he subsequently endorsed the Amendments, he found no reason to change his understanding of their meaning. See Alan F. Westin, "John Marshall Harlan and the Constitutional Rights of Negroes: The Transformation of a Southerner," 66 *Yale Law J.* (1957), 653–54 and *passim*.

10. Brown, "Dissenting Opinions of . . . Harlan," 321, 352, 335–38.

11. Schmidt, "Principle and Prejudice," 468. Schmidt argues that *Plessy* classified railway seating as within the realm of social relations and hence outside the ambit of the Fourteenth Amendment's requirement of equality. But Brown's meaning, I believe, was that *if* accommodations were equal, *then* any feelings of inequality were the result not of the law but of what he called "social prejudices." In the nature of things, he contended, constitutional amendments could not have been intended to change such feelings, for the feelings were impervious to legal alteration.

12. *Chesapeake and Ohio Railway Company v. Kentucky*, 179 U.S. 388 (1900).

13. Tourgée, "A Bystander's Notes," Chicago *Inter Ocean*, 26 May 1897, in Tourgée Papers; *Downes v. Bidwell*, 182 U.S. 244 (1901); *McCabe v. Atchison, Topeka, and Santa Fe Railway Company*, 235 U.S. 151 (1914).

14. See Catherine A. Barnes, *Journey from Jim Crow: The Desegregation of Southern Transit* (New York, 1983), 21–131 and esp. 35–51; Richard Kluger, *Simple Justice: The History of* Brown v. Board of Education *and Black America's Struggle for Equality* (New York, 1976), *passim*; *Brown v. Board of Education*, 347 U.S. 483 (1954); *Gayle v. Browder*, 352 U.S. 903 (1956). In the transportation area, the Interstate Commerce Commission also played a crucial role by striking down both the application of state laws to interstate transit and company regulations mandating separation on interstate routes; see Barnes, *Journey from Jim Crow, passim*. On the

issue of when the Court explicitly extended *Plessy* to segregated schooling, compare Paul G. Kauper, "Segregation in Public Education: The Decline of *Plessy v. Ferguson*," 52 *Mich. Law Rev.* (1954), 1145, with Harris, *Quest for Equality*, 102–3, 130–31.

15. Note, "The Fall of an Unconstitutional Fiction—The 'Separate but Equal' Doctrine," 30 *Neb. Law Rev.* (1950), 72–73; Laws of Florida, 1939, excerpted in *State Laws on Race and Color . . .* , Pauli Murray, comp. (n.p., 1950), 82; Laws of South Carolina, 1917, quoted in Charles S. Johnson, *Backgrounds to Patterns of Negro Segregation* (1943; reprint ed., New York, 1970), 171. For the full array of laws in effect as of 1950, see Murray's compilation.

16. Walter E. Weyl, *The Passenger Traffic of Railways* [Publications of the University of Pennsylvania in Political Economy and Public Law, No. 16] (Philadelphia, 1901), 27–28 and 28 n. 1; Barnes, *Journey from Jim Crow*, 18, partly quoting from Ray Stannard Baker, *Following the Color Line: American Negro Citizenship in the Progressive Era* (1908; reprint ed., New York, 1964), 31, Gunnar Myrdal, *An American Dilemma: The Negro Problem and Modern Democracy* (1944; reprint ed., New York, 1962), 635, and W. E. B. DuBois, "Race Relations in the United States," 9 *Phylon* (1948), 243.

17. For example, John Hope Franklin, *Racial Equality in America* (Chicago, 1976), 65; Germaine A. Reed, "Race Legislation in Louisiana, 1864–1920," 6 *La. Hist.* (1965), 392.

18. W. Ernest Douglas, "Retreat from Conservatism: The Old Lady of Broad Street [the Charleston *News and Courier*] Embraces Jim Crow," *Proc. of the South Carolina Hist. Assoc.*, 1958, at 5; Albert N. Sanders, "Jim Crow Comes to South Carolina," *ibid.*, 1966; at 36–39; Linda M. Matthews, "Keeping Down Jim Crow: The Railroads and the Separate Coach Bills in South Carolina," 73 *So. Atlantic Q.* (1974), 121–28.

19. Charles E. Wynes, "The Evolution of Jim Crow Laws in Twentieth Century Virginia," 28 *Phylon* (1967), 416–21; Margaret Law Callcott, *The Negro in Maryland Politics, 1870–1912* (Baltimore, 1969), 133–34; J. Morgan Kousser, *The Shaping of Southern Politics: Suffrage Restriction and the Establishment of the One-Party South, 1880–1910* (New Haven, 1974), 188–95, 231–36, 250–64; Joel Williamson, *The Crucible of Race: Black-White Relations in the American South Since Reconstruction* (New York, 1984), 243–44; Dewey W. Grantham, "The Contours of Southern Progressivism," 86 *Amer. Hist. Rev.* (1981), 1037–50.

20. C. Vann Woodward, *The Strange Career of Jim Crow* (3rd rev. ed., New York, 1974), 72–82.

21. Brown, "Dissenting Opinions of . . . Harlan," 338; *Brown v. Board of Education*, 347 U.S. 483 (1954); *New York Times*, 23 May 1954, sec. 4, at E10. Specifically, Justice Brown wrote: "He [Harlan] assumed what is probably the fact, that the statute had its origin in the purpose, not so much to exclude white persons from railroad cars occupied by blacks, as to exclude colored people from coaches occupied or assigned to white persons." Regarding the *Civil Rights Cases*, Brown similarly confessed, "there is still a lingering doubt whether the spirit of the [Reconstruction] amendments was not sacrificed to the letter . . . . " Brown, "Dissenting Opinions of . . . Harlan," 338, 336.

22. On the Court's failure to overrule *Plessy*, see, for example, Kauper, "Segregation in Public Education," 1151–56; Harris, *Quest for Equality*, 148–50.

For the *Gayle* suggestion, see, for example, Barton J. Bernstein, "*Plessy v. Ferguson*: Conservative Sociological Jurisprudence," 48 *J. of Negro Hist.* (1963), 196 n. 2; Albert P. Blaustein and Clarence C. Ferguson, Jr., *Desegregation and the Law: The Meaning and Effect of the School Segregation Cases* (2nd ed. rev., New York, 1962), 208–9, 282. In *Gayle v. Browder*, 352 U.S. 903 (1956), the Court cited two other cases besides *Brown*, but these were themselves *per curiam* decisions relying on *Brown*. Using *Shepard's Citations* to resolve the issue is suggested by Paul Oberst, "The Strange Career of *Plessy v. Ferguson*," 15 *Ariz. Law Rev.* (1973), 415 (which also offers other insights into the mini-debate about the overruling of *Plessy*). For judicial comments that *Brown* overruled *Plessy*, see, for example, *Browder v. Gayle*, 142 F. Supp. 707, 715–17 (M.D. Ala., 1956); *Bradley v. Milliken*, 484 F.2d 215, 249 (6th Cir. 1973), quoted in *Milliken v. Bradley*, 418 U.S. 717, 767 (1974) (Justices White, Douglas, Brennan, and Marshall, dissenting); *Florida Department of Health and Rehabilitative Services v. Florida Nursing Home Association*, 450 U.S. 147, 152 n. 6 (1981) (Justice Stevens, concurring).

23. See *Brown v. Board of Education*, 347 U.S. at 494–95 and n. 11.

24. Ralph A. Rossum, "*Plessy, Brown*, and the Reverse Discrimination Cases," 28 *Amer. Behavioral Scientist* (1985), 792; Kluger, *Simple Justice*, 705–6. Readers familiar with the controversy over *Brown* will recognize that I credit (or charge) the Supreme Court with giving less direct weight to social science testimony than do some of the critics of Warren's opinion. Neither the opinion (when read closely) nor Kluger's careful account indicates that the Court itself rested its conclusions on *independent* evaluation of the empirical evidence—nor, of course, had Justice Brown done so in *Plessy*.

25. *Bolling v. Sharpe*, 347 U.S. 497, 499–500 (1954). Warren indicated his constitutional test in this fashion: "Classifications based solely on race must be scrutinized with particular care, since they are contrary to our traditions and hence constitutionally suspect." *Ibid.*, 499. As authority he cited the Japanese Relocation Cases from World War II, which upheld racial classification on the grounds that after close examination the Court could not say that the classification was not reasonably related to the conduct of the war—which was essentially an adaptation of the *Plessy* test, albeit with some tightening.

26. See, for example, Blaustein and Ferguson, *Desegregation and the Law*, 156, 198–209.

27. *Regents of the University of California v. Bakke*, 438 U.S. 265, 318–19 (1978) (Justice Powell, separate opinion). Justice Blackmun in particular charged that by allowing race as a factor but rejecting preferential quotas, Powell had elaborated a distinction without a difference. *Ibid.*, 406 (Justice Blackmun, concurring and dissenting). See generally J. Harvie Wilkinson III, *From Brown to Bakke: The Supreme Court and School Integration, 1954–1978* (New York, 1979), 301–6.

28. *Bakke*, 438 U.S. at 415–19 and 417 n. 19 (Justice Stevens, joined by Justices Burger, Stewart, and Rehnquist, dissenting and concurring).

29. *Ibid.*, 326–27, 355–56 (Justices Brennan, White, Marshall, and Blackmun, dissenting and concurring).

30. *Ibid.*, esp. 388–89, 392–93, 397–98, 401–2 (Justice Marshall, dissenting and concurring).

31. John C. Livingston, *Fair Game? Inequality and Affirmative Action* (San

Francisco, 1979), 85–88; Ronald Dworkin, *Taking Rights Seriously* (Cambridge, Mass., 1977), 225 and *passim*; William Van Alstyne, "Rites of Passage: Race, the Supreme Court, and the Constitution," 46 *Univ. of Chic. Law Rev.* (1979), 792–803, partly quoting from *Plessy v. Ferguson*, 163 U.S. 537, 550 (1896) (Van Alstyne's emphasis).

32. For example, *United Steelworkers of America v. Weber*, 443 U.S. 193 (1979); *Fullilove v. Klutznick*, 448 U.S. 448 (1980); *Bratton v. City of Detroit*, 704 F.2d 878 (6th Cir., 1983), cert. denied, 104 S.Ct. 703 (1984). For critiques, see, for example, Terry Eastland and William J. Bennett, *Counting by Race: Equality from the Founding Fathers to* Bakke *and* Weber (New York, 1979); Edward J. Erler, "Sowing the Wind: Judicial Oligarchy and the Legacy of *Brown v. Board of Education*," 8 *Harv. J. of Law and Public Policy* (1985), 399–426.

33. Booker T. Washington, *Up from Slavery* (New York, 1901), reprinted in 1 *Booker T. Washington Papers*, 267; *New York Times*, 6 Dec. 1985 at 17.

34. Cunningham to James H. McKenney, 24 Sept. 1896, in Clerk's File, Plessy; Mandate, dated 18 May 1896, and Notice of Remand, dated 28 Sept. 1896, in *Plessy v. Ferguson*, No. 210, October Term, 1895, filed and entered with the clerk of the Louisiana Supreme Court, 2 Nov. 1896, in Plessy La. Case File; Notation of Disposition, on Information, *State v. Plessy*, No. 19,117, Section A, Criminal District Court, Parish of Orleans, in photocopied case file, Nels R. Douglas materials, The Amistad Research Center, New Orleans; Citizens' Committee, *Report of Proceedings for the Annulment of Act 111 of 1890* (New Orleans, [1897]), 6–8; Tourgée, "Bystander's Notes," Chicago *Inter Ocean*, 26 May 1897, in Tourgée Papers. The minute clerk's notation on the Information indicates that Plessy changed his plea from "not guilty" to "guilty." Since he had apparently never pleaded "not guilty," the plea to the jurisdiction having been his initial plea, I am following the statement in the final report of the Citizens' Committee that he "entered" the plea of "guilty." (*Report of Proceedings*, 6.) Neither the final report nor Tourgée's column describes the form of the Committee's testimonial to Tourgée or its contents.

35. Otto H. Olsen, "Reflections on the *Plessy v. Ferguson* Decision of 1896," in *Louisiana's Legal Heritage*, Edward F. Haas, ed. (Pensacola, 1983), 182–83; New Orleans *Daily Picayune*, 9 July 1898 at 7; Olsen, *Carpetbagger's Crusade*, 337–49. The date of Plessy's death is from his tombstone in St. Louis Cemetery No. 1, New Orleans which lists his age at death as sixty-three. (I am indebted to Lester Sullivan of The Amistad Research Center for this information.)

36. Citizens' Committee, *Report of Proceedings*, 7; Tourgée, "Bystander's Notes," 26 May 1897.

Table of Cases

255

Index

In the following entries, "Louisiana proceedings" refers to the local and state proceedings in *State v. Plessy* and *Ex parte Plessy*. *PvF* indicates *Plessy v. Ferguson.*

261